MW00444566

Down Below

Reminiscences
of a World War II
Engine Room Merchant Seaman

Edward "Ted" Jones Whitehead

Copyright © 2018 Edward Jones Whitehead

All Rights Reserved. No part of this publication may be reproduced in any form or by any means, including scanning, photocopying, or otherwise without prior written permission of the copyright holder.

Disclaimer and Terms of Use: The Author and Publisher has strived to be as accurate and complete as possible in the creation of this book, notwithstanding the fact that he does not warrant or represent at any time that the contents within are accurate due to the rapidly changing nature of the Internet. While all attempts have been made to verify information provided in this publication, the Author and Publisher assumes no responsibility for errors, omissions, or contrary interpretation of the subject matter herein. Any perceived slights of specific persons, peoples, or organizations are unintentional. In practical advice books, like anything else in life, there are no guarantees of income made. This book is not intended for use as a source of legal, business, accounting or financial advice. All readers are advised to seek services of competent professionals in legal, business, accounting, and finance field.

ISBN: 978-1982087241

Art and Photography credits
Original cover drawing: S/S Lily by Arme Navee Chumpalee
Back Cover–1943 Edward Whitehead photo: A local Swansee photography shop
Back Cover–2017 Edward Whitehead photo: Chris Rodgers
Back Cover–Merchant Navy in WW2–Convoy PQ 17: Mike Kemble website
Cover Design: Deborah Wheaton

First Printing, 2018

Printed in the United States of America

FOR MY DEPARTED BROTHERS AND SISTERS

AND

FELLOW ENGINE ROOM CREW MEMBERS

TABLE OF CONTENTS

Note: All S/S designated ships are British except the S/S Lily (Greek). D/S ships are Norwegian.

PREFACE

I have developed this book as a dramatised version of my Merchant Marine/Merchant Navy service during World War II. Some liberties were taken since memory over the passage of time can play tricks or have small fissures but the unfolding of the memoir is directionally correct with remembered dialogue and incidences filled in with tone if not perfect Memorex precision.

I have preserved in here some of the colloquial classics of my Welsh youth, such as the use of myself instead of me, ourselves for us, etc. Spelling and punctuation are based on British standards.

Additionally, I thought it would add a dimension to wartime life to apply British currency figures used in the book. Historical prices can be converted into equivalent present-day prices by using historical inflation rates. For accuracy, amounts are expressed in 1943 mid-war values. Because of inflation since then, £1 is equal to £43.30 sterling today. The multiplier for 1943 versus 2017 is therefore obviously 43.30%.
Source: stephenmorley.org

Data for 1949 onwards comes from the Office for National Statistics document RPI *All Items: Percentage change over 12 months*. Data for 1751 to 1948 comes from the 2004 paper *Consumer Price Inflation Since 1750* (ISSN 0013-0400, Economic Trends No. 604, pp 38-46) by Jim O'Donoghue, Louise Goulding, and Grahame Allen.

WWII British Coins
Farthing (1/4 penny)
Half Penny
Penny
Three Pence
Shilling (Bob = 12 Pence)
Half Crown (2 ½ Shillings)
Crown (5 Shillings)
Currency
£1 (20 Shillings) £ = pound

And finally, at the end of the book I have included a Glossary with definitions of mostly nautical terms used in the book.

CHAPTER 1 STARTING OFF

It was in early August 1941 when I walked out of a house I was boarding at near Witney, the blanket-making town in Oxfordshire, intending to hitchhike my way home to South Wales for a two week holiday away from my council job. I walked the long mile to a Minster Lovell Petrol Station, where I might get a lift.

Few cars stopped during the next twenty minutes, so I retraced my steps a short way back and dropped into a small tavern, known by the villagers as The Pike. After sharing a few words with a drinking mate, he told me to jump into a van for a ride to a busier filling station on the road to Burford – seven miles distant.

Weather had been good for crops, and harvesters had been making overtime. Their well-tanned faces in the fields that we passed became part of the rural scenery. One might think the war was non-existent around these parts during the summer days of '41.

My friend deposited me at a favourable place for pickups; it was a canteen for long distance lorry drivers. I picked up a cheese roll and a cup of char at the counter and seated myself at a table near the door. Here I could read the faces of drivers entering and leaving and possibly hear the chat and learn if they were bound for Cardiff, South Wales.

A few circumspect glances informed me that I might not be alone in seeking a free ride, but these others had little need to sit near the entrance. They were uniformed men representing the armed forces. More often than not they had no need to beg a lift. Drivers with spare seats in their big trucks would offer them a lift when passing their tables.

There was plenty of time before sundown, so I took it pretty easy, lighting up a smoke after nibbling through the roll and then sipped my sugarless tea, biding my time for my opportunity. Slowly and surely my eyes focused on a shiny, brown face with a smile on it.

He would be fortyish with receding, crinkly black hair. I waited for his jaws to demolish his so-called meat pie, and as he lit up his fag to accompany his diminishing cuppa, I moved swiftly. The cigarette had relaxed him, and when I strolled over to his table and asked him if he was going in the direction of Cardiff, he nodded.

He politely placed the butt of his cigarette on the ashtray, and with a drawl as soft as his smile, said he was going only as far as Chepstow, where he would sleep overnight before continuing his journey. I stood there with my thoughts doing rapid calculations.

There were many hours left before blackout time with daylight stretching to 9pm, but chances were I would not hit a canteen as good as the one I was in, and should time catch up with me, hitching lifts at blacked-out traffic lights was out.

Just as he stubbed his butt into the ashtray and stood up to leave, I accepted his kind offer to share his cab. Holding twelve pounds in my pocket, I felt I could afford an overnight B and B stay. And pleasant company was this driver since feelings are closer than words when only two are together.

Here was daddy cool himself with a flexible hand on the wheel, nursing the speed of his truck, as he seemingly nursed some deep down personal plans in the same way. Occasionally, he passed small talk as a matter of courtesy, and he must have been closely acquainted with valley people in his suburb of Cardiff because when I mentioned the Rhondda, it seemed to relax him.

Naturally, I put up at the same guest house as he did in Chepstow to be sure of the final leg of the journey. One did not take second notice of the smallness of the rooms of which there was a half a dozen since a lot of care and hard work had been put into making them a pleasure to sit in.

Our hostess was thirty-something, vivacious and made one feel at ease. She had a reddish tinge in her light brown hair that made her as attractive as her cosy rooms. My driver was obviously a regular lodger the way she welcomed him, and there was no doubt she valued the visits of these drivers at her place, in case they might be able to pick up some extra items of food she was short of. I paid ten shillings for my bed and breakfast, but with a permanent food shortage, she gave value to her rationed meals. A bumper meal of homemade scones sat on the breakfast table to help fill the stomach with the meagre ration of bacon with a single egg. They tasted delicious. The rest of the trip to Cardiff spun off like a melody.

The final dropping-off place was at the central railway station in

Cardiff. I spent a half crown for the fare up to the Rhondda Valley. I then enjoyed the mile long hike up to Cwmparc where the incline not only slowed my body but also my mind.

Down at a meditative level, I thought that the magnetic pull of home territory weakens with time. Pleasant face talk and utterances greeted me on the way up, and I thought of quaffing a few beers with teenage friends at the local, but there was little impetus to hang out in the village for a whole fortnight. Having drifted off to England to seek work the year before, my relationship with local skirts was still in the formative stage.

Links had weakened in the interim due in some respects to a small bombing raid on the village. They did severe damage to the small community, leaving 400 roofs open to the sky. As I entered my house, I foresaw that the topic of conversation would soon come around to the Blitz. I was told there had been a very large attendance at the funeral for the twenty-seven victims of the recent bombing. The only compensation was that the homeowners were left with a higher property value due to excellent repair work.

After my sister welcomed me through the passage into the living room, I passed her three pound notes for a fortnight bed and board. She placed one note back in my palm and told me to enjoy myself with it; there was plenty of work and cash brought along by the war effort.

Had those familiar rains come from the usually misty hills, I would have lingered out my fortnight, getting bored during the days and spending long evenings in the pub the rest of the time. The first three mornings waking up in sunny weather changed all that.

Instead of lying abed until noon, the blue skies allowed the sun to rip light between the curtains on the third morning and told me to forget about bed. It tempted me to the outdoors and adventure. As images of a sandy beach played on my mind, I decided I was in the wrong place.

I feel women are up on men when it comes to fine perception because I was handed back yet another pound of my rent money when I told my sister I was going to the coast for a few days, and that I would not return. I bought a train ticket to Barry twenty miles away.

I became pensive on the train ride, secluded in a compartment with no one to talk to. My daydreaming mind was focused on yellow sand, as the old steam train rattled on. I took my feet out of the high-stepping exit door as the sandy scene disappeared with the departing train, whilst I belatedly found myself on the wrong platform.

I found myself standing on the Barry Docks Station instead of the terminal called Barry Island, where the fun fairs and sand castles took old and young from the real world. With my brain switching from disappointment to seeking a quencher for my thirst, I made a course for the first pub in view. I was directed to Thomson Street.

I came to the first pub, right near to the docks, a granite-looking structure with a name that was unreadable due to coal dust blowing from the coal-holding wharves. It was a terraced hotel with steps leading upwards. Then I noticed men entering a door beneath. There I followed two stalwarts in high rubber boots, overlapping serge trews and talking in a language I had never heard before. I trailed the clumping of boots into a cellar with a lot of laughter going on.

At my impressionable age of eighteen years, the atmosphere was pure magic. There were more of the long-booted ones in this cellar, as well as men with flat caps and dirty hobnail boots, who I learned later, were stokers, as apart from the deckhands. Watching some of the customers swaying in front of the bar, I felt high before I even bought myself a pint of ale.

In a port like Barry, where it was mostly a one-way trade with cargoes of coal going all over the globe, there was a valid reason why men in the deck department wore those wellington boots on a hot summer's day. Walking on the wharf itself meant plodding through lots of thick coal dust and then brushing the same coal dust off the deck, must have been a continuous chore with a final big wash down with the water hose.

Two cheerful barmaids served the salty clientele. At the far end of the bar, the big-bosomed one pulled pints of ale for a group that seemed intent on explaining a joke to the hostess in chatty but broken English, which by the nods of the barmaid seemed well understood because she released the handle she was tugging on and let go a few hearty guffaws.

The slimmer of the two breezed up to give me her attention, and the humour in her eyes after digesting the jokes made me feel warm. "Deck boy?" she queried as she worked a foamy top on my glass. Seeing confusion in my face, she screwed up her eyes understandingly. Another dungaree walked up to the counter near me, proffering two glasses for refills – a half pint tumbler and a wee one for spirits.

I was about to carry my bitter liquid to a vacant place on a long, rugged bench, at a table of bare plank wood, but the server would have none of it. The side look of an eye and a raised hand was a signal to stall. Turning her attention to the body next to me she asked, "Same again, Olav?"

A smile grew on the other's face as a reply. She took his coins and handed back a full glass of ale, but retained the double tot of whisky with

4

her hand, holding tight onto the glass. She now favoured me with her attention. "Now look here, Dai, and with such an accent like yours, you're down from the valleys, so your name must be Dai. Tell me the truth. You've come down to this dump to look for a job on some ship, haven't you?"

When I entered the cellar such an idea hadn't entered my mind, but intuition was telling me that the barmaid was reading my inner depths, and I answered with a head nod. She must have caught the slight excitement in my shy eyes and handed over the tot to the stranger with a request to try and get me a berth on his vessel.

Olav was more cleaned up than the rest, wearing shiny blushers instead of rough cut rubber boots and a clean pair of jeans beneath one of those sleek, thin, navy blue sweaters over a white shirt. I have only seen this type of sweater with Norwegians, and I think it keeps the heat in as well as the cold out. But I think vanity had the better of him to wear those high boots in warm weather.

I trailed him to another part of the wide room and sat at a small mahogany table at another section of this wide drinking den. My new friend first introduced himself as bosun, or deck foreman, of a small Norwegian coaster called *Bjornvik*, but his ship was not here in Barry but rather thirty miles distant in the port of Swansea.

Seeing my disillusioned face, he smiled off any disappointing thoughts with, "You no worry about cost. I make much overtime. I pay you the train fare to Swansea." After a while I noticed that he kept scanning the bar at rapid intervals, and when the slim barmaid had time to idle, she went over to him. That must have been the cue he was waiting for as he walked over for refills. He confided that although a couple of whiskys were not allowed in wartime, sometimes she broke the rule for him. Noticing my eagerness to have the opportunity to work on board my first ship, he promised to leave shortly.

This generous person offered to spike my ale with a portion of his precious tot, but I was wisely too eager to make a good show for the job to accept the offer. At 6p a shot (valued at 3p in the old currency), his double cost one shilling – three time my pint of beer, or at least nearly three. He was on holiday like myself, having been allowed three days off by his captain.

Ascending the streets into the sunlit street, he informed me that his beloved here in Barry happened to be the barmaid's sister. He said the evening train from Barry Island would be crammed with children, tired and sandy after a day on the beach. But as it was early afternoon, we had a compartment to ourselves to Swansea.

My mind was inflated at the prospect of sailing on a real ship. The chance of a lifetime beckoned, but it was still on the verge – not within grasp yet. Ever since my elder brother Jack returned from sea as a deck boy two years earlier, before he opted to enlist in the Air Force, it gave me a few sleepless nights wondering what it would be like to go to sea.

All keen, I waited for Olav to let me know what work I was being offered, but being reticent about disturbing his pensive mood, I became that way myself and it all came back to me when those many years ago I sat on the Barry sands, building small castles with my little bucket, and then totally forgetting about the castle as soon as my eyes were diverted by smoke on the horizon from one of those departing steamers.

That was when I was six and every year after, when I returned to Barry with my family for the annual outing, there was only one thing on my mind – to gaze out at those ships transporting the black coal cargoes out into the magic unknown. I wanted to watch until they dipped over the horizon into an unknown yonder.

Now that the barmaid had fired my mind with adventure, I was intent on following Olav like a zombie. The call of the waves was hypnotising my mind; I took in the idea of a future at sea completely, and it was not a case of will I but when. Looking sideways at me, I think my friend appreciated my state of limbo.

He probably had his mind well-occupied with the barmaid's sister, maybe working a different shift in the same cellar, which I now learned was called The Chain Locker. He came out of his mental state before arriving in Swansea and put me in the picture. The deck boy on his ship was a young Belgian who had returned on board some days ago drunk.

He had complained to the crew a number of times about having trying thoughts concerning his family back in Belgium, and especially his sister, as that country was under enemy occupation, and on that particular day when he was flat out crocked, he went amok with a newly installed anti-aircraft gun on the bridge.

He fired a string of bullets into upper space, and the skipper gave him a week to return to sanity or face the sack. Arriving at Swansea station, there was no such thing as walking to the ship. We dipped our heads into a taxi and away we sped. We would have enjoyed a pleasant stroll down the hill so I noticed, but the cab gave me an entrance into the Swansea docks.

The policeman at the gates thought me automatically a crew member. Going up the gangway, Olav explained that his vessel could not sail deep-sea, only coastwise, because she was of small size, only 1200 tons. But to my young, ignorant self, I felt I was walking the deck of something that would defy any ocean.

There seemed to be only one solitary crew member aboard when we entered the crew mess room, a cubbyhole of a place seating ten persons. I was introduced to the loner who my mate explained was the donkeyman, the man who kept the cargo winches and pumps going in port on one boiler, nicknamed the donkey boiler.

This man, as short as my friend and not looking at all like the big, tall Vikings we imagine, pulled off a white tablecloth from a stainless steel oval tray on the table. After the two men had a brief conversation in their own language, they switched to English for politeness sake, and I was invited to finish off some of the cold meat cuts.

Bread and butter was passed so I could make a few sandwiches for myself. I was halfway in the process of making my sandwich, when Olav called me over to the open door of what seemed to be the kitchen, and walking over to the stove, he drew my attention to an open pot and asked me if I would like to try a bowl of sweet soup to start off with.

Olav fetched a bowl and spoon and I didn't need coaxing to grab the bowl. He ladled a wallop into it and asked me to give it a try. Whatever it was, due to the prevailing scant rations of sugar in the UK, after the first spoonful of this liquefied, dried fruit, I was instantly in love with the stuff.

A big smile broke out on the petty officer's face as he saw me scoffing away. He told me to eat as much as I wished since when the drunken mob returned on board, the taste of boiled raisins and dried peaches would not go well with alcohol, and it would have to be dumped for the fishes anyway.

I took him at his word and downed a few bowls, making myself somewhat bloated after the short session in the bar a few hours back. But I still managed to mop up with a sandwich back in the mess; the sea air must have had something to do with my healthy appetite.

I then asked Olav what my chances were of being employed. He answered that the donkeyman had gone amidships to locate the captain and find out if the deck boy was still a crew member. When that person returned, though he conversed with my friend in an unfamiliar lingo, it was not difficult to face read and to realise that that there was no vacancy; the skipper had decided to give the Belgian boy a second chance. Sadly Olav informed me he could help me no further. The ship would put to sea within twelve hours.

Disappointed I may have been as I descended the gangway, I realised the barmaid in Barry had brought a deep-seated longing to the surface. I was destined to live a life on the ocean waves, almost as if it was an instinct.

Passing The Plough on the way to the dock gate, I read the ship's name on the bow, *Bjornvik*. For some reason I sensed there may be a few more *Bjornviks* to board before being accepted in the seagoing fraternity. I would prove myself such a pest that one of them would have to hire me I hoped!

Silly fumes from the couple of beers I had downed in Barry had evaporated, and I was pensive walking up the main street of Swansea – Wind Street. I entered the bar section of the first pub I set eyes on namely the Bush Hotel. It was not thirst that drew me in but the chance to hobnob with like people.

I needed cheap lodgings and had not found any in my search. I got chatting at the bar with an elderly person with an Irish accent, and he took to a window and pointed directly, more or less to a narrow lane. "That's Saint Mary Street," informed my guide. "Walk halfway down and you'll come to a wide, black door on your right. Give it a hard push, walk through the passage, and you'll come to the kitchen." "And then?" I inquired." "And then Mrs Ramos will take you in. I know she will. I stay there myself," commented my informant. "How much does Mrs Ramos charge?" I quizzed. Irish: "Bob a night." "Thanks a lot," I answered him fumbling in my thin windbreaker pocket for the necessary seven shillings to keep me under a roof for a week. It was now evening, and like early morning traffic, buses and cars sped by carrying the productive elements of the workforce back to their home fires.

I took time and noted the Bush Hotel as an important landmark before stepping down an ancient lane of cobbled stones. The entrance to this medieval street was flanked by ruined masonry on either side, the result of a bombing raid six months before. One was the totally ruined St Mary's Church. The only remnant of masonry on the other side was the untouched lettering of A. Samuels – Jeweller.

Strange when looking back across the road, the Bush Hotel seemed unmarked, as was the building right next to it, with the heading Posada Espanola, a loading house for Spanish nationals. Making a rough count of houses as I dipped down this cobbled street, I noticed it had about twelve houses on each side.

And age revealed the road like an old spring mattress that had sagged in the middle. I have found that such streets have a friendly, communal atmosphere; else people would find it difficult to live with houses so close

8

together. A lady I was about to overtake must have noticed that I was a stranger and questioned me if I was searching for someone nearby.

To make sure of my address I asked her if she knew where Mrs Ramos lived. She pointed out a nearby big, black door. There I rapped a wide panel above the brass doorknob, and getting no response after a tardy two minutes, remembered the words of the Irishman and put my shoulder to the door gaining an easy entrance.

I was met by the oval face of a pretty, young lady as I entered the kitchen. She looked me over and turning around yelled, "Mam, there's a new lodger." "Ask the man where he comes from?" The voice had a foreign accent and I assumed it was Mrs Ramos. The pretty face returned her attention to me. "My mother wants to know where you come from." "Say I'm from the Rhondda Valley."

The creamy swan neck again reversed itself. Every time she turned, I had a chance to observe this sweet female at close quarters. I hoped this question and answer business would go on for weeks. She hollered, "He's a Dai from the valleys," and after which the face swung back for my admiring inspection, and it returned the bonus of a smile.

I got surprised by my own embarrassment. The half open door was opened wider and the young lady introduced herself as Julietta. "My mother said to make you a cup of tea." This was spoken in a cool, friendly manner, and the ease with which she poured the tea and the way she passed the cup showed she had complete trust in valley boys. But I was too overwhelmed to have trust in myself.

"You may as well sit at the table," she said, guiding me to the chair; then after pouring herself a cuppa, she joined me. It was her turn now to do the studying. I sat in a question and answer mood, which made me feel a little uneasy, but she was not too probing. We exchanged ages and I thought we were the perfect match – my eighteen to her seventeen years.

From this topic, we moved onto jobs, and the coolness of her conversation, as well as her doing most of the chatting, put me at ease as she elaborated on bed making and the sweeping up of fag ends! Of course, my ears were more tuned in to the intoning of a purry voice than the actual info imparted, trying to guess if she had fallen for me?

Then her mother entered the kitchen. In response to Ma's "Hullo", my embarrassing response told her my face had grown redder than my ears. Further conversation between the two brought me down to earth when I learnt that Julietta already had a lover boy, soon to return from across the sea – a Portuguese lad. This sailor boy liaison was no doubt encouraged by her Portuguese mother, and I sensed that the only reason I was in favour with the pair was because there were not too many young faces entering the establishment. Her Mam asked me to sign the big book after I passed her seven shillings for one week's rent, and she left me in the care of her daughter.

I was poured another cup of almost sugarless tea before being led upstairs to be shown my sleeping accommodation. Climbing creaky stairs I began having ideas, but the respect shown to valley people forbade underhand advances. First, she opened a door at the end of a landing, and I viewed six beds, all covered with hairy, military-style blankets; they covered greyish white sheets.

She mentioned she wished one of the beds was vacant for me, but regulars rarely gave up one in this room. Then we turned to the major dormitory with twice that number of beds, where I was informed that the doors remained permanently ajar so that the drunks would not keep opening it and banging it shut after them.

I did not need to hold a high intelligence quotient to know what the pail in the middle of the room was for, as it squatted between the double rows of cots. My smoking habit was not yet cloggy enough for my smell buds not to recognise the odour of stale urine, entering the nostrils as it evaporated in the summer air. Any romantic feelings I had for Julietta also evaporated!

After showing me a middle bed on one side, Julietta left me standing there in a half-stupor, wondering what the morrow would bring. Don't think I was a big sis; for the past seven months I earned my living by leading a mare around the back streets of Witney, pulling a mobile tank in the wee hours of the morning. I was emptying buckets full of human excrement into it.

You'll get used to anything for good cash. The little sadness I felt looking around that dorm was only a passing thought of 'you get what you pay for' and a night's flop for only a shilling would be the cheapest doss-house for miles around. One needs cash to survive an uncertain future and after a moment's thought, I knew I had made a wise choice.

As I returned downstairs, I realised that even if the broken springs of those ramshackle beds were curved like shaving bowls in the middle, at least I would not be picked up and questioned by police; the best law is to keep away from the law. I passed the kitchen on a thick rug and noticed the two females had their backs turned towards me.

I took a quick look around before leaving the passage. The elder one was retreating to the further end of the kitchen. Because she wore black, it came as a surprise to me that she was wearing something else on her back as well. It was like she had a bowler hat stuck between her shoulder blades. It was a hump.

There was something I had forgotten and returned to have a word with Julie about the toilet facilities downstairs. She took me to a door beneath the staircase where there were towels under a corrugated shelter and an open yard where there were several latrines. Returning to the kitchen, we met a young lad helping himself to a slab of cake on the table.

My bed maker was swift to introduce me to her younger brother, Antonio. During the long school holiday season, most children wear smiles, and Antonio's bright eyes laughed into mine when we shook hands. Before making my exit, Julietta reminded me to be in before 11pm. As I paced up the alleyway, I reasoned that the 11pm curfew was something to do with blackout regulations.

Then on second thought, I felt pretty sure it was to keep out late and aggressive drunks. The human mind always seems to compare, and as I walked up to Wind Street, I felt what a lucky soul I was to be fit in body, when in Thirteen St Mary Street, a humpbacked lady had been struggling for years to rear two beautiful offspring from her deformed body.

She ran a houseful of night campers at the same time, who paid her no more than one shilling per night to battle on with. A minute earlier, I had not entertained pleasant thoughts of the mysterious occupants of my new, big bedroom, but now I felt on top of the world.

After crossing the other side of the main road, I was in no hurry to enter a bar. Had I not socialised with warm-hearted people like Julie and her mother, the grip of loneliness one can absorb in a strange place would have sucked me into one of the drinking houses. Instead I dared to enter the precincts of a small structure with doors wide open. It had a square metal sign swinging above it stating Flying Angel Mission to Seamen.

Beneath the caption was the figure of a lady in blue with wings. I made my entrance unchallenged. A small counter offered various sundries for filling the stomach, and a pretty, young thing gave me her attention. I ordered a cup of tea and speculated on a fresh pack of twenty smokes.

My feed on the *Bjornvik* had sunk by now, so I added a small slab of cake to take over to one of the small tables. From the sunlit outside, my eyes had not quite adjusted themselves to the dimmer electric lighting, and gazing from my table down this lengthy room, some amenities caught my eyes. I caught sight of a billiard table and a ping-pong one beyond it.

I was not the lone customer. At the next table, other young voices drew attention. They were friendly voices, and when I dared to look their way, one of the threesome offered me a seat at their table, which I accepted. The urger introduced himself as Dave and his two mates as Billy and Ivan.

I still had small change from the shilling piece and considered that the outside world had treated me marvellously that day with such small expense to myself. What with the Viking paying my rail fare and his other kindnesses, plus then finding the cheapest accommodation in town, I felt I could not put a wrong step forward.

I felt in a good mood as I sat with the other teenagers, eager to prolong their company, so I offered cigarettes all around. But Dave, speaking for the others, turned the offer down. "No, you keep them to yourself. We've just cadged a packet of twenty from a sailor down at the docks. Have you been down there today?"

I surprised even myself at my quick "Yeah". Dead silence followed this answer. I realised they wished to learn more. I tried to put on a look of experience when they hunched shoulders around the table, pricked up ears and bent over in my direction. "What ship?" queried Dave.

Impatiently, I had finished my slab of cake, which as small as it was, had weight, was slippery in the throat and slid down comfortably on top of the sweet soup. I lit a fag, leaned back and sent smoke above their heads, trying to recall how *Bjornvik* was pronounced by the Norwegian bosun and successfully twisting the J into a Y, I got it off my tongue good.

"Norske boat, hey," commented Dave, and admiring looks made me feel high. Then I slipped up a bit by asking what 'Norske' meant. "Norwegian," they chorused. Then the next question was shot at me. "Been to sea before?" The speed of my brain realised I was unable to pull off a lie so easily, and the only reply was that a little blood had rushed to the wrong side of my face.

The boys understood since they had no seagoing experience either, and they became more relaxed, knowing we were all equals. We all lit up smokes and had a period of trying to blow curls out of the smoke until someone could think of another item of discussion. As we puffed away, one lad broke the silence by asking where I lodged.

My reply told them that I was not too flush with cash. Then Dave told me that he and Ivan were ok for a night's kip, but Billy was short of 4p to make up the bed money to stay at the same place as myself. Had he noticed the 4p change I had at the counter from my shilling piece?

Anyway I dipped down and parted with it, even eagerly, because I sensed that these boys were keys to job info about shipping, and I had ensured myself that I had at least one friend in the new room I was to occupy that night. At 8pm, we left the premises and still found enough daylight to take us a stroll down to smell the sea air at the docks. I was introduced to the inside of another seamen's mission – a very old place in Balaclava Street. It was conveniently near the Number One Dock Gate; the very one I had walked out that day. Inside the mission, a stout lady sat beside a big, steaming hot-water urn behind a small counter on which some hefty china mugs and stale-looking cakes sat.

The main attraction seemed to be the long pool table at the distant end of the room, with the usual padded bench beside it. The gang let me into a tip that if one had nowhere to go, one could always sit around this place as long as you wished; they would even allow you to catnap on the long bench as long as someone was playing billiards.

It was getting dark, and as the place had no fresh visitors besides ourselves, we left and walked up Wind Street before the blackout fell. At Saint Mary's Street Billy and I branched off and made for the black door. Julie took care of Billy, and I went ahead upstairs. I was glad of Billy's company that night since it held me back from seeking company inside a pub.

In my fresh determination to ship out, I was beginning to plan ahead to conserve cash for the trials ahead. There was a light in the bedroom, and an elderly person was lying awake in one corner, looking as if he wished to be left alone. Mrs Ramos offered my mate another corner, which he was only too glad to accept.

After she left, Billy came across and advised me to tie my shoes to a leg of the bed but softened the surprise on my face by adding, "The seamen are OK; all they do is drink and talk in their sleep; they won't steal anything, but sometimes there are other people."

Then before turning into his own cot, he added, "Just make sure you have everything in the morning and sleep with your clothes on." Actually, I enjoyed a fair night's sleep after such a hectic day and only woke up once when someone emptied his bladder in the bucket. Then with the early summer dawn showing through the windows, I awoke and then later would fall back into short naps.

There were several risers around 6 to 7am, who spoke in hushed voices about a very early opener called the Cape Corner in Balaclava Street, which I later learnt was open from 6am to 8am to allow dock workers a few pints of ale. When Billy came across to my bed at about 8.30 am, there were only three of us left in the room.

This other person, a brawny man in his thirties, had a word with us before leaving. When we said we were seeking work aboard a ship, he had only one piece of advice to give us and that was to forget the whole idea, a romantic fantasy. He had a very rich Irish accent and became very descriptive about storms he had encountered at sea. It appeared that he had just paid off a coasting vessel, in which one of the crew had been washed overboard coming round the northern coast of Scotland.

When he left the room that fear he instilled in us was ousted by another. Billy was wiser than me in certain matters, and I was glad for his advice. He told me that in some flophouses, straw mattresses bred fleas, but that Mrs Ramos had a good name on that point, which eased my mind.

Julietta entered our dormitory about 9 am. The good weather was holding and lying abed late was out of fashion. My mate and I were covered in minimum clothing of T-shirt, over-shirt and pants with my extra clothing in my holdall, the canvas one I had brought to Swansea with me, and would usually leave under the bed during daylight hours.

We left Julietta to clean up the room and took off to Flappers, the Flying Angel Seamen's Mission, to clean up rather than use the wash place below. Billy also had a canvas bag, a small one containing a towel, a bar of soap and a two piece put-together razor. He had high hopes for this day, had Billy, and let me know that we should take time to clean up, in case we had to face up to a ship's officer for a deck boy's or a galley boy's job.

As we cleaned up at the washroom in the mission, I handed Billy five shillings for himself but also to pick up any sundries we needed, like razor blades, etc. My mate was an inoffensive type, about my own stamp but frailer, so there was no way I would be dominated in the partnership, and I got an appreciative returned look on his face for the handout.

Sometimes the mission got donations of food from farm owners who were not stingy with dairy produce. I asked Billy on that occasion, "Why don't other people walk in from the street and help themselves?" Billy: "If you are over eighteen, you have to show identification as a seaman before service is given to you."

Me: "But I am over eighteen." Billy: "Yes, I know, but when you first came in, the counter girl was doing some guess work on your age, but you mixed with our gang and that changed things. We three are only seventeen, and the Padre knows that we try hard to look for work. Besides he knows my father and Ivan's dad."

After the clean-up, we returned to the counter and passed 'hellos to handsome'. We were in luck. There were but a few meat pies, which did not look too meaty. So for the speculation of a shilling, we were served a pyramid of small triangular sandwiches of spam and cheese, daintily cut by Blodwen, the counter girl. Billy took the big plateful to a table, and I followed with two mugs of tea. The tea was short of sugar, but we could help ourselves to saccharine tablets on the counter. It was lucky to have a counter girl to back up the young fellows seeking their chances to ship out, and she pepped us up. Having looked under the counter at the list of ships in port, which she would hand to the padre when he arrived, she let us know that the port was only half full.

If that made us gulp the tea, she added that there was a lot more to expect over the next week. Then a gentleman in his forties entered. He passed a good morning to Blod, and also asked Billy about his chances of shipping out. He was answered with a wag in the head and returned a 'Keep Trying' smile.

He moved off and disappeared into a side door near the end of the counter. "That's Padre Edwards," said my friend. "Keep in the good books with him." I always soaked in any advice Billy offered me. After breakfast I was about to light up, when Billy cautioned me to return the cigarettes to my pocket, saying that Mr Edwards didn't like seeing young people smoking.

"We can enjoy a fag on the way down to the docks," he added. Since both of us were looking forward to a whiff, the small dilly bag with my towel inside was handed over the counter for safekeeping, and we toddled off. The August weather of 41 degrees gave out a lot of optimism. "Thanks for saving my skin with the 4p last night," Billy dropped this grateful comment nonchalantly.

"I would have given you a bob if you had asked for it," I answered. "Not if you'd have been smarter you wouldn't, because it's best not to let on you are holding more than us," he uttered. Silence followed as we sauntered along under the bridge connecting to Balaclava Street. Billy understood he had put his foot in it, talking against friends, but he continued.

"If I must speak the truth and I don't really mean to speak bad about Davy, but he was holding 9p at the time, so he could have passed the 4p I needed. He spotted the change you slipped into your pocket and was after it," he ended. I was all ears. Was I in luck? Here was a real mate; I was favoured above others. Then we grew quiet.

There was a wide railway bridge we passed under, like a small tunnel, and our shoe leather could be heard. To break the silence I asked Billy why he was barred from his home.

"My real father left us a couple of years ago, and my mother remarried and had a baby with this new feller about five months ago. My stepfather comes from a very religious family in West Wales and used to question my sister and me a lot about where we'd been and on and on, telling us we had to be in the house by 9.30 pm each night."

Me: "How old is your sister?" Billy: "Nineteen." Then he stopped for a while as if in thought, and then he guided me across the road and towards the Number One Dock Gate. "When we pass the gate, walk near so I can see who the gate officer is," Billy said. I looked sideways together with my mate through a small office window; a police officer was inside. My mate ordered me to double back.

Billy read the uplifted eyebrows of the guard, who had come to the door. He explained to him that I was also on the lookout for a job on a ship. I felt police eyes carrying out rapid judgement on my face, and as the phone rang from inside the office, he waved us on. An elderly man, he had probably allowed quite a number of young adventurers' freedom of the shipping area district.

Perhaps he had been acknowledged as a friend from many a first tripper on their return. "What if I could not enter the docks on my own, Billy?" "There's another gate further along, but Dave is pretty wise and advised me not to try gate two if we can't enter the main one, seeing that these guards keep in contact with each other."

Me: "So what do I do then?" "Go to Port Tennant. That's a mile away. You follow Balaclava Street and then follow the dock fence around." We were now passing two smaller type vessels, one tied outside the other, and both had white ensigns on the flagstaff with Union Jacks in the corner.

"We'll give those a total miss," said my friend. "They are navy ships; fishing boats converted into minesweepers. They don't go much further than outside the Bristol Channel." Way ahead loomed the bows of a less sleek but much larger vessel. "We'll board that one," said my guide. "She's flying the Red Duster flag." And then he didn't allow me the embarrassment of asking what this 'Red Duster' meant but with a side glance passed on a titbit.

"A red flag with a Union Jack placed in the upper corner is a British merchant ship." I followed him up the long gangway at the stern end. At the top, Billy looked around and seeing no watchmen to avoid, waved me on in a walk to amidships. He located the ship's galley and right away approached the cook asking if he wanted any potatoes peeled. I stood outside the open door and failed to notice a dark shadow in the recess.

The cook's reply was for us to have a bit of a chat with the shadow, his offsider (assistant) – the galley boy. Presently, a young lad from the back of the galley passed us with a bucket of unpeeled spuds. We followed right behind him until he placed the bucket beneath the outdoor pump; he gave the handle a few up and down jerks and then gave his attention to Billy.

Although our spud barber came from a suburb of Swansea, and way out from Billy's neighbourhood, something in the teenager's mind drew him towards us. He confided that as this was a Friday, the last day of the week for offices in general, and he had an appointment that afternoon with the immigration department.

"Unless I pay them a visit with permission from my parents to sail, I could be in trouble with the Shipping Office." We said we would gladly relieve him of his problem if he could get permission off the cook. The cook agreed to let him go, and the lad passed us two sharp knives and a couple of apple boxes to sit on. After filling a bucket of water and putting it before us for the peeled potatoes, we took over gladly. I don't know between us two who the worst at ripping off thick skins was. We peeled away, looking at each other and comparing, but we didn't find it easy, trying to peel off thinner skins. We feared the cook might take over the job himself, so we tried to improve as we proceeded.

Before he left, the galley boy said that the cook was a kind man and would ask us to help him clean the pots and pans so we would be sure of leftover meals. Left to our task, we soon lost ourselves in conversation. My friend realised by now that he had become my mentor and drew attention to the importance of boarding ships.

"Nearly everyone going to sea starts off by being hired as a galley boy," he explained. "And then when an opening comes up, whether it is for a coal trimmer or deck boy, you can ask the captain to give you the job." At that point I asked him to finish off the story of his home life. "I'm not the only one barred from home now," started Billy. "My sister has been kicked out as well."

"One night she returned home around 11pm, which really made my stepfather very angry. After demanding where she had been so late, it wasn't long before she confessed that she had met a boy near the docks, and that was the last straw. He thought the very worst and informed her that harlots would not be allowed under the roof of his house, although she was allowed to stay the night."

Billy concluded, "My mother pleaded with my stepfather, but it was no use. She could not protest very well, holding a five month old baby, and in the morning my sister packed her belongings and left. I told my sister that I would act as a go-between and pass messages to Mam, but after a week, I was found out and chased from the house as well."

After a brief silence, he changed the subject. "Ted, you didn't find it easy climbing that ship's gangway, did you?" I had eagerly followed the footsteps of my mate up the steep gangway. However, Billy was way ahead of me clambering up, whilst I laboured trying to plant my feet on the loose steps. I was but half way up when my leader stood on the steel deck smiling down.

I struggled up grasping the rope guides and trying not to trip over the steps, almost unbalancing at times as the ropes sagged. I tried to make up for that weak demonstration by pointing to Billy's peelings which were twice as thick as mine. I enjoyed a bit of teasing myself, and by that remark, the question in the air was, 'How many times had he peeled potatoes on board?'

The cook came through the galley door and stood over us for a while. I sensed he was giving us a critical stare, which he was but not for long; he must have noticed a lot of peelings at double thickness. Laboriously, we continued in our attempt to fill the bucket, although my thumb was starting to ache and throb a bit.

Both of us dared to look upwards, and the downward looking face began to grow a faint smile. Such reassurance did we feel that we put our best into the task, even if it did take a long hour to fill his bucket, still inches from the top. Noticing him looking at ease, we reminded him that all the eyes in the spuds had been taken out.

We had probably lost him a quarter of his spuds, but satisfaction rested on his face. The satisfaction we began to realise was that the skipper knocked all hands off so they could have a long weekend with their families. Not only did some cancel their noon dinner, but most had also cancelled their evening meal, which our potatoes were for.

My mate then explained that when a boat was lightship, or empty of cargo, the skipper would let all the crew go except the donkeyman, cook and one officer of the deck and one of the engine room; it could take days waiting for a coal-loading berth. "You'll find a difference walking up the gangway when it's loaded. The ship is low in the water and the gangway is only a short one," he concluded.

The cook shouted from the door that if we waited until the crew had already eaten, we could have whatever food was left over, and Billy muttered an aside to me, "I bet he wants to go ashore early as well for a few drinks and will ask us to wash the pots and pans."

And that is what happened. When he handed us our plates of roast beef and mixed veg, he told us we could take home any plum duff left over. Even though we had a fair filling of sandwiches for breakfast, being young fellows, we still managed to scoff some plum duff on top of our dinner.

With the rationing in force, this was a meal the locals would not find it easy to put together for a Sunday splosh. The cook lingered long enough to fill the large sink with hot, soapy water and left the pots and pans for us. And once we found ourselves in charge of the galley, Billy opened a cupboard door and nicked a small, empty flour bag.

Curious, I stuck my head forward and saw several of these bags in the cupboard, neat and flattened lying on a shelf. "He won't miss just this one," said my mate. He located a roll of brown paper, and he wrapped the pud and stuffed the weighty items inside the flour bag.

Then we took off, leaving the pots and pans clean if not in the right places. "I may as well walk you around the dock," said Billy. "Then you'll know where to go by yourself." He pointed out that although we were in the main dock area for discharging cargo from overseas; Port Tennant was the busier place. That's where they loaded coal from the valleys. Our day had brought some luck.

Billy also told me to look out for any legs that had a western ocean roll so we could find out if the owner of those supports could pass on any info in ship jobs. Me: "What's this western roll, Billy?" Billy: "My real father was a sailor, he used to walk a little wobbly, and when I asked him why he carried on like that, he told me that all sailors have a western ocean roll."

We semi-circled the whole basin, passing seven ships in the process of which we expected sailors to come down gangways for shore leave like our first ship. We were disappointed and sat on a capstan each near the stern of a ship to rest our full bellies. I was determined to become part of that mob that walked with a roll.

The few dockers we passed all had straight legs. Expecting no more luck on that lucky day, we sauntered off in the direction of the gate. My mate examined each vessel on our return walk, then stopped looking at them and told me it was time we stepped into the old mission where we could catch up with Dave and Ivan.

As we walked, it was agreed that if there were any teas bought, I would be the banker so they would be unaware my mate held any cash. Coming to the end of our walk, we found an extra small battleship had tied up to join the two minesweepers, except this one was tied to the quay. Dave and Ivan were leaning over the vessel in reaching distance of two naval ratings (enlisted men).

There was a third youth with them, wearing a naval tunic. "Watch him," warned my buddy. "He's the smartest in the gang, quicker eyes than Dave. If you have nothing, he'll help you out, but if you are carrying cash, he'll smell it out like a bloodhound and pass you a lot of smoothie talk."

As we neared, the new boy leaned over to grab something from the rating. Then he backed off and joined the other two. They all waited for us, and I was introduced to Adam. Billy was not far wrong about my new chum since Adam was not long in spotting the flour bag.

Although he himself was clutching some kind of booty, he snooped around the bag saying, "What's inside there, Billy boy, come on and tell us?" Then I noticed the round mischievous eyes in his face, and the smile in them deluded the onlooker. He seemed to sense he was looked upon as smart and played the part like a real charmer.

My mate shrugged him off; it was then decided to sort things out at the old mission. The police were changing at the gate, and the gang gave friendly waves to them. The new boy seemed to be familiar with the guard taking over and shouted, "Hello, Dai!" and gave him a puckish smile. We hung on as the officer returned. "Time you got yourself a ship, boyo. What's that package bulging in your pocket?" and added, "I hope there's no thieving going on with you boys?"

Adam: "A naval party gave it to me, Dai." "Ok, carry on but watch yourself tomorrow; there's a lady police officer on duty, and she'll take no nonsense." He didn't wag his finger at Adam, but he wagged his head, as much as to say, "That impish face puzzles me, but at least he's honest."

We left the gate, and a few yards on the other side of the road, we entered the Old Seamen's Mission. Four circular tables of ancient marble, sitting on wrought iron stands, were set a little away from the small counter, the big half of the mission area being occupied by the billiard table; two men were into a game of pool.

We seated ourselves at tables, Billy and myself on one and the others on table two. The stout lady at the counter had her eyes aimed at the direction of the billiard balls to kill boredom, and for a moment we did the same. One of the players, a short, stocky type, leaned over the green cloth and clocked an eye at us before taking a shot.

There was recognition from Dave, who waved at him. Billy planted the duff in the centre of our table. I stood up and asked the boys what they would like to drink? Being a hot day they voted for cool drinks. I speculated 6p on a flagon of red pop. Our server released the cork from the bottle top with casual expertise.

As I lingered for glasses, I overheard some nattering behind me in loud whispers. Adam asked, "Who's the new boy?" Billy: "He's a valley boy, and he's looking for a ship like us." Adam: "Did the copper at the gate know him?" Me: "Why?" Adam: "Well, he never asked what was in the flour bag Billy passed to him." Billy: "Dai DID study his face."

Chat changed when I passed the glasses around and followed with the bottle. Billy then asked Dave, "Who's playing pool with your friend Ben?" Dave: "Dunno." "I do know him," broke in Adam. "Geez, you know everybody, do you?" The tone from Dave was a little sarcastic.

But he was eager to find out as well and continued, "Well, who is he then?" Adam: "He's a Canadian not much older than us, but he looks older and is much bigger."

Then Dave broke in saying, "I now remember Ben telling me about a Canadian who was paid off as a galley boy for fighting with the chief cook."

Adam had the last word. "He's the biggest bum in Swansea." From the other table, remarks were thrown into the air like: "I haven't eaten all day," and "I am starving, I am," and "Me, too," sounded a bit louder. Addressing me, Billy said, "You can share the cake between us if you like," then turning to Adam, he demanded five cigarettes each for both of us from his cache in return. Because Adam agreed so readily, I suggested dividing the duff, and he accepted the weighty and flattened dessert lump of sugar and dough smeared with jam and stood there waiting for a knife.

Audrey, the woman at the counter, brought a large plate and knife from there. Glasses of pop helped digest the sweet meal, and when the others were glorifying in mouthfuls, my partner lowered his voice and warned me a second time about Adam.

"Adam has had a lot of chances to ship out but pulls back at the last minute. He has no mother; however, his Polish father is good to him, especially when drunk. When he's boozed up, he makes his son lazy. He drinks in the Bush Hotel. That is where Adam is always poking his nose, and if he finds his dad, he never comes out with less than five bob.

"Later on his father will have mean periods, and then Adam will screw anybody, so watch out for yourself! He knows now that you are holding some cash, so he'll be onto you." "Thanks, Billy," I answered. The other boys moved their chairs so we could join them and make a big ring around the duff. There was just enough pop to go around, and although my mate and myself had a small helping of the pudding, we were already pretty well-stuffed and enjoyed watching the others gorge themselves.

21

Whilst we sploshed the gooey down with red water, Adam placed two tins on the table. As if there was a bond between them, Davy also rose, walked over to the long bench and ripped off half a front page from an old newspaper.

He placed the paper near Adam, who poured loose tobacco on it from one of the tins. The rest of us gathered around these two, and then Adam upended seventeen cigarettes from the second tin. He passed ten smokes to Billy to conclude his contract. Dave glanced at the other seven, as they rolled across the table, but Adam decided they shouldn't be touched until the tobacco was used up.

Then Dave got to work; he grabbed the double Rizla papers and skilfully pulled one off as we all looked on in admiration. His long fingers lightly placed two fingerfuls of tobacco between thin rice paper, carefully wrapped it around and then gave a final lick across the glue edge.

To finish off, he tucked it over and smoothed it again to make it look more circular. It surprised me how Dave asked Adam how many smokes he wanted rolled in such a friendly tone, and when Adam suggested he make five for now and five for afters, he didn't hesitate but got stuck into his task; then after a minute the idea surfaced in my brain that he enjoyed doing it.

He knew he was the only artist among us who could manufacture smokables with loose tobacco and bits of paper. We all marvelled at the act, including the counter girl. "How clever!" said Audrey. Dave was cleverer than that. Whilst the tobacco lasted, Adam would need him by his side; he would be indebted to him.

It was common knowledge now that I had held cash in my pocket; enough to keep me supplied with the usual tailor-made cigarette, so Billy and I were not asked if we were willing to partake in the rolled ones. I knew beforehand that the two sailors on the destroyer had gone out of their way to please Adam, after he had explained to them which pubs cornered the pretty lasses of Swansea.

"But why?" I asked Billy, "Didn't they give him something different, like a shilling piece to spend on himself?" Billy replied, "Because a tin of fifty players cost a shilling and seventeen fags cost only 4p. If a ship sails out of British waters and the crew is allowed duty-free spirits and tobacco, my dad always used to bring home a bottle of whisky and two hundred cigarettes."

"Adam is wiser about the business than me. Once he knew the ship came from Gibraltar, he was after smokes. Sometimes you will see him outside the Bush selling duty-free smokes to sailors on shore leave." After

Adam replaced the remaining tobacco back in the tin, the three of them went back to their own table.

There was low talk from that direction, and it was not long before I realised what was in the wind. Adam returned to our table, sat himself down, and out on his charming smile and silky voice, he told us that his sailor friend Ben would soon be finishing a game of pool, and Davy would ask him what ships were due in port.

He wanted to find out if it was worth our while visiting the docks on the weekend for jobs. Billy pressed his boot over mine, and I read his lips "Blodwen" and collected the silent message – not to mention anything about the shipping list news she had passed on to us. Then he started talking about scrumpy cider, quite the potent brew but very inexpensive.

Adam concentrated on this subject, saying his mates were thinking of paying a visit to a certain pub for a pint of scrumpy each, provided I forked over the necessary shilling. "It's only 4p a pint," he finished. "However, it will cost 1s4p," countered Billy. Adam: "No, it won't. Ivan is going back to Sketty where he lives."

The game of pool at the Old Swansea Seamen's Mission was over, and the Canadian left through the doorway while Ben sidled up to Dave when that person waved him over. We all stood up ready to leave, and Ben followed the Canuck through the doorway. Adam picked up the bread-knife and passed it over the counter to the young, stout brunette.

"Thanks a million, darling," he said. The smile she beamed back at him told us the comment had made her day. Not many young people called at this place, the majority being retired seamen or younger ones who had more interest backing horses than women.

If my reply to Adam about paying for a few drinks of cider had been in the negative, I doubted if the gang would have left that place in such a chummy and confident manner. Going up the road I had my doubts if seventeen year old teens would be allowed inside a pub and voiced this opinion to Dave. He waved off my doubts with, "They don't push you back if you enter two at a time. So long as you don't barge in as a gang, it will be OK. You and Billy go in first; we'll loiter outside for a few minutes and in the meantime, grab a table far away from the bar and that's where we'll join you."

We returned the way we had come. A leg stretch to the end of Balaclava Street, turned right at the bridge, and we were back in Wind Street.

The two leaders, Dave and Adam, were pushing each other in a boisterous and playful manner. I felt sure they were going to call a halt at the Bush Hotel, but they turned down my own personal alley, St Mary's Street. We passed the big, black door and called at a pub at the end of the street called the Cross Keys, a small place, just suitable for a small street.

"Why did they pick this pub, Billy?" I asked. "We are not allowed in the Bush; popular pubs on the main street are strict on serving juniors. Anyway, this is the best place because Adam hangs out a lot here when he's out of cash." Small the pub may have been, but it had the usual diversions that conform to the British pub that make it unique.

We passed the open door of the Cross Keys enclave with seats for only two or three elderly ladies to natter, and inside this cubbyhole was a door that led to a small room where business people could wheel and deal. We passed through the lounge, which was spacier but still not accommodating for many people and then we went into the bar.

Here the dartboard was given its quarter space of room for elbow exercise. This was where any type of dress was welcome, dungarees or plus fours. The dartboard here looked very new and non-punctured, and I was to learn that there was a reason for that. The clientele was international and a calling place for the Spanish nationals living at their hostel next to the Bush Hotel.

Different bars have distinctive atmospheres, and my feelings were in tune with this one. Its quiet was not that of a subdued nature, but it had a 'pull' to its atmosphere. Just as I was drawn very much to the atmosphere of the Chain Locker in Barry with its attraction of free, loud expressions of mirth, even if the guffaws seemed a little rude, I was also drawn to the Cross Keys but with the opposite effect, like a magic secrecy in the air, and by that I mean those 'instant' first impressions one takes in and never recur. I paid for two pints of cider and was handed a cheeky smile with my change. Billy had collared the table most distant from the bar, and after collecting change from my shilling, I carried the two pints over.

Passing a table on the way, I overheard the smooth lingo of an alien tongue. I queried Billy on our neighbours after placing the glasses on the table, and he let me know that this place was the hangout of Puerto Rican sailors. He also let on that later on around 6pm, you have a lot of painted dolls coming in to entertain them.

First impressions can sometimes be right; I still felt the atmosphere held mystery and romance, like it was floating in the air. Billy was now explaining to me about the tarts that made this place their rendezvous. "They are all local girls, but some of them are Spanish speaking from crossbred parents." Then who should enter but our two mates.

As they made their way to our table, I was surprised when the barmaid who had served me gave Adam a cheery "Hello" as he passed, and the young lad then stepped back to have a word with her, as Dave stood by him, before they reached our table. Billy let me know that Adam was frequently brought inside here by Puerto Ricans.

They would trust him with a carton or two of cigarettes to sell, and since he always returned with the cash, the barmaid held him in high esteem. With the shortage of smokes in the UK, it wasn't difficult to up the price, even though they were U.S. brands like Lucky Strikes or Camels.

UK Players cigarettes were charged 9p for twenty, which amounted to 7s 6p for a carton of 200, whereas a duty-free carton cost only a quarter of that; yet on American ships the cost was even lower. I went to the counter to pay for the ciders, and Dave carried them over to our table.

I was getting very interested in the knowledge Billy was feeding me and was avid for more, but Dave had more important news to put into our ears. "It's no use going down to the docks until Tuesday. Ben told me most of the ships in port won't be there for a day or two, and the only ones coming in at the weekend will be one Greek and an American ship."

"What's coming in Tuesday?" asked Billy. Dave: "There are two flying the Red Duster and a Norske."

There was a twinkle in Adam's eyes and turning to Dave he asked, "Was that ship you saw American or Panamanian?" Dave: "Dunno. I can't tell the difference with those two flags. Why?" Adam quaffed his scrumpy and answered, "I'll talk to Rosie at the bar." Dave asked, "Tell her what?" Adam: "She can expect a few customers at the weekend; there's always Puerto Ricans sailing on American and Panamanian ships."

Before walking over to the barmaid, he bent low over our table so that customers at the next one could not overhear. "If the cider gets you tipsy, don't mention the word 'Dago' and spoil things." We agreed with head nods.

When Dave and Adam went to visit the toilet later on, Billy took the chance to caution me. "It's up to you, but you'll regret it if you call more than one round of scrumpy; it makes good people quarrelsome and dopey later." He was a good mentor, was my mate, and I decided seriously to take his advice. The other two had already returned to the table, and I passed a shilling to Adam to order four more refills.

The warm weather might have quickened the thirst, but it was a wiser move than I thought at the time of giving in to buy booze after everybody's belly was full of duff. There was no hurry in emptying the sweet liquid, and by the end of the second round, there was no urge from anyone for a refill.

We waved Rosie goodbye and sauntered through the door, a little unsteady on our feet. With the humid air outside, everyone showed signs of drowsiness. We made our way to the nearby mission floppers. The other two left Billy and myself at the first whilst they carried on to have a snooze at the other mission. Blodwen handed me my dilly bag and Billy's canvas one, and then we bought two coffees.

I had an inclination to pump some more information out of Billy about the shipping game, but first I wanted to query him on his source of info. "How do you know so much about ships, Billy? You haven't even been to sea." "When my real father shipped out, he used to take me to the shipping office with him sometimes," Billy said.

"What happens when you go in the shipping office?" I asked. Billy answered, "If you are first trippers like me, and you hand him a note from a skipper who has offered you a job, he may tell you to run along to the immigration building, which is not far along Balaclava Street." Billy was going on like a river now and I sucked in every drop.

"If you are under twenty-one years of age, you will need your parents' consent. Padre Edwards here may help you since he is used to sending telegrams."

Now that the others had left us, I felt a bit loose and invited my mate to try and enter the Bush Hotel for a drink of ordinary beer. "I've had a drink in there before," said Billy, "so their barmaid must have passed me for eighteen, so we should give it a try at least." There were no questions asked, just like when I entered my first day in Swansea. Rather than lean on a counter, we drank at a table. The cider had dried in my mouth, so I took a big gulp from my pint glass first go.

When someone went to the toilet, they went part way through the lounge bar. I sat sideways to that door, and I took a big squint each time. Billy did likewise, passing the comment, "There's loads of skirt in there for anyone with extra cash." This got me thinking about money, and I probed, "How long do you have to be on a ship before the captain pays your wages?" Billy: "When you sail deep-sea, you sign for a voyage. As soon as you sign the big book in front of the shipping master, he will ask you if you want five pounds in advance of your wages." Me: "You mean five one pound notes before you even start doing any work?"

Billy: "He has to give it to you if you want it; every captain has to. But it is not in cash; it is a white note that cannot be cashed until the ship sails." Me: "I don't understand." Billy: "Don't worry about it. There's not one in a hundred that fails to turn up when the ship sails, as he has to pay back the money before he ships out again. You will have no problem changing your note into cash."

"Outside the shipping office door, you will always find a note casher. If there are two, you are in luck because they compete and will charge you 2s in the pound on top, but if there is only one, you will have to pay him half a crown for every pound he accepts. This means that when you pass him a five pound advance note, he will return you five pounds minus 10s or minus 12s 6p. Able seamen and firemen can draw ten pounds, but deck boys, galley boys and trimmers are only allowed five."

After that chat we left the mission, I decided we should speculate a few coppers at the wash and brush-up cubicles near the railway station. We talked a lot on the long downhill walk back about what it would be like when we joined the same ship together – the warm evening building up in our imaginations.

I was awoken by my mate on Saturday morning. It was gone 9am and most of the lodgers had vacated beds. My mate laughed at the drunks complaining at my loud snoring of which I had been unaware.

We walked out into bright sunlight and made for our first stopping place. Entering the mission, we said hello to some new girl at the counter, walked past the ping-pong table and entered the wash-up room for a face wipe. I handed my towel back to Billy to put in his bag and returned the short distance to our dormitory to hang the towels at the bottom of our bunks.

We returned to Wind Street. My mate remarked that he felt he carried a small brick in his head, and I felt the same way; that was always the curse of cider drinking. We felt that a hot cuppa at the dock's mission would melt that imaginary brick.

Before entering the mission, Billy urged me a hundred feet further along, and we came to a sturdy, embellished stonework entrance. A notice on the wall stated that this building was the Board of Trade but more commonly known as the 'shipping office'.

We idled along further to an ancient inn. It was built in the old stonemason style and called the Cape Horner. We went no further, but I was pointed out the immigration offices as well as the customs and excise building. I asked my mate why we shouldn't carry on to Port Tennant and explore the dock area for jobs. However, he insisted that all we would receive there was coal dust and a need for a fresh shower.

He let me know not to bother with Port Tennant, only as a last resort, because most ships had full crews and were under orders to sail. We doubled back to the old mission and clumsily kicked a few stones.

On entering, we found we had company. I recognised the big Canuck at the far end of the billiard table bench. Also, two strangers sitting on the near side of the bench were eating from a spread out newspaper. The Canadian waved us over. In the newspaper were plenty of bacon rashers and sausages, and Chuck, the Canadian, told us to dip our fingers in, as there was plenty for everyone. I nibbled at a sausage, found my sense of taste returning and enjoyed a second one.

Billy had even a smaller appetite than myself. My main urge was to drink and if the tea didn't satisfy, it meant I might speculate on a beer. I felt sure Billy felt that way too, so both of us walked to the counter. We turned to go out when Chuck called us back to introduce us to the two new faces.

Duncan was in his mid-twenties and his mate a little younger. He asked if anyone had a fag to spare, and I handed him one. His chum told us his name was Alex and that he was a Geordie. Alex was pretty chatty. "You boys, looking for a ship?" "Yeah," both of us chorused. Alex: "So am I. I'm spent out from the last coaster I was on, but don't worry, there'll be a few jobs going next week."

Both of us walked over to the counter and ordered coffees instead of teas, then took over a table. I recalled what Blodwen had mentioned about a lot of shipping arrivals in the coming two weeks, and that it looked like more men were coming to Swansea to try their luck. I suggested to Billy we keep in contact with Alex.

The coffees had small effects on our combined headaches, and there was only one thing for it – the hair of the dog – another pint of beer to get the blood circulating back to normal. I suggested to Billy that we bring along Alex. "It's your cash," he replied. Then there was a pause. "But I'm not objecting."

We lit up another fag just as Alex was making his way out. I offered the packet to him when we passed, and he didn't resist but came and sat by us. He lit up and thanked me profusely. I asked him if he would like to join us in a drink. "Wouldn't I!" Obviously he felt like a hair of the dog too, as we took him to the Cross Keys and settled at a table with three pints of ale. "Why did the other fellow in the Mission call you Geordie?" I asked. Alex replied, "Anyone from Middleborough to the River Tyne is a Geordie, and I'm from South Shields, which is near Newcastle."

Then he opened up a lot and told us he was bedded at a cheap flophouse near the railway station. He complained about a previous shipmate he met the night before. "I enjoy a drink with a friend, but when a man is plain broke, there are other things on his mind, and this shipmate of mine kept standing me drinks on an empty stomach. When the pub closed, I even had to bum some fish and chips money off him."

I looked at Rosie, the barmaid, and wondered if she had taken a fancy to me because when I bought the ales, that big smile she gave me was very real. Girls at two other tables were local, but I didn't know about their swarthy boyfriends; the tables were too distant to overhear their conversation.

Whilst Alex was in conversation with Billy, I took off to the toilet. My head was clearing fast, and I was coming back into the real world. I did not want to wind up like Alex and locked myself in a closet to check my cash. I dipped fingers into my rear pocket and brought out what notes were left from the twelve pounds I had in my possession when I left Witney in Oxfordshire a week before.

I was astounded at only counting four one pound notes and one ten shilling note. Where had all the cash gone? My side pockets were heavy with coinage since I had started my spending spree, which I didn't bother to count, as it might give me another fright, so I walked back to the table and put on as bright face as I could.

Alex was doing the nattering, and I seated myself by his side as I did not want to miss out on any info from a real seafarer. He was on about 'live wires', and I interrupted him to understand what the term meant. He let me know that live wires were men who had just paid off a ship and were flush with cash.

Then he repeated the axiom about live wires. "If you meet one you've sailed with, he'll buy you all the beer in the world, but when it comes to parting with a quid, they back down." He asked us if there were any vacancies at Mrs Ramos' lodging house since he heard it was the cheapest lodging house in Swansea.

Then Billy informed me. "He pays 2s at his house and everybody is drunk and too noisy at night." The ale was not softening my resolve to make sure my rent was paid up but hardening it. There and then I decided to pay two weeks rent in advance as soon as I returned to Mrs Ramos' friendly habitat.

The single pint seemed to have a good effect on Alex as he played the gent and stated that he wanted no more. Billy felt the same way so that made three of us. We walked out of the door, and before leaving our new friend, I put a shilling piece in his hand for cigarette money. We made our way back down the narrow street to St Mary's.

I left Billy at the black door; he said he was going to kill time at the nearby mission. I was glad to find myself alone in the long dormitory upstairs, and making doubly sure I was alone, I spread out all the coins I possessed on the blanket. Not only was there enough to pay two weeks rent from the loose change but with seven shillings left over.

When I paid Julie (which I now called her), she handed me some magazines she had kept from lodgers that had left, and I took them up to my bed and put them under my pillow. All except one called 'Titbits' of which I made a quick scan.

Then I went back to the Cross Keys. My mind was set on some sandwiches I had spotted at the bar. They were set on a platter beneath a semi-globular glass cover. There were longish rolls with thick ham slices between them, and when I had mentioned this to Alex, he said that a Puerto Rican cook from one of the ships had brought a leg of ham to his favourite barmaid.

Rosie served me a shandy at the Cross Keys and still took a special interest in me. The three girls with a similar number of partners had exited one of the tables since I had left, and only three men remained at the other table. Said Rosie, "You are looking for a ship aren't you, boyo?" "Yeah, that's right," I replied.

"Adam has had plenty of chances to ship out, but he is never really serious. You are different; I can see it in your eyes." She handed me the two rolls I had ordered with the sweet shandy but had already warned me that they were on the expensive side at 3p each. As I was about to carry them to the table, she told me to hang on.

She then leaned over the counter and addressed one of the trio, "Any jobs going on your ship, Manuel?" and pointing to myself asked, "Can you find work for this young man?" "Maybe, if he got his papers?" and turning in my direction, Manuel invited me to sit at his table.

It was a round table so that you could sit yourself down on any part of it. His two partners stopped looking into their wine glasses and shuffled their seats to make room for me. I carried my sweet ale there but left the sandwiches on the counter; something important could turn up.

Conversation started out with pleasant, small talk, but it was soon obvious that I had not yet adapted to the jargon of the merchant seamen, which sort of deflated the situation. Even so they were not short on sympathy; I learned quite a bit from them. They were crew members on an American ship.

They made me aware that they worked under the discipline of a strong union and could not recommend any new crew members unless they could produce some valid seagoing experience and a passport. I had neither. The serious business being over, I took my sandwiches and washed them down with my glass of sweet ale. They offered a refill, but I was too bloated to accept, although I did not turn down an offer of Lucky Strike smokes before leaving them.

I made headway to the nearby mission and found Billy sitting by his lonesome – listening in to two old codgers sitting at the next table, throwing seafaring yarns into one another's ears. A stiff-looking, prim lady sat behind the counter reading a magazine; she looked in her thirties.

Billy suggested we take a walk to a sandy beach, and I was with him. I needed to know some places to escape to when the situation looked none too bright. We soon discarded footwear for a stroll along the beach at Mumbles Road, only a short walking distance away. We stripped off upper clothing and lay back in the sun.

For a lot of white sand and beautiful weather, I was surprised to find only small pockets of people here and there, but Billy explained that there were such a lot of choice beaches further along the Gower Coast that people could be selective. Then I remembered having packed bathing trunks in my case, which was still under the bed in the dormitory.

Days passed. Pubs were such a source of information and with good feelings that dispel loneliness in a strange place so that without realising it, my bank was slowly but surely getting frittered away. After a week I saw Billy for brief intervals at the missions, and he must have sensed that I didn't have the cash to renew his bed money.

When I did catch up with him, he said his sister helped him a lot, as she kept the friendship of a steady sailor who was making good money. What I liked about his attitude was that he retained a gut feeling, like myself, that our ship would turn up. We had determined our path come what may.

After the fortnight's bed payment ended, I awoke one morning fumbling through my pockets and found myself in possession of nine shillings. Being all alone in this room and in the world as it were, I understood seven shillings of that nine must be paid for my bed. I descended downstairs and paid Maria for a week's lodge. She always gave me encouraging hopes, and I walked out of the door with my head still held high.

During the last week in August 1941, Billy and I decided to board every ship docked in the port of Swansea. Getting the nod from gate police, we put our best foot forward, yet we had no luck with job openings, until the third vessel we boarded. It was not long past midday. Although the cook needed no galley boy, he did take kindly to our circumstances.

He told us we could eat whatever was left in the pots and pans, provided we cleaned them up after us. Destitution was tracking us now, and hunger gnawed our innards, so we were only too glad to oblige, feeding our faces like a pair of gannets.

We had no luck job seeking but left the dock with full stomachs and had company on the way up Wind Street. There were familiar faces from the missions, looking for jobs like ourselves with no luck – one loner and two young guys paired up like ourselves. It seemed everyone was rowing against the tide on this day. At the bombed church we separated, Billy going his way, and I went in the direction of the black door. I decided to make use of my bed to conserve energy.

That big feed held me together for the next two days. On the third day I failed to rendezvous with my mate in the Flying Angel Mission and took off to the one in Balaclava Street. In the second mission I came across Chuck, the Canadian. I was a dud at the game of snooker, and he offered to show me a few points of the game.

It was then he must have noticed I was acting kind of listless. He pulled me aside and said, "Look here, buddy. You need a goddam feed like myself. Follow me." I followed like a sheep, an awfully hungry sheep. I had no inkling what he was up to, but he was so earnest in his quest that I had difficulty in keeping up with him.

All I could get out of him was: "We'll have to get out of the main drag before we start operating." He repeated this a few times, and then we turned up a steep, long lane. We were moving to houses on a higher elevation that looked more high-class. We settled in a street that had a harbour view and sat down on a small, low wall to catch our breath back.

He must have felt the heat more than myself as he wore a thick, tartan shirt. From a breast pocket he drew a packet of loose cigarette tobacco and turning to me asked if I could roll a cigarette? "No, I have never done it," I said. "Well, watch me." and he placed spongy, stringy tobacco across the palm of one hand, and with the heel of his other thumb, he rolled it around. Then he separated the neat little ball in two, placing one part under his tobacco holder so that the small breeze would not waft it away; then he pulled the other part sideways and long ways and then rubbed it rapidly back and fro with fingers pressed together.

The explaining takes longer than the actual act, which took next to no time, and when it took shape, it looked like a firm, thin brown stick. He told me to remove the Rizla paper from inside his tobacco pouch and pass it to him. He circled the stick of tobacco with the thin paper and tightened it by rubbing two thumbs gently in a circular motion, licked the glue edge, and deftly smoothed the finished product with his fingers.

The first 'Make' he passed to me, and then manufactured one for himself. He took matches from his pouch, and we both lit up. "Smoke away," he advised. "And take it easy, we got time aplenty." Noticeably the rolled fag eased my hunger. I felt giddy at first because it was stronger and more pungent than ordinary tailor-made cigarettes.

From then on, he strolled easily along, studying the houses, and as I trailed slowly after him, I quickly felt less weak. "Top dogs live in this neighbourhood," he commented. "I've done this stretch before. Watch this," he said smiling. Looking back at me he directed his footsteps to a noticeably high-fashioned door, Chuck didn't hesitate to give the shiny, brass door knocker a good clang.

The door was soon opened by a tallish, athletic-looking person, just starting to grow a middle-age spread. He must have been someone in a 'boss' capacity or he wouldn't be wearing a collar on such a warm day. He condescended to address us after a sharp scrutiny.

"What do you want?" The question was to the point. Then Chuck took over. "Excuse me, sir, but we are merchant seamen in a desperate situation. If you have a bite left over from your last meal, we would be grateful if you could wrap it up and give it to us as a handout?"

It was not difficult to read this man's mind. He must have been thinking after his ears registered the strange accent, 'Shameless cheek of these seamen. Don't they know we're on rations this side of the Atlantic?' He stared past my eyes. Had I been cross-examined? I felt sure I should have bolted; those eyes were certainly very questioning.

But his gaze had no such effect on the Canadian; Chuck was as nonchalant as you like. The householder retreated along the passage. "He'll give," said my mate turning around. "By the way what's your name, buddy?" Me: "Ted." Then sounds of a tinkling piano echoed from a side room, whose door was ajar and broke the silence.

The main door was also left half-way open. And our man was soon back. The front door opened wider, and it totally surprised us since the door had erased the sound of footsteps on the hall carpet.

My mate swung around rapidly from chatting to make a half bow to the long fellow, who handed him a square parcel. The bloke didn't smile. Just passed it to us and closed the door directly after.

He proved a Good Samaritan all right. When we whipped around the corner of the street to examine the contents, there were newly made sandwiches made with fresh bread. Our prize was half a dozen thick slices with meat between all of them.

Admittedly, the butter was sparse and the meat slices on the thin side, but the smell of homemade bread made up for all that. My friend rewrapped the parcel, and we made our descent in the direction of Wind Street. Presently we came to a side lane with some large stones and settled ourselves down in this hideaway.

The brown paper packet was opened up again. Chuck handed me a sandwich, took one himself and laid the spare to one side. I bit through the thickness of my sandwich and tasted the sweet sharpness of salted ham. It was delicious. Whilst both of us were munching away, my mate lifted open the third sandwich and took a smell of the paste filling and exclaimed: "What the hell is that stuff?" Chuck blasted.

It only needed a short examination with my eyes. "Spam," I replied. "A new kind of meat developed early in the war; a kind of meat that will self-preserve like corned beef." He let me know that the Spam sandwich was totally mine, and I thanked him. With two thick sandwiches, normal thinking soon took over my brain.

"Guess you were hungry," Chuck smiled. "I noticed the way you wolfed down that hunk of bread and meat." I then opened up with a comment. "That man must have used up some of his personal rations to feed us?"

Chuck: "Maybe so, and maybe not so. That guy wasn't keen on socialising – like he was trying to hide something. My guess is that he has a contact that raises a lot of pigs because that ham sure has a lot of salt in it, so he would have a leg of pork hanging up in his kitchen." I replied, "You're a real detective, Chuck." Chuck: "You've got to be a real face reader in this situation to survive. What d'ya say we make another visit to that guy's house later in the week?"

He read my silence. He was asking a big question. I doubted if I had the nerve to face up to that pair of piercing eyes again. We might not be so lucky next time. He had been studying my facial expressions all that time, and then he turned to me. "I was only kidding, Ted. That guy would sure call the cops if we showed up at his house again."

And with that, he broke out into a great guffaw. The laugh caught on as I was doing the face reading now, and I could just imagine both of us scampering down those short, few steps in front of the ornate doorway, when we heard the telephone in the hallway being set down after a police call. We parted at St Mary's Street, still laughing and joking at what might occur should we pay a second visit to our Good Samaritan.

Entering the lodging house and making my way to the kitchen, I paid Julia and Maria some long due smiles and asked if Billy or anyone else had called around about me. No one had been around, but I was passed a small batch of magazines, more glossy ones this time. Going up to my room, I felt I would survive this day and the next.

Well, the next day came along, and I wandered listlessly down Wind Street and entered the old mission. Alex the Geordie caught my eye, sitting on a long bench while watching two men playing a game of pool. I joined him. After a while, he nudged me, rose up and walked in the direction of the entrance. I followed him. At the doorway, he waved me on. As we walked up Balaclava Street, he told me that he had important news to share.

"But first, let's get settled in the other mission; I want this news kept quiet. We'll have a cuppa and something to eat." "But I'm broke, Alex," I replied.

"I can see that, pal, but a ten shilling note was passed on to me by an ex-shipmate yesterday, and I'm trying to use it wisely, at least until tomorrow." Me: "Why tomorrow?" "Wait until we sit ourselves at the floppers."

Pleasant Blodwen was at the counter to give us service. There was not much choice of eats, but our sweetheart was helpful. Pointing to a large glass jar full of small, flat cakes, she confided to us, 'Someone came in this morning and donated these Welsh cakes." "How much are they?" I asked. "They are lovely and fresh and worth a penny each," she replied. Alex bought a dozen, costing him a shilling, and Blod made a pyramid of them on a wide plate. My mate carried them over to a back table, and I followed with two teas.

I noticed Alex had picked a far table to sit on, so there would be some special news coming from him. In a low, confiding voice, he passed on to me what I was waiting for. "As you know, Ted, I have sailed on coasters for over a year and was advised to come to Swansea to get myself signed on deep-sea ships. The Shipping Master told me my only hope was to pop into his office now and again."

"I called in there this morning, and there was no business going on. I found the head clerk all alone behind the counter and asked for the Shipping Master himself. I was told that person was preparing to pay off two crews in the afternoon, but perhaps he himself could be of some help to me."

"I spread out to him my tale of waiting for a job break that was a long time coming, and he sympathised. He saw I couldn't last much longer, and I didn't want to return to coasting. He then suggested, "Do you mind sailing on foreign ships for a while? Some of them pay higher wages than us, and it's just the food is different." "Would that help me to get on British ships when I paid off?"

"Of course," he answered. "Once you have sailed deep-sea and completed a voyage with good recommendations, any port in the UK will register you as a foreign-going seaman," and he added, "There's a war on, you know."

"As we chatted away, the big office was still empty, which is unusual for these places with skippers coming and going all the time; so being impatient, I asked him to tip me off about these other ships, and pointing to the window facing Balaclava Street and the dock area behind it, he let me into something."

"He said that on the following morning there would be a free-for-all for jobs against the iron fencing surrounding the docks. Two ships, one Panamanian and one Greek, needed fresh crews. If you lined up against that railing fence at 9am, you may get picked out by one of the two skippers, who will turn up at that time. He told me to keep it mum so that you are the only one I am passing the tip onto; I don't forget the time you helped me with a fag and a drink."

"How about my mate Billy?" I questioned. Alex: "OK, but only him, otherwise we might spoil everything for ourselves." He was thoughtful for a moment, sipping tea and chomping into the cakes, and then he continued. "The clerk told me that I stand a good chance with my discharge papers from coasting, and you can bet that most of them will have no papers to show, so you stand as good a chance as any."

Me: "But won't there be experienced seamen there?" Alex: "Yeah, but the papers they will be holding won't be of much use, mostly bad discharges." Me: "What does that mean?" Alex: "It means they have been fighting or drunk and disorderly or vandalising on the last ship they were on, and they have been paid off with bad remarks in their record book."

Like many rumours that had come my way, prospects had fizzled out, but this time I felt my chance had come. I decided to put on an extra effort getting myself cleaned up and ready for the morning line up. Alex passed me a fag, and we lit up after scoffing down the sweet, floury cakes. I was given two cigarettes for later, which I placed in my shirt pocket and I left Alex who had ideas about searching for a friend uptown.

I went on my lonesome down St Mary's Street, full of thought and expectancy, gave the black door a hard push and made straight for the kitchen. Julie was cleaning up the dishes and put on an encouraging smile for me when I told her I might be onto a ship at last.

"Billy told me that you cleaned up at the Mission in Wind Street. Is that right?" Me: "That's right, why?" Julie: "It's just that my mother is out shopping, and she'll be visiting friends at the same time, and it could be a few hours before she returns. Why don't you use our bathroom at the other end of the kitchen?" I was glad that I had stayed at number 12, St Mary's Street; to be on family terms when you are down and out is an advantage not to be scorned.

On the coal stove, there was a large copper pot full of hot water plus a square tank at the side of the fireplace, so I was not short of hot water for a lie back in the bath, and as Maria would not be back for a few hours, I took my time and lay back in the steamy, old tin bath. I later spent the evening in the dormitory reading magazines.

I slept well that night with no fear of late rising. Mrs Ramos herself had said she would instruct the early-rising lodgers to rouse me. On this particular night, I slept with my jeans stretched flat under the mattress to give them a presentable crease for the morning.

Julie must have talked her mother into inviting me into her kitchen that early morning for a friendly cup of tea with saccharine. Then off I went, pacing down Wind Street, hoping to meet Billy on the way. After emerging from beneath the bridge and entering Balaclava Street, my ears were struck by a chattering intercourse of voices!

Having left the house at 9am sharp, it could not have been less than ten minutes later when I arrived on the scene. There was certainly a lot of talk going on opposite the shipping office. Had I missed out? Panic seized me, as I ran the last few yards as fast as my legs could carry me.

I saw that there in the spot were several broad-shouldered men with open booklets, chatting to a man in epaulets. One of the men had a particularly tough face with a longish scar, arching down along his jowl. Altogether the setup made me feel small. I made a random check for the face of Alex among the groups of men, and I was relieved when I spotted him leaning up against the fence, talking to Billy who he had run into and alerted about the hiring.

After a few hellos, I asked both if they had missed out on any vacancies. They wagged their heads, and then Alex cleared the air. "Hang on for a while, Ted; we're waiting for the skipper of the other ship to arrive." Me: "But who is this man in uniform talking to those hefty sailors?" Alex: "He's the skipper of the Panamanian ship."

Alex: "He only wants four ABS." "What's ABS?" I questioned. "Able Bodied Seaman. You've got to have over three years' service on deck before you get issued with an ABS ticket." Me: "How long have you got, Alex?" "Only fourteen months." Five other men were leaning against the rail, close to where the foursome was bargaining with the skipper of the Panamanian ship.

"The captain won't take on those men, because he doesn't like the reports in their record books. They are just hanging around to see if their mates will get a something. Turning his back to the others as if to keep something secret and then facing Billy and me as we leaned against the rail, Alex rubbed his hands with glee. And then he said, "I've heard a whisper that the Greek ship is looking for a galley boy, a cabin boy and an ordinary seaman." "What's an ordinary seaman?" It seemed my mate enjoyed answering maritime questions as much as I liked asking them. Alex: "That ordinary seaman's job is for me. For the first year at sea, you rate as a deck boy, and after that your pay goes right up as an Ordinary, an OS."

Scanning the others, he confided, "Looks like we'll get the jobs because I can't see any other young guys here except ourselves." The four sailors who had been trying to persuade the uniform, turned to their mates in a jubilant mood and chatted happily away with them before rejoining their new skipper, and they all walked off.

The other fence leaners, somewhat dejected, took off towards the old mission, hands in trouser pockets. Only us three were left. "I told you so," said our mentor. At first we didn't notice a person carrying a briefcase, as he strode out of the nearby dock gate. He looked your ordinary civilian type with a trilby on his head.

Presently, someone in sea boots and work gear was tagging after him, and as they moved in our direction, I heard the broadest English ever come out of their mouths. Clearly these men were foreigners and we were caught unawares when they asked us if we had seen any sailors around.

Without thinking, Billy responded immediately that there were five sailors in the mission opposite. The trilby then turned to his offsider and said, "Manuel, go and fetch them." Alex was now alert to the situation and turning to the speaker asked if he was a captain. "Yes, I am captain of *Lily*. Why you ask?" "Well, us three are looking for work on any ship we can get." The skipper returned him a quizzical stare. "You have papers?" and quick as lightning, young Alex drew a thin blue book from his hip pocket and handed it to the skipper.

It seemed that the skipper had a little difficulty with the wording. Pointing a finger at the wording 'OS', "What this mean?" he wanted to know. Alex: "That means ordinary seaman, sir, and if you look further along the line, it's got GOOD stamped on the report." Captain: "I understood that word, but I didn't understand what ordinary seaman is."

Then up walked a person in uniform. Alex passed onto me that his epaulette registered him second deck officer, or second mate.

Standing beside the skipper, he seemed more conversant with the British style of ratings and explained to his superior that an OS was just another word for a sailor who could steer a ship and understood knots but was limited in the technical side of seamanship like splicing wire ropes or rigging a bosun's chair for painting aloft.

"I have a sailor coming from Cardiff tomorrow to join my ship," put in the captain. "But if he does not come, you shall have sailor job." The skipper read the pain on the face of Alex, and like an experienced seaman knew he would be a willing deckhand. After hesitation he said, "I can give you coal trimmer job until we need more sailors. Is same pay."

As five men emerged from the mission, the skipper turned to have a word with his second mate. I thought he was going to forget about Billy and myself, and my heart sank. Then as the mate examined record books of the others, the skipper turned back to give us attention.

Captain: "Are you two boys also looking for jobs?" "Yeah!" we shouted in unison and waited breathlessly for the next question. Captain: "Can you show me papers from your last ship?" Switching his eyes from one to the other of us, Alex was on the point of trying to explain the situation to the captain; however, that man turned around to him and said, "I understand. They have not been on boat before," and he just stood there in front of us, thoughtfully and silently. He then approached me personally and squeezed my shoulder. "You are strong. My cook, he need someone to help him. You can do that job, yes?" I nodded in affirmation, afraid that if I spoke, I might say the wrong thing; I was that excited.

Then he moved closer to Billy and, eyeing him as well, must have concluded we were mates. I thought he may have hesitated to engage my mate because he had a frailer body. The skipper turned aside to have a natter with his junior officer. The mate ceased talking to the other group and came across to us and asked us if we didn't mind eating Greek food.

I would have eaten anything for the chance of shipping out, and the other two must have felt the same way, because the three of us were very eager in accepting a different diet. Then the mate concluded his talk with us, whilst the captain attended the others. He confirmed that the three of us would be accepted as members of the crew of *S/S Lily*.

All we had to do was hang around until the other five men had been dealt with. My joy was boundless and as far as I could see so was Billy's. Alex, however, was of a more silent, serious air. Coming out of his seriousness, he explained that a coal trimmer's discharge was no good to take to the board of trade when we returned from the voyage.

Then he brightened up when we reminded him that the skipper would give him first chance of a job on deck when a sailor paid off, and anyway, if the sailor didn't turn up from Cardiff the following day, the deck job was his.

An argument broke out among the other bunch, and presently, two men returned to the mission cursing. Then a third and fourth man followed, leaving only one pasty-faced person, reasonably tall but dressed in worn clothes and heavy boots. I had often seen him playing pool with Chuck in the mission. We soon heard the officer tell him what berth the *Lily* was docked at, and that the quarters were on the forepart of the ship, and then he turned his attention back to us.

He made it a point of addressing Alex first. "Remember to come aboard tomorrow, and if the sailor has not come from Cardiff, you can have his job." "What if he turns up?" Alex asked. "Then you can take the trimmer's job." Alex: "How much a month?" "Twenty-five pounds."

Alex: "That'll do me, providing I can get work on deck when a deckhand pays off." Officer: "There are two men in the crew with sailor rating, so you have a chance."

Then he attended to us. After letting Billy know that the captain had indeed accepted him as cabin boy, he continued, "The captain tell me you have no seaman's papers. You must go to immigration for permission to leave the country. The ship will not sail for one week, so you have plenty of time. You know name of ship?" "Yes!" came three eager voices. When we separated from the officer, Alex said he needed a cuppa to think things over and invited us to join him, so we pushed off to the convenient Old Swansea Seamen's Mission nearby.

The stout counter girl, Audrey, was eager and happy to serve us. "I was watching through the window," she remarked. "Which one of you was chosen by the captain?" "All of us," answered the proud OS. "Well, don't forget to come and visit me when you return from the voyage," she uttered coyly, and we answered that we certainly would.

At the table next to us were two of the chaps who had been turned down. Alex asked why the skipper hadn't hired them. They replied that they were qualified firemen, but the skipper needed only one plus a trimmer. They decided among themselves to allow the Canadian with them to take the job. The rumour was that the ship was bound for Canada, and he wanted to return to Montreal where he lived.

"Didn't you fancy the trimmer's job?" Alex asked. "It wasn't worth it.

We make the same on British ships. How much does a fireman get on Greek ships?" one man asked. Alex: "Thirty two pounds and with no tax." "Gee, that's top cash. Did the mate tell your lot what your wages were?"

Alex: "Billy gets twenty pounds as cabin boy; Ted gets twenty-two as galley boy, and my own wages come to twenty-five, whether I take the job as OS or trimmer, and remember no tax." "Well, good luck to you, boys," they concluded and left.

Alex: "I think I'm going to have to visit immigration as well myself, fellers, because the mate didn't realise I was only a coastal seaman, and I didn't want to upset him. Let's push off now while the day is early," he finished. On the way out, we remembered to give the counter girl a smile, and then made straight for our office down the road.

We found three men at hand behind the counter; one middle-aged gent was sitting in a far corner, studying a ledger, while two younger assistants were only too glad to be of help. We approached the nearest one. He told Alex to hand his discharge book to his assistant to deal with and then turned to Billy and myself. He leaned over the counter, and in a fatherly tone, let us know that because both of us were under twenty-one years of age, the first thing we had to do was to get permission from our parents or next-of-kin to leave the country.

He impressed on us that though it was only a formality, it basically was – no permission, no shipping out – and if and when we received this document, their office must be informed before anyone else. Both of us left the building, silent and thoughtful, leaving Alex still talking to his man.

As we walked along the street, Billy remarked, "I hate to see that stepfather of mine, and I think my real father is still at sea," but he brightened up when I told him he could get a signature off his mother. Until he had confided his problem to me, I thought I had the biggest problem in the world, but now my sympathy went out to him.

I wouldn't like to ship out without Billy, but then my brain tussled feverishly with my own dilemma. How was I going to get enough cash for train fare home to coax permission out of my eldest brother? I handed the problem to my mate. "I've been an orphan since nine, but I have never lived in an orphanage, only with my brothers and sisters. Do I have a choice of who to ask?"

Billy couldn't answer that one, and it looked like I would have to visit my brother. Then my mate had a brainwave. "We'll have to ask Blodwen to put in a word for us to the Padre; I hope she's at the counter right now." The dark cloud of despair quickly lifted from our minds.

We sighed with relief as we entered the Wind Street Mission. Our heroine was at the counter, but she let us know that it would be a full hour before Mr Edwards would arrive at his appointed time of 11am. We took a pew at the nearest table so Blod could share our problem, and she dived into it.

"Look, Billy, your father is at work now, so why don't you pop up and see your mother? You can get her written consent before he returns." Billy hesitated, and our angel first bided her time. Then she encouragingly said, "I shall go ahead and tell the Padre about your problem, and if you are in difficulties, he will assist you further." My mate chewed over this advice for a while before agreeing.

"Coming?" asked Billy, and then I hesitated. Blodwen then urged me to get along also, after she assured me that she would let Mr Edwards know about my problem as well. Instead of pairing with my mate on his long upward trek to his mam, I took the route down to familiar St Mary's Street. I entered the lodgings intent on sharing my problem with Mrs Ramos.

She often gave advice to seamen lodgers. The kitchen door was ajar, but I entered hesitantly as there were more voices than usual, and not only were they chatting in a different language to English, but the tones sounded like they were in a real party mood. I tapped the door nervously, and Maria's hand opened it wide and invited me in with a smile.

Maria returned to her seat at the end of the long, oblong table, whilst on the long side sat a young, sunburnt man, somewhat taller and more bodied than myself. Julie waved me over and introduced me to her beau, the one she had talked about, Tony, her boyfriend.

He addressed me in acceptable, passable English, a little slurred by his Portuguese accent, and let me know he had just returned from Canada. At first I thought there was refinement in his demeanour, but on a second look, his body advertised strong peasant stock and some coarseness.

Both women were curious how I got on at the dock fence. When Tony heard me utter the word job, he was eager to say, "Come on board my ship; I help you get job." "What ship is that?" I questioned. "The *Lily*, a Greek ship." I played a clever game then. I could see Tony was well-fed, so the food on board must be ok.

I asked him if it had a happy crew. He then broke into Portuguese with Maria. She in turn explained his response for me. "There are different nationalities on board, but most of the crew are Portuguese, and the officers are Greek. Tony told me to let you know that if you keep company with our nationality, they will look after you."

Then I let the cat out of the bag to say, "Sorry for keeping it back, but I have already been offered a job on the *Lily*, though I have a big problem on my shoulders. I have to ask permission from my next-of-kin. It's a long way to the Rhondda Valley, but I hope the Padre at the mission will help me."

There was joy in the three faces when I mentioned being offered a berth, yet there were knitted brows about the business of obtaining family permission. I was surprised how really concerned they were. A few seconds later the two females gave up and looked for the solution from Tony.

With surprise he looked at both of them and speaking in English, uttered the following. "I know it is wartime, but captain, he send many telegrams." It was Mrs Ramos who understood first what was in his mind. Turning to me she asked, "When do you have an appointment with the Padre?"

"Eleven o'clock," I answered. "Well, do ask him if he can send a telegram to your brother for his consent for you to join a ship; there's no need to travel all the way home," Maria replied. Seeing the tension disappear in my face, they all became jovial, and the mother, turning to me, said, "Have a real cup of tea with plenty of sugar. Tony has just brought a fourteen pound bag back from the ship."

It's remarkable how we make problems when none exist. It must be the tension of excitement that prevents one from thinking clearly. It seems the answer has to come from the mouth of another and then it's so simple! An enjoyable cuppa, several Welsh cakes and plenty of empathy put me in a good mood to return to the mission.

At the mission I could hardly believe my good luck after seeing the Padre conferring with Blodwen as I entered. I found that he turned his attention to myself and shook my hand. I didn't even need to bring up the telegram idea because he asked me to step into his study and give him my family name and address. After filling him in with all the details so he could telegram my next-of-kin, I felt all of my worries draining out of my cranium.

I left my headache in the hands of Mr Edwards. Emerging from his study, he suggested that I might have to wait until the following day for a reply. Perhaps being broke was a blessing in a way; else he might have smelt alcohol fumes on me.

Then it came to my mind that my brother Jack had shipped out as a deck boy on the *New Westminster City*, one of Smith's Shipping Line of

Cardiff only two years before, so he must have had consent from my oldest brother. Now I was doubly assured everything would turn out fine.

Tony had earlier promised to take me on board the *Lily* for dinner; so after everything was settled, I returned to number thirteen, and soon both of us were on our way down to the docks. The *Lily* was only the second ship from the gate, and Tony led the way up the gangway. After showing me the galley amidships and introducing me to the cook, he told me I could enter the open cabin opposite the galley door. I gave it a look around.

It had two portholes, a washbowl and two bunks, one above the other. The cook told me the top bunk would be mine. I stepped back over the high storm plate as Tony led the way out of this inside alleyway, which was blocked at the far end by the engineer's mess room. Being warm, summery weather at the time, I did not appreciate how cosy such quarters would be with the winter months coming.

As I was interested in seeing the crew's quarters, I tracked my mate as he went to retrieve some leftover baggage. The small amidships cargo hold was discharging general cargo, and we evaded the swinging derricks easily, but on the forewell deck we stopped; long planks of timber were sweeping through the air there.

My guide led me across to the other side of the ship, clear of cargo operations, and I followed my mate in descending to the lower well deck in reverse. I found it difficult in edging my feet backwards on the steps of the iron ladder. Tony let me know in his own words that this was a safety measure I should work on.

He said that when you grasp the side rails in this certain way in rough weather, you would not easily be bowled over by a rogue wave. As we walked along the main deck, it gained an incline the nearer we approached the fo'c'sle, which he called the elevated structure before us.

After passing the lofty foremast, we came to the last cargo hold, behind which there was a steel wall, sheltered by an overhang of steel plating, protruding through the deck of the fo'c'sle head above. My mate grabbed hold of the handle of an iron door and jerked it open, and we entered the quarters. Again we came to that same barrier of the 18' high protective storm-plate, which I had to step over.

This was another habit I had to get used to, as all hands had to lift their legs over this obstacle umpteen times a day. We had entered the left side of the ship, which Tony called the portside. This was the deck department or sailors' sleeping place, known as a communal forecastle, where everyone slept together.

With two small portholes and a paraffin storm lamp suspended from the deck head, it was a shadowy place to get around. This area was directly inside the steel door, but one entered by a passageway between two private cabins, which on either side was occupied by the carpenter and bosun. Tony made his way to the three double-decker bunks against the steel wall, dividing the centre of the whole forecastle, like splitting a v-shape in half.

On the other side of this wall or bulkhead were the quarters for engine room workers, like firemen and trimmers. Tony grabbed some odds and ends from his former bunk, and we took off to the galley to try out the menu of a few bowls of spaghetti with fresh vegetables and mutton thrown in the mix.

And from this happy and promising start, I was to find my world turned upside down thanks to the *Lily* taking U-boat torpedoes in March of 1942.

CHAPTER 2 – *S/S LILY*

SHIP NUMBER ONE

I asked, "How many men ya' lose?" The seaman I had addressed would be in his thirties. He turned a tired face to me from his stretcher and answered weakly, "Just a few firemen. What ship did you come off?" Me: "The *S/S Lily*." I then shifted a couple of pillows under my shoulders so I could take a look around and see the line of stretcher-bearers.

I was boarded at Ward One, Royal Canadian Naval Hospital, at the port of Halifax, Nova Scotia in Canada. A holdup at the end of the ward prevented survivors from torpedoed vessels from being wheeled to another wing. This was March 1942.

The occupiers of the beds on either side of the trolleys being transported along the aisles were all frostbite victims. Some like myself were less prostrate. More serious cases resulted in amputation of toes and greater parts of the lower legs through gangrene, yet exposed hands somehow overcame the terrible results of exposure.

We all felt fortunate that we had been plucked out in time from the icy waters of the North Atlantic – some from rafts and others from lifeboats. There were many a frozen carcass being tossed around out there that would never make it.

The man on the stretcher preferred to turn his face away from me and gaze at the ceiling instead. He looked so pathetically weak that I thought he would pass out if I continued our conversation, so I held my silence. Presently the blockage at the far end cleared, and orderlies renewed wheeling their languishing patients to waiting beds.

Since a Canadian corvette had rescued me from a lifeboat a week previous and had transferred me here, several casualties had proceeded past my bed, and it unnerved me to overhear the comment made at times. "We only lost a few firemen" as distinct from the navy term 'stoker'; the same ratings in the merchant ships are called 'firemen'.

Although this was a naval hospital, only six ratings from the navy occupied beds here, the rest of the remainder being mostly seamen of merchant ships. At the time of my entry, my own rating had been that of coal trimmer, which is a status below that of fireman, supplying the coal needed to burn in the furnaces and working in the supply bunkers on deck above the stokehold.

Lying in bed I had sweet memories of joining the *Lily* in the port of Swansea, South Wales during the end of August 1941, and where I had spent an enjoyable week under beautiful weather conditions for spending shore leave. As it was my first voyage, several impressions came across my mental scanner, like the two vessels that were tied up fore and aft of our own berth.

The three vessels were aged tramp ships, waiting to load cargoes of coal. The one ahead was named the *Santiago* and flew the flag of Panama. Each time I passed her, there was always an argument going on board in foreign voices, like it was a mutinous crew of cut-throats.

Directly astern of us was a British India vessel and next to her, the Greek *Anna Mazaraki*. Some from the *Mazaraki* used to board our vessel for a chat with some of their countrymen. It seemed that most, if not all the Greek merchant fleet had made for British or Allied ports, when that country fell to the enemy.

I learnt they were not keen to live under Hitler, after being so many years under the Metaxas dictatorship, and Britain had consented for them to set up an official union of Greek seamen. The *Lily*, although under the Greek flag and registered in Piraeus, Greece, came under what was known as the 'London Greeks' ships that had their offices in London.

There were various nationalities aboard the *Lily*, as there are aboard most tramp ships, although officers were Greek personnel. When we sailed out of Swansea to rendezvous with other vessels forming a convoy at Milford Haven, we found the *Mazaraki* at the same anchorage and in the same group that sailed to Canada.

As a further coincidence, we also tied up side by side in Notre Dame Docks in Quebec, Canada. At 1 East, Notre Dame Docks, a massive poster advertised 'WELSH COAL BEST IN THE WORLD', so the friendliness between some *Mazaraki* crew members and their mates on the *Lily* continued as in Swansea. They had visited many times; their smiling faces were welcome on board by other members of the crew.

But when they boarded on the third day in Quebec, they wore no smiles, and we wondered why. Wartime regulations specified that sailing times and destinations be kept secret, but radio officers would sometimes break tension with shipping news, once they understood there were no blabbing types aboard, so married men could inform their wives when they could be expected home.

The sparks aboard our neighbour ship had leaked out that the next port of call would be Benghazi, a port in Libya, and a main hub of the allied war front. The skipper on board had refused to negotiate with their union rep for extra danger money for carrying ammunition, and the crew were thinking to strike.

They had come on board for support to back them up in case of a strike action. The Greek bosun on the *Lily* tried to explain to them that a strike in wartime was anti-union, and he offered an alternative which was to refuse to wash the coal dust from the holds to load ammo.

They returned to their own vessel to vote on what action to take. About 9.30am the following morning, a gathering of our crew on deck witnessed the decision the *Mazaraki* crew had finally come to – excited elements on board had carried out a vote to strike. Three paddy wagons were parked at the foot of the gangway with police strolling back and fro in the bright September sunshine. Their crew seemed in a cheerful mood. We watched them step down the gangway and enter the rear doors of the vans to be driven to prison.

Three days later, as the crane grabs were scraping the bottoms of our holds for the last lumps of coal, our ship was way up out of the water. During break time, someone went to the ship's side to pour coffee dregs over.

Fifty feet below something attracted his attention, and he waved us over. Curiosity drew all hands to the rails. Sure enough the *Mazaraki* mutineers were strolling past our ship on their way to their own. The long, uneven line trailed from the stern as they approached amidships where we were gathered, when one of them stopped and looked up.

He cupped his mouth to shout – "No more porridge!" The smiles on the faces of his mates assured us that they had won out.

Their cargo holds had been washed down by the officers and were ready for loading ammo. A day later our own ship was also washed down, and we shifted to a grain silo to load. Two other vessels were tied up ahead of us waiting their turn, so we enjoyed a few more evening visits to the bright lights of Montreal before returning to a blacked-out Britain.

Two days before we were fully laden, the *Mazaraki* crew gave us a wave as she passed our berth on her course down the St Lawrence River. Thumbs went up wishing them luck with their deadly cargo. When our time came to follow it downstream, we knew there would be no more coincidental meetings with her in the future.

Our next port of call was Levis, half way to the open sea. We tied up there to take water bunkers and final stores. I joined the mob outside the galley door as Sparky gave out news. Normally, it was passed on by the cook.

We learned that a launch would be supplied at 6pm to take anyone across the river to spend an evening in Quebec City. There was little interest, as most men had spent up in Montreal. This unusual shore leave had been granted since the ship was not due to leave until late the following morning. The blue sky kept everyone on deck socialising, so when the chaplain arrived on board, he drew attention when he explained to the crew about the Mountain Hill dance.

There would be plenty of free snacks, and those who were broke could still enjoy a good evening out. Several took him up on the offer, and when they returned on board, a rumour from them circulated that a Greek vessel had exploded on the lower reaches of the river. The news left many uneasy in the mind. Unspoken thoughts left a 'What if?' question mark in the air.

To ease tension, two men ascended to the bridge to have a natter with Sparky. The messengers returned, confirming our very worst fears. The *Anna Mazaraki* had sunk below the waters of the estuary with the loss of all hands. Patrol vessels were baffled and assumed that a submarine had entered those waters, camouflaged as an iceberg. But thankfully the reports were wrong. The ship would live to sail until May 1942, outliving the *Lily* by three months. And it wasn't torpedoed as passed on by my informant; it ran aground on Sable Island, Nova Scotia.

Then we headed for Halifax Harbour with the September weather continuing a balmy Indian summer. One afternoon, standing on deck in the enjoyable afternoon sunshine and listening to the faint din of windlasses, orders came through for ships to take their positions in the convoy formation, ready to sail. A lot of the crew came on deck at this time, and I was attracted by others looking in a certain direction. From a distant point one of the vessels, seemingly an oil tanker was running amok and heading in our direction. Movement of ships were at slow or half speed, but this odd one out seemed to be speeding up.

Coming closer into view, it was indeed an oil tanker, and it was rapidly cutting through the placid waters of the basin; faces took on seriousness. There she was, dead on, heading into the hull of the *Lily*.

With her belly carrying 15,000 tons of easily ignitable fuel, even a minor collision could spark off an explosion. Fortunately, both our anchors had been hauled up, dripping from the briny at that point before they had locked in the spurling gates, while a fast thinking engineer down below had put the engine in reverse and drew astern in the nick of time.

But not quite; I saw the skipper and chief mate run quickly to the forehead. The prow of the tanker had nicked our bows just below the anchors which meant that the *Lily* must have had an excess of cargo in the after cargo holds, and her bows were higher out of the water than normal. The gash we received in the bows ensured we would miss the convoy.

Our hearts sank a little as we watched the merchantmen file out into the open sea, bound for the one and only destination – the western approaches of the British Isles. It was fortunate that the excess grain in the after hatches enabled the buoyant forepart to dance away when struck. Repairs would begin the following day.

We were left with the whole enormous anchorage practically to ourselves. We wondered when the next group of ships would appear on the horizon to keep us company. We had not very long to wait. After four days, what seemed like twenty or more merchantmen appeared to be entering the bay, and men grouped on deck for some familiar sight, maybe of a former ship they may have sailed aboard.

The nearer these cargo boats ploughed into this inland field of water, the more intense the scrutiny became with hands cupped on foreheads. Some wondered if they were seeing correctly, and there were gasps of astonishment when it was discovered that these ships belonged to the very convoy that had left us behind.

Surprise faded as the ships re-entered the harbour. What kind of catastrophe had happened? We could scarcely wait for one of the returnees to sail close abreast of us as they spread out over this big pond.

One ship did approach fairly close, maybe forty yards away. Four or five tars leaning over the bulwarks of their freighter must have recognised the name of our ship.

They must have surmised that we were leaning over the rails to discover why they had returned. It was a bit far to throw voices, but hand movements made it that they had suffered losses to the enemy. Interpretations were confusing until Sparky came down from the bridge and let us know that insufficient escorts could not prevent fifteen vessels from being sunk by submarines. This was out of a convoy total of forty-five ships.

What further mishap could there be to prevent us from joining the next convoy formation and setting a course homeward bound? We missed passage with this unlucky group of ships, and it was early November before we grouped ten abreast on a northeast course to Iceland. We were about sixty in number.

A few days of tossing about tested the repairs. Twenty tons of cement had been poured into our forepeak to check the damaged section. Luckily, stormy weather failed to cause any further damage. Three weeks later, thanks to our naval escort, we reached the North Sea without one of our number lost to enemy action!

Nearly out of coal bunkers, we broke off from the convoy, coming down to the northeast coast of England, and called into Tyne Dock near Newcastle for extra bunkers to carry on to London, our port of discharge. I was still galley boy at that time, and the cook assured me if I wished, I could now take off on the train to Wales and see my family.

Together with the ship's third engineer, we took the train south to Cardiff. Then we took the early train from Newcastle, and by late afternoon, we were chugging up to the Rhondda Valley on the old steam train. I alighted at Treorchy Station. Being a roamer at heart, I was never too fond of staying home for over a week, but during wartime these home visits held special meaning.

I boarded the bus for the final mile home, the longest mile. With a few friendly faces favouring mine, I felt that beautiful tingling sensation which is the rewarding experience of a homeward bounder. Surging with excitement, the door of my old home got a good rapping. My elder sister welcomed me in and before I reached the living room and fireplace, I felt the warm air surrounding us.

I have heard since that a coal fire in the house gives out a healthy atmosphere, and if my reasoning is right, it is because it encourages the circulation of air, as the air going up the chimney sucks more air into the room, and sitting before that big, blazing fire, I was certainly good and truly 'At Home'.

The house was in the best state it had ever been. When my parents passed away in the early thirties, there were eight brothers and sisters left in the house, which was a bit crowded with four children and four adults. The oldest two brothers and sisters kept us four younger ones under the roof after it was learned that the combined pension of four orphans each week was equal to the earnings of your average labourer.

But the war had changed the house population. Two brothers were in the army, one in the air force, and my eldest brother, a coal miner, had married and moved three miles down the valley. With one sister recently passed away, that left only two sisters in the house, the eldest and the youngest, plus a third person, the husband of my eldest sister.

I had interrupted my sister in her usual early evening task of rolling down black paper curtains over the windows to comply with blackout regulations. Stan, my brother-in-law, held out a welcoming handshake before slumping into a recliner chair, after assuring himself that no cracks of light would show through the curtain.

He had just washed up at the local pithead baths after a daily stint at the coal mine. Although he would be eager to learn about my first trip to sea, he held himself in restraint of any questioning, as it seemed his wife Beryl wished to convey important news to me. After brewing some tea, she placed the pot on the hob above the oven.

Then she passed on the very bad news that my brother Ken had been reported missing since the fall of Crete a year ago. I showed no strong emotion over Ken. I put this down to wartime psychology, although at the time I never realised this. In other words I lacked an emotional response because my mind would not believe the worst.

There was a shortage list of commodities in '42, and the tobacco shortage hit the miners most. Most of them enjoyed a plug of chewing tobacco to spit out the coal dust, and it did a lot more for their health than other forms of tobacco; however, my brother-in-law preferred cigarettes. He was overjoyed when I opened my kitbag and handed over a carton of two hundred.

They were the duty-free ones allowed by customs. In return he invited me into the pantry to show me that he was beating the rations. There was a large leg of pork suspended from the butchers hook. I gladly ate some ham sandwiches offered by my sister, and time went swiftly by as I told shipboard yarns.

My sister, noticing the hour hand on the mantelpiece clock, warned me to move if I wanted to catch a pint of beer at the local, as there was a beer shortage. I took the cue and slipped on a leather windbreaker purchased in Montreal. And then I slipped out into the crisp, dry night with a half moon to guide me to the nearest watering place.

After three nights restful sleep on a spring bed at home, I was eager to return to the S/S *Lily* and spend a few more months on a harder bunk of straw. The familiar surroundings had done me a tonic, especially so when notice had come through on the radio of President Roosevelt's speech following the bombing of Pearl Harbor.

After standing alone against the power of Nazi Germany for over two years, with only silent, stubborn determination against economic hardships and reverses in combat, Great Britain was able to record a date to remember in December when the USA decided to ally herself with Britain to defeat the fascist aggressors.

On my journey back to London, one could not fail to notice the vibrancy and the good expectations reflected in the faces of ordinary people. I stepped off at Paddington Station and proceeded to the information desk to request how I could get to the West India Docks. The lady there providing me service was more than polite.

We couldn't fail to weigh up the feelings after the good news from the USA. Not since the Battle of Britain had the heart of a nation in peril suddenly responded with such a mighty throb. I joined the human stream through the turnstile and muddled my way throughout the underground until I surfaced at Aldgate East Tube Station, from where I took one of London's red double-deckers direct to the end of the commercial road as instructed.

Wild Road was at the junction where the commercial road ended and the East India Dock Road began. It was a short jaunt down the road to the main gates of the dock. The policeman at the gate looked up the name of my ship in the office and directed me to walk as far as I could along the dock road, past Canary Wharf to Dog's Island.

Fortunately I was only carrying a small, light suitcase, but before I got too tired, I sought reassurance and asked one of the workforce there, who assured me that The *Lily* was unloading cargo into the grain silo at the Millwall Dock at the far end.

It must have been around 3pm before I entered the cook's cabin amidships, where I had spent months as a galley boy. I found the chef dressed up and packing his belongings. He had a kitbag there and a sizable suitcase packed to bulging plus a few small crates well-covered over. One assumed that ships' cooks certainly departed with more than just personal belongings during wartime, which was understandable since food was a most coveted possession.

He told me he had already received his payoff and was now awaiting the arrival of a taxi. For three months I had been sweating on raising my wages by taking a coal trimmer's job. The cook already knew that I used to spend my time at sea visiting the stokehold at the bottom of the ship, learning how to throw coal in furnaces.

The news he passed on to me was that there was vacancy for one trimmer open, and he had recommended me to the skipper for the position. He told me to make it quick to the officers' saloon where the captain was now signing on some new members of the crew, in case someone else filled the trimmer position.

The captain was seated on the opposite side of a long mahogany table, together with some unfamiliar, important-looking faces which I learned later were higher ups of the company, just arrived down from the city for the afternoon. I put my shaky signature to my new contract as coal trimmer.

When I returned to the cabin, I found the cook waiting for my help because he had a lot of booty to carry down to the awaiting taxi. When I remarked to him that the captain was in a jovial mood, he commented that the skipper was also packing his bags and leaving after being relieved by a new captain, who was expected at any time. Then before entering the taxi, he looked me straight in the face and stated seriously, "I think you should leave that ship, too."

I was flabbergasted! One minute he was recommending me for a better monthly salary, and the next his whole attitude and tone of voice had changed. The cab driver was busy stuffing the cook's luggage in the boot and on the roof rack. The widow he was in love with certainly wouldn't exist on bare rations. After he dived into his seat, he passed the final comment to me "Leave ship. Ship will sink this trip." and sped off.

My arm wilted in waving him off as this fatal omen sunk into my mind. Back on board my mood changed. I was again thrilled with my new promotion. I entered my old cabin for the final time – my comfy two-berth cabin, heated nicely by sitting over a hot engine room, just the accommodation needed for a North Atlantic run in winter.

I packed my belongings in a kitbag and suitcase and dragged my feet to an open fo'c'sle to my new sleeping quarters in a communal sleeping compartment where nine men shared a half V-shaped area together. This was the only part of the contract I disliked. Before stepping down to the forewell deck, I dropped my bags for a minute and looked ahead a hundred feet at the cover in the forecastle.

Then I walked onto the wall of steel in front of me. Having visited these quarters before, I knew the firemen and trimmers slept on the starboard side, so at the top of this sloping deck, I walked around the top of the Number One Cargo Hold to give the ring on the iron door a twist to let myself in, clanged it back from the inside and then latched it closed.

I was familiar with the short, dark passage between two small workshops where engineers made on-the-spot repairs to the steam winches. I stopped for a moment to rub my knee. I still had not gotten used to the steel barrier 18 in. high at the entrance to all quarters called the storm plate. In my excitement to get into the warmer air of quarters after throwing my baggage through the door, I had hurriedly lifted my leg over the plate and grazed my knee. It was very silent as I entered quarters, and I wondered why no one was around. I entered the semi V-shaped open fo'c'sle. The wider part was where I stood, and the deck sloped upwards between bunks, coming to a point towards the prow. The chimney pipe from the potbellied stove pierced the centre space of quarters. Five bunks were in a straight line against the steel bulkhead, dividing the firemen from the deckhands.

Four other bunks sloped in line with the starboard bow. This accommodated the complement of firemen and trimmers. Naturally, there were only portholes above the bunks on the outer bow section. They were always open in port to take away any bad air added by occasional fumes blowing back from the stove.

By the glow of a paraffin lamp, I made out a form with its back to me, slumped low over a stove. He seemed singularly well-dressed and hearing my footsteps on the bare wood deck, his face turned about, pushing an American Stetson hat up past his forehead.

I stopped and let him look me over. He then rose from an empty vegetable crate, as no chairs were provided there, and in an amicable way came towards me, hand out friendly-like, ready for shaking. He introduced himself as Johnny, an American citizen of Greek parentage, who had left the American Merchant Marine to do his part for Greece as a fireman.

He now regretted his patriotic duty towards Greece, as it would take time to get himself back in a union that had better conditions for seamen. He appeared more of a northerner than a Latin type, being tall and broad with an oliveness absent from his facial colouring. At twenty-five his attitude and talk marked him as a weathered seafarer. Furnace heat had left a faint pink on his cheeks now.

Johnny's nature was affable, well-meaning and open, and I soaked in all the hints he could pass on about trimming coal because all firemen started as trimmers. He urged me to seek work on modern type ships as soon as I became good at my job, as open fo'c'sles were substandard.

These quarters had disappeared with sailing ships he argued, and if there was no war on, Lloyds Insurance would demand the *Lily* be scrapped. When I asked him where the rest of the crew was, he said they had gone ashore soon after they had signed on because all necessary work had been completed in the engine room and stokehold.

He said he would be going ashore himself shortly, and if I was staying aboard, to keep the fire well-stoked for a warm night. Being the last man to sign on, my choice of bunk was nil. Kitbags had been slung over eight beds, and the ninth bunk was beneath the hawse pipe. Everyone had avoided this particular sleeping berth because every time the starboard anchor was lowered into the sea, it caused one almighty din from chain links.

I threw my luggage on this bunk; it was right at the bottom of the central tier of beds. There was another crate lying around, and Johnny told me to draw it up close to the stove. He passed me an American cigarette and both of us lit up.

He asked me if I had ever been present when the anchor clattered through the hawse pipe. I had been up there once, visiting a friend, when the windlass above us had released the big steel cable through the spurling gates. The whole fo'c'sle shuddered when the cable left the chain locker beneath. That mental image must have twisted my face a bit because my new friend burst out laughing.

When he rose to make his exit, he asked me to follow him so that I could pick up my linen allowance from the chief steward; there were plenty of folded blankets lying over beds. Before stepping down the gangway he insisted that I keep the stove topped up with coal so all the black gang (stokehold workers) could enjoy a warm night's sleep.

I entered the saloon which was empty except for Stamatis, the steward, who was preparing the table for evening meal. He left off his task to take me to the linen locker and handed me two sheets and two pillowcases. I soon returned to quarters to make up a presentable bed, tucking in the blankets deep under the straw mattress. After which I took Johnny's place and bent over the glow of a well-cleaned fire.

A day later after discharging our cargo of grain, we sailed north, picking up ships on the way from the Rivers Humber and Tyne on the northeast and broke off from the convoy on the Scotland coast to bunker coal at Methil. Within forty-eight hours we were part of another group, heading across the most northerly part of the British Isles. Our destination there was Loch Ewe, the harbour of one of the western isles, where convoys were made up.

We arrived there Xmas Eve. It was the season when heating living quarters was essential, but having the stove lit when sailing around the wild northwest in winter was surely out of the question. The reason was obvious. Every time the bows plunged into the white horses, smoke blew down the skinny smokestack of our stove instead of upwards, nearly suffocating all hands. Since leaving Methil, my workload had been light as the topped up bunkers taken in Scotland needed no trimming, and the rolling of the ship took plenty of coal down to the stokers.

I can never remember a happy crew when a ship swings at anchor for two or three days since anchorages are in the sight of land and the land beckons. Here is a feeling of stagnation, which is absent when a ship is under way, even when ploughing through those massive wintery waves of the North Atlantic. We made the best of the Xmas break as we could.

There was practically a brand new crew, both on the deck side and our own, and during this festive period, we mixed and got to know more about each other. Most of the days spent in this harbour were spent sitting around the hot stove, feeding it lumps of coal and feeding each other's loneliness with yarns. Of us three trimmers, the other two, like myself, were in their late teens but with more experience. Frenchy, a dreamy sort of guy, was from Le Havre. He informed me that he was saving his earnings to buy his sister out of occupied France. Slim Jim was from the island of Jersey, also under occupation; he was a spent, sombre type.

Both were friendly towards me, and I was not in want for advice, which all new starters badly need. I had already familiarised myself with the two four hour periods of duty each day called watches and found that each watch had its advantages and disadvantages, and if two of you wanted the same watch, you came to an agreement by cutting cards, aces high.

Few rarely like the watch from midnight to 4am, called the 'Dead Watch', yet Jim the Jersey boy opted for it seeing that in his way of thinking, the days went by faster; every time you went on a watch at midnight, you entered a new day; Frenchy wanted the 4-8 watch, and I ended up with the 8-12 watch.

I was to learn later that the men would put up strong arguments to claim this watch, as it offered a full night's sleep from midnight to 8am, but I was to learn that in winter climes, the favourite watch was 4-8 because the morning and evening breeze blew more air down the ventilators.

Convoy speed was reckoned at that of the slowest ship, usually a worn-out ten-knot tramp ship, well past its prime at seven knots. If there was good steam coal on board, it made it easier for the firemen, and they were easy on the trimmers in supplying them with coal. The first thing a fireman did when he came below was to clean a fire.

The fire was left with one side full of bright embers and the other a layer of dead clinker. The clinker was drawn, and the live embers were winged over with a thick poker over six feet long called a slice bar, similar to a crow bar with one end hammered into a wedge shape to pierce and lift clinker from the back of the furnace and to allow air to be drawn through.

What urged us trimmers to speed up shovelling was that as soon as the two feet by two feet square hole in the deck was filled to the top, we could knock off work. It meant that the firemen would have a good reserve of coal near their fire doors for several hours ahead.

My recognised finishing time was forty minutes before the two firemen I served. By speeding up my shovel or 'banjo', I could finish work at 11am or 11pm, and that gave me an extra twenty minutes to wash myself early.

Since there were no facilities for taking a bath in the fo'c'sle, the chief engineer allowed all engine room hands to make use of the rear part of the engine room on the bottom deck, where hot water could be gotten from a thin pipe coming from the condenser and with space enough to splosh around.

I was passed a tip that has lasted me all my life, and it has to do with the use of the sweat rag issued to all black gang firemen and trimmers monthly. The rag is a large, square cloth, punctured with holes and usually tied around the neck. As its name clearly advertises, it is used to wipe sweat off face and body. Someone showed me how to get an entirely clean bath with hardly a speck of coal dust left on my body.

It is very easy to demonstrate but difficult to explain, but as far as it goes, the idea is to keep dipping the rag in and out of the water rapidly so it hardly discolours. At first it seems time-wasting to wring out the rag before each time it's dipped; however, it soon becomes a habit with plenty of water left over.

Eventually, we left Loch Ewe Harbour just prior to the New Year, and the whole group of ships wallowed in a gale-force westerly wind. We were somewhere off the west coast of Ireland the next day. Such was the disastrous weather that it was only towards evening that we came in sight of other vessels. No naval escorts were in the vicinity; they were probably spread out, bringing struggling merchantmen back to the fold before nightfall, like marine sheepdogs.

Wireless operators on all ships must have been working overtime, keeping contact with the commodore of the armada. The following day was a repeat performance, and looking at the wild briny, one wondered if we were progressing at all. After midday, a vessel was sighted, then another, this last being followed by a destroyer.

Someone was on the bridge of a battleship holding a loud hailer, and I was informed that he was Harry, the captain of that vessel, telling us to raise more steam to keep our ship with the convoy. According to orders, we were proceeding in a north-westerly direction to avoid contact with U-boat packs.

More escort vessels were supposed to be waiting for us off the coast of Iceland. We never approached anywhere near Iceland. On the fourth evening, no other boats showed up, and we spent the whole night pitching and tossing in a full-blown storm. Morning found our wheelman steering in an easterly direction at the orders of the captain.

He had decided to return to Whitehead Bay on Erin's north coast. We dropped anchor there on a cold Saturday night, and the following morning the sun broke brightly through wet clouds. The air grew clean and crisp, and it was noticeable that the harbour was half full of ships, riding at anchor, on becalmed water.

No running water was pumped to quarters. When we wanted a drink at night, we drank from the mug floating on a wide bucket, half full of drinking water and suspended from the deck head by a butcher's hook. Sunday being the usual wash up day on most ships at sea or in port, there was a trail of men with buckets in hand.

They walked back and fro between the fo'c'sle and the amidships pump. One time a man returned and brought a fresh snippet of news almost as fast as the War Office received it. The report was that most of the ships in the area were from our own company with reports of lifeboats washed away, etc.

This kind of news in wartime was not unusual, because all lifeboats were swung out, readied for lowering at a moment's notice. The Atlantic was proving more hostile than the enemy; ferocious weather scattered the whole convoy. When a sailor came along with his bucket, we heard even worst news. An oil tanker, further south in another convoy, had broken her keel and had split in half.

On this particular Sunday forenoon, the weather grew summery. As often occurs, calm weather follows a storm, but this was really unusual weather for the month of March. It was so sunny that all the hands decided to eat their dinner on the cargo hatch near quarters. Someone brought out a gramophone and put on a record of 'Beneath the Lights of Home' by Deanna Durbin.

The soothing, comforting voice of Miss Durbin caught the ears of the lookout sailor on the wing of the bridge, and momentarily forgot his duties. He neck stretched over the monkey island, the bridge on top of pilot's house, in an effort to catch the song words in the silence of the bay. One of our gang walked over to the side of the ship to empty the remains of his plate over the bulwarks.

Then he turned around smartly and there was a look of terror in his face. He gasped out that he had spotted a floating mine close by. We all rushed over except for one thoughtful person who removed the needle from the spinning, musical disk. The lookout man was very alert by now and waited for a message to pass on to the saloon where all the officers were dining.

The urgent message was passed on to him, and he disappeared. Two firemen thoughtfully made a bolt for amidships in case they were needed to raise steam. After we had seen the spiky mine for ourselves, bobbing up and down gracefully in the water, there was a lot of men filing through the iron doors to grab a life jacket.

After the rushing around, there was a quiet intensity, as expectant faces riveted eyes upwards in the direction of the high bridge. The skipper came out of the wheelhouse with a loud hailer through which he ordered all hands to put their life jackets on. Those that had not already donned a bulgy 'Mae West' were back indoors to pull them from beneath their pillows.

A fresh face appeared above and stood beside the captain; it was the radio operator and he was whispering in the other's ear. The ominous silence of the next minute seemed like an hour. Then our master put the blower to his lips again and transmitted the awaited message: "Everything is Ok. You can remove your jackets."

The shore station has just informed Sparky that the mine we saw was dead, useless. It has been defused but had been accidentally allowed to drift back out. There was certainly a sigh of relief all around, and one man was detailed to rewind the gramophone and let Deanna tell us about the cosy lights of home. How much longer would the luck of the *Lily* last we wondered?

We left Whitehead Bay in what could be labelled a small convoy; only thirty-three ships took a westerly direction. Destinations during wartime were kept secret up until the last hour of sailing time, although sometimes the giveaway was cargo, but the *Lily*, lacking any cargo, the next port of call could be anyone's guess.

The orders came through to reroute the course back to Iceland. Fair weather had told us that the western ocean had gotten over its wild temper; then we were cheered by a report from Sparky that our loading port would be Canadian but not sure which one.

Later, upon leaving Reykjavik, Iceland, we struck foul weather. It was generally understood that U-boats would not attack in rough weather conditions, but at breakfast every morning report that came through via the galley was upsetting. As you were handed a plateful of fish or whatever, the last part of the menu was "One ship lost last night", which had been authentically passed on by the radio operator three mornings running.

What was most frightening was that the ships were torpedoed at night when any form of lighting was non-existent. Men were scared in case their ship drifted away from the convoy one dark and moonless night. Although two escort destroyers had been added for our safety at Reykjavik, if the helmsmen was not very adept at steering on nights of choppy seas or the lack of steam was holding up speed, stragglers became victims of the unseen enemy beneath the waves.

With four hundred miles to go before reaching Newfoundland,

Canada, the *Lily* going south found itself alone on the whole wide ocean after a night of gale-force winds. By noon the weather had begun to subside, but the sea remained choppy beneath a sky of uncertain cloud signs. Then it happened!

It was maybe 1pm, after everyone had digested his midday meal, and the galley boy and myself were chatting a bit inside his workplace. After helping him to wipe up the pots and pans, he allowed me to tuck into any leftovers I fancied, and then he went off to his cabin, leaving me to wash out the final pot. There was a rich, thick soup in the base, and I poured it into a bowl.

It was just the stuff made to bolster a man from icy-cold weather. I rinsed the pot and bowl and left them upside down in the sink, and then left, stepping over the storm plate at the galley door, turned around and gripping the steel sides of the doorway, took a last look at this warm, cosy area where I had worked for months.

I wish I had never grasped those door sides, because the vibrations from the shuddering body work of the empty ship stung my hands. In the galley pots and pans were dancing in the air. The shuddering passed through my body from the base of my feet to the top of my head. It was like an earthquake at sea and had a shattering effect on me.

I spun around to look for an escape, but seeing another explosion in that direction paralysed me. Blue smoke came out of the empty cargo hold, and hatch board covers were flying sky high. Perhaps the second torpedo was even more disastrous since the whole ship's structure from the stern to amidships rattled uncontrollably.

It may have been only seconds before I could regain my mental equilibrium, but it was still jarring my system when my feet got mobile. People were running past me in a state of shock as they emerged from their cabins. I trailed a stout-bellied, middle-aged greaser, who nimbly raced up the perpendicular iron ladder.

The port lifeboat, already slung out on its davits, was lowered in no time by a few hands. Later on I realised I let go a few ropes skilfully myself, although I was very unlearned in this business. No words were spoken yet actions were skilful and speedy. Stone Age desperation had released the language of gestures and telepathy.

Looking back at those frantic moments, I found that my mind was so governed that my hands were making rapid and skilful use of ropes passed me. It seems one learns instantly at the gates of the next world. In the mad scramble down the rope ladder, the boot of another above me caused my hands to become dislodged.

How I missed what was below me in that plunge seaward was a

miracle. I was hauled into the boat minus my boots, which could have helped me survive. Perhaps even the baptism in those cold waters may have prepared me for worse to come. Fortunately, I was the only one to be pulled over the gunwales; the rest made it into the boat so that we could pull away from the ship rapidly.

Within minutes we were forty feet away from the doomed vessel and abreast her port side. We all sat on the thwarts of the life boat as onlookers, watching the death of our home sweet home, not realising how spectacularly the scene would evolve. It was a lucky escape for all hands except Antonio Pereira. He never made it out in time

He must have been in a deep sleep when the ship was holed twice. Possibly the forepart of the vessel would be little affected by the vibration, being divided from the rest of the ship by the bridge work, and as he was fortunate enough to sleep in a two berth cabin, he was unaffected by the mad rush in the open fo'c'sle when alarms were raised.

He became the focus of all our eyes as he emerged from the fo'c'sle door and belatedly raced wildly along the foredeck. Before he reached amidships, the bow gradually surged upwards, revealing a dripping keel. We held our breath, wondering what our victim would do next. Waves started to sweep over the poop deck, and the stern started disappearing under the waves.

There he was, still up at the forehead, swinging from the ship's rail, which he was grasping frantically. For some strange reason, by my way of thinking, the bow rose in a vertical position, and then, half above water, stood perfectly still, as if waiting to have its picture taken.

Fortunately, we had safely distanced ourselves. Then an internal explosion rocked the *Lily*, sending smoke and ash high in the air; the boilers had exploded! Someone close to my ear said, "Antonio can't hang on there any longer."

The explosion of the boilers had caused the doomed vessel to surge even further upwards towards the pitiless wintry sky in its final dance of destruction. Then it dropped without warning – like a stone into a briny stream with our mate hanging on to the very end. Then an unbelievable event occurred. Just when we had decided that Antonio had entered Neptune's realm, his body shot up into the air. We were not the only witnesses; our partners in the starboard lifeboat were now visible. We had already arranged ourselves so that everyman was positioned on the thwarts ready to row.

And row we did for dear life, struggling in the waves, as did the crew of the other boat. Guiding our tiller, the chief mate informed us that such events had been recorded before, when a body had been caught in a submerged bubble and then had been rescued from his doom.

I suppose there is a loose brotherhood of the sea, even in wartime, because yet another party had obviously seen what happened. The U-boat surfaced and attempted to rescue our man. We had raced it to the victim, and the skipper of the sub must have decided to allow us to pluck our mate from the freezing water in order to track down another straggler from our unlucky convoy.

Both our boats reached Antonio at just the same time, and as he was hauled into the other boat, it was very noticeable that his body had turned a pale blue complexion from his immersion. Now that we had helped our last man, everyone showed a buoyant attitude that no lives had been lost. The skipper confirmed this with a head count.

One man was transferred from the captain's boat to ours to even the numbers; we had had fifteen men to his seventeen. Both boats kept as comfortably near to each other as possible so that the chief mate and skipper could work on a plan of action. All hands were eager to do a spell of rowing whilst the sea was yet manageable, and we still had energy.

But the captain advised that everyone now make themselves as comfortable as possible for the night ahead. The wind was blowing from the northeast and would soon take us into the shipping lanes. With a sail up we would have a better chance of being picked up.

Before the early winter twilight merged into the black envelope of night, a few able-bodied seamen assisted the bosun in stepping the mast and hoisting a trysail. As the night grew, so did the sea. Small troughs of water developed into very big troughs. The weather was taking on an unpleasant aspect. The choppy sea was no more.

We were being raised skyward on high waves, and contact between the boats became lost. Flurries of spitting foam over the bows ensured we would suffer a cold, miserable night. The spray became dangerously plentiful and with increasing regularity. Perched aft near the tiller, the mate focused a battery torch on a small compass and, after some study, ordered all hands to keep below the thwarts and as central in the boat as possible.

As the wind had now switched around and was blowing from the west, a sea anchor was slung over the side to prevent us from drifting too far into mid-ocean; the bosun then lowered the sail and spread it over our huddled bodies. We met the morning of the second day on a lonely ocean, less happy than on the previous day.

The dog biscuit allowance was dished out, yet strangely enough, considering the low temperature, few takers. Was exposure already beginning to lower the sense of taste? Or had someone been rifling stores overnight? The ration was not offered during the rest of the day, as no interest was shown by us.

The mate timed it as 11am when we sighted the captain's boat; it took skilful manoeuvring to bring both boats to close quarters with waves reaching peaks of twenty-five feet. An accident would have been unavoidable if we dared to come too near to each other; we just closed into sufficient distance so a bailer could be thrown into our boat.

Now we had two bailers each, and it was a matter of life and death to keep bailing out the continual showers of spray water; we already sat in a pool of icy water to keep balance. Also, half the men were bootless in our boat, either by having to make speedy exits from their bunks or had lost them scurrying down the rope ladder.

The temporary meeting of our boats produced a tonic effect. Tired faces threw sympathy to tired faces and seemed to rekindle with faint smiles a fire of survival. This extra boost was certainly needed as sleep had eluded everyone overnight. The weather continued to worsen as night fell.

Monotonously, the white horses on the waves sprayed us in regular fashion. Thankfully, our man in charge, the well-shod and oil-skinned mate, sat in the stern and kept strong discipline, urging each and every one to take turns in bailing out water. Once in a while when he needed a break at the tiller, the bosun would take a turn, stepping from his seat onto the prow.

Without these two expert sailors, the boat would have foundered. Whilst the chief mate sat at the stern steering the boat and keeping discipline, the bosun continually prodded and nudged the rest of us zombies with the aid of an oar to keep to the centre of the boat.

As dawn broke on the second morning, snowflakes were observed melting in the salt air and spray. Our chief mate was still amazingly alert and skilful as ever; he seemed well-prepared for each challenge; for now we just wallowed in each wave and crested them like a cork. Calculating and sizing up the waves from the troughs gave men needed interest and eye exercises, and it was generally agreed that the waves had risen to thirty feet.

Before midday arrived, the mate saw that he was not getting through to the boys anymore. The seriousness and necessity to continue bailing caused him at one point to threaten a lax sailor by pointing a revolver at him, which he drew from his left-hand pocket of his oilskin coat, as his right hand was continuously on the tiller. It was obviously an excellent psychological persuader.

By afternoon the wind had dropped, the air was clear and the waves were subsiding. This let up was most welcome, and very little spray now broke over the gunnels. A furry sun split a sticky, grey cloud, and this small omen from the upper firmament had a positive effect on the boys when I was reading their faces.

There was now a gleam of interest from the blank eyes, although on the whole we were a pretty mute lot except for the chief officer and his offsider, the bosun, who were now speaking together in low tones. Since the wind had dropped, the water we were sitting in measured only about four inches and was splashing back and fro.

The mate, noticing this, told the bailer to take a rest. The bosun then unlocked a low cupboard beneath where he sat and drew forth a bottle of rum. A noggin was passed to each man in turn. Tongues thawed out at this little treat, and for the next half hour, we livened ourselves with a bit of small talk. There were even a few faint smiles exchanged.

The liquid boost was not enough to normalise us because when the dog biscuit ration was offered around, there were still no takers, and that could only mean that numbness had sunk deep enough to rob us of our primary instinct – hunger. Alcohol had been the catalyst for bringing to life a response from our senses.

Grateful mention was made of the sea anchor; its cone bobbing up on the end of a line over the bows. As bad as the weather had been, steering head on was preferable to being swamped by riding broadside into one of those towering waves; without the anchor our chances would have been suicidal.

The mate found weather conditions safe enough to allow the crew to seat themselves on the cross-pieces, the rowing seats or thwarts. He meant it as a leg stretcher, but as much as we'd have liked to bring ourselves up on the seats, that wasn't so easy. Numbness had climbed the legs like an anaesthetic, so leg movement did not react in the normal way.

Life only seemed to register itself in the upper thighs. Some preferred to keep their legs doubled-up, as normal movement proved strange and quite awkward. Then came the general realisation that those without footwear possessed feet twice the usual size. The force of feet swelling had split the boots and shoes off others, and an excess of fatty flesh expanded above the foot area, trapped inside the leather. Personally, there was no feeling below my knees. I assumed that this was general. To an extent the leg stretching procedure could be directed by the thigh muscle.

We were still battling against unfriendly seas so that some time had to be allowed before again all hands got themselves in a crouch at the keel centre. I was really thankful that my mind was astoundingly calm given the circumstances. I put this down to the slowing down of thought processes; they were literally ceasing to function. As the sun set that night, we still had not sighted the captain's boat, and although gale-force winds howled, sleet fell before the dark hours set in. We were still riding on fairly high waves by morning, but with a good man at the tiller, it was not that dangerous.

We were lucky to have two such men who realised that the smaller the boat, the easier it would be to ride the long, deep troughs. The wind lessened to a degree of safety, and there was less tension aboard. The bosun, after being handed the key by the chief mate, opened the small locker under the stern seating and brought out the rum bottle; a generous tot was handed around.

If it brought a small smile to one's face, it was also not without the almost pleasant thought that one would be unable to carry on with another night of exposure. Only those well-clad with oilskins and rubber boots would survive, and they were too few. Too many faces advertised this premonition.

Around noon, except for taking one's turn at bailing out water, inertia was definitely taking up lodgings in the hearts of most. Even the loud mouths were dumb. This was sad because weather conditions were improving.

Then one man gazed with eyes above the others and continued to stare over the horizon as if in a trance. I noticed him blink, raise a right hand over his brows and take another fixed stare. He practically barked in a weakened, tremulous voice for the others to do likewise. The group in the middle of the boat would only look in one direction, downwards, but the weary chief officer used his reserve energy from concentrating on the compass to take a glimpse himself.

That was when I cupped my hand over my eyes in the lifting and falling swell, and as gloomy as the daylight was, I could swear I could see a tiny pipe rising and dipping in the far horizon. A smokestack could only have a ship beneath it, and a tingle of excitement, of hope in me, could not be drowned.

At first the glazy-eyed bosun could not make out the mate's orders to unlock a certain compartment under the thwarts, but being handed the binoculars, he found energy came back to him very rapidly. Within a minute a flare was being rocketed into the bleak sky.

Minds and bodies stirred into a collective rousing. The men fed their minds on a bit of hope. Imagine you had purchased a lottery ticket, and the wind blew it away. Next day you learned the results and found you had the winning numbers. Emotionally you became very upset and developed suicidal tendencies.

You may have been living a pleasant existence with a regular job and good pay; however, the fact that you had tossed away a few million quid knocks you. Anger has raised your temperature alarmingly to a feverish state. Now imagine sixteen men sitting in icy water for three nights and days. Hope in the form of a friendly ship faded as it ignored them. Here again, anger raised the temperature of men's minds and bodies, but the heated words passed around were the very best medicine that could have been asked for.

As the ship sailed away and left them to suffer, it also left them in a far livelier state than before it had arrived on the scene. At first they were drained of emotional feelings. Then, like a catalyst, the sight of a ship's funnel stirred hope in their hearts, causing warm blood to circulate in their bodies. It seems that in a way that anger heats up the bloodstream more than hope, and it must have been a godsend to the mate, when he saw his physically helpless men gesturing wildly over their misfortune.

Not ten tots of rum could have had the effect of reviving them as much as their emotional anger. From then on, all eyes were peeled and alert to spot anything, maybe at least a change of scenery on the horizon. In the late afternoon that same day, as night was beginning to cast its early winter shadows at maybe 4pm, an object was spotted bobbing up and down.

There was no hesitation this time about opening the locker for distress signals. All the distress signals were shot up into the air – the lot! It was a gamble that paid off. In fading daylight, Morse signalling was beamed out to us, and a short time later, coming in our direction, was a warship that seemed like a destroyer.

It turned out that the craft was a Canadian corvette. Brought out in WW2, it was known as unsinkable. It was remarkable how this vessel could roll over the danger of forty-five degrees without mishap. As it appeared on the scene, it never stopped rolling, right down to the water's edge, or so it seemed. Lots of uniformed ratings were on deck, and they seemed well-prepared to rescue us but in a method that was indeed unorthodox, yet certainly the speediest.

Actually, there was no reasonable alternative; two or three of our crew might have been able to climb a rope ladder, no more. Here was the scene as this man-of-war moved alongside us.

There were about eight tars grouped around the amidships area. Ship's rails were removed for a gap of around twelve feet. On each side of the gap, two burly sailors clutched the rails, biding their time. Ten feet behind them was a winch facing the side of the ship. At the rear of the winch sat the winch driver looking on. He was looking between two men holding onto ropes circling winch drums.

Each rope line was lashed around the waist of a pair of brawnies so that should they slip when the corvette keeled over, they could be hauled back. These two men, who seemed to have excellent sea legs and looked like weathered seamen, came together as the warship's hull rolled far over as if she would touch the waves while the two well-stropped huskies leaned over with it. Dipping their bodies in unison, they grabbed hold of the first man available by arms and feet.

They did this movement each time with the roll of the ship, and as the deck of the warship rose upwards, each body from our boat was given the heave-ho onto the wet deck and slid along the steel deck into the arms of waiting stretcher bearers. With the others I was carried to the sleeping quarters.

I soon found myself snugly tucked into a swinging hammock. No sooner had everyone been rescued from a sad ending, and all settled in, than an explosion shocked our systems. Could we be saved just to lose our lives in a speedier way? Soon we were assured by the ratings that a shell had been put into the life boat so not to leave any evidence.

Then came the good news. We were not the only survivors on board; up in the stern sleeping quarters, rested the remainder of the crew of the *Lily* from the other life boat. What we were most grateful for was that the captain of the corvette had detailed his crew members to tend to us so that we were well-looked after, and our needs attended to. They even gave up their hammocks for us. It is not pleasant lifting men up and down from a swinging hammock in a ship that rolled like a drunken sailor, yet the tars were only too glad to be on call. I truly felt well-nursed and well-fed on our three day journey to Halifax Harbour. Since most of our crew suffered from frostbite, it was a race against time to get medical attention before gangrene set in.

News reached us from the other end of the ship of the sad demise of three of our mates. The ones who passed away had all joined in London, and I had hardly enough time to know them. Of the trio the fireman spoke of a likable third engineer. Of the other two, one was Johnny, the Greek American fireman and his trimmer Slim Jim from Jersey Island.

It was these three who suffered the severest shock, being on duty below when the first torpedo struck amidships. From what we heard, the three unfortunates had a swift burial at sea, whether they would have wished it or not, to make more room for those who still had breath in them.

The chief steward had been in a coma for the last eighteen hours in the lifeboat, but no word came along if he was out of it yet. It was remarkable and good to learn that Antonio was in no worse condition than ourselves. The fantastic survival story of this Portuguese fireman was amazing. Six months previous, off the coast of Iceland, the same man was shipwrecked off a fishing trawler.

On the corvette, I had ample time to think about my future during those three days coursing to a safe haven. I thought mostly on a pair of feet that had swelled to a massive size, but at least my appetite was healthy. Perhaps I owed this fair state of health to the rich soup I had guzzled just before the *Lily* blew up.

The young tars who attended to us certainly did their best to make our layup as pleasant as possible. One of my aides filled my mind with anything I didn't know about Halifax. I had been there a couple of times but always at anchorage. This was the main port/city of Nova Scotia, and according to one of the young sailors, had four hospitals, all major ones.

There were the army and naval hospitals, and for the civilian population, an infirmary and a general hospital. I was amazed to learn that most beds in all four were taken up by merchant marine casualties. It was only recently that a large building had been commandeered and transformed into a hostel to house the less serious cases of merchant seamen picked up in the Atlantic. These Canadians were making a tremendous sacrifice by allowing the likes of us preference in medical attention over themselves.

On the third day, we entered Halifax Harbour in late morning with a lot of hustle and bustle in the fo'c'sle. No doubt there were a great number of homesick first trippers among the naval crew who were as excited as us to be returning from the dangers of the western ocean.

Joy at returning must have filled them that extra energy plus, which made light work of their tasks of lifting us out of hammocks and helping us to walk unsteadily on the deck where we were lined up to sit close to the gangway, ready for disembarking under a wintry sky.

The jumpy little warship no longer pitched and tossed but still waltzed rhythmically from side to side, almost like a normal ship. Then it hoved to and was tied up at the quay. We sat in a row of blue jerseys supplied from the ship's stores, as mooring ropes held fast, and the gangway was lowered – each man with a pair of outsized bare feet still thawing out.

A snow plough had cleared the dockside, leaving crisp hillocks of white snow as a background to a half dozen waiting medical vans. Men were leaning against them, holding stretchers; we were safe and dry. As our exiting began, the stretchers were only used for the more desperate cases. Most of us, with a little aid, were able to make that strange walk to transport as if that area just below the knee was walking on air. Mostly that was what the assistance was for; since we failed to sense when our feet were touching the ground, and each time my foot did touch, my aide moved me forward. He must have done this job many times because I reached the van in a short time.

Except for the officers, all the crew of the *Lily* ended up bedded down in the Royal Naval Canadian Hospital. Within an hour of being shown our beds, we were truly pampered with encouraging small talk and advice with the medics making the rounds, followed by other staff taking our temperatures. What the sailor told me on the corvette I found out to be true in the naval hospital. Only ten naval ratings and half that number of civilians, occupied beds here; the rest of the patients were off merchant ships.

A cigarette and chocolate man came along with his trolley, handing out whatever we needed on credit. And before night fell, a steaming hot cup of chocolate was placed on our side tables. By lights out we were left to a world of our own. A cigarette had followed the hot drink, and then I promised myself a sound sleep. After three nights of merely catnapping in the corvette's hammock, I quickly dropped off and must have slept for several hours soundly.

I awoke under a blue pilot light, pinpointing the darkness about me. That faint spot of blue added to the calmness of night, and propping myself up on pillows, I palmed over the top of my bed locker for a cigarette pack. Getting my eyes accustomed to the darkness, I sighted a white clad form coming my way down the aisle between the two rows of beds, which stopped beside my own. She was a tall lady, quiet-spoken and had a very comforting tone to her voice.

She asked me if I was feeling ok. I let her know that a sensation of pins and needles was running up and down my thighs. She lulled me with advice that my body was in a normal healing process and went away. She returned shortly and handed me aspirin tablets which I swallowed, and then I asked her the time. It was 4am.

When I dropped off next, I must have slept heavy because I had to be shaken for my early morning hot drink with probably an important pick-me-up inside it. The pins and needles were at work, but not as irritably now that I was getting used to them. I welcomed them as a matter of fact if that was all there was to redeeming life in the legs.

Wheelchairs in our ward were reserved for amputees, but most beds had a pair of crutches besides them, which we were encouraged to use if visiting another. Except for visiting the toilet, it was three days before I decided to explore the ward on crutches. In the sun room at the end of the ward, I encountered familiar faces of crew members, some playing cards and others looking on.

On my way back, I was requested a fag from one of the beds. I handed the man a cigarette and to be social asked the usual question, "What ship did ya come off?" "The *White Lily*," he answered. Me: "Say that again." "The *White Lily*," he shot back. The unusual fact that our ships had similar names kicked off a friendship that was to continue.

'Scouse', his mates called this young deckhand from Liverpool, and I sat at the foot of his bed to hear about the fate of the *S/S White Lily*. His yarn was unusual because the vessel he was on was not sunk through enemy action but by successfully avoiding the enemy.

After entering the Caribbean Sea from the Panama Canal, loaded with general cargo from Australia, the skipper set course for the Florida Keys and joined a convoy assembling at Key West. There was no mishap as the fleet proceeded up the east coast of the U.S. At Cape Hatteras, North Carolina, wild weather scattered a lot of ships, but naval escorts soon rounded them up.

Off the coast of Maine, stormy weather was waiting, and powerful winds on the outer flanks of the convoy formation caused them to lose direction. At sunrise *The White Lily* came out of the black night, finding itself alone and deserted.

The skipper continued on his northerly course, but afraid of being spotted by a lurking U-boat, chose to hug the coast and this proved his undoing. Before he was about to rendezvous in Halifax Harbour with the convoy, some fierce offshore winds forced the freighter onto a rocky promontory on the 'blue nose' coast of Nova Scotia, and without too many injuries, the crew were saved from the wreckage by coastal defence vessels. Scouse happened to be one of the injured with his knee put out of place escaping the wreck.

But back to my story – ten days later it was fortunate that one of the first men to get himself fit and well was our skipper. Like the chief mate when the *Lily* was struck, he was allowed to leave the private residence where he was recuperating and pay us a visit.

When he was going around the beds, handing out pay packets, I was sitting at the edge of my bed, dangling alabaster-coloured feet, still somewhat bloated. I was chatting to a shipmate, who was also sitting upright on the bed next to me. We were both handed packets. I tore mine open in a rapid fashion without reading the sum written on the front. I was dumbfounded when I withdrew the dollar notes. My mate also looked at me apprehensively. "I think I've been overpaid," I opened. "Same here; keep it mum. How much did you get?" I flashed him four hundred dollar bills, and added, "And there are smaller ones still in the packet." Altogether I was in possession of $465 Canadian.

This was more cash than I ever dreamed I would get. My mate had collected more than 500, and his final comment was, "It must be correct because the shipping agent was handing the skipper the dough after reading the name and amount on the packet; I took note of that." Both of us went through the same motions of stuffing the windfall under pillows, laying the head back on it and contemplating what to do with it. When reduced to sterling, the payout was not such a staggering amount. At 4.30 to the pound, my tally made a few quid over a hundred pounds.

Even so, I had reason to feel extra lucky. Toes were scrutinised every morning by the medic. Providing circulation continued to increase down the lower legs, and the health of the individual was optimum, then the patient was left to improve by himself. Should the man's health be under par, ice bags were wrapped around the feet to assist circulation. When I asked the quack why such treatment was not given to me, he responded that it sometimes had adverse after-effects; therefore, it was only done as an emergency measure.

Lying back in my hospital bed at Halifax, Nova Scotia, I was in an optimum state now that the pins and needles sensations had faded from my lower legs. There was no doubt I was on the way to recovery. Some of my shipmates were not so lucky. Some were minus toes, others worse off.

Surgeons were kept busy eliminating smaller or larger sections of the lower limbs that showed the smallest signs of gangrene specks. Compared with other inmates, our crew got off lightly. Hearsay had it that had we drifted another hundred miles eastwards, all hands would have perished within thirty-six hours. Fortunately, our ordeal took place within the current of the Gulf Stream. That slightly warmer water temperature saved our lives.

Half a dozen of our men were operated on by surgeons. This did not stop unfortunates from getting around. They were to be seen steering their wheelchairs in the direction of the sun room and also the games room.

The popular game in that room was poker, the curse of all sailors. Within a fortnight one of our firemen was bereft of his whole payout. This forced him to stay abed, the only consolation being a visit from charitable organisations of kind, mostly elderly ladies to buck him up. At weekends, I doubt if any patient failed to have a visitor.

The lady who attended me was a captain's wife. She was Belgian as was her husband. I do not know who she missed more, her husband away at sea on his freighter or her native Antwerp, as she spoke of carefree cafes and sailors stepping out to melodic accordions; she enchanted me with her descriptions.

Some visitors offered open homes when you were discharged from hospital. Others advised and recommended lodgings. My personal best offer came from another patient in the ward. As mentioned, this was a naval hospital, with few naval ratings being treated. I also came across two civilians in my adventures on crutches.

One patient was a young French Canadian and in the next bed to him laid a member of the Canadian Mounted Police. This Mountie became my information centre. Whenever I wished to learn anything about the big city outside the hospital walls, I would make for his bed and have a few words with the young farm boy at the same time.

Soon Frenchy was coming around in his wheelchair to pay me a visit, and I thought if he had to use that form of transport, he could be in a bad way. However, he showed no signs of a visible accident, and I never inquired what his ailment might be. Being farm bred, it was only natural he would be curious about the wider world and its big cities.

He would question me about the different ports I had visited, and his eyes lit up when I filled up his curious mind. I never realised how serious his ailment was until one morning, when I paid him a return visit, his bed was empty. The Mountie told me he had gone to the toilet but would be back soon if I cared to hang on.

In his absence the Mountie confided to me that the young lad valued my company highly. It seemed the policeman was under some kind of strain himself, as he was unable to raise his head and as he wished to confide something to me, he asked me to bend an ear to his mouth. After turning his head towards the toilet area, he hurriedly turned my way.

Even after he explained the technical name of Frenchy's ailment, I failed to retain it. What did shock me was his final words, "I don't think he has long to live but don't let him know I told you." After that I did my best to please the young man and I was well rewarded.

Although the boy's parents did not visit me, the Mountie informed me that Jules had mentioned me in letters home, and his parents invited me to stay at their farm in Quebec Province for recuperation after I was discharged from the hospital.

I held this offer in mind until just before I was ready to leave the hospital; however, by then both my body and mind were in a fit and adventurous state. I had swallowed the wandering bug, and the briny air was circulating in my blood. I was for chasing after another ship job.

In early April, Scouse received a clean bill of health, and before his departure, paid me a call with a new kitbag slung across his shoulder. He informed me that the hospital van would drop him off at the newly renovated building now dubbed The Allied Merchant Seamen's Club.

I shook his hand and promised to pay him a visit when I was discharged myself. By this time I had made a big spending spree with the trolley man and had a collection of clothing, buying something new off him each week so that I now was well-rigged out to face the outside. Then, a few days after my mate had left, I was discharged myself and fortunately was destined to be transferred to the same club.

Bright sunlight was melting small islands of snow into slush, and the vestiges of winter surrendered to the season of spring. When the orderly opened the door of the medical van, I stepped down on the padded snow and found myself at the club's entrance in Barrington Street, holding on to my belongings and waiting hesitantly.

The club door swung opened and a burly six footer emerged. The bouncer/doorman seemed very motherly and cooperative. Grabbing my kitbag he sailed through the foyer which had a small area with a mat to rub the snow off one's shoes and proceeded through an inner door to a much larger reception area. Stamping some slush on the mat, I followed and he guided me to one of the reception booths.

I then dug my hand into my new leather jacket and handed an identification card to the receptionist. I was about to request if there was a vacancy in the room of a certain friend of mine, but as I was only familiar with the name of Scouse, I bit my tongue and held my peace.

After some scribbling by the lady behind the counter and being directed to the stairway, I was handed a card, together with a room key, and she said with a smile that someone in that same room would be glad to see me. I had a nice surprise when who should I meet in the room but my Liverpool pal, Scouse. I then realised that he had made arrangements to have me as a lodger in his same place.

It was a two berth apartment, and after sitting in a joyful silence on our cots facing each other, he informed me how lucky he was to have copped this particular pad. Most rooms had four, and sometimes six occupied beds. I then drew out a packet of Sweet Caporal cigarettes from my shiny, black leather jacket and waited for words to follow his questioning stares.

Scouse: "Where did you get that terrific windbreaker?" The words dropped from his lips in all earnestness. "They're not too expensive at that hospital sale; the man used to wheel racks of them around the wards; they're a popular buy," I informed him.

Eyeing my thick yet quite sleek gabardine trousers and buckle shoes covetously, he said, "Do you know, mate, I've gone to all the clothing shops in Barrington St, but that hospital bloke sells the choicest gear." He then suggested we go down to the canteen for a cuppa and a look around at my new habitat. The foyer was only one floor down, and turning left at the bottom, we pushed past swinging doors into a wide hallway.

"This canteen turns into a drinking bar after 6pm in the evening," Scouse informed me. "And on Wednesday and Saturday evenings, an improvised stage is set up in the area near the counter, which is normally used for spare tables, trolleys and chairs."

He guided me to a seat at one of the twenty or more square tables, seating four and then took off to the self-service counter, leaving me to look around at the different groups, yarning away at other tables, and returned with two steaming cups of coffee. A sprinkling of seamen sat around, sipping their mid-morning coffee here at the Allied Merchant Seaman's Club at Halifax, Nova Scotia. Their minds were into the popular tunes being piped through on the radio between interludes by insistent adverts. Some had their noses into newspapers. Scouse dished out the info I was waiting for.

The bar opened at 6pm and shut at 11pm. The whole city was devoid of any drinking outlets. I also learned from my mate that all banjo players, amateur singers, or anyone gifted artistically to entertain his fellow salts on concert night was encouraged by the management to put his name down.

He then laid out his personal problems to me. He couldn't wait to return to Liverpool and to his girlfriend he was planning to wed. The company's agent paid him a weekly visit and handed him whatever deduction he wanted from his wages.

He had spent five months working on the *White Lily* and would not receive his total wages until he returned home." What about recuperation cash?" I questioned. "That is what is worrying me. There are still three crew members recovering in hospital, and the others have already found their passage back home. You see, Ted, I'm in a different position than you. My ship was not sunk by enemy action. I could claim a lot more cash or maybe a lot less," Scouse worried.

He ended up by mentioning that if the British Seaman's Union, the NUS or National Union of Seaman devoted more time to a seaman's monetary protection, he could receive a good claim through a marine court to start his marriage off; then he changed the subject. "I intend speculating on a purse belt," he said, looking seriously at me. "I want my personal belongings, like documents and cash, sticking next to my skin."

At that point in the chat he decided to give me a guided tour of the place. I found no game room there, but there was a fair enough set of books and magazines in the library, though very few readers. I then followed him to a glass panel in the foyer. It was against a wall and he told me that if I was eager to ship out to visit it each morning.

Pointing to one of the kiosks which was used to aid men looking for a berth on a ship, he mentioned that there too many names on the registry, and the jobs on the panel were jobs that had been turned down.

Before returning to the dining room for the noon meal, he said he had decided to rig himself out after my fashion. It seemed the tailor called around the club once a week.

It was good news to me that my mate cared little for swilling down beer; he cared only for his sweetheart and a future with her. Therefore, the first night after two bottles, I killed the urge for a spree and spent the quieter evening in the cosy surroundings of our two berth cabin. It's amazing how long two pals can carry on chatting on different subjects when adult life begins to open up in front of them.

The following morning there was a full house at the breakfast gathering, and I wondered how so few had a drunken lie-in from the night before. Not only that, but half the sitters lingered over the breakfast table. I learned from my mate that most of the inmates were hotfooting it to consuls and shipping companies. I assumed that most of the go-getters were from English speaking countries, who would naturally suffer from homesickness to a degree.

In regard to other nationalities, most of these residents came from countries under the occupation of Germany or Japan, so what was the hurry to get out of pleasant surroundings like Canada? Whatever the nationality, could a lot of them be impatient to get to some port where a pair of candy legs was waiting for their return?

For the first three or four days I enjoyed the benefit of being well-heeled. I kept doing the rounds of reading the dailies in the library, jawing with all and sundry about the tables and wondering where the rest of the *Lily* crew had gone. I recalled how helpful visitors used to call around the hospital beds, offering patients free recuperation in their own private homes.

So, how many men were quartered in the suburbs, and did they call to the club for the sake of buying beer? But this still didn't answer the question of how my whole crew had disappeared into thin air. And around that time came the clothing man with his trolley, and I bought a fedora, or trilby type hat, to add to the mature look of my eighteen years.

I started to spend time at the evening drinking sessions looking for a familiar face. After a week of this, my feet were now in such good shape that I ventured down the main drag, Barrington Street and its offshoots. Then the 'shipping out' urge sucked me in.

I scrutinised any fresh notices put up in the foyer and stopped at shipping company offices on my walking excursions. Returning one morning from a fruitless search, I entered the club, pushed open the swing door to the dining room and was pleasantly surprised to find Stamatis, the steward of the *Lily*.

He was sipping coffee alone. Having been just released from medical care, he relayed news to me that I had been unaware of. After being eighteen hours in a coma after being rescued by the corvette, his healing had been longer.

When Stam left hospital, Antonio, our miracle survivor of the *Lily's* torpedoing, was still under observation, having come through a bout of pneumonia. And Mitso, our donkeyman, was still in care, but would be released as soon as they could find a shoe for one of his feet which had to be amputated. Six others who had suffered cut-offs from the feet would be permitted to remain in the hospital until passages back to the UK could be arranged

"But where were the other crew members floating around?" I asked. My informant told me that most had opted for a free passage to New York, where the Greek consul was trying to recruit crews. An idea then occurred to me to pay a visit to the Greek consul here in Halifax and maybe get a transfer to the Big Apple.

I mentioned this to the Stam and he invited me to come along with him on the following Monday; it was now Thursday. I was then asked about my identification, and Stam told me it was important that I change my hospital release document for a more valid one from the consul. Although I was impatient to go along myself, it was preferable to allow a few days to pass, as my shipmate might assist me in getting a free ride to New York.

I filled enjoyable evenings that weekend, being welcomed at tables where sat groups of twos and threes. On one occasion I heard a familiar brogue and introduced myself to some Cardiff boys. A chair was pushed out for me to join them, and I found that they were tied up at a wharf.

Scouse joined me in a few beers one evening, and I tipped him off about seeking work on ships tied up in port. Crews could be contacted here in the club, where they would naturally be attracted like bees to a honey pot, as it was the only oasis for relieving one's alcoholic thirst. I mingled with all kinds whenever invited for a drink at the tables; as most residents were survivors of enemy action, there was a strong fraternity among all nationals.

On Sunday night, I over drank and could not clearly remember who were my drinking partners, but one item of gossip stayed in my mind. A couple were over lamenting on the wartime perils at sea. I felt it was uncalled for, considering that merchant seamen had a free and easy lifestyle, and our earnings topped most of the cash payments received by members of the armed forces.

That uneasy feeling stayed in my mind, and the following night lying abed in a more sober state, I thought on the statements of some of my fellow seafarers. It was the utter seriousness in their voices that brought back the vague memory of words and faces. They seemed to exaggerate the amount of ships sunk by enemy action.

What was surprising in that club was the number of survivors from neutral countries sailing on allied ships. When ships docked in places like South America, sailors from Spain, Eire or Portugal would receive uncensored letters from home, giving shipping losses from the other side. Could the losses be higher than our own censorship allowed us to know?

These men scorned the safety of their own protected neutral fleets in order to support the alliance and would no doubt keep mum about reports from home that would disturb the minds of shipmates, but alcohol is a tongue loosener. It was one year later that I heard from American newspapers that allied shipping losses had well surpassed the loss of over one thousand in 1942 alone! Perhaps censorship is a necessary evil after all, but at that time, I could not comprehend that the North Atlantic was Hitler's greatest success story in the destruction of allied convoys.

On Monday, Stamatis said he felt his feet were still not in the best condition and would have to wait until the next day; I agreed. Tuesday morning came around, and I was waiting impatiently at the breakfast table for him. Scouse had got to the table even earlier; the job search must have hooked him as well. Usually his first words at the table were: 'Heard the news?' He seemed to pick up rumours quicker than a woman. This morning was no different.

So I opened with, "Well, what's new, pal?" Scouse: "Admiral Darlan has given the French fleet to Hitler." Darlan had been the only real friend of Britain in the Vichy government of France, and I just knew this couldn't be true. I tried to digest this report together with my bacon and eggs; no tough food rationing on this side of the Atlantic.

"Who told you this, Scouse?" Scouse: "Heard it in the foyer when I went out there to look at the job list." If the news was unfortunately true, I would accept it in the same way most people would – that the reverse is expected in wartime. I swallowed the fried eggs nonchalantly, waiting for the Lily's steward's decision on job hunting.

Taking the cup from his lips, my mate bent over and confided, "By the sound of their voices, some of the geezers on the other tables are getting panicky; they must have heard the bad news." They weren't the only ones; it was affecting me as I was itching to join a homeward bounder. Both Scouse and I were chasing jobs.

As soon as my mate left the table, I made a point of observing the international set grouped around respective tables. They appeared not as congenial as usual. I overheard some audible, angry tones.

Along came Stamatis, who passed me a good morning, slapped down the daily in front of me and joined the queue at the self-service counter. The headlines were there all right, but I was still reticent, as it was a Montreal paper, and that meant a French Canadian influence, and the French Canadians were very tardy in the Ottawa government in agreeing to support Great Britain in the war.

My table companion read English as well as his native Greek, plus he was a strong anti-fascist, so I awaited his opinion of the news.

The only comment he gave out, between chews of pancake, was "Not good". By the time he made it to his coffee, he made a further comment, "Very bad situation for England." His mind must have been trying to come to a conclusion like myself. I was brought back to earth when Scouse returned to let me know there were no vacancies for ABs, and he was ready to take the position of OS to get his passage back home.

Before leaving the table once more, he asked me if I would mind shipping out on a Norwegian vessel. "Fine, if the cash is ok and she's heading for Blighty, I'll jump at it." Scouse: "Well, you'll find a notice in the glass pane in the foyer, which says that a coal trimmer is needed, and the ship is definitely headed for Liverpool; says so on the board."

Now giving my attention to Stamatis, I realized leather jackets were not for the steward. It was not his line. He had purchased a jacket in a light cloth about 2' lower than normal – an American innovation, in grey with rather outsized pockets, from one of which he drew a local edition of a newspaper in Greek, just a small issue. Before he put his nose into it, I let him know I would meet him in the foyer later.

I glanced at the advertised notice pointed out by Scouse; it stated that the D/S *Ingerfem* needed a coal trimmer. Right after this statement was the wording I was looking for most especially. It was bound for Liverpool, just as Scouse had said. I just had to share my excitement with someone.

The doorman was just leaving the information desk on his way back to the stool between the double doors. When I pulled him up and passed on my lucky break, I realised immediately that someone might beat me to the job and confided my fears to the bouncer's ears. He would have none of it.

He assured me that 'Down Below' workers were looking for less hard ways of making a living, like oil fuel steamships or motor ships. Then quick like he said, "How are you for dough? I mean do you have much? Because if you have some, there's a guy selling one pound notes behind the Bank of Nova Scotia."

I turned this juicy piece of news around in my mind, and it became more interesting by the second, so I quickly requested how I could make contact with moneybags. "The guy will be at his stand from 9am till noon." As I left to go to my room, he wished me a successful trip back to the old country.

Back in the room, with only myself there, I removed the purse belt from my waist, unzipped my long pouch and examined my banknotes. Since the old man had dished out the bounties at the hospital, my fortune had been reduced by roughly $100. This left me in possession of $340, or approximately 70 pounds, which was still a lot more cash than I had ever been blessed with.

An idea entered my head that I might be able to restore the original value of the handout, by trading $130. Shrewdness got the better of me and gingerly I lifted four $20 bills from my belt and then slipped them back into a different compartment of my wallet, sitting in my inner jacket pocket. In my centrally-heated apartment, I lay back on my bed telling myself that spring was in the air, but a glazed window told me that the air still had a knife's edge. I upped myself and prepared for it.

The sea was always near and when I opened the window to test the gentle wind from the harbour; its keenness caused me to zip up my windbreaker. And facing the mirror, with a cigarette sagging from my mouth, I planted the trilby over my tousled curls at a rakish angle. Sure enough the great actor Humphrey Bogart's double peered back at me out of that mirror; thinking of the financial deal I was about to arrange, I felt like MR BIG.

CHAPTER 3 –*D/S INGERFEM*

SHIP NUMBER TWO

I left the room, walked down to the foyer and joined Stam. Both of us stepped into Barrington Street. Sauntering along the sidewalk of the main artery, one observed the uniforms of three separate navies. With all these seamen flooding the port, Canadians were in the minority since the bigger warships came in under British and American flags.

Perhaps only other merchant seamen can identify the brotherhood from different civilian groups unless they are a leg watcher. Except for officers in uniform, one would see a sailor from a cargo vessel dressed in unorthodox styles. They left tailor shops differently garbed and shod than when they entered the premises. One might see a sailor walking out from the tailors, wearing a high-priced top coat with threadbare oilskin trousers protruding from the bottom and a brand new canvas kitbag slung over one shoulder.

Short-order cafes were in abundance the whole length of the street, and there was not too much sitting space in them since there were no drinking bars to take in the excess manpower.

We called at the Greek Consulate further along the street. It seemed we had arrived a bit early, but the squat, though intelligent-looking person before us instructed us to go to a certain address in the street to have our photographs taken fast, and by the time we returned, his secretary would have arrived to deal with us. Our identity documents were made out by the time we returned. The consul and my mate hit it off well together and chatted away for a long five minutes.

Then my mate steered me up a side street, and we dropped into a small comfy Greek cafe. This time when I probed Stamatis over cups of coffee, he was more optimistic about the French fleet affair. The consul had let him know that there had been no official handing over of the fleet.

Hitler was urging his puppet, Laval, whom he had upgraded in the

Vichy government to force the hand of Darlan, but the consul had insisted that if it came to an order, then Darlan would scuttle the main fleet in Toulon, or else allow it to escape. (Neither would be the case –the RAF bombed the ships into hulks.) I would like to have hung around and chatted with the sociable daughter of the cafe owner, but I had to be off to the bank on my important money-changing business.

The 'pound man' at the 'bank' must have read me or my rolling gait because he waved me over to an alcove in a thick wall. After a few opening words, we turned our rears to the passersby and scrummed over, hat brims touching. In exchange for the four twenty dollar bills from my wallet, I stuffed forty-one pound notes.

The big, new wallet was well-stretched and took up all the space in my inside jacket pocket. My 'banker' had rapidly counted out each note, which proved he was no stranger to handling currency notes. I left him feeling 'High' as the saying goes, excited at what I had pulled off. Soon I was in search of another consulate, the Norwegian one.

I located it after worrying a few locals with questions and jauntily entered a door beneath the coat of arms of Norway. After handing the pretty secretary there my identification from the Greek consul, I proudly pointed out the part where the captain had recommended me as a reliable coal trimmer.

She whisked me into a side door for a medical check-up, which I passed the medical test easily, and the job was mine. The secretary's face was not so cold when I returned to the counter. She even risked a faint smile when she took me to the window to point out the pier where I would catch the launch which would take me to the *Ingerfem*, which lay at anchor. I was told to be at the pier at 10am the following morning with all my gear.

I dawdled on my way back to the Greek cafe, feeling that my main morning tasks had been completed, and I had a day to waste. As I entered the cafe, I was still trying to guess why the lady secretary at the consul gave herself airs when I had entered. Then I remembered I had not bought stokehold boots and other work gear, so I doubled back to the shopping centre.

I put it down to a thing she might have had for men in uniform, and an approach of a low paid engine worker was not in her dreams. What a different welcome I received in the cafe. The pretty, young lass with the olive skin and winning smile still passed me pleasantries when she served coffee.

It turned out Stam had left earlier after another customer entered who had said that with more loses at sea, it would be best that Stamatis gave up his career and stay ashore in Canada. Perhaps the steward thought if he lingered any longer he might be persuaded in doing so, having been already torpedoed three times.

My club roommate joined me at early morning breakfast the next day; we discussed how he had not been as lucky as myself in getting a passage back home. But he shook my hand and wished me well when he saw me off at the door.

The sea breeze was somewhat strong as I passed a half mile down Barrington Street, and as I turned down the small hill towards the jetty, I looked out on a squally sea beyond the row of launches. Spits of brine wetted me as I drew towards another young sailor who was obviously waiting for a passage as well.

He took the same launch as myself, and we hopped aboard as it drew alongside. Along the quayside, a row of white-capped U.S. Navy sailors stood around awaiting their own particular ferry. They stood back so that spray would not gust over their uniforms. It so heartened me to think that the great might of the U.S. Navy was now joined on the side of Britain.

My companion was also joining a new ship's crew, and as our small launch chopped its way through the ruffled waters, his body signals let me know that he didn't want to talk much – his brain was probably going through something like my own. Butterflies always made their presence in my stomach on entering into the life of strangers.

The coxswain of the boat asked me to unlace the top of my kitbag so he could put the ship's mail inside, and when we moored on the lee side of the *Ingerfem*, he manoeuvred his craft so it hugged the hull of the ship. A heaving line was lowered from above, and the bag made fast to it and was hauled aloft. A rope ladder followed.

Ascending those steps seemed like a small ordeal. However, willing hands were there to assist me over the gunwale, and with a final effort, I threw my legs over onto a capstan. I was immediately introduced to my new cabin mate, Ole, who was about my own size, barring the fact he was broader of shoulder. I let him guide me aft to quarters below the poop deck.

I took a liking to my two berth cabin right away and stashed my gear on the top bunk, claiming ownership after I had untied the bag and passed the mail to my new cabin mate. Steam pipes from the engine room ensured that a large radiator kept the cabin warm and cosy. He suggested that he take me to the skipper to sign on, since he was waiting for me in the saloon, where I went through the procedure of signing on just about last.

The next person I was introduced to was the second engineer, who informed me that on the first day when joining a Norwegian ship, time would be spent attending to your cabin, seeing that it was clean and tidy. He stressed that Norwegians always treated their living quarters not in the ordinary way but as a 'Home'.

He then ordered Ole to show me the duties of a coal trimmer. We returned to the mess room on the poop deck. There were half a dozen or more sitting around speaking in English, although most were Norskes, and later I was to learn that English truly was the language of the sea, bridging different nationals on board a ship.

After the poor accommodations on the *Lily* up forehead, where most times rough weather prohibited any decent eating as the bows continually pitched and tossed, men preferred to eat standing up in the alleyway outside the galley and socialising at the same time. Here living at the stern was a completely different situation with electric lighting plus hot and cold running water.

Admittedly, a trimmer on the *Ingerfem* had a few extra duties, but they were not unpleasant. At the end of each watch, you were expected to bring food kits or containers of food from the galley to the mess room, and after the meal was over, you washed the dishes and returned the kits. Dirt marks on the insulating woodwork over the bulkheads had to be washed off at weekends, in addition to the mess room floor being scrubbed.

These tasks were done consecutively by the three trimmers, which made it easy cleaning the quarters only once in three weeks. We did not sail until midnight the following day, so I had plenty of time to look over the stokehold. I was relieved to find that trimmers were excluded from putting ashes on the furnace pits after the firemen cleaned out their fires. My duties were thus reduced in this part of the routine.

At 7.30 am the next morning, I was already rigged out in my new stokehold boots and work gear, ready to tear into my new job. The throb of the propeller under the stern vibrated through the ironwork. It was fair weather out on deck, and for a moment I was busy watching all those other stern crews pushing rows of ships with fresh supplies to the UK's western approaches which would feed and arm the only country in Europe still not under the dictate of fascism other than neutral Ireland, Sweden and Switzerland.

I had been up and about since 7am, swilling coffee and enjoying a smoke before the 7.20 am breakfast bell. I knocked down my meal pretty quick – it was the first time I had tasted fiskeboller or fish balls. Apart from lacking any spicy sauce to liven up the flat taste, I found the aftertaste was better than the eating.

Ole was the shorter of the two firemen, and the three of us strolled amidships for fifteen minutes for that hour of duty. The boys seated themselves outside the fiddley door (part of stokehold), before going below for the four hour stint.

One of the firemen, a young, tall blond picked up two empty 7lb fruit tins from inside the fiddley. He took them to the galley, a few yards away, and used the outdoor hand pump to fill them with water. He instructed me to lower them on the hooks of the wide ventilators as soon as they went below. We sat outside the door on the lee side, the other one being closed against a shifty wind.

Inside the fiddley, dirty pullovers hung over the handrail, dry and warm from the heated air rising. It made no difference how dirty they were – on board the *Ingerfem*, the men showered the coal dust off themselves in the crew's quarters. There had been no such washing facilities on the *Lily* so men washed up in the engine room.

The idea was that in the stokehold, men worked at the furnaces, either stripped to the waist or in singlets, irrespective if it was a North Atlantic winter or the tropical south. Climbing from the hot workplace and sweating, it was a wise idea to cover upper bodies with a woolly covering against the colder elements until they reached the poop deck.

I was also told by Ole that the trimmer usually brought back the pullovers to the fiddley. Before I went in the bunkers, my cabin mate told me there would be little to do, as fresh bunkers had been taken on in Halifax. He told me that after he had lowered the water cans, there would be no need to come down to the stokehold.

He and his mate would clean out the ash pits and throw buckets of water on the ashes before hauling them up in a drum. They would let me know when they wanted me to haul up ashes, by rattling the inside vent with the stout iron chain and hook. All I had to do was stand by.

My two firemen were happy men to work with, and I handled the job to the satisfaction of the other two trimmers and the deucer. Fish was high on the menu with these northerners, and after a week I began to acquire a taste for fish myself, or should I say it grew on me, just like the Mediterranean diet of the Greeks had.

There is never a calm Atlantic, but our trip was fortunate weather-wise. It was a happy-go-lucky crew, and I seemed to get along well with all the hands, especially the steward from Manchester, and the other trimmer, a Spaniard – both lads in their late twenties.

Ole and I had a bureau in our cabin with our sharing the four small drawers. The photographs above it were screwed to the bulkhead above. They were Ole's parents living in German-occupied Bergen, Norway.

Then something odd happened. We were two weeks at sea when the 4-8 trimmer put me on a shake for breakfast. I scrambled out of my bunk to get dressed before my mate in the bunk below awoke to give him more room in the cabin. I then felt a numbness in my hands as I was lowering myself down to the cabin's deck.

I sat on the small stool in front of the only furniture in the room, the pine bureau with its flat top for writing letters. Still half asleep I stared up at Ole's treasured photos of his parents and then guided my eyes down to my hands, which I placed palms upward on the desktop. They were somewhat swollen yet causing no discomfort. There was just a touch of awkwardness about them; they lacked grip. I found little difficulty in putting my work clothes on except for tugging on the boots.

Up the ladder to the mess room I went. To make sure I spilled no coffee, I removed the sweat rag hanging from my trousers' belt and gripping the under part of the mug, I held it under the percolator, turning the urn on and off with my other hand. The blonde fireman was bent over his own coffee so he didn't notice anything unduly strange about the way I handled my mug.

Heaving up ashes through the ventilator pipes would soon test my hands, but it was asking for a miracle for an improvement to happen in such a short time. Try as I might, my hands failed to handle the winder firmly. This Armstrong patent device would not respond to hauling up thirty kilograms of ash and clinker. Then I descended the iron steps down to the stokehold and showed my swollen fingers to the firemen. They sympathised and said the ashes could wait until I had seen the second engineer.

Into the engine room I went. However, it was hard to explain to the donkeyman, who was standing in for the engineer whilst he was at breakfast because of loud, discordant noises coming up from the main engine and steam pumps, so my displaying the state of my hands did most of the explaining. He shouted in my ear "chief's cabin!" and pointed upwards.

I ascended from the engine room and cornered the chief just as he was leaving the engineer's mess. Taking serious notice of my hands, he guided me along the alleyway. Then he stopped and asked me if I had undergone a similar ill before. I told him of my lifeboat experience. He nodded and told me that my duties would now cease.

Then he led me back to the mess, and after saying something in Norwegian to the second engineer (deucer), that person drained his coffee, butted his cigarette on a tray and left the table to accompany me. He told me the reason for hurrying was to catch the second mate in his cabin. In the absence of a qualified medic, the second mate had the honour of acting as the ship's doctor.

In the mate's cabin I was asked the same questions as by the chief. After some considering, the mate concluded that the swelling was a reaction from my recent exploit and fully agreed with the chief that I should lie up and do no more duties. He said he was sure the captain would pay me off in Liverpool as a cure would not be rapid.

The hands gave me no pain; they were just a damn nuisance. I had to use gloves continually to drink tea or coffee, as my fingers remained unable to grip the handle of the cup. Apart from this small irritation, I enjoyed the five days it took to arrive at Liverpool with an enjoyable leave at home planned. My mind was bathed in a holiday mood with summer not far away.

When the saloon steward offered to scrub the sweat and coal dust from my money belt, I was amazed how dry the currency notes still were. These waist belts were roomy enough to carry lots of documents and cash, and as soon as it was dried out, back went my possessions into rubber bands. The belt had proved its worth, being next to my sweaty skin since leaving port except when taking a shower.

Just in case there was some doubt about my pound notes, I entered a pound note withdrawal on the sub list, handing it in before entering port. The convoy had experienced no rough weather so far, and the forecast ahead was also good.

It was only on that final night, whilst crossing the Irish Sea that a disturbing event occurred. There was an exuberant mood that dark and cloudy night, and at about 10pm the small firemen's mess was packed to the bulkheads with visiting deckhands and stewards. They were bragging for the loudest of the bars, molls and acquaintances they were familiar with in Lime Street in Liverpool. As my gloved hands nursed a cup of coffee, I enjoyed the yarning.

Then one man whose hearing seemed more acute than normal called a hush; faces turned a more serious hue as some understanding dawned on them of the strange droning sound overhead. All hands traipsed out onto the poop deck, eyes trained skyward. Were they friendly planes? What was lurking above those starless, black clouds? Misgivings were confirmed when a sailor ascended from the afterwell deck.

He clued us in with the latest news from Sparky, enclosed in his cabin hideaway. The wireless operator's contact had informed him that several hundred enemy bombers were returning to Germany after a devastating bombing blitz over Belfast, Northern Ireland.

We sat out a tense hour in the mess room with our life jackets on.

Providentially, the large spread of clouds blacked out the giveaway smokestacks of the fleet, just in case any of the bombers had not disposed of all their ugly, satanic cargo. It was a relief to hear the last of them.

Before turning into our bunks for the night, several of us walked back out on deck for a bit of reassurance. The warm spring air had turned chilly in the night, and I scrambled my funny hands through the sleeves of my thick, Canadian lumberjack shirt. We walked around on the deck for a while, basking in the friendly throbbing sound of the prop which was vibrating a homey arrival in port. The buzz got around that we would tie-up in the morning at Garston Dock, ten miles up the River Mersey.

Around 6am the next morning, the clanging, clanking and banging, as steam forced its way into winches, woke me from an uneasy sleep of anxious dreams. Dazzling sunlight flashed through the cabin's porthole circles, and the reassuring thought that I was back safe and sound in Blighty put me in a positive leaning for the day.

A sailor informed us at the breakfast table that we were expected to take our dutiable allowance of spirits and cigarettes to the saloon when we finished filling our faces because the customs officers had already boarded. I still hold the memory of that morning in Garston Dock when all hands filed into the skippers saloon.

Customs officers were seated on one side of the long, polished table, whilst the crew filed along the other side to answer questions and sign the manifest sheet. Exchanging a lot of friendly words with a sailor in front of me helped ease some of my nervous energy of now being safe in England.

Only when the sailor's turn came to be questioned, did I realise I had missed out on catching questions being shot at the others in front. I was unprepared when my turn came. The usual questions I replied to in automatic fashion. Cigarettes - how many?" Me: "200." The face studied mine. "How about any spirits?" Me: "Just a bottle." Customs poured a refill of coffee for my questions, and he took time off to lift the cup to his lips.

"Well," I thought, "that is it." and directed my feet after the man in front of me. The sailor moved on from the manifest sheet after he signed his name, and I took his place.

The customs officer pushed back his peaked cap, just as I was bending over to put my name to the big sheet. I was abruptly brought up short. "Hang on there, Mr Whitehead," came from the peaked cap. "There is one more question. Did you acquire any pound notes during your stay in Canada?" "Yes," I answered.

My reply had been as sudden and unexpected as the question. It was such an unusual question that I was caught completely off guard. I felt like a mug and somewhat dumbstruck and deflated for owning up so readily. I detected a grim inner alarm that it was goodbye to my easy cash. I was requested to produce the stuff.

The officer sat back and added some more sugar to his coffee. He probably thought I was going to run off then and there to my cabin to fetch the goods, and I was hoping he would concentrate on his sweet beverage, whilst I did some fumbling beneath my shirt. With the state of my hands, it took great effort to loosen the buckle of my pants.

The man in line after me understood my condition, and whilst I hugged the side of my pants to hold them up, he removed the waist belt. He dumped the fag pouch in front of his majesty's customs, whilst I tried to cover up my embarrassment. My pink face brought on a few smiles, and I did not attempt to replace the belt. Then came the verdict. "I am afraid that these currency notes of yours will have to be kept in our custody. They have to be checked in case they are forged." "What if they are Ok?" I asked. "Well, we'll have your address from the captain, and we'll keep you posted. If the notes are OK, you will be notified and the cash returned. You see, old chap, they have a little factory going way down in Argentina, which our government is well aware of."

"They make very good duplicates of our currency and these are distributed throughout both Americas. Sorry I have to take them off you. Are you the person paying off now?" "Hmm," I muttered. As I was about to pass along the table in half shock, his voice followed me, "Don't worry, you'll have your money in a couple of weeks if the notes are genuine."

His apologetic attitude eased my pain. At least I had plenty of dollar bills for a lengthy holiday, my two months' recuperation leave. At the end of the long table sat the captain and the Norwegian consul paying out money. After signing on the dotted line, I received twenty-eight pounds for my trip, which was less than a month and was definitely more than expected.

When I returned to my cabin, Ole was waiting for me with my kitbag across his shoulder. He carried it to the bottom of the gangway, and after placing it on my shoulder, waited until he was sure that I could make it to the dock, a short distance away. The bag needed little grip, and arriving at the gate, an unusual request was put to me.

A police officer stepped out of his little office and without further ado asked me if I could supply him with a box of matches. He said he was not interested in searching my bag for dutiable goods; all he wanted was matches. He sounded like he must have needed them badly and I quickly agreed.

I dropped the sack at his feet and said "My hands aren't in the best shape; if you untie the bag, you'll find matches at the top." There were several Canadian jumbo-sized boxes looking up at him. He eyed me quizzically. "Grab one of them," I urged, and they were in fact large boxes, enough matches to last him a year. I had made his day for sure; he seemed overjoyed.

Not only did he order me a taxi, he took over from the driver in stashing my belongings in the boot. On the way to the railway station, I laughingly related this deal to the taxi driver. He briefed me with the news that the match factory at Garston had scored a direct hit in a recent air raid, and the locals were without these useful items.

Arriving at the station, the first porter I came to grabbed my bag and asked where I was bound for. When I answered South Wales, he trolleyed my bag to a platform, where he told me to catch the next train to Crewe and then make a change from there to Cardiff. I offered him a bob, but he said sixpence.

This attitude was definitely not a peacetime one of grab-all. Sitting on a bench at Crewe station, waiting for my Cardiff train, I felt that I had had a lucky break at the dock gate. At the bottom of my bag were several plugs of chewing tobacco, which I had not declared to customs. They were very popular with miners for spitting out coal dust. I intended on winning a few smiles at home with them.

I had a long wait at Crewe, nearly an hour. You could feel the atmosphere of a nation at war here because it was a busy intersection. Platforms were swarming with men from all the services, swilling down mugs of tea or rushing to and from trains. Thick china mugs were left around carelessly on seats and window ledges.

I was later to learn that outward appearances in Britain counted for nothing. By the time I stepped off the last car in Treorchy, this charged feeling of camaraderie was infecting me; here was the character of a unified nation.

I was now on my last mile getting home, and for once there was no familiar face to greet. However, that homecoming feeling could not be upended; every pore of my body registered exhilaration. It was early evening when I stepped through the front door of my house. I was welcomed not only with a steaming, hot cup of tea from the teapot on the hob of a bright coal fire but good family news to go with it.

My brother Ken had not fallen by the wayside after all; he had been hiding in the hills of Crete with others of the Welsh regiment and was now in a German stalag (prison camp). Jack, my senior brother by two years, was now a rear air gunner in bomber command.

That evening I was not feeling like paying the local a visit and making a fool of myself trying to lift a pint of bitter with my funny hands. It had been a hectic day and so I took to my bed. I could hardly believe I had slept from early evening into afternoon of the following day, but when I arose and located a timepiece, I found it to be 2pm.

For the middle of May, the weather was as good as you could get in the UK. It was awfully inviting to say the least. If it would keep as sunny as this, it would indeed be a merry month, but British weather can be the most unpredictable on earth. I lay in bed for an extra few minutes, enjoying a stretch and looking forward to the rest of the day.

But how in the heck was I going to lift a pint of beer with these bloated hands of mine? Later enjoying some tasty bacon sandwiches with tea downstairs, my sister let me know there would be no need to pay a visit to the town surgery. The local nurse would pay regular calls each morning.

Rashers of bacon from the dried, salted and smoked pork shoulder hanging in the pantry put a good base in my stomach should I overdo any tippling at the pub. After washing the food down with a cuppa, I went to the rear door, where on a slight elevation, I looked down into the valley and tasted a perfumed breeze from the mountainside; my smoking habit had not grown enough to keep me from enjoying nasal flavours.

The weather was warm enough to stroll outside minus a jacket, but vanity won over my mind, and with clumsy hands and the help of my sister, hands and arms found their way through the sleeves of my flashy, zip-up leather Canadian covering, and I was then soon off with plugs of tobacco stuffed in pockets.

I made a short stop across the road to hand over one plug to an elderly miner. I planned to refuse cups of tea until I arrived at the last house of call in my circuit. My mind was set on the taste of the hop at the local. Like it or not, I was forced to unzip my jacket, when I emerged from my final visiting place. My fingers were developing tricks of their own, as I placed two thumbs together to pull down the zip.

Now, in the middle of the afternoon, the day had warmed up. I escaped to the coolness of the pub, where I ordered a half pint glass of beer; I would not be caught spilling beer with a larger glass. At that time of the day, the elder males were making their living cutting coal way below the surface of the earth, whilst the few customers in the Park Hotel were definitely all strangers to me.

Seeing me drink in a truly awkward way, I received blank stares, which seemed to say: 'Where are the bandages?' The new boss had an indifferent look and I stayed glum. Obviously they must have thought I had burnt my hands in some way, but since I was not familiar, neither were they cooperative. This was not what I had looked forward to.

So this gave me the option of returning home and discarding the jacket. A couple of hours passed rapidly as I sorted out my belongings, and after a snack found the evening had cooled rapidly outside. So back on went the jacket and down the road I sailed. Men were home from work now, and I decided to stop at the Park Hotel for a few snorters of spirits to perk me up.

Poking my nose inside the door, I had a quick look around, and with no friendly faces to welcome me, I stepped into the Italian cafe next door. At Tortello's I found old school day friends sitting around a table, buying up anything that was edible. People always seem to enjoy food more when there is a shortage, and as for cash, there was plenty of that around, now that the mines were working full blast.

Maybe these friendly faces warmed my spirits more than a few tots of whisky. I was given a hearing to gab away and was soon yarning with the best of them. Someone suggested that the weather was warm enough to stroll up pathways, and away we went allowing the aromatic breeze to waft away our personal problems on the grassy landscape of the mountainside.

The five of us made the climb in the hope that a group of girls might come along with the similar idea. We returned well before blackout time, since sunset was now growing later into the day, and although we failed to come across any skirts on the way, it gave me the mountainside roaming bug. The mountainside all around was my playground as a boy and just running into the wind after school gave me a thrill.

There are some enjoyments one cannot put into words. During those days motor transport was still a rarity especially in this end of the valley. Sheep had the freedom of streets and back lanes, living off food scraps thrown to them, and kids spent most of their time walking up streams and maybe fishing.

As everyone was now working, I looked forward to wandering on my lonesome over mountain tops where sheep were fat and healthy, living in the long grass and grazing their heads off. On the following days, I could hardly wait for the calling nurse to attend to my hands so that I could be back up on those green hills before the weather changed.

For some reason these walks brought back a kaleidoscope of sweet memories away from school and home quarrels. After several days of mountain climbing, the healing process of my home area brought a healthy glow to my cheeks, and on most evenings, I enjoyed socialising in the Italian cafe rather than the hotel.

After the first week at home, my hands began feeling a grip returning to them – though slowly at first. It was a fortnight before the Cwmpark lady healer confirmed that my hands were back to a normal and fit state. Armed with her stethoscope, she stopped her daily visits of monitoring my health. The weather still proved promising, and I aimed at spreading out my two months convalescence in as enjoyable a manner as possible.

The balmy days of June proved even more satisfying than those of May, and I kept the afternoon mountainside walks, spending the evenings with some friends at Tortello's Cafe; weekends meant a get-together at the Park Hotel. I was often plied with questions and satisfied their curiosity with yarns I had overheard in the mess rooms of both ships I had served on.

There was good reason for not bringing up any of my personal experiences. One evening as I stood at the bar alone, without any of my teenage friends present, one sly-eye about five years above my own age urged and probed me regarding my narrow escape from perishing in a lifeboat. To give him and the others there an idea of our plight, I recalled observations from the chief mate in our boat.

What did I receive in return for being helpful? With only critical glances, they might have said out openly because it was well-written on their faces. Who was this eighteen year old blowing off about his experience of riding thirty foot waves in an open lifeboat in rough weather? It was too much for their understanding.

Perhaps if I had stuck a flowing white beard on my chin, they might have given me credit for my effort. Yet in Cardiff bars, these tales were passed regularly amongst seamen and were enjoyed as acceptable experiences of how men escaped the wrath of the sea. These locals might have been conditioned by movies with heroes dressed in a peaked cap or uniform.

Those blank stares determined me never to give that pub a second chance to downgrade me. One unusual story went down well though, and I was asked to repeat it. It concerned a steamer called the *S/S Pegasus*, which was torpedoed at night in October 1941. This vessel was struck nearing home waters. The engine room received no tin fish, only the stern did.

This gave all hands a chance to get to the life-boats. If you meet any wartime seaman, he will let you know that the primary fear in all men's minds was being torpedoed or shelled at night. It must have been a grim affair with all deck lights out to conform to blackout regulations. They all succeeded in reaching the lifeboats, unhooked the hooks from the davits and pushed off.

Since both boats were on different sides of the ship, a head count could only be made when both boats met, which was not easy on a black night with a high sea running. But, alas, there was one man who never made it – a tardy fireman, who being the last to ascend the stokehold ladder, first slipped in his hobnail boots in the excitement of the moment, then fell back, sustaining an injury to his leg, and this caused him to limp up instead of run.

A timber ship is liable to collapse if the explosion causes it to list far over on its beam ends because the cargo is stowed ten to fifteen feet above the main deck and held in place with a set of chains seized around stanchions on either side. This unfortunate loner, finding himself left behind with rough seas building up, used the best survival tactics he could think up.

He descended from the boat deck and in the darkness entered the first cabin in the amidships area where he grabbed any blankets he could feel. There are always a couple of life rafts on the boat deck, and this is where he decided to sleep for the night in case the ship foundered, but up to this time the cargo was keeping it afloat.

He unleashed the tie rope and secured himself to the first raft with it. Morning came and this Robinson Crusoe found the ship in fair trim. She was not listing, and because of the high cargo (which in itself was insurance against being sunk), only a second attack from the enemy could cause it to sink. As far as the damaged stern was concerned, there was a dip in the deck cargo at Number Five Hatch where the explosion had occurred.

As long as the ship remained afloat, he thought it not worthwhile checking out the damage and putting his life at risk. He was more concerned in foraging through the chief steward's larder to feed his stomach; then he carried canned supplies up top to deposit in his raft.

After locating canvas from the bosun's locker to cover his raft against the elements, he spent most of the first day on the bridge, using the skipper's binoculars, looking for the two lifeboats but without success. Even though gale-force winds rocked the ship that night, he still slept under the blankets and canvas in the life raft.

Endlessly, one phalanx of waves after another buffeted the ship for the following three days, and just when the poor chap thought he was a goner, the wind and sea dropped. He crawled away half-crazy from his wet blankets to realise that the ship was still afloat, and the crippled vessel had not suffered a dangerous list.

Still having the sanity for appreciating a shower, even if it was a cold one – what did he do but have a privileged one in the captain's private quarters. He then decided to take up his private abode there until rescue arrived. The cold weather had kept a lot of the eatables fresh while there was lots of tinned food. He made himself a cold breakfast, flopped himself rapturously into the skipper's bunk and fell asleep. He stayed there resting until morning.

He was now feeling confident enough to realise a timber boat might not sink rapidly, and from then on, it was high living, selecting for himself a variety of nourishing foods. He lit the galley fire where there was a large heap of coal at his service, and although he was no cook, discovered he could boil water and experiment.

From boiling water for making coffee, he advanced to boiling potatoes and then tried his hand at other vegetables. When the ship's bread ran out, there were biscuits of every description and porridge for morning breakfast; then there was frying up some bacon and whatever eggs held on to their goodness. Imagine the surprise of a Scottish coastal patrol six weeks later when they boarded the seemingly abandoned cargo steamer.

They found a middle-aged person wearing big, clumsy, stokehold boots, lying flat out on clean linen in the captain's bunk. He looked well-fed and was snoring to beat the band. The wife of that man had written of his experiences in a long letter to his close friend, the *SS Lily* cook.

CHAPTER 4 – *D/S LOKE* (Pronounced Lokee)

SHIP NUMBER THREE

WALES

Apleasant surprise welcomed me at the end of the first week in June. It was a message from HM Customs to the effect that forty pounds awaited me at the Midlands Bank in the neighbouring town of Treorchy. I had not finished my designated leave yet, and now that I had given up hope for a refund, I found the bank was going to fund a holiday twice as long.

Excitement bubbled within me when I met up with the gang in the cafe that evening, and I suggested we go somewhere on a spree. They were all teenage coal miners who welcomed the idea. When Saturday came around, all of us took the six mile train ride to Tonypandy or 'Pandy', as it was familiarly called.

Young chicks were drawn to the weekend dance room there, so after a couple of pints of beer each, we joined the stompers with my new found 'riches'. I felt like Mr Big and wished to pay more than my share of rounds. But, although I was stashed aplenty with dough, the gang wouldn't hear of me paying even one round. They told me it was sadly the beer shortage, not a money shortage that was the bugbear.

Pub crawling in another town was a necessity, not a girl search in wartime as most pubs kept most of the beer for their own customers with less allowances for strangers. Then it was back to the dance hall for another half hour session before making the rounds again. I had been pleased that my feet tested well at the stomp.

Lying abed Sunday night, after spending earlier that day sobering up, I realised that I had good friends after all. The boys were treating me to drinks as their way of letting me know that when I went back on my travels, I would be missed. They put me on a pedestal, and with my hands and feet in tiptop form, I was feeling fit and adventurous. Wanderlust was surely biting me through and through with no let-up and only thoughts of escape to a seaport.

By midweek I was riding the train down to the port of Cardiff with the intention of having a check-up with its navigation doctor. I had been briefed by another merchant seaman, whom I had met in a local pub, that once a seafarer passed his medical, he was automatically registered with the Mercantile Marine Manning Pool.

He advised me that everyone was paid the same – three pounds and ten shillings a week until his name came round on the roster. Lots of thoughts went passing through my mind as the slow Bute Road tram carried me to the dock area with its maritime offices. Although shore life was beginning to bore me, there was still no hurry. There were options open to me now. After sailing on tax-free foreign ships with much higher wages for qualified firemen, how long would I be ashore to receive pool money, maybe two weeks at the most? My friend up in the valley had told me he was never longer than three days on pool money, and his leave with pay was only six days per month.

The excitement of this first offer was wearing off; with cash one feels independent and I wasn't short in any way. Also, conscription had come into force, and I wished to get that off my chest as soon as possible. I stepped off the tram at the terminal building and asked the first passer-by for directions to the shipping office.

I merely had to step one block in reverse and that sturdy structure beckoned me through its dusty yet rather ornate arched doorway. I pushed open the very first glass door I came to. A very long, thick mahogany counter looked lonely for the few people doing business there. An elderly person gave me his attention as I approached.

With no others waiting behind me, I took time explaining my case and told him I was very concerned about getting the conscription business off my chest. "Forget it, Whitehead," was his comment. "We are very short-handed as far as merchant marine ratings are concerned; try and join any of the forces, and you could be in trouble for refusing to go to sea. The government is at this moment considering releasing a lot of people from prisons to fill the gap."

I sighed and thought glumly, 'What an effort it had been for us young guys trying to ship out, not ten months back.' Having put me at ease on that point, I told the superintendent, for that was what he was, that I wished to know if I could have the choice of serving under other allied flags instead just sailing under the red duster.

He told me I could rest assure on that point. He explained that as nationals on these vessels decreased, the positions had to be filled with

British seamen anyway, and the choice would be mine. Men ignored the bigger wages on these boats because it meant a change of diet and being treated as a foreigner. The diet part didn't worry me – I was adaptable there.

The only drawback with the Norwegians was that they were big fish eaters if you could call that a drawback. And I never met one who was unable to speak English. Also, from what I had seen of other ships when boarding ships with Billy in Swansea, accommodation standards on Norwegian ships were very high, and I appreciated the thick, wooden insulation in the quarters.

After I stepped out of the building and walked to the facing square, I drew the small pay book from my hip pocket and reassured myself that inside was the discharge paper from the *Ingerfem*. I then pulled up to the first man who looked to me like a seafarer.

I asked him if he could direct my footsteps to the Norwegian Consulate. Actually it was only a stone's throw away and recognising the royal coat of arms over the doorway, I entered and bounded up a narrow staircase. The door was ajar and I dared myself to peek in. The lady in white, behind the counter, must have read the query in my eyes and answered, "This is the Norwegian Consulate. Can I help you?"

I forked up my discharge paper and placed it on the desk. "What are my chances for shipping out soon?" She took the document and disappeared through a door behind her. She was not long in returning. "We are always short of coal trimmers. Only yesterday we signed on two, and before the end of the week, we will need more." Had she said the opposite, that there were few chances, I might have jumped at the first offer.

That's how the mind works. I supposed with the summer weather being truly summery, I had choices both ways now, either to join the pool or to take a little longer and enjoy the weather. She asked me my address so a telegram could be sent to me when a job turned up. I hesitated. Seeing me waver, she didn't push.

Next, instead of taking a tram, I decided to walk the long mile back to the railway station and call in at a few pubs on the way. About the nearest was the North and South in West Bute St. It was a real hangout for seafarers, being nearby to the pool offices, and I got confirmation there about receiving pool money. According to what I learned, once you registered with the shipping federation, you were shipped out within days.

I now had double confirmation of the short time ashore once I joined the shipping pool. The only way to extend one's leave was with a doctor's note. My mind was now clearly made up upon receiving the same reports in both pubs, so I continued my walk up Bute Road, calling in for a feed at the Greek restaurant at the top where I had a dish of well-spiced rabbit.

Back home, I realised that being a freelancer gave one privileged freedom and staying with the Norwegians not only gave me that extra freedom but also surplus cash. Firemen on British ships were getting twenty-four pounds a month before tax deductions, compared with thirty-two pounds and no tax after elevation from trimmer to fireman in allied ships.

Long summers in Britain are a rarity, but if Britain was suffering setbacks in the early war years in the field of conflict, the summers were unusually good, and with a lot of grazing land turned to growing more foodstuffs, the harvest must have made up for a lot of supplies being lost at sea. However, I knew the mist and rain would soon be on its way. And after those first signs of rain, I would take the first train to Cardiff and pick up a ship from the consul.

That extra forty pounds I had gotten was getting me lazy with beer swilling. But for the next three weeks, the weather wouldn't stop being good, and it was in the first week in July when I joined my second Norske boat, the *D/S Loke*.

The consul handed me the train fare to Swansea where she was berthed. I arrived at the main gate of Swansea Docks at around 2pm and there was a lady police officer at the gate who directed me to the ship's berth. The *Loke* was a 3,000 ton freighter, pretty small for deep-sea trade, and the skipper was waiting in the saloon to sign me on so he could go ashore himself.

I was handed a fresh blue pay book and introduced to the deucer. The watchman at the gangway told me that most of the crew were ashore since the ship was all ready for loading coal and would shift to Port Tennant a mile away the following day to come under the cranes.

I quickly found the donkeyman in the after crew quarters, which was a duplicate of the *Ingerfem*. He handed me the key to my cabin and told me to return it to him if I was going ashore so he could pass it to my cabin mate, another trimmer, when he returned on board. The petty officer was a friendly person, not one of your big-boned Vikings but a smaller brand, thickset and chubby in his late twenties. When we had a cup of coffee together, he filled me in with the usual details.

Although she was a small steamer for trading overseas, he assured me she could ride the Atlantic rollers with the best of them, being a flat-bottomed boat. I knew that she was on the Atlantic run, but where was she bound for? He told me the first port of call was Halifax, Nova Scotia, and then to await further orders.

I was glad I still had dollar bills in my wallet, which I hadn't changed into pound notes; it meant I would have no need to draw from my wages. The petty officer told me the other trimmer was a Norwegian lad of my own age who had newly joined the ship like myself. He surprised me by letting me know there was down below only a crew of six men – three firemen and three trimmers.

I was told that the ship was waiting for one more trimmer to be hired, and then my advisor asked me if I knew the whereabouts of the Bush Hotel. The very sound of that name brought a smile to my face. It seemed that my four workmates had made this pub their venue if I wished to look them up. I made up a cheese sandwich, and after scoffing it down, took off to the hotel.

I had always thought that the Bush had a special license because on the way up Wind Street I pushed on the doors of a few pubs to check for a familiar face, but they were all shut for the 2pm – 6pm break time, and the Bush took the overflow of afternoon drinkers. I went into the bar section and waited my turn at the centre of the bar.

Familiar chatter in the Scandinavian tongue reached my ears from the elbows on the wooden counter, but just to make sure they were my future shipmates, I asked the barmaid if they were members of the *Loke* crew. She said they certainly were and were kicking up a bloody rumpus because the bar had run out of whisky.

With a pint of beer in my hand, I walked around the angle of the bar and introduced myself to the foursome. Each one fired a question at me in turn: "Are you the new trimmer? Shake hands." "Where's the other trimmer?" "Have you been on natural draught boilers before?" and finally, "Is this your first Norwegian ship?"

The eldest one with a flat cap, slanted to one side, told the others to shush and drew me aside. When I assured him that I had sailed under the Norwegian flag before, it seemed to settle his mind. First he gave me a rapid briefing of the job, and he then opened his thoughts. The four of them were really hoping that it would take a few days to pick up the last trimmer.

They wanted a few more days whooping it up. Then he called on Johan, a young fellow with tousled blonde hair, to take over from himself. Johan was a bit younger version of the *Ingerfem's* thickset Ole. I liked him right off, plus he seemed a strong, reliable working partner. He queried me if I knew that the trimmer's duties included washing up dishes after meals.

I satisfied him on that point, and then he introduced me to the working arrangements on this new type of stokehold. Although there were two boilers, with three fires in each, only one fireman was needed on watch, as the boilers were of a smaller type than the big scotch marine boiler with forced draught appliances to urge any lower grade coal to burn.

There was one extra duty I was to learn. Because there were only two on watch, and being a trimmer to one man instead of two or three was light work, the trimmer was expected to clean one fire each watch. This was no problem to my way of thinking because it meant that I could learn to be a proficient fireman.

Having assured myself that Johan was my cabin mate, I drank up, waved the gang goodbye and took off across the road to pay a visit to Mrs Ramos. It turned out not as sociable as I had hoped. Julietta was in a more sedate and serious mood than her normal happy-go-lucky self. The only time she beamed at me was when she mentioned that her fiancé had received permission to leave the ships and work in the Swansea shipyard.

They were already engaged to be married, and her eyes were telling me that marriage couldn't come fast enough, and as her brother, Antonio, and her Ma were out, I felt it rude to stay on with a lady in love. On my way down Wind Street, I found out what a difference a year makes on the waterfront. Not one familiar face in either of the two missions, so I decided to return on board and sort out my kitbag.

Usually, if the crew had cash in their pockets, they would catch a snack ashore and stay around their favourite pub until the money ran out, but in a port where residents lived on rationed food, meals were more inviting on board, especially if boiled cod was on the menu, an item the Norskies were in love with.

All hands were present for that evening meal including the new trimmer, Frank from Plymouth. Frank had one of those faces you couldn't read. He was a fairly slim man in his early thirties and of medium height, who had been discharged from the army with a leg injury. But he seemed to have passed the doctor OK with his stiff leg, though it seemed to have some effect on his face.

That evening, after the five o'clock eating, men walked up on deck with a cup of coffee or tea to socialise since the mess room was below decks on the *Loke*, with the deckhands' cabins on the port side and the firemen's on the other. In an exchange of talk, I was introduced to the two other firemen, a Latvian (or Lett), a pleasant, quiet-spoken man and a Dane with a Canadian accent, having lived over there for a number of years. Both men seemed in their thirties with neither very tall. I then moved myself to the starboard side of the ship to sit on a bollard and leaned against the handrails.

After taking his cup below, Frank returned to the poop and drew a lot of eyes. There was something about his walk that caused people to smile. It was as if one lower leg had been removed from the knee and replaced out of kilter. With the tautness of his facial muscles, combined with his stiff strutting around, he certainly stood out as different.

And sooner or later it was inevitable that someone was going to stitch a nickname on him. It came much sooner than expected. Obviously, the cod had not quashed the beer mischief in one of the sailors, because as Frank walked into the circle of firemen and sailors, the eldest fireman stood up from his orange box and went to shake hands with him. "You are the new trimmer in my cabin, so you will be on my watch. What is your name?" "Frank." "Frankenstein," blurted out of the fireman. Then the unbelievable happened, the new trimmer beamed a smile.

But even the smile had a stiffness about it, and so it stayed in that position as if he was waiting for his photograph to be taken. The boys could see that the new crew member was a good sport, and that cue set them off on a round of hilarious laughter, not the scornful type but more like a round of applause.

It took a while, but soon enough Frank's face sent out messages. Pass a comment in the wrong way, and the response was a look on his face that read 'Up you, too!' He was the kind of person who could take a joke and hurl one back as well and that made for a happy ship. And that's how Frank was christened Franken.

Later on, inside our cabin, Johan let me know that there would be little shovelling during the next couple of days, as we would load full bunkers at Port Tennant. Then I removed myself from the small cabin since he wished to put on more attractive clothes; he had a date uptown with his newly acquired sweetheart in the Bush Hotel.

I was betwixt and between about stepping ashore, but after a game of cards with Franken in the mess room, I decided to stay on board and plan for Canada. My mate had just done a long train journey from Plymouth with the usual wartime holdups, and he also decided to rest up.

The following day our ship was shifted to Port Tennant, and after loading cargo, sailed off for Milford Haven. We were less than one full day in that harbour when the convoy we were attached to sailed at 2am. Most convoys seemed to set sail in the very early hours. Before sailing, Rolf, the eldest fireman, had switched cabins with the Lett, and by this move I was on the 12-4 watch with Rolf. As we were only going half-speed until the fleet cleared the harbour, my watch mate gave me tips on how to clean a fire rapidly so no steam was lost.

It usually took up to three weeks to reach the other side of the

'Western Ocean'; the convoy sailed at the speed of the slowest vessel, which averaged seven knots an hour. But on this voyage, the weather was exceptionally favourable, so we sailed into Halifax Harbour just over two weeks after leaving Milford.

CANADA

The Dane, who often spoke of his mysterious ex-wife in Canada, at that time reported to the second mate that he would need a visit to the doctor with an equally mysterious back ailment. The skipper was now ordered to go ahead to Montreal to discharge the cargo, and having contacted shore about the availability of a replacement for the fireman, learned that no firemen were on the roster. The Dane said he could bear his pain until Montreal, and we sailed.

After discharging coal at East Notre Dame Docks, the cargo holds were washed out and we sailed for Sorel, a port on the St Lawrence River. We were expected to lie alongside there for a week, loading grain for the UK, and where the crew meant to take time off.

It was a countrified sort of port and stood out in its charming self at the height of this summer. The wharf was only large enough to take one ship at a time. Except for there being no loose skirt around, we were content being accepted most sociably in friendly cafes where beer was freely served. Market day was Saturday; the day when most of the crew went on a bender. The locals also looked forward to this day for some carousing themselves, and folks from the outlying farms arrived on ponies and buggies.

When we returned to Halifax, we picked up two fresh firemen due to another fireman also paying off there. One was a Chilean by the name of Guillermo, who was in his early twenties, and the other, his mate, who by his own account shipped out of Swansea often and was from the Shetland Islands.

"Call me Shanghai," he said upon introducing himself, and when I mentioned Mrs Ramos with a lodging house in St Mary's Street, he let me know he was often a lodger there. Rolf decided to switch to the 4-8 watch to work with Johan, as they were the only two Norwegians in the stokehold gang, and my new watch mate was now Guillermo.

That left Franken to supply coal to Shanghai. Shanghai Grant, a lanky 6'4" in his socks and bi-lingual like a lot of Shetlanders, being able to talk in both English and Norwegian. His Spanish was passable, too, and this was helpful to the South American.

When I spoke with the man from Chile on the 12-4 watch, I observed that his brief knowledge of English was richly decorated with four letter words. Guillermo might have admired the grand bearing of his language tutor, Mr Grant, but I thought that if he did not break off his partnership with Shanghai, socialising with the opposite sex in the English language would be out. With his 'effs and B's', the gangly Chilean used ruder language than an Australian gold-miner.

I was still pretty fresh at the seafaring game, and a year or two later, I was to learn that most ships carried at least one man of Shanghai Grant's type. They would join a ship carrying an old kitbag or shabby suitcase, with only a pile of magazines from a seamen's mission inside.

Older hands could soon spot these types, and come tea or coffee break, they would start the ball rolling or yarn swapping with "I think we have a 'schooner-rigged' man along with us," which usually brought on spontaneous laughter. Mariners who joined ships without working gear were 'schooner-rigged'. And they were nearly always alcoholics. If not, they were fast moving on that path, and their cavalier attitude had a comedy effect on other crew members.

Weeks at sea are never boring with such characters on board. The Norwegians must have spotted Grant right away because he could speak in their own language. It was only when I showed the large Shetlander his cabin with Franken that I totally understood the general humour his presence aroused.

I watched him empty his kitbag. All he drew out of it were very big, outsized work boots – nothing else! I was about to leave him when the big man tagged onto my shoulder and asked me to direct him to the locker room where one could change into working gear. He wanted to know which locker was stowed with gear that had been left behind by other stokers.

He rummaged through torn clothing and old boots and picked out the largest pair of trousers he could find plus several singlets. Two pairs of boots in good condition had also been left behind but were too small for him. Then my mind clicked that he must always keep back some booze money to speculate on work boots for his outsized feet.

Shanghai was on the 8-12 watch. When I descended the stokehold at midnight on the first watch out from Halifax Harbour, Guillermo and myself couldn't help smiling at the scene in front of us. Shanghai and his trimmer were preparing the fires for cleaning by winging red ash over to one side of each furnace, leaving dead clinker on the other side to be raked out.

They were using slice bars, sort of like crowbars but over six feet long. When the pair went off-duty, we would rake out the clinker from the dead side. The raw-boned figure of the Shetlander brought broad smiles to our faces. He happened to be cleaning the low, central fire which caused him to stoop low and the bottom of his pants were a good 4 inches above the tops of his sockless boots. Although precious booze urged this wild character to be economical with clothing, I was to learn later on the Swansea waterfront that they knew him for being very generous with handouts on payoff days. On that special day, down and out seamen would not go without a drink or a feed.

As days passed, I kept improving my skill at shovelling coal into fires after I had filled coal bunkers. Every chance I got I would go down and help the fireman. Ten feet above the steel plates of the stokehold deck, the open ends of the circular, wide-mouthed ventilator shaft blew down cooler sea breezes on both sides of the stokehold. It was a good place to stand and cool oneself after pitching coal in fires.

Every steamer had a valve box which was centrally positioned against the steel wall facing the boilers. At sea this box had a lot of sacking piled over its whole length and was used to sit down for a break between shovelling, slicing and raking. It was also a favourable position to watch the steam gauge.

The valve box was about eight feet long and eighteen inches high and beneath the lid were hidden several steam valves used by the donkeyman in port to turn steam on and off. Since the valves were never used at sea, firemen cushioned them with castoff sacks.

Welsh coal firemen could have an easy time of it, once they learned the technique of burning different coals. With this coal type, you filled the furnace way up to the crown once you had built up a good base of red embers. It wasn't until years later that I understood how such a big, dead-looking fire could generate so much steam; I just followed suit from the more experienced hands.

Then it was finally explained to me by a young, intelligent-looking stoker. "So long as you have a bright front," he pointed out, "and the rear end of the furnace is not blocked by clinker, by thrusting the long slice bar over the fire bars and lifting the back of the fire which breaks up the clinker, you'll have no problem."

Then he explained that most of the steam is created by the smoke continually streaming over the narrow opening between the top of the mound of coal and the crown of the circular furnace. Half of the heated smoke bursts into flames when it comes to the soot box or combustion chamber behind the fire. The remainder of the smoke is exploding in the forty or fifty tubes running the length of the boiler.

"By the time the remaining smoke passed into the funnel," he had gone on, "it was practically only a wisp of what had streamed over the coal in the furnace. After pitching or shovelling into his fire, a fireman could look forward to thirty or forty minutes of sitting down on the valve box or getting his breath back under the ventilator."

It was about 2am one eerie morning when I sat with my Chilean mate on the valve box. Guillermo kept his eyes regularly pointing to the steam gauge so we could stick needed slice bars under the fires when the steam dropped. As we had just finished pitching, it would be a long sit down. I had already filled the bunkers, and it would only require a topping up at the end of the watch.

Lifting the water billy, suspended from the mouth of the ventilator, I noticed it was only a quarter full. After taking a deep swig, I passed it to Guillermo, and then ascended to fill it at the galley hand pump. This was also an opportunity to find out the latest news from Sparky's radio.

With blackout regulations in force, iron lids (called 'handy billies', positioned above the fiddley) were lowered before dusk every evening with pulleys. The leeside sheltered from the wind was next door to the fiddley, so I fast bobbed around the corner and filled the billy from the outside pump under a half moon.

I descended to the glory hole again and passed the wide-mouthed can to my mate so he could take a few gulps. I took a swig myself before suspending it beneath the weather side vent. While replacing it on the hook, I naturally had to look upwards. My eyes caught streaky flashes of light through the fiddley door.

Rather than panic my mate by revealing what I had seen, I remarked that I was going to quarters to prepare coffee and sundries for the oncoming 4-8 watch keepers and up I ascended. There were always several worn-out deckhands' sweaters hanging on the handrail topside so I put one over my shoulder to face the cold, night air.

Stepping out on deck, I felt that the moon had somehow become enlarged, and the sky was further lit up by a carnival display of lighted flares being shot up into the nether ether by what looked like the outlines of destroyers. They were weaving in and out of convoy lines.

The illumination made it easy to seek out a sailor on duty watch. I soon caught one of these sailors coming down from the wheelhouse. He passed on a message that the radio operator had passed on to the mate on watch. Due to the fair weather, subs had been able to infiltrate the convoy to select and attack the innermost vital vessels instead of picking off stragglers on the outside flanks.

I had already heard the vibrating thuds of some depth charges being dropped so that I knew what he meant when he said that destroyers were passing through the lines of ships trying to sound out the underwater enemy. By the time I had returned to the stokehold, Guillermo was lifting a billycan of water to his lips, whilst standing beneath the vent, flushing his sweaty body with the cooling sea breeze.

He had just sliced the six fires, and broken clinker settled on the fire bars. No tools were stood up in case they fell on someone, and shovels, rakes and pokers were just dropped on this deck after use and kicked against the brickwork under the boilers to shift as they pleased with the roll of the ship.

The slice bar still had a very red end, and after a deep swallow of water, my mate sat himself on the valve box. Both of us were silent for a short spell, and I thought I would share some cheerful news. I remarked on the fair weather we were experiencing. He swerved around fast, concentrating his eyes directly on mine.

He had no need to scramble some English words together to explain himself. His unspoken question and direct look sent a clear message: 'Don't waste my time. What the hell is going on up topside?'

I had forgotten that he could feel depth charges vibrating down through the iron work, and anyway, it was possible that the engineer had paid him a visit from the engine room to ask for more steam which they usually did in emergencies. It took a minute before I could collect my thoughts. Then I told him what I had heard.

Naval exercises ceased by 3am, and I went to awaken the 4-8 men about twenty minutes later. They were already up and about. There was minimum social chat, and it was obvious they had learned all about the recent action from the deck watch since all hands lived close together.

I had already topped-up the bunkers, so I washed the coal dust off myself and prepared to have a talk with my offsider over a coffee and a smoke when he came up. I just couldn't turn in at my bunk right away after the night's events, even as bleary-eyed as I was. But my mate drank his coffee as broody as the rest – so no gab exchange.

It was never easy sleeping through the morning unless you had been in bed all night, or you had a belly full of booze. My slumber was light, and so I was back in the mess wide awake when Franken's boots banged on down the steps of the wooden ladder. The heavy foot falls due to his limp were something he couldn't help.

There was a faint clatter as he pushed the metal tray of fish balls on the table. I was more eager for the other trimmer to spit out the early morning news than to scoff down any breakfast.

Lingering over an early morning coffee with Franken, who was puffing blue rings of smoke into the air between sips of java, I sensed that he was about to reveal to me some kind of confidential report. He took one more sip of his hot drink, set it down carefully and pinioned my excited eyes with a blank stare. His neutral look couldn't hide the pleasure he took from my impatience. Then he broke into a half-toothless smile and brightened my day with the news that our escorts had flushed out the subs that had been lurking in our sailing formation.

During the following watch all went OK and without incident. We had a following sea which still blew enough wind down the vents to prevent the workplace from overheating, and with the best coal in the world – Welsh, of course – top steam was no problem. Up on deck the sun was out shining clear and bright. Which meant all hands would gather on the poop deck for a get-together after the evening meal.

These good weather conditions failed to cause any cheer at the table. There seemed to be edginess among both sailors and firemen. Jittery responses greeted any attempt at talk after eats, but as expected, all hands not on duty carried their mugs of coffee topside. There was a definite feeling that fears had to be brought out into the open.

Using the capstans to place our cups on, men sidled around each other, trying to create a social atmosphere, or else sat along a bench. Others hung their heads over the rails, watching the waves push a fleet of seventy ships to the safety of the western approaches.

Shanghai then seized the chance to make a star turn for himself this particular evening. As the gaunt frame strutted across the stern end of the poop deck in big stokehold boots and trousers six inches too short, we learned that his past had not all been seagoing.

Here was probably the oldest seafarer on board, now in his early sixties, clumping back and fro on deck against the setting sun. There was something theatrical about the pose he struck. When he stopped pacing and faced his shipmates, he drew all eyes. Before he had been mumbling, but now he was boldly pronouncing.

He orated over our mistrust of those who were escorting us – our naval protectors – and against the background of the flagstaff and a red evening sky, he reminded us of the darker times in 1917 when his old regiment had been posted to the Western Front.

Before us stood not fireman Grant but Corporal Grant, speaking in a tongue that no other than Churchill could command, chastising us for putting down our protectors. There was nothing to worry about he concluded. He had lived through more dangerous times and stressed this more in the Norwegian tongue than in English to get his dramatic effect across.

It was certainly well-timed to break the tension. Several voices requested him to embroider on his speech; it was going down well. But he returned to his pensive pacing back and fro. By a look around at the faces, quite a number of the boys seemed to have used this interesting interlude to find their own tongues and socialise in the normal way. Anyone who has sailed deep-sea when TV was unknown and when even owning a radio was rare on board ships knew that having a 'card' on board was a necessary tonic to drive away problems that stowed away in the mind, either after ill news from home or tension on board.

Filling bunkers the next time I went on watch, I found that wheeling barrow of coal in this shadowy world had driving force about it, like the barrow had wings. The wheel needed no oiling. The barrow had a certain lightness about it as it was upended into the chute for the man below.

When the 4-8 trimmer, Johan roused me at 7.20am, my aching bones registered a premature invasion of privacy when there was yet four hours to go before my turn of duty came around. I peered at the big alarm clock lashed to one of the screw dogs on the porthole and realised he had woken the wrong trimmer. I pulled the blankets over my eyes to shut out the world.

The only time I rose for breakfast was when I failed to sleep. On Johan's second attempt to rouse me, the mention of a life jacket turned my ears into alarm bells. That constant companion of mine, Mr Blind Fear, put wings on my feet and spirited me through the cabin door, while trying to haul up my pants and drag my jacket at the same time.

I was forced to calm down in this moment of crisis so that I could dress properly and wrap the Mae West around me; never get caught with your pants down is a useful motto in any emergency. Yet just before my final escape up the ladder, I dared myself to double back and admire a plate of untouched breakfast on the table.

The fried eggs, sunny-side up, gazed at me pleadingly like big eyes and together with the sausages not to resist, and that brave little voice inside me gave the order to gobble down a big mouthful with my bare hands. In a disgusting, savage fashion, I crammed my mouth with a double handful of sausages and eggs.

Then I flew up on deck, ready for a long sit down in the life boat. The poop deck that morning was full of men gathered in small groups; life jackets tied neatly around their waists. I was the odd one out still fumbling with my strings.

Since we carried a cargo of grain, our vessel was positioned on the outside line of the fleet formation. Glancing out at the convoy, there seemed to be seven lines of ships, with ten ships to a line. I joined a group leaning against the handrails on the ship's port side and became a spectator of a tanker attracting attention. It was on an inner line of ships, and we had a clear view of the victim engulfed in smoke and flames.

Then eyes diverted to a cargo vessel directly abreast of us. She seemed to be progressing normally, but there were men pulling away from her in a lifeboat, and soon the big freighter did the dance of death. Just like the antics of the *Lily*, she dipped her after end and sunk her stern into the sea waters before shooting her bows upward in that classical farewell pose before becoming history.

Ahead of us the sun was rising bright and clear from the liquid world. The sea was ideal for launching boats, and behind the silent gazes, I was not alone in thinking that our turn could be next. A minute or two after the foundering of those two unfortunate vessels, silence broke and men said hopefully that destroyers were closing in on the U-boats.

Someone spoke about the 4-8 fireman, and there was sympathy on his behalf. "I wouldn't like to be in his shoes," commented one. "What about Frankenstein?" spoke up Johan. "He would be washed up and finished by now, but he has stayed below because the chief has asked for more steam." Then Rolf nudged his offsider to check the time.

Johan stepped halfway down the ladder from where he could see the mess room clock, "There's twenty minutes to go," he reported back. I was amazed at what had gone by in the past fifteen minutes. Rolf and his mate took a chance and went down to quarters and took a bite before duty called at 8pm.

I was very glad they were out of the way for what occurred next. Someone was banging on the iron door of the toilet under the ladder leading down to the well deck. A short time later the second engineer was hollering from amidships: "Has anyone seen Grant?" There was a lot of head wagging in response.

Then the deucer cocked his ears to that final voice. It was from the man banging on the toilet door that I recognised the sharp voice of Franken, Grant's trimmer, "He is here in the bloody shithouse!" This drew the attention of all those still on deck, and they leaned over the handrail facing amidships. Under their gaze, Grant sheepishly followed Franken back to his workplace, receiving a scornful glance as he passed the engineer.

This early morning episode drew to a close with everyone letting off steam at this finale of a tense half hour. Despite the strained emotions, people were going through, a few laughs and giggles were let out at this latest incident.

The rest of the voyage was calm seas and starry summer nights to aid our way along the deck during blackout hours. As the Welsh anthracite petered out, it cost the firemen extra sweat to keep up steam but not such a great deal when keeping up with a seven knot convoy. Our destination was Swansea and they started bragging how they would win the heart of a chick at the Bush Hotel.

Shanghai preferred the society of the Cape Horner, the nearest pub to the main gate. A sublist was put in. It was expected we would dock on a Wednesday which meant that there would be a two day wait until the cash was dished out. Personally, I still had cash in my money belt but never let on about it in case someone borrowed some and paid off the next day.

WALES

We were steaming up the Bristol Channel on a balmy Wednesday morning when I heard the news at the galley that we would tie up at Weaver's Dock for a week. As soon as I found it convenient to see the skipper, I paid him a visit and requested a few days leave to visit my family and he agreed.

There were furrows on many brows that night when we docked in Swansea. Everyone was looking forward to going ashore for a visit to the Bush if they could get their hands on some cash. For one pound you could buy forty pints of beer. For half of that – ten shillings – one could still have a belly full at 6p a pint.

Before we left Montreal, the coaling company had handed each crew member a seven pound parcel of preserved food. I offered my cabin mate ten shillings for his parcel, and he was overeager to barter so he could go up the road and look for his girl. I knew the older crew members would sell because these Norwegians were a thirsty lot.

First, however, I had to think of customs. They would not bother to board a ship at 8pm, and Weaver's Dock was the easiest one to get out of. The bows of the ship were even poking over the dock fence which separated it from Balaclava St. I went down the gangway and made an examination of the fence. By going between two bent bars, I could miss the main gate and walk directly onto the street; it was dead easy in the blackout. I had bought eight food parcels and was dressed in my going-ashore clothes. The parcels fitted into my kitbag and with a 56lb load slung over my shoulder I scrambled.

After edging my way through the fence, I rambled along putting on speed as I walked through the arch and slacked off as I entered Wind Street, where I wiped the sweat off my face. As easy as the escapade was, I had taken no chances. When I arrived at St Mary's St, I turned between the cathedral ruins and the shell of Samuel's, the jewellery shop.

I lowered my load at the black door of the shilling-a-night lodging house. Then I put my shoulder to the door and dragged the goodies into the passage. I took a short pause to wipe a film of sweat off my brows with a hankie. It was a warm evening, and I wished to enter the kitchen in a cool manner, sort of triumphant.

I planted all 56 pounds of my treasure between the two smiling faces of Julietta and Antonio, both sitting at either end of the long kitchen table. Mrs Ramos wiped her hands at the sink and turned to greet me. She joined the smilers when she noticed the squarishness of the kitbag, realising that it was more likely goodies than clothing.

With a half-used tea towel, she wiped a section of the table after noticing that I took on a smiling face also and told me to lift the goodies onto it. Surprises often make pleasant starts to reunions, especially in times of war shortages. The first thing I did whilst the other six eyes were on the bag was to relieve it of one of its parcels.

"Open it up," I directed Maria. Her brows lifted a bit in a cautionary manner as she questioned, "You no take from cargo?" "No honestly, Mrs Ramos, take my word and open it up; Antonio is getting impatient." Mam grabbed a bread knife and broke through the seals. Two eager faces leaned over.

When the last bits of cardboard were torn away, the young lad's eyes gloated over the tins of ham, spam and other delicacies mostly unavailable in wartime Britain. Antonio was urgently ordered by Maria to shut the kitchen door firmly, and she again gave me a questioning look.

Women can be pretty good at reading faces and satisfied that my booty was legal, she told Julie to put the kettle on in the coal fire. While the kettle was boiling, I confided my plans to take the train home the next day. She was clued up to my scheme now and asked if I wished to leave my treasure in her care overnight, so I had no need to request her to do just that. Antonio was told to release the bolt in the door.

As she poured boiling water into the tea pot, which Maria held steady for her, I was reassured that nothing would go amiss overnight. Maria realised that I had intended to give her something out of the smaller parcel; however, when I told her she could have all of one of the boxes, weighing 7lbs, there was a lot of pleased beaming.

People were using small sweetener pills to add to the small ration of sugar, and sweet-toothed Antonio only needed that small nod from me to lift out the 2lb bag of sugar. At 13 years, a boy's appetite is very healthy, and one member of this family was surely looking forward to a small and tasty fireside party that evening.

The tea drinking warmed us into some conversation, and at this opportune time, I approached Maria on the business of looking after a Spanish-speaking man. I let her know that Guillermo would be paying off in a few days, as soon as a new fireman could replace him.

It was still broad daylight when Julie walked me to the door to see me off. She said there would be no worries about my shipmate; her mother would treat him as one of the family.

I seemed to have arrived in Swansea when the weather was at its best, and with clocks changed so that summer evenings lasted an hour longer. At 7pm I was returning to my ship in broad daylight. I first called into the nearby mission and after a cuppa made a long look for old acquaintances. My eyes registered only strange faces. In the pleasant evening, walking down Wind Street, I avoided the temptation of pub doors and imagined Antonio sploshing extra spoonfuls of sugar into a cup of tea.

My paid leave off the *Loke*, whilst in the port of Swansea, was on condition that I did my stint the following morning alongside the other 'down below' crew – cleaning flue tubes running through the boilers, which swallowed smoke through the combustion chambers at the end of the furnaces and conveyed it up the funnel.

I found only the donkeyman in the mess room when I boarded, and over a smoke and a hot drink, was told by him that the crew had gotten hold of enough small change to wash their throats at the nearby pub. At one end of the table, a canvas cloth had been laid down on which stood several storm lamps and domestic ones for use inside our quarters.

I was told all three boilers had been shut down and within an hour the coffee urn would be cooling off, and hot drinks could be made from the galley stove amidships. He said he would be soon trimming the wicks of the lamps on the table and topping them up with paraffin.

As he was on duty overnight, he informed me to get into my bunk early for a sleep as he would be calling all hands in the black gang at 5.30am the next morning. I had cleaned soot out of the boilers before, and the hottest job was lying on the fire bars with a small bucket and shovel, whilst removing a pit of soot behind a small wall at the rear of the furnace.

When I mentioned to the d'man that the boiler had to be shut down for 24 hours before anyone was allowed to enter a furnace, he said that sometimes a senior fireman (the one who had been on board longest) would have a word with the chief to take a chance on getting this filthy job over and done with in less time.

All I could think was that the d'man was spending the whole night flushing cold water through the boilers. A lot of rules could be bypassed in wartime. The special jobs were called job-and-finish, and the oldest fireman usually decided when to start in the morning.

I lay abed that night going over that stinker of a stint in my mind. You mucked it together and knocked off after the spot was cleared from the back ends and was hoisted on deck in a big drum. One point about the Northmen was that they could have their guts awash with booze but still would turn out for duty early dawn.

The donkeyman brought a big jug of hot coffee from the galley next morning, and we were all woken at 5.30am prompt. There was little talk among the six of us as we clumped along the deck in our heavy industrial boots and climbed down the iron steps of the fiddley.

Once below, all butts sat on the valve box as we lit up cigarettes to wait for our foreman, the donkeyman. In the high summer month of August, the open lid of the fiddley grating on the upper deck gave out enough morning light to help you find your way around. However, for the purpose of a dark furnace and shadowy area tube cleaning, our boss arrived from the engine room with several duck lamps.

These simple lamp types were really economical. They were shaped like inverted cones, no more than seven inches high with rope wicks sticking out of the narrow top.

Cigarette butts were stubbed and flicked into ash pits, as men rose from sitting positions to face this tour of duty. Dizzy heads kept silent and were uncomplaining. From the passageway leading into the engine room, our boss called Guillermo and myself over and shined his torch against the hull of the ship.

In front of a disarray of planks and a mangle of ropes, we picked up lightweight rods and took them out to the waiting pair of workers. By our third bundle, the pair had nearly finished a five foot high scaffolding against the far boiler. We formed a little chain gang for passing out planks to make a staging area above.

There was only enough metalwork and timber to complete two small sets of staging. Now the stokehold was a busy scene with the d'man and a trimmer bringing foot-long steel rods and brushes.

Even though strong sunlight was now sending long rays into this gloomy pit, forty feet below, duck lamps swung on meat hooks under the covers to allow men a clearer view. At one end I was stationed with Guillermo. He climbed up a few short steps, remained there and was handed a brush in a fairly new state.

Whilst the three firemen and a trimmer sat on the valve box enjoying a smoke, another trimmer and myself plunged our brushes with a 2 inch radius into the tubes. I remembered the golden rule of pushing the soot back into the soot chamber. It was to make sure the brush was going one direction and to keep pushing but never reverse if the going was hard.

It was better to call up a stronger man than try to loosen the brush by pulling backwards because then it would set firmly and was harder to remove. There would be about six rows with seven or eight tubes in a row; however, when we got to the last two low rows, we were told to step down for a breather.

Then the staging was dismantled rapidly with skill. Wooden horses two feet high and covered with a few planks replaced it from which one man could crawl close to the high fires. Before entering them, firemen finished off the pair of lower tiers of tubes. With old steel brushes burnt almost to a frazzle, the experienced firemen first loosened the blocked tubes by thrusting and drawing a few times and then set to work with good brushes.

Letten, the lead fireman, told Franken to go into the engine room and ask the d'man to visit the cook about keeping our breakfast hot and also to get some needed sacks for our project. Franken returned saying all had been arranged and that the galley boy was collecting empty potato sacks in the store room that would have been thrown away any minute.

A voice echoed down the hollow ventilator shaft. "Under below," followed by a heap of dusty sacks clumping down on the floor. Two firemen spread sacks over the fire bars inside furnaces.

Then Guillermo entered on our side full length; I squeezed half my body in to hand him a bucket and small shovel. He already had the duck lamp in front of him. He was clothed in thick overalls especially reserved for this particular job to combat the overheating of the ironwork and lay down sideways on a thickness of potato sacks.

As he placed the lamp on the miniature wall behind which soot accumulated, I noticed he was very fast with his shovel work. When I withdrew my head out through the door, I realised why I had to put my sweat rag across my forehead. It was that sweaty, even though the sacking prevented heat from rising from the fire bars whilst radiation from the surrounding ironwork made me feel a little bit faint.

This did not prevent me from taking on the challenge when my mate asked me if I would be game enough to shovel soot out of the low fire, the central one between the other two high ones. After the second bucket full, I hopped off the planking to allow my mate exit, legs first.

Once Guillermo had lowered himself from the low platform, he made straight for the valve box and seated himself on the low platform over the asbestos padding. A red face was detected through a soot black covering and it seemed a little blown out. He then asked me to bring him the water tin; I lifted it off the hook beneath the ventilator and brought it over. He gulped down some big swallows and handed it back. By the time I had donned the outside overalls over my other clothing, the red colouring had vanished from the fireman's face, and it returned to the colour of a frying pan.

Before entering the oven-like sauna, I recalled the motto for cleaning soot out of a dead furnace – SPEED! – before your body had a chance to swell up. My mate had scrambled out of his oven within ten minutes of entering, and with my fit, young body (even with a pretty heavy smoking habit), my legs must have been out of the door within five minutes.

Then I realised that men with a lot of size and flesh were never allowed this task; I felt that in that brief period, I had swelled up a bit. If fear had spurred me to make a rapid execution of filling two buckets of soot, then fear was a good ally.

I collapsed on the valve box, and my senior rating did me the honour of fetching the large, empty fruit tin from beneath the vent so I could gurgle away cold water at my pleasure. By the time he had dismantled the planks and the two small wooden horses and had set them up in front of the other high fire, I had normalised. I was able to help in removing buckets out of the door.

We had been working between two and three hours now, and we then got busy returning everything to where it was before starting the clean-up, whilst two men got busy removing soot. Whilst one went topside to wind up the big drum to dump the soot on the main deck, his mate shovelled it in down below.

Before we climbed out of the glory hole, the deucer entered from the engine room to let us know that money was being handed out at 10am. Some boiler makers entered after him, ready to check the fire bars and any other jobs that had to be done, while our d'man started lighting up his donkey boiler to get the electric dynamos and steam winches going by early afternoon.

Up on deck, we all lined up with buckets at the water pump outside the galley and filed along to the well deck and then up to the quarters below the stern deck. It was the only time that you needed to return to the pump for a second tubing as soot was harder to remove than dust from steam coal.

It was optional for a chief engineer to hand out cash for 'job-and-finish', but that morning we were all paid the sum of three pounds, recorded as overtime. This amount was equal to the weekly wage of a common labourer at this time, but it was a wise chief that paid it out when you consider the effort made by a group of drunks to turn out before dawn.

The thought on all minds was to get themselves cash at an early part of the day so they could invade the town bars in search of booze and romance, but holding up cargo discharge for a day would have cost the company a lot of wharfage charges.

Walking along the deck that morning to the gangway, I was met with envious eyes from deckhands who were stripping tarpaulin covers from cargo holds. They had a full day of work in front of them and I was off for days.

I was soon whistling my way up Wind Street. A cup of steaming tea was waiting for me in the kitchen of Mrs Ramos. She knew the train times and sent Antonio out to get a taxi. With my bag of goodies slung over the shoulder, I was through the door, placing it carefully in the boot of my transport and was waved off by three smiling faces.

Wartime trains were generally late; however, I enjoyed the half hour wait with a lot of camaraderie around. Any gloom that hung over the British spirit after Dunkirk in 1940, when we faced a Europe dominated by a well-armed Germany, had vanished. Should the enemy submarines actually cut our supply lines and leave us to starve, we had an ally in the USA that would not allow that to happen. How could we lose?

I wore a lightweight, cream-coloured windbreaker, unzipped right down; it was noticeable by having a big Canadian maple leaf printed on the back. Soon it was a moment of true nostalgia as I rapped at a familiar door, inside of which I had been reared. The news that entered my ears when I sat at the living room table was more uplifting than in the recent past.

Only recently my elder sister had bore a baby boy. Apart from this news, her husband was over the moon with glee when I revealed the food parcels in my kitbag. Except for an evening in the local and a natter with old school friends, most of the weekend was spent in bed.

For a young man, a house is usually the place to get out of except when a traveller, so I gave it a lot of gratitude, spending hours lounging around. After spending all my sleep time on timber boards separated only by a mattress not a lot thicker than a palliasse, two or three nights on a spring bed was a luxury.

Those few days were very blissful in themselves. The feeling of complete ease had evaporated the tension associated with sleeping when the underwater enemy was always in one's thoughts. Apart from the rest, I was much less excited about homecoming than I thought I would be.

Three nights back home was enough. Now that my batteries had recharged, I was fit and ready to return to the hustle and bustle of a busy seaport. So it was one of those old carriages that I got into at the

Treorchy Station, with pretty high steps and no passageway separating one compartment from another. I ended up with one all to myself and did a good deal of future planning.

My mind mulled over which were the best pubs in Swansea where the girls hung out. I concluded there and then that waterfront pubs not only had choice but a constant supply; however, there seemed to be something missing in those tarts. They were living a false life, gambling their lives away in order to get a certain degree of economic security.

Once they had been hooked into the delights of wining and dining in between their efforts of pleasing men whilst lying on their backs, it was a risk that if a Mr Right ever did come along, the half-drunken life of the seamen they courted would push him away. That experience was painted all over their faces, which Mr Right, with a fat bank account, could see right through.

Wartime meant more employment for women, who were not too eager to throw themselves at men, and who were looking forward to enjoying a career life. Here was more competition for men to chase after what they thought was Miss Right but our lifestyle could not easily square to such a decision.

What was on the less cool minds of the female sex was the idea to have a good time before we became underwater heroes. This was the general trend among single men. You could say that most officers on board ships were in a serious career, and if they were not married, they were saving up for the nuptials. Among the crew, married men were in the minority, usually holding onto well-paying petty officer jobs like boatswain, carpenter and donkeyman.

These various thoughts reflected back on myself and why I never found it easy to pick up a respectable female partner. I concluded that the only advice I could take was what was preached into my tiny ears in childhood by dad: 'Be thankful with the blessings of God.' Whoever she turned out to be would be one of my blessings.

My compartment filled up at Cardiff, so my decision was to lodge in a cheap hotel near Swansea station. I had been given time off to visit my family during the whole six days we were expected to be tied up in port, and my idea was to hide away from the waterfront pubs for a day or two. However, that evaporated too when I got off and thought of visiting Mrs Ramos and maybe getting acquainted with one of Julietta's friends. These girls used to sometimes enter the big black door to talk with the young lady of the house.

But I did the right thing and took a taxi to the ship, where I walked up the steps of the bridge ladder, knocked on the door of the chief engineer's cabin and let him know I would be ready for down below duty in the morning.

It felt right to be back, sitting around the mess room table after dinner and listening to the yarn spinning about weekend follies. The day before – a Sunday, Shanghai and his trimmer Franken had brought some ladies on board from the local Cape Horner for an evening meal.

With strict rationing ashore, these ladies probably looked forward to a nice tuck in, but the special Sunday meal had already been served up at midday, and since then the cook had gone on the bottle. These ladies of easy graces knew ships carried some good food supplies since they were regulars at the dockside pubs. However, that evening meal was served to a drunken crew by a drunken cook.

The meal was a large bowl of potatoes cooked with their coats on and served that way, and another large bowl of Norwegian fish balls left over from breakfast was warmed up. Most of the crew couldn't care less, being under the influence; intelligent taste was lacking.

This food offer was treated as impolite by the gentler sex, and the guests showed their feelings by swearing louder than hardened sailors in descriptively malicious tones to their benefactors who had brought them aboard ship for such a rough meal; the fish smell even swept through brains swamped with beer and spirits.

The crew enjoyed the verbal assault enormously and could eat no more, in order to give way to boisterous laughter; small glasses were brought out of cabin doors together with a bottle of duty-free whisky to decorate the table. The ladies were not shy in coming forward for refills to smother the fish taste.

Certainly, with the big Shetlander on board, there was never a dull moment. The crew were now sobering up after the wild weekend, and when they sat around the table for the 3pm break, they looked forward to hot coffee in their system to erase the alcohol effects. However, no sugar could be found in the food lockers or elsewhere.

Fresh stores had been collected the previous Friday, as had been done every Friday, but after searching high and low, I was requested to pay a visit to the chief steward. So off I went amidships, hoping the chief would be in a good mood. I needed to do no coaxing; he filled my empty 7lb fruit preserve tin with no facial expressions, meaning that his mind was occupied with more serious business.

Under general questioning the following day, our shipmate Grant admitted to petty thievery. His only defence was that a local harlot needed sweetening up. Kitty would be well over sixty years if she was a day, and when the young deck boy started giggling through his teeth, the rest couldn't hold back. Most of the lads were acquainted with the six-footer's lady friend, and Grant was fortunate that the case ended in a chorus of laughter.

The following day both the Chilean and the giant Shetland Islander joined the skipper in a short stroll up the road to get paid off at the Norwegian Consulate. After bringing grog on board the night before, Shanghai was very well-oiled when arriving at the consulate. Guillermo then returned on board with the skipper so he could pick up his kitbag of clothing. I hung out at the mess table whilst my now ex-watch mate revealed the final blunder of the famous Shanghai Grant.

As Guillermo's story went, the captain had already departed with his documents and my fireman hung on so Grant could return on board with him. Still a little high with drink, he started showing off his linguistic versatility, calling the representative of the Norwegian government some rude names in that person's own language.

The argument was supposedly over the shortage of one shilling in his payoff. The rep did not enjoy haggling with a 6'4" uncontrollable drunk and telephoned the police. Then the law put him on the Black Maria van for a night's cooling off in jail, whilst Guillermo returned alone.

As for Guillermo and me, my mate uttered his gratitude for my help in arranging his Ramos lodgings on our way there. Upon arrival we all gathered around the long table of the back room with the Ramos family, with a mix of English, Spanish and Portuguese words flying around. The young boy, Antonio, was eager to find out about this new Latin country called Chile, which pleased his mam, Maria.

Later Mrs Ramos guaranteed that she would arrange for emergency rations and coupons for Guillermo as her special guest; he would eat in the privacy of her family. I then realised on the way back to the ship that my shipmate's education in the English language had been in the hands of Shanghai, and most of the conversations between them were decorated in four letter words. One thing about male adults generally was they usually held back from bandying around bad language in the presence of women, and that idea put my mind at rest.

Fifteen months on, I was back in the port of Swansea and called on the friendly family in St Mary St. My reception was not so agreeable. The Portuguese proprietress of the lodging house pulled up a chair for me in her private back room. We were alone sitting at the table, and she said she would like to discuss some serious business connected with myself.

She recalled that when I departed from her house the last time, the following days were enjoyable with her son and daughter urging the new lodger to speak in Spanish. There were several words they could not interpret in Portuguese or English. But mother knew these words very well; they were bad words, common swear words.

Maria pretended that she did not know them, but asked Guillermo to keep his conversation to the English language. Under the schooling of Grant, you can imagine what he came out with at the table after a few glasses of wine at the nearby Cross Keys.

She said she was unable to bear the horrible swearing that came out of his mouth in front of her offspring and gave him his marching orders then and there. She had gotten this business off her chest and both of us felt relieved. Before I left, she warned me never to bring any other brutes like Guillermo into her establishment again.

Then a day before we left port, Lett the Latvian, who had been on board longest, missed a step descending the shaky, metal stokehold ladder, slid down onto the steel plates and suffered a serious injury to his hip; he had to be paid off. There were now no firemen left.

Soon I discovered that two Norwegians were on their way from London. To make up for the other one, Johan, my cabin mate, was promoted to fireman. Young Dave from the Swansea area was signed on and was accepted as Johan's offsider so that myself and Franken could familiarise the fresh fireman with the stokehold.

It meant that I had to move in with Sverre, a tall, lanky Norske, whilst Dave took over my bunk. This fireman got on well with Franken, but I was the only trimmer he took a dislike to. He had been living in a London area where there was some distrust held against Welsh people, and he had caught the disease.

Wartime regulations prevented the crew members from learning the ship's destination, but before leaving port, some rumours (although not mentioning any particular port) always gave guidance like 'The Malta Convoy' or 'The Russian Convoy'. However, since there were no rumours, it was taken for granted that the company was chartered for the Canada run.

CANADA

And that proved to be the case. Coal was loaded at Port Tennant, a mile away from where the ship lay, and as usual we crept out of the dock in the early hours unseen, bound for the convoy round up at Milford Haven. Here we learnt that our black cargo was destined for Nova Scotia.

With fair weather the crossing was faster than usual. Nothing eventful took place except news from the wireless operator via the cook that after the cargo was discharged, the *Loke* would head south for the Brooklyn Navy Yard in New York for a refit and have a small deck built above the poop deck aft to house a 4 inch gun. Everybody had been guessing what new port the fresh charter would bring us to so now the mystery was out.

We spent five days in Halifax alongside the wharf which gave me a chance to hunt up familiar faces and places. First, there was the Greek-American Mitzo, whose half of one foot had to be amputated due to frostbite after the *Lily's* sinking. I came across him in a cafe in Barrington Street. He had a special shoe and acted normal, but it prevented him from sailing again. However, he was happily settled in Canada now. He took me to his apartment above one of the many cafes in the main street. In the five different rooms he pointed out, there were nationals from five different countries, who had escaped Nazi Europe.

Out of all those rooms, there was only one resident he disliked he told me. He was Bulgarian. Many people are brought up with some national prejudice fixed into them from an early age that is hard to get rid of, and it is often a next door neighbour or a neighbouring country which was this case.

Since Nova Scotia was what is called a 'Dry Province' in Canada, the only place to go for an alcoholic drink was the Allied Merchant Seaman's Club, where I only lingered but a short time since there was nobody around I recognised. So I returned to the *Loke*.

Back on board, I found that the padre from the local mission had left a load of magazines. The best thing of being British on a foreign ship was that we were free to commandeer this free literature and take them to our cabins.

But, unfortunately, a sad event happened before leaving Halifax. A Swedish freighter drew alongside the *Loke* and looped her mooring ropes to the bits of our vessel to await a berth. It was a quiet evening with most of the crew aboard. There was a deep stillness, replacing the throbbing beat of the propeller.

There were not even sounds coming from the donkeyman's radio, the only one in quarters. Even the card game on the mess room table was seriously silent, and I took to my bunk and held a magazine to my eyes. In the bunk beneath me not even Sverre could break into my thoughts with conversation as I studied full page pin-ups of the female form. Both he and his friend who had joined from London were invited on board the Swede for a tipple of some duty-free whisky; however, only Sverre accepted.

It was a choice night to enjoy sleep, and I felt good waking up in the morning. I was up early on deck and splashed out my liquid intake. Coming out of the toilet, I noticed the Swedish ship had its national ensign flying at half-mast over the stern and assumed that maybe some royal personage had passed away in Sweden. A deckhand, who had been on night duty, informed me that three of the Swedish crew had been asphyxiated by fumes.

We in the Black Gang noticed that my cabin mate was not at the table, and troubled faces looked at each other across the room; Sverre was nowhere to be found and it turned out that he was one of the three. By mid-morning we received the full news. The trio of victims had been seen swallowing raw liquor straight and making a lot of noise as drunks will.

They were told by other crew members to shut the door. All doors, or as many as possible, were left open at sea during wartime in case of emergency, although a lot were left hooked for privacy. So it became a habit in port only to lock the door when going ashore.

These deaths were certainly unusual and that cabin door, where the three men were found lifeless in the morning, must have had one of those soundproof doors. The cause of their death was traced to a cigarette stub causing a fire that was more smoke than blaze.

His shipmate who had lived with Sverre in London through its night bombing was terribly upset for a few days after since he had to report the news to his mate's wife living in that city. Not only that but whenever the topic arose about how easy it was to pass away with the combined fumes of whisky and smoke, his mate would talk about the days just prior to the outbreak of war, when both of them served in the Norwegian Navy aboard the same battleship.

It was better for him as well as the rest of us when we left Halifax and its sad memory and sailed to New York, only a few days further south. Now everyone looked forward to some exciting times in the Big Apple.

USA

I was not alone in being a newcomer to the port of New York, and others joined me at the rails to gawk at the mighty skyscrapers. The famed Statue of Liberty loomed out of the clear, morning air of early fall, and we finally docked at the extensive naval dockyard in north Brooklyn. However, it was morning before we were slotted into the assigned dry dock, where ship repairs began straight away. Even the galley was closed down for overhaul, and the word was that repairs would take three weeks.

That morning we were briefed that from now on meals would be provided at the big diner outside the dock gates, which swallowed a big workforce working at the seven dry docks all bunched together in this waterfront corner of Brooklyn. I doubt there was a repair yard anywhere in the world that came near the size of the Brooklyn Navy Yard.

After dry Halifax everyone looked forward to a tipsy evening out when we received our subs, and by most comments there were going to be big cash withdrawals. However, there was even more exciting news in the pipeline. After a three week repair job on our vessel, a cargo of rice would be loaded for the tropical island of Curacao.

A lot was happening all at once. We were ordered to be ready at 3pm with our personal effects and kitbag of clothing to travel en masse by subway to Pacific Street, still in Brooklyn, where we would lodge at the Norwegian Seaman's House.

The new working hours were very favourable. Instead of turning up at 7am, followed by an 8am breakfast, there would be no need to board before 9am, and finishing time from work would be 4pm. Officers were put up at a different address but their duty hours were the same.

The noon break at the big diner made everyone feel at ease. The counter seemed a mile long with a flimsy curtain separation about two thirds along. At the curtain on the bar only liquid refreshments were served including alcoholic drinks. It entered our minds that this place could be a good spot to spend an evening if one did not wish to drift around.

The entranceway did not advertise a large inside; however, when entered it took a full minute to digest the size of this space. There must have been hundreds of chairs, four to a round table plus it had a very informal, comfortable atmosphere.

All forms of dress were worn as most of the customers were ship repairmen and the crews of ships very busy getting ready for sea. The dungaree was definitely the uniform for daylight hours.

The hostel we stayed at was somewhat new with a lot of pastel colouring on the walls. It was ideal for our needs with a large bedroom for each man plus writing desks and magazines close to the dining room. We used it mostly for a sleeping place and for morning coffee.

The diner was a magnet for us firemen and some of the deckhands. During our first week's stay in New York, this was our watering hole. Big as it was, it did not lack homeliness and had a lot of camaraderie from men serving the self-service counter. Most of all it did not lack young ladies who were on the easy-going side.

So why go elsewhere? Like the usual run of waterfront females, these ladies were commendable in their socialising. We found this out the very first day.

Hanging on at the evening meal, the near part of this eatery really looked enormous because only workers on the late shift scattered at different tables. We decided to wash our meal down and led our feet to where music was being pumped out from a jukebox beyond the curtain in the bar area.

The people who sat around this room were all in dress clothes. With water still available on board, we had come ashore after a wash up so we did not feel out of order, even though our small group of four all wore jeans.

Even though this section was not as spacey as the central part, the shiny dance floor had a circle of about thirty small tables surrounding it with lots of other tables and chairs in the background at each end for lovers who preferred to snuggle or talk seriously of their plans.

We lingered until 6pm before a group of ladies entered, and then some more arrived. Such a large set-up could afford to deliver excellent meals at a low price, and we soon found that after a few rounds of bought drinks, there was a round of drinks on the house. Perhaps the smiling bartender recognised fresh faces, and this was a good way to welcome them.

A lot of popular jukebox numbers were attuned to waltz or foxtrot dancing, and Johan became a draw with the girls who wished to spin around with a waltz. As enjoyable as this was, when we drew cash from our wages the second weekend, we had general agreement to adventure into Manhattan.

We still took coffee breaks on board since the steam urn was still working. There was a group of Swedish welders employed aboard, who joined us in a cuppa during the breaks. They talked a lot of 'The Great White Way', referring to midtown Manhattan, and described the theatres and other places of amusement in the famed 42nd Street area.

They made mention of the Stage Door Canteen at Times Square, where men from the services could go and meet a film star. But since only uniformed men were allowed in, we were advised to pay a call at the less famous Pepsi-Cola Club, a few blocks further along Broadway, where seamen from the Mercantile Marine outnumbered the uniforms and drinks were for free.

Actually, the biggest itch for us crew members was to be able to walk around under the bright lights until way after midnight and still be able to catch the subway back to our hostel. The underground rail never closed until 4am, when there was a break until 6am, and then the early morning workers piled in. Britain under the blackout must have had the world's friendliest pubs, but the night out was finished and the streets silent by 10.30pm, and so on this second Friday night, we looked forward to the novelty of hanging around at night a few hours later than in old Blighty.

Back at the Navy Yard, a metal platform had been built above our living quarters on the stern deck, and it looked like there would be no need to set up an awning when we later sailed into the Caribbean Sea. Two days later a four inch gun was slung over by a crane to rest on the platform.

Three gunners from the Norwegian Navy now joined our crew. I got chatting to one of these ratings, which led to us stepping ashore for an evening out. After cleaning up at our hostel, we took the short subway ride to the diner/bar, where I planned to introduce him to some of the ladies our crew had been on casual terms with.

We wasted a half hour downing a few glasses of beer but not a girl turned up, so we went Manhattan-bound. The Norwegian Navy had the smartest of uniforms, and I had thought he would be a magnet for the ladies at our local; however, we certainly didn't lose out later that evening.

We entered a subway station to take a train. The moment we dropped our nickels into the slot at the turnstile, I felt a lot of good vibrations.

People were not just passing through the stiles; they were whizzing through. However, our footwork was not quite in harmony with this transport system. We were dawdling and following Gunnar, the navy gunner, I glanced back and expected to see annoyed faces, but I sensed at that split second strong goodwill. I was unable to lip-read, yet the file of people to the rear seemed to be saying, 'Hold your horses! Take it easy!' and all eyes were pinioned on the Norwegian uniform.

Terrible War! However, didn't it produce a unity of good emotions with others? Stares, friendly gazes and smiles were clapped onto my mate as the train rattled on. We disembarked into the maelstrom of Times Square, and we rushed upwards into the bright, electrified night lights and flashing neon signs.

Here was the centre of nightlife in the city. We did a pub crawl along the bars of 42nd Street and its environs, strolling from shiny bar to shiny bar, cooled by a near ripe moon as we gazed up at the theatre lights and mingled with the crowds all out for a good time.

In half the bars we entered, free beers slid along the counter from well-wishers. We would have to be thick in the head if we didn't catch on to the raised voices on entering these horseshoe bars. Obviously, the high-pitched tones were meant to include us in town gossip and the small talk of guys and dolls.

Big cities can give off a feeling of very big loneliness, especially to a stranger, so these good feelings were a welcome change. The sight of a uniform in New York City during the war years brought the best out of people, and I had the feeling that the Norske uniform had an appeal that caused that feeling to be even more obvious. I paid a few more visits to midtown Manhattan but with civilian-dressed shipmates and sadly never again experienced the same deep camaraderie as on this special occasion.

When alone, I would spend the best of an hour or two in the Pepsi-Cola Canteen, not for the free drink which apart from hot drinks was only cider which I had little taste for. I would have a few dances, and for some reason, nearly always slow waltzes, which was OK by me, since I was no better at shuffling the leather along a shiny floor as any other of the pretenders.

Most of the volunteers there were thirty-up and talked sensibly about job promotions. Their sympathy was none too warm but very real. Men who always look romantically at the female sex do not sense what realists women are.

The Pepsi-Cola guests were mostly merchant seamen, so the music that came out of the speakers was nautical, and the final song before closing time was always 'When the Lights Go on Again'. The ladies knew it all by heart, but the only part I was sure of, since we were all invited to join in, was 'When the lights go on again al-l o-ver the w-o-rld'.

Then after a fortnight in dock, news came through that a week hence we would shift the ship to a loading berth. It was confirmed that we would be taking a cargo of rice to Curacao in the Dutch West Indies. Very few had credit to their wages as everyone had let loose.

So we were glad to get away to build up a cash surplus; we then sailed to join a convoy group in Guantanamo Bay, Cuba. When we left New York City, the nights were drawing in and the breeze coming up the Hudson River was not warm anymore. Everyone's mind was now focused on spending time on a tropical isle with dark-skinned maidens running around.

Our small group of merchant ships and naval escorts steered south, and romantic notions were left to the rising steam. The only joy we looked forward to was rushing under the ventilator shaft after attending to the furnaces. Natural draft boilers depended on wind to raise steam and also raise men's spirits.

CURACAO

However, oxygen was in short supply as the temperature rose on deck. This meant that a fireman had to slice under the furnaces more often with his crowbar-type poker or slice bar, and those breathing exercises under the vent were precious moments. Enough steam was raised to keep up with the convoy, and over a week later we steamed through the fairly narrow entrance dividing the only town in Curacao,

Willemstad, and into an excellent harbour.

The fireman on my watch, Friedhof, had joined in New York at the last minute; in his fifties he had the same philosophy as Shanghai Grant in that he only stayed on a ship long enough to collect a month's pay, which would pay rent for the next month. I liked him because he saw the world through humorous eyes.

He had reason to show humour that morning after breakfast when we climbed up on deck and found ourselves freed from the sweaty stokehold for several weeks. We all appreciated that brilliant sunshine coming down from the blue heavens. It was like we had dropped anchor in a calm lake.

Men leaned over the rail awaiting news from the agent. An elderly seaman let us know that there would be no customs as this was a free port. Nobody seemed to take notice, yet everyone actually did. Always there would be men hiding cartons of cigarettes to sell for a profit, and I had four stowed in the darkness of the steering flat myself.

They would be of no use in such a duty-free port but handy to sell if funds were low. The agent brought mail and cash in Dutch Guilders, and most of the news was that we could look forward to a three week stay at the minimum, whilst cargo was being discharged by our own derricks into barges.

There may have been some firm resolves since we left our last port to stay on board and build up cash, but I don't know if you have heard this before. When a ship is at anchor, the shore is twice as appealing as when it is tied up to the wharf, so it was again the same procedure as in the Big Apple and that was to draw cash to the hilt.

Recuperation from the sweat loss en route would go better with some tots of rum ashore it was generally felt. We were assured of a constant launch service, which made a circuit of all vessels at anchor, and a large one it was, picking up crews mostly from oil tankers.

So there was no particular hurry to clean up the next day after the evening meal. The dock's watchman was told to invite himself into our mess room for a coffee or a bite anytime, as he could then supply us with all the island news. And he soon let out an unbelievable story.

Curacao, being a small island with not a large population, news got around fast. Considering that the harbour entrance would be among the world's narrowest for ocean-going vessels, one would assume that in times of war, a boom defence would be put across this narrow slit of water, but there was none.

And this was a vast complex of pipes that refined oil coming from Venezuela – the biggest in the Caribbean. It was utterly amazing that a simple protection had been overlooked. The watchman recalled that recently an enemy submarine had slipped into the harbour, and after sinking several tankers, returned to the open sea under the cover of darkness.

The narrow waterway split Willemstad, one side called Punda and the other Otrobanda. Near the mouth there was a net to capture fish at the change of tide, and it was also at that narrow that a good man could hurl a stone from one side to the other. The ferry boat that crossed from one side to the other only plied the water up to 11pm.

The climate was hot although not sultry; it was a dry heat so that short trousers and a T-shirt met one's needs for going ashore, although some preferred to decorate their bodies with flowery shirts bought in New York. The half-day Saturday stint of work was waived by the second engineer, and when we got our subs on Friday, we decided to take a long weekend ashore.

For some reason I drifted away from the rest, and with a beer here and there, I practically encircled the small, brightly lit town. The night seemed to belong to seafarers – Dutch naval ratings and Venezuelan schooner crews, more so than international crews of merchant seamen. I saw no docks at the edge of town, just a rickety jetty where scows still had a cargo of bananas from the nearby mainland of Venezuela.

I enjoyed walking on my own as there was a pleasantness in the air. The only locals I came across were some young mulatto ladies serving at soda fountains and short-order counters, all American-style, and it occurred to me that, as far as the oil complex was concerned, they had taken over when Holland came under enemy rule and what followed was an American township more or less.

I bought myself a hot dog at one of the stalls and dawdled, taking a quick glance at the stars above. This climate was so glorious after a hot stokehold. The walk did me good, easing my leg tendons from the ship roll walk habit.

I bought a can of beer at one of the small drinking counters. The other drinkers there were largely American. Then I became interested in black faces looking out of square gaps that were not windows. The upper part of one of these big, rambling wooden structures interested me most. There was Spanish-style music blaring out of it.

Entering this place, I went right upstairs. I arrived at what seemed like a high loft of a vast barn. Drinkers sat on benches which looked like raw flat timbers as were the tables where they placed their drinks. In this hall there were but a few white-skins like myself.

I decided to seat myself at the edge of the dance floor where the white-skins were and was invited to the table of two American seamen.

They pointed to one of their friends on the floor. He was dancing with a very curvaceous creature of light brown skin. I looked around and saw a group of similar ladies and decided they must be Latinas.

On the way back from the toilet where I had relieved myself, I stopped at a table. It was full of local drinkers, and one turned to me after knocking back a tot of rum with a very sociable smile on his face. This gave me the nerve to ask him if there were any females in the place who desired a partner. He pointed to where the female loners sat around a table, sipping from bottles of coke.

When I passed by their table, all I could work up was eye talk. As yet I had had an insufficient alcoholic boost. I remarked to my U.S. friends at the table that the local males were a friendly lot. "They should be," I was told. "Those guys make a darn sight more bucks than we do." Me: "I thought U.S. ships paid the top wages."

Then he mentioned that most of the local men drinking in this bar were crew members of what he termed 'The Mosquito Fleet', which was a fleet of small tankers that brought crude oil from the Gulf of Maracaibo at mainland South America to the refining plant here on the island.

These guys are on double the wages of a Dutchman, and that was two hundred dollars a month. I later found that Dutch firemen and able seamen were the same as Norwegian wages – $130 a month. However, at the rate of exchange then, $200 really was a big monthly payment, equal to fifty pounds sterling. The provision was that members of the fleet had to be bona fide born and bred on the island.

It was still only 9pm when I left and decided to go walkabout the smaller bars and return then with greater confidence in winning the heart of a lady. I caught up with shipmates at a hot dog stand, and together we drifted to one of the cafe bars.

We gathered around beer cans, and I opened our conversation by commenting on the lovelies I had spotted at the big watering place. A Second Steward took me up from there and offered what he himself had overheard. With a bit of alcoholic boosting, there was a consensus on discussing our eternal temptation.

Our speaker informed us that on the upper floor of the big bars, all one had to do to catch a mate was to walk up to the table where the senoritas sat away from the couples and say the word 'Taxi!' or 'Mat!'. Although Spanish was understood, these two words were grasped.

Then the chosen damsel would arise from her chair and beckon with her hand. You followed that hand downstairs and into a taxi. "What next?" came a query as deeply interested as if a highly scientific question would be answered. We all scrummed over the table to listen to this professor's words. "The taxi takes you out to a lonely beach."

The speaker slowly tipped some beer down his throat and kept us waiting. "You are charged one florin by the driver, and then he asks you for another five florins. If you don't pay up, you don't have a mat. It's strictly business; he probably gets another florin from the young damsel for playing middleman. The mat he takes from the boot is long enough and wide enough for two to snuggle on after being unrolled."

Ears were still waiting for more, but our champion ended, "That's all. The driver always pulls up a short distance from a palm tree, and she will lead you, mat under her arm, to a spot beneath the fronds." He then felt another swallow of cold beer was earned after the lecture. This Second Steward seemed to have adopted the airs of the officers he served.

For around US$3 it seemed a small sum to share your feelings in nature itself. There was a lot of Indio blood in these lassies from South America's interior or did that steward expand our imagination overly with slow, impressive words?

However, there were cooler heads among the group. Whilst I was still fantasising about the naughty girls, one young man piped up that he planned to go to the launch so he could write a letter to his beloved in Swansea. There were mixed feelings to his idea but his influence was strong and affected us. We decided we would get a good night's sleep and leave flirting until the following day.

These colonial islands certainly offered inexpensive entertainment so there was a good chance of stretching our guilders and at the same time roister around. Before leaving coins were passed into someone's hand, and a large bottle was purchased to take with us. I couldn't remember the brand of the rum, but it was all good stuff in the West Indies.

After a good lie-in Saturday morning, I walked up on deck and found a few lads busy washing up their work clothes and decided to follow suit. I found a large bucket and went amidships to half fill it at the galley pump and asked the cook if he had some hot water on the stove, I could mix with it.

He was always helpful and after steeping my sooty gear into it, I peeled slivers of green soap on top and churned it with a broom stick. I left it on the stern deck where it could sit in the sun until afternoon. I had no appetite but that small effort caused me to enjoy a cup of coffee, sitting with it there on a bollard.

Before catching the liberty boat ashore in late afternoon with the others, my two sets of pants and vests were drying on a line in a lighter shade of grey. We joined other smiling faces on the launch with the same 'Party' state of mind, mostly young mustangs.

Parties of two and three went this way and that on the quayside. I took off alone and dived into a native rum shop and tested a shot to nerve myself for a visit to the music loft. This time I walked directly to the lonely ladies table and looking at one young, brown-eyed beauty, I mentioned the magic word "Taxi!"

She bowled me over with her speedy response, and I was soon rushing after her down the wide staircase. I was led through the narrow street to a waiting taxi. Everything occurred as the steward had spelt it out except the night before I had planned romancing on a moonlit beach.

This affair took place on a sunlit beach near a lot of high tropical foliage for two people to examine each other's body. It is said that night is made for love but beneath a parasol of spreading leaves, I added a page to my romantic history. In broad daylight I caressed a lady I would have preferred to win.

Later that evening found most of the crew loitering in the small bars, not very capable for a launch trip. I was pretty unsteady on my own feet so I turned to a stranger at a nearby table and asked if there were any inexpensive lodgings in town? He turned out to be a crew member of a Norwegian tanker who had made a lot of trips here, and after swallowing his can of beer, directed me to follow him.

He led me to the wharf where schooners and luggers, some loaded with banana cargoes, lay alongside. Choosing one of these Venezuelan craft, he stepped aboard. No one stopped him, not even an elderly mulatto sitting atop the cargo hatch cover. He politely smiled at the intruder. Pointing to a coil of hemp rope, my guide said, "That's where I'll sleep tonight; pick your own place to lie down; everything's OK." I had not yet reached a yawning point and thought it a pity to waste the remainder of such a pleasant, starry evening, so I returned ashore with my new mate to enjoy a beer and a few tots of rum and coke to follow.

We returned to the schooner later on with a small flask of rum for a livener in the morning. Actually, it was cheaper drinking rum than the imported American beer. I had overtaken a few shipmates along the way, who were even groggier than myself. They were very happy to accompany me to the line of small craft.

Those dependable sea legs kept them from tripping over ropes and rigging gear lying over the deck. When the man on the hatch, who might have been the skipper, passed a friendly nod, I knew it was OK for three extra loafers to lie horizontal on his deck.

I told my mates to find a rope coil to flop on and did the same myself. I dropped off right away and waking up with the rising sun, I realised that there is nothing like the smell of hemp rope to put one off to sleep. From that night on, whenever I found it hard to get shuteye on a warm night, I went up on deck and dropped myself on the flattest coil available.

It was better than a pillow of hops to send one off to bye-byes, and it melted the morning hangover as well. I sat alone on deck, waiting for one of my mates to surface into consciousness, when a boy, just coming into youth, approached and handed me a black coffee; he was wearing a sombrero-type straw hat nearly as big as himself.

It curled up at the front sufficiently enough to reveal smiling eyes set in light brown skin, nurtured under Mother Nature's sunlight. I had learned enough Spanish to return "Gracias" and that made his mouth open, beaming out a quite excellent set of teeth. Used to drinking hot beverages without added milk, I really enjoyed the morning service.

I offered him a florin; however, a few hand motions from the eternal watchman discouraged me. How could I thank these people? Three local deckhands emerged from below deck and settled themselves in the wheelhouse after saluting my presence with hand waves. These straw-hatted men with beardless chins showed they had Indio blood in them, and I felt they would have made an excellent camera shot.

I then had a notion. Feeling inside the rope coil, I brought out the small rum bottle. As there was no speech, or very little when I joined them, I held up the flask. An open palm was waved in front of me, and one man left to return from below deck with several metal cups.

He passed these to the young lad. Not long after, the four of us were enjoying a South American special – hot coffee spiked with rum. The stream of chatter in Spanish awoke my friends. They did not relish coffee with no milk but were quite keen on a noggin of rum before departing, and then we left the rest of the bottle with the Latinos.

We drifted along the quay and looking ahead noticed the ferry disembarking passengers from Otrobunda. Considering that this was Sunday and that people were out and about doing their visiting, it seemed that perhaps this was too early to return aboard.

We did cross but lingered on the way to the launch pier. We emptied our pockets to see how our finances were and felt we had enough to return and get ourselves into a shady rum shop. We crossed again on the ferry and did just that. It was OK in those establishments to put a bottle of rum on the table.

Together with several tins of coke, we joined the rum and coke groups that were very trendy here. We settled in for a lengthy bout of tippling; however, by late morning, we presented a drowsy foursome and decided to return to our floating home after all.

Again, we crossed on the ferry, but on the other side, there was some lingering. One of the lads gave out his thought that during the midday heat we should seek a shady spot to lie down, and after a short nap, adventure along the shore of the inner harbour. After all it was a Sunday with zero duty demands on us, and agreeing to this first suggestion, we strolled under hot, dry sunlight which was not driving us mad. This dry heat was not oppressive and a half mile further along the inside shore came drowsiness.

We had lost the town by now, and noticing a family of palms huddled together a short distance ahead in the sandy landscape, we settled for its shade. Talk warmed as we sat in a circle. Hearsay had it that for nine months of the year not a spot of rain fell on the island, but when it did come down, rain clouds dropped everything they had gathered in one go. And by all accounts, the wet spell was due very soon in this current month of November.

We had picked a good spot, as eyelids soon started dropping, and it was now siesta time. Even if the lizards were darting around, making a nuisance of themselves, the soft tidal breeze put us all into a glorious sleep, and we forgot all about them. We finally returned on board after waking from this sandy world, determined to do the same again.

During one of the weekdays I took the liberty boat ashore before the evening meal and enjoyed a big plate of chop suey in the Chungking Restaurant for a change. This became a regular habit of mine to miss a meal when going ashore.

It was towards the end of our stay in Curacao when I again called in at the Chungking. I ordered a plate of chow mein there, and the normal oriental music was now missing. My usually jovial waiter was also silent and rather slumped. When he brought the meal, the pall on his face was very noticeable.

I asked him if he had received sad news. "Vely sad," he replied and off he went to serve another customer. When I stood up to pay him, I asked him to open up his mind to me, and what a mouthful he came out with. "Twelve Chinese sailors been killed in prison." and the tone of his voice was unmistakable – he was telling the truth. I decided not to question him as he was obviously very upset.

I kept this news in mind to let the crew know, but when I went on board ship, the news was already general knowledge. According to the watchman, the whole town knew about this extreme racial abuse. It appeared that some European-flagged ship had been crewed by Chinese, who had gone on strike for higher wages whilst at anchor. As all allied ships had received extra pay for wartime risks, the Chinese crew felt that their own wages should be upgraded as well. The white officers knew they had the power of wartime emergency law on their side to lock up any rebellious mariners and called the police to jail the crew.

I was unable to find out the details of the confrontation; however, the bludgeoning of twelve seamen to death was a hell of a price to pay for this violation of wartime regulations. I imagine that other ships' crews in the harbour were as mad as ourselves, and I can only assume that no American ships were in port because the National Maritime Union would certainly have taken action to force an inquiry.

We were now told we were due to sail shortly, as the last of the cargo was being discharged. Our next port was Port-of-Spain, capital of the islands of Trinidad and Tobago. The company had signed a six month contract to take bauxite from the upper reaches of the colonies of British and Dutch Guiana in South America to a depot in Trinidad.

Supposedly, it would be shipped to Mobile, Alabama to be processed into aluminium, which the American Air Force was in great need of. Before sailing we experienced a few days of the island's wet season and were glad to leave as the rain bucketed down.

Since I was now a qualified firemen, my wages now shot up from twenty-four to thirty-one pounds a month; however, it did not go without a challenge to my constitution. Teaching an ex-motorman of slight body his coal-trimming duties would not be easy I thought, but he turned out to be a willing learner and had young manhood was on his side – he was twenty-two years old.

It was a queasy kick-off to be a fireman, sticking my face to those red hot fires after such an easy three weeks of just helping the engineers do adjustments in the engine room. The run, however, was only a few days of sucking sweat out of my sinews. At first I thought my sweat glands would cease working after pitching coals on six fires at a time.

I would then rush under the ventilator and swallow a litre of water and yell at the trimmer to keep the hanging tin full of liquid. With slack coal (small bits of soft bituminous coal) and little wind to keep the embers red, I had no time to smoke a cigarette but had to rush back to my task of spiking beneath the coals with my lengthy poker.

TRINIDAD

It was my own watch, the 8-12, that took the *Loke* into the harbour of Port-of-Spain. It was a great relief to me when the donkeyman entered the stokehold at 11am and told me not to build up steam as we would be reducing speed shortly. When she slowed to half speed, I collapsed my butt on the valve box after gurgling down my usual quota of water and lit a cigarette.

I wondered where I would get the strength to climb that iron ladder when knocking off but was amazed after a long sit-down that I regained my old energy again. I had faced and won my baptism in sweat as a fireman, and when the d'man came to take over the glory hole, I climbed that ladder more spiritedly than I thought I could.

Nature's heat causes some people to be fussy with their meals – just picking here and there; however, with manual exercise in steam heat, it may have caused queasiness at times, yet most of the time, firemen and trimmers were the hardiest eaters on board. There was hardly ever a time that we lacked appetite as energy was immediately needed to be burned up.

It was 11.30am when I ascended and what a glorious sight met my eyes. The port city sat back against a background of a green hillside, glistening seemingly straight up from the water's edge. Our anchorage, however, was pretty far out, or we might have seen the hillside had a slope. A passing deckhand questioned me if I didn't think this place was more stifling than Curacao. To be diplomatic I agreed that there was more humidity about, but after the intense heat of my workplace, the faint breeze wafting across my nostrils was heavenly. The shimmering waves of hot air had little effect on me.

After washing the coal dust off my body, I put my teeth into some tough, reddish kind of meat that the Norskes seemed fond of, a sort of cousin to corned beef as it had a salty tang, but it was tougher. It went down the gullet well with mustard and assorted veg.

No one was too upset when news came out of the galley that shore leave was not allowed. After the joyful days of rum and coke on Curacao, it was time to build up our wages again. We were alongside the dock the following morning, taking in bunkers and fresh food stores, and then back to the anchorage by afternoon to ready ourselves for a short voyage to a new port.

BRITISH GUIANA

On the dead watch, the 12-4 fireman took her out at midnight, and we were on our way to Georgetown, capital of British Guiana, and after the beautiful holidays at New York and Curacao, I was prepared to put my shoulder into some honest toil, hot as it was. The run was short which gave us some time to recuperate – only three days to the Demerara River, where Georgetown guarded the entrance, and with hard Welsh coal it would have been maybe twelve hours less.

It must have been considered a pretty safe run since we went without any convoy protection. On my way to the glory hole, I passed a deckhand coming off watch duty, and he pointed to a similarly deep-sea craft as our own, steaming in the opposite direction. He let me know that it was the Norwegian *Ingertre* on the same bauxite run as ourselves.

And presently, it was back to the routine of pitch, rake and slice. My breakfast had been well-digested, and I tore into cleaning out two fires, since I had not the time to educate my new trimmer with the technique of cleaning the ash and clinker from a fire yet. However, having done so and having then pitched coal on the other four fires, I allowed myself a gasper of half a cigarette after a short session under the vent, gurgling water.

Naturally the steam level dropped with the new fires still needing building up, but as there was no need to keep up with the speed of a convoy and after that there were no more smokes, allowing my lungs to energize my body between short breathers under the ventilator and gulps of water.

I no longer took my duties as an almost impossible burden. I had passed the endurance test and looked on life in much the same way as Friedhoff, my humorous chum, who had paid off in Curacao. The pain barrier had already been crossed on the way from that island.

As soon as we passed the estuary of the Demerara and dropped the hook abreast of Georgetown, we learned that a German cargo ship had been scuttled broadside to the river to block the passage of any ships upstream to the bauxite mines. Since then a channel had been dredged around it.

Two tugs came alongside the ship, and the captain of one ordered us to reverse direction so that the ship's stern pointed upstream. Heaving lines were thrown down to them and were pulled in by their thick wire hawsers. The tugs then began to tow us from the stern.

The new run was turning out to be a better one than expected as our speed was only half speed astern to assist the tugs. The stokehold was still a roaster because it was still jungle country all the way, with a thick growth of trees hugging our boat on either side. Even before I went down at 8pm, I noticed smoke from the funnel making a straight line to the stars.

At sea you were usually sure of the morning and evening breeze; now it took me less than an hour to come to terms with the new situation. The breaks were longer than when we were going at full speed, so during these intervals, I sat on my empty drum and stayed under the ventilator. There was no draught in the ordinary sense, yet enough oxygen to pump the lungs with less than a normal effort. I would not need to worry about waking up with a muscle-bound body cramp.

The ship's engine went at slow speed when taking the bends of the Demerara River, which I thought was a good thing except that air was reduced to a whisper because only the movement of the vessel stirred the needed oxygen in the first place. If I sat on the valve box at these times, I would have been sitting in a puddle of my own sweat.

It was refreshing to come up on deck after duty in the cooler night air and wash up. Thirty-six hours after leaving Georgetown, we tied up at a jetty by a new town called McKenzie. All this time, the horizontal line of smoke rising from the *Loke's* cigarette-type funnel showed that the wind failed to penetrate the dense, green shrubbery surrounding our passage upstream.

We tied up that evening, and as soon as the deckhands had stripped canvas from the cargo holds and removed the hatch boards, a chute was lowered from the silo of bauxite, and by nightfall we were making the return journey.

No one had been allowed ashore at this new settlement. From the ship's rails, we spotted the makeshift start of a town with prefabricated housing for the natives, looking like boxes, but not with too many signs of life. The bosses must have had their quarters a mile further on where the mine was worked.

We felt that there was very little to go ashore for in this big, fresh clearing of rainforest, deep in the interior where natives had yet to learn how to wear clothing. There was reinforced steel wiring surrounding the outpost, and the information we gathered was that uniformed Americans were posted at several gates to either stop or permit the forest people to enter.

From the officer's mess to the galley, news trickled through that one barrier for entering town was a lack of a civilised, western appearance. There was a humorous side to this order. At each entry point, the sentry had inside the gate two piles of female clothing.

One stack was for knickers and the other one was for bras. If any female wished to enter, she was handed these skimpies. There were some on board who would have given a lot to stand duty as sentry for one night. On this flat clearing, one would have expected the higher land to produce a cooler climate; however, the only difference but also benefit was that the mosquitoes that had plagued us were much scarcer.

During the river journey both ways, off-duty men sat near the rails or leaned over them watching the river people, but on the upward journey, the tugs didn't allow small craft from coming near due to the backwash from the three propellers. We sailed bow first on the return trip under our own steam and still at half-speed to manoeuvre around the bends where the river was very narrow.

The canoes, as speedy as the *Loke*, even though only small paddles were used, raced alongside us. They were as curious of us as we were of them. In the middle of these small craft, there was usually a female who sometimes had little or nothing to cover her private parts. It certainly provided food for yarning from our stand point on board.

In daylight you realised how necessary it was to slow the engines down to navigate the bends. Sometimes the steamer would make wide sweeps, and if the bend was narrow, the thrust of the ship's wash would force wooden pillars to sway violently, causing panic in the inhabitants they supported.

Many a native house must have been wrecked or half-wrecked with the regular passage of steamers. And when possible they showed their anger from our intrusion into their homes. Sailing down river with a full belly of cargo, the *Loke* was low in the water, and we were easy targets for young fellows on the river bank to hurl mangoes at anyone passing on deck.

TRINIDAD

We were at this time headed for the bauxite depot at Chaguaramos, which lay about ten miles from Port-of-Spain. This would be our regular Trinidad base. Our arrival was on a Wednesday, and the chief was firm that no cash would be given out to us until the soot chambers had been cleaned out. With the bulk cargo removed by sucker pipes and a two day waiting time before discharging, we had an easy day Thursday.

The fires were pulled, the boilers shut down, and by Friday morning the furnaces were cool enough to enter as it had been over 40 hours since shutdown. That morning we got into the job before the day warmed up, and after washing up late morning and picking up our subs, there were few words passed amongst us.

But I analysed those few words, and they were similar to ideas of my own. We would all take the crew bus put on for us at 12.30 pm and then be off to the capital. We had all drawn money up to the hilt, and whereas I thought I alone thought that if I still had cash in my pocket on Monday, I would not return on board until I was spent out. But I wasn't alone. When we were seated on the bus, all of the black gang opened up and revealed they had the same idea. All we wanted to do was escape from that iron lung of our workplace and spend some time in the cool shade of a rum shop. There was also a U.S. club for seamen on the waterfront, and that is where the bus dropped us.

All dressed up in flowery shirts bought in either Curacao or New York, we dropped into the club for a round of beers before separating. The wooden structure we were sipping at was fairly large. We also learned it had inexpensive single rooms as well as a restaurant, and before leaving we decided to make it our meeting centre.

It turned out what was on everyone's minds was that if we overstayed our leave, it would be best to go back in a group because if it was about keeping up work discipline in this out-of-the-way port, where would they pick up experienced firemen?

That short spell in the club, with its hypnotic spinning ceiling fans made me promise to visit the place regularly. We also learned that there was another club for mariners called The Torpedoed Seamen's Club, but it was only residential.

Then off I went on my own, happy that if I could hold on to some cash, I had the choice of staying at two hostels, rather than sweat in the hot quarters on board ship. I purposely only had soup before leaving the ship in order to keep my appetite for a Chinese restaurant. Later, after some chop suey, I sauntered around the town, eyeing up the girls at the market near Prince St and explored alleyways and side streets.

Then I dropped into a rum shop. The locals there invited socialising and told me that the big event of the week was that very night – it was a calypso concert, when anyone and everyone created their own songs and music. At least one band would be in attendance.

Downing a couple of rum and cokes to sink the chop suey, I was then off to the residential lodging house. I liked the place and booked a room for four nights. I was learning that Trinidad was half price to Curacao, regarding drink and food, and cash could go far if a man was careful.

I did feel a guilt twinge at deciding to return aboard as late as Tuesday because even then I might not start work before Wednesday, but like the others, I joined in the testing game. Deckhands could face immediate dismissal, but we realised that coal-burning vessels were going out of fashion, and not many fancied handling the furnaces.

I decided to give the calypso concert a miss that evening, though I promised myself attendance at another time. Instead that night I enjoyed good sleep on a spring mattress, not surrounded by ironwork, but with the pleasant aroma of woodwork. That weekend I moved between the clubs and rum shops, mostly planning for my next jaunt ashore; moving around was the only way I could keep the booze at bay.

There was that urge in me to squander hard-earned cash. Yet a few days civilized living restored my strength of mind and purpose; so after breakfast on Tuesday morning, I set off to the American Club to pick up the bus to the bauxite depot.

The bartend, however, told me that there was a main depot for loading the mineral right there on the docks. Drivers were on regular runs from there to Chaguaramos. My very first request for a lift from one of the drivers on one of the big trucks told me to jump up, and he'd get me there.

He turned out to be a good partner to ride with. He seemed very glad to help me out, and I wondered why. It was only later that I learned that America had an agreement with Winston Churchill about leasing British colonial islands in the Caribbean. It went back to 1940 when Britain stood alone and needed U.S. battleships.

And the Americans had given the residents employment with high wages. Later on I found out that these drivers would not hesitate to give one a lift either way. I alighted off the truck and edged my way behind other transports before sneaking up the gangway unseen.

I passed the time of day a bit with the shore watchman on top of the gangway and then hurriedly made for the galley where I found a carefree, happy crowd of deckhands and my own gang. Over a cup of coffee, they told me I was not the only absentee. Even some officers had gotten into the same game.

Later I was not long in changing into work clothes and reporting for day work but not before listening to the bosun, who had just come down the ladder and told me to hang on. He told the men at the mess table that he just had a word with the chief mate who disclosed something of importance.

When the agent boarded earlier that morning, he had a coffee in the saloon with the ship's captain and officers and reported that the other Norwegian ship, the *Ingertre* (which I had spotted earlier) was on the same bauxite run as ourselves. The skipper aboard that craft usually allowed the crew shore leave after normal workdays.

Their captain suggested to ours through the agent that it was better to give the crew extra time off rather than their paying a visit to a doctor and paying off that way. His reason for easing up duties was that if one man succeeded, there could be a rush to the medic. He recommended to his officers that only necessary tasks be done, or he could be short of a crew.

The captain aboard our ship then asked the officers what they thought about the matter. The chief mate stated that with all the bauxite dust covering every inch of the ship (even entering the tiny apertures of the quarters), there could never be any paintwork done, either by the deck or engine room department. Another mentioned that the *Loke* was a twenty-year-old rust bucket, and the owners would be only too glad to save cash by not ordering drums of paint from New York whilst we were under this six month charter.

I now felt more confident to face the deucer; however, he was absent, being down in the engine room. Instead I found the lanky third engineer. He gave me a big smile from where he sat on the big end of the main engine piston, with a massive spanner in his hand. He arose and waved me into the stokehold.

There we joined Johan, who was sitting on the valve box smoking a cigarette. He passed me one; I sat on the box with the other two and lit up. I was relieved very much when he let me know that the second engineer had told the donkeyman to let us run our own race.

This news pleased me no end. It looked as though the donkeyman would run the show from now on, and to keep this new system up, we would carry more responsibility. He then let me know that by the last word, the ship would move to the main port to load stores on Friday.

The present situation was that Dave the Swansea lad was in the port bunker, wheeling coal from the recesses to the chute that emptied into the stokehold bunker. As for the other two trimmers, Franken and Thor my offsider, they were even now still adrift ashore with Henrik the fireman, and Johan guessed they would soon board as their funds would be getting low in the rum shops.

I decided to wheel a few barrows in the starboard bunker and work up an appetite, so I left Johan staring up at the steam gauge on the one boiler that kept pumps and winches active. He was relieving the official d'man, who was in town on a shopping spree. Just in case I passed the deucer on deck, he would notice me looking slightly black and dusty, and this would assure him that I was not lying around drunk.

Throughout the dinner break, the able seamen were still in a happy mood with the new arrangements. There were eight deckhands, and they had just finished cutting cards to see which half would be allowed to go ashore, whilst the other four stood on duty to batten down the hatches.

I questioned Dave about arrangements for the engine room crowd. "Johan can tell you all about that, but I know that the second and third engineer are taking day duties in turns, same as the mates on deck," then he passed on a message from our man below for me to relieve him for his dinner after I had eaten.

Having eaten, it was my turn to gaze up at the steam gauge. Before leaving me to it, Johan asked that I touch no fires because there was little steam being used on deck, and if the steam rose too high, it would clamp the half-circle blowers in front of the ash pits which would prevent any air getting through the fire bars.

He then added that with the new system going into place, the donkeyman had advised that as soon as we stopped discharging cargo, we all should make a fast clean-up of the engine room. In this climate the skylights had to be kept open, and the engine room was full of grey mineral dust. We didn't want it to get into the generators.

Later, we sailed with all hands from Port-of-Spain, en route for Paramaribo, the capital port city of Dutch Guiana, with a day's gliding through those placid, shark-filled waters. Talk around the mess table was still about organising for the new system. It was very unusual for us to shoulder an additional amount of responsibility.

The captain and chief engineer could not make it official, or a stiff reprimand would come from the company; yet the same company would give good recommendations to a skipper who could hold onto the crew. As if we had not enough rest ups, we went into dry dock for engine room repairs. Whether it was the bauxite damaging the works, I never learned.

DUTCH GUIANA

The only thing concerning about these short runs was that it was impossible to save money unless we started a new system with our selves. This latest colonial enclave turned out to be more attractive than Port-of-Spain. It had one central feature of enjoyment right close to the dock area called Paris Dancing.

I don't know where they dug up the word 'Paris', because the bench seating around the dance floor was rough-hewn timber, as were the tables, unless the proprietor was a Frenchman. It looked like seamen were allowed to mingle with American big spenders, high class personnel involved in Alcoa mining projects. The talk was a change from the usual, salty conversations concerning booze and girlies. Any information we wished to learn about these new mining towns was freely passed on.

We were told that we would be picking up a load of bauxite at a new settlement called Moengo, up on the River Suriname. The trip upstream would be no different to what we had experienced up the Demerara, being towed astern to a newly-formed settlement, but it would take half a day longer to reach this new destination. Having learned this, we knew what to look forward to.

Meanwhile, on our second day in port, the company agent brought dollar bills on board. It was Saturday and time for enjoyment. A young ordinary seaman came to my cabin after picking up his sub and asked that we go ashore together since he wanted to keep away from the drunks. I felt the same as he did.

We called into Paris Dancing to exchange our dollars into guilders and enjoyed a can of beer before stepping out. As usual there was no actual evening as we knew it. In the tropics, it was daylight at maybe 15 minutes to 6pm and by 6.15, the curtain of night had fallen, and the stars had appeared above.

Treading along through the dimly lit streets of this Dutch colony, a flash of light came from an open doorway, and as we passed, small arms grabbed hold of us and pulled us inside. These were young, feminine arms that tugged us into the living room with little resistance on our part.

Actually, we became curious and most surprised to find ourselves surrounded by what seemed like a troupe of young girls. An olive-skinned gent was seated there with them and informed our gaping eyes that all these young ladies were over twenty and refugees from Java, a Dutch Asian colony (Now part of Indonesia.)

The man spoke to one of them in Dutch, and we were guided to a small table. Chairs were pushed under us, and we sat facing our host. He looked Portuguese with a touch of South American Indio in his blood and was quite the friendly person.

We soon learned that these diminutive females had just landed and were eager to make a living in their new colony, and he was helping them. Then two coffees were placed in front of us whilst I lit up a cigarette and pondered on how these very many chicks managed to lodge themselves in a house made for far fewer.

We soon became aware that one of the rooms was used for their present occupation, lying on their backs with a stray sailor to copulate over them. The only English they seemed to have learned so far were two phrases: 'Short time' and 'Four guilder'. When I stubbed my cigarette, this idle hand was grabbed by one of those oriental fairies, as I held onto the cup with my other hand.

A voice kept repeating into my ear "Short time!" As I am the sprightly type, I am not slow in taking up such an offer, but I DO have taste, and I held off to gas with the boss of the lasses, who said 200 of them had landed together. My mate jumped at the proposal to make instant love, and I promised to hang on there until he left the special bedroom.

I supped another coffee whilst he took fifteen minutes to fall in love. And after he recovered his senses, we left the man at the table surrounded by his pixies. He then joined the girls outside the door to wave us goodbye and told us to spread the word around about his lovelies.

No sooner had we turned the corner of this street than we bumped into another group of these doll-like creatures, beckoning us to make love to them for four guilders. We politely waved them away and beat a retreat to Paris Dancing – back to the rustic benches and tables.

We found a lot of elbow-leaners stretched across the long bar, both male and female. As most of the cash was sucked out of the Americans, the tunes coming out of the jukebox were rowdy, pleasant USA. Some Americans were seen at the far end, being served short-order snacks, and therefore, they didn't need to leave the cool timber surroundings.

After a few beers, my mate urged me to return with him to the house of love. However, we never made it. On the way, two lovelies in their late teens approached us in friendly talk. Chatting under the dim street lights, we fell for a plan which the girls set up. In the gloaming, I couldn't make out their nationality, but they were of a light skin, or should I say lighter skin. Perhaps they were true Carib people.

I opted for the slim one with large eyes. We paired off and sauntered along under a starry sky. We then halted at some rooming place, and in the shadows, both lasses spoke with the proprietress. Then we coughed up the cash to rent a room for the night at a reasonable rate.

Sometimes you bed down in cool silence and do a little kissing and snuggling, but this dual one-night marriage kicked off with friendly, small talk across the bed, as if we had known each other for quite a while, and in the darkness there were giggles and pleasantries thrown between the parties.

For a potluck romance, it turned out to be the best ever. Walking back to the ship with my mate the next morning, I felt like I was walking on air. When morning had released our tangled bodies, not only did she spurn the florins I wished her to accept, but did so with a thankful smile.

I wistfully hoped we could meet again, yet strangely enough, for all the love that she showed in her eyes, she made no request for a future date. And stranger still neither did I request a further meeting. Yet I was still on cloud nine when I boarded the ship.

Year after year I have often thought of that sweet chick, and I often wondered if both girls were daughters of rich merchants, who wanted to break with their confined society. The final glance from her eyes when we parted told me that it was the first time that there was someone of the opposite sex who adored me for what I was.

I spent that Sunday afternoon walking around this quaint town, and passing another house with an open door, I was invited in by a middle-aged European. He turned out to be a Dutch settler and somewhat on the religious side. He definitely was not an out-and-out Dutchman.

There were traces of indigenous blood in his complexion, and in an agreeable way, he told me he would like to help me in some way. He

145

turned rather serious at one point, warning me about going with diseased women. He then eyed me up and down, and I wondered what was on his mind.

He told me that if I ever had any ideas about leaving my vessel, he could put me up at his house, and what got me really interested was that he could also fix me up with employment at the American outpost in Moengo.

When I left and steered my feet in the direction of Paris Dancing, I gave quite a lot of thought to what my new acquaintance had passed on, while I spent the rest of shore leave at this convenient watering hole.

Back on board and travelling upriver, the *Loke* was churning through the water at half-speed as usual and it proved to be a windless passage. I, surprisingly, worked through my 'saunas' like a real pro. It's amazing what you could get used to. The river was so narrow in places that I wondered why we never ran aground on the return trip with a full belly of bauxite.

Tree branches would snap against the ship's side, and walking on deck, it was wise to duck at times. The river bottom must have been very slushy. If we thought the river folk on the Demerara were poorly clad, when we throbbed our way into the upper reaches of the Suriname, we found both males and females without any covering whatsoever.

They were starker! These natives were of a different complexion also. Instead of women wearing shiny black hair sweeping down over their shoulders, these ladies, sitting in the middle of row boats, had more of a curly, crinkly hair style, no lower than the neck. This seemed to prove the hearsay stories in Paris Dancing that slaves were brought from Africa to build dykes for which Hollanders have an obsession; these new arrivals didn't find it too difficult to disappear into the same type of forest from which they had earlier been dragged.

What was even more annoying was that the downpour of showers daily was more frequent than on that river in British Guiana. Here it was a regular three times a day, and the mosquitoes would let you know when they materialized biting like Hades. Even so, if you had washing on the line, out would blaze the sun and leave things dry in ten minutes.

If we thought the McKenzie clearing looked forlorn, Moengo was absolutely desolate. In McKenzie, except for the absence of hotels or bars, the prefab housing was in neat rows. Not much doing about with the settler street population strolling back and fro and entering doors which possibly were stores that didn't announced themselves with sunshades.

Here in Moengo, the prefabs were more scattered about, and the area looked messier with people lolling around instead of being on their feet.

The place was so alien that no one felt like taking a walk and exploring, which was unusual. It was possible that a few gourds of jungle juice had been sneaked through the gates by some locals, who may have sold this alcoholic beverage to the workforce.

Perhaps it was a lower water table than at McKenzie because with different breeds of flying insects like midges and other flying teeth, the mosquito net was our best friend during sleep. It was a necessity!

TRINIDAD

Cruising back to Trinidad this time, several on board had requested to visit the doctor on arrival. There were various complaints, no doubt some invented, and this was what most skippers feared in an out-of-the-way port with very few qualified seamen.

Paying off sick was the only workable way of breaking a contract. And with Norway under German occupation, the 18-month contract was more flexible than for British ships. In ports the size of New York, where there was a good supply of seamen, men could be paid off at request.

Now that the doctor game had begun, we found our values, and I planned for a more sensible shore leave. I would attempt not a three day stopover in Port-of-Spain but would hang out until the fourth day if that covered the weekend.

My plan was to spend more time at the residential club than the one on the waterfront. As pleasant as those drinking bouts were, I intended to give up throwing too many dollar bills around. What the Dutchman said about working in that jungle cleaning up on the Suriname with the Alcoa Aluminum Company stuck in my brains, and I did not want to dislodge it.

It seemed to me that round trips to Chaguaramos and back would average two weeks. It was already arranged that watches would take turns at cleaning out soot chambers, doing their own boiler only. With the small amount of coal used on these short runs, being cleaned out every six weeks would keep the tubes very clear.

Now that wages had shot up to $120 a month, equal to thirty pounds sterling, I might be able to get a nice holiday ashore. From now on I would draw no more than $15 each time the sublist was handed in. Even if I drew cash at both ends, there would still be enough left for a nice tropical holiday if it was possible to leave the *Loke*.

At this time we entered the smaller port for discharging our ore. I was the only one that didn't go ashore, and I planned from then on that there would be no more impulsive dashes there, as soon as we tied up in Chaguaramos. This time the soot cleaning had to be done by Thor and myself, and we had to be ready for duty Monday morning when the boiler had time to cool down.

I had first soaked my washing in a bucket before we ate, and after breakfast, enjoyed sitting under the shade of the gun deck with a cigarette and a cup of coffee, musing on what kind of employment was on offer in Moengo, that jungle outpost up the Suriname.

There was a regular washboard on legs on the poop deck, and when I was bending over washing my work pants, up came the d'man who told me he could never remember me staying aboard on a Saturday. I let him know that I had letters to write back home, and that is just what I did.

On Monday morning, Thor and I worked really hard for three hours, removing soot from tubes and back ends. As the cleaning was now done on a regular basis, the black powder was easily pushed through the tubes with wire brushes. I felt glad of that sober weekend on board because this task needed a lot of agility to wriggle over the double thickness of sacking laid over fire bars.

With only one bucket of soot to remove, I made a quick retreat. I still felt in good shape but sped to get the job done quickly, removing myself was important, so as not to let my body swell. What might seem like an ordeal was reduced to a healthy exercise.

I felt good, sitting on the valve box and swallowing water, whilst the d'man and the trimmer removed the scaffolding and cleaned up. I went up topside ahead of them as Thor was hoisting the ash bucket of soot, dust and rubbish.

After I washed up, I lay back in my bunk, resting under the electric fan until midday mealtime. After that Thor and I both left the roasting cabin to hitch a lift into town. I didn't ask Thor how long he planned to stay away from the ship, nor did he ask me. Everyone was playing his own game.

I intended making a four day break of it, and then to come on board Tuesday night. If the deucer did not berate me over this extra leave, I might land a longer stay on the *Loke*; else my plan was to leave it. We spent the best part of that sunburned afternoon in the shade of the American Mission, drinking ice-cold beers before separating.

I made my way to the residential hostel past the market. On the way I bought a paper, and on entering the 'Home', booked in for four nights and took a siesta, leaving the local rag on a chair beside my bed. As I dozed, it seemed to me that as far as this part of the globe was concerned, the U-boat menace had lessened rapidly.

That gave me some peaceful thoughts before dropping off. After an hour or so, I woke, stretched, yawned and picked up the newspaper. It was not until I came to the back page that I realised that there was little censorship in the local media. The news my eyes were first glued to was a minor headline; however, beneath it was scarifying news.

Twenty-two ships were reportedly sunk off the coast of French Guiana, and this attack occurred only the day before. The story went on that they were part of a north-bound convoy. Most of the convoys I had been in had consisted of sixty to seventy vessels.

All kinds of questions flooded my head. Where were the escorts? How large was the convoy? Amazingly these ships were torpedoed in the light of day. This action must have been very well-planned by the enemy. On the coastal strip of Guiana, could submarines have hidden there? In past centuries, Caribbean pirates made use of the Guiana coast to hide from justice. Definitely things to reflect on.

But too much for me then so I rose and walked out of the room. Soft drinks and general items were sold at this lodge, as would be expected, and I switched my taste to a can of coke and went out to the veranda to join a group of new faces. Their general talk told me that these boys had just been discharged from hospital. I joined in on the conversation and learned that they had survived a sinking.

During my visits to the US club, at no time did I hear about shipping losses in local waters, yet it was obviously happening. These new boarders had survived on rafts when their vessel sank off the northern Columbian coast. They were Scots, the crew of a Scotch company line doing regular trade in these parts.

I fail to remember the company name, but as one of their vessels was due to dock from Jamaica soon, they were not interested in seeking another berth, as they continued on full pay and would soon be repatriated. If nothing else prevented me from quizzing this crew, such news that was coming to my eyes and ears caused me to take a more serious view of life.

However, there were also day-to-day things to work out. At the rate of the Trinidad pound to sterling, if it cost two pence for a drink of coconut from the market, it meant only a penny compared to UK currency, and the nut was hacked with a machete right in front of you. You were then handed a straw, and you then boosted your body with a pint of valuable energy.

At 240 pence to the British pound, it showed how inexpensive life could be in this colony for a sober being. Why was it hard to live a good, normal existence? Yet for all the crews guzzling beer at the US club, the normal life meant walking no further than the nearest rum shop.

And it was this second mischievous beverage that got the better of me, especially on the following trip. I drew more cash from my wages, way above what had been my intention. Rum and coke was not only inexpensive but the choice for all types since you could doctor it to whatever strength you wished.

But the imp gets your pockets empty either way. The stronger the drink, the further away you are from the real world, and if your dosage is weaker, it means you are chained to the bar longer, and can you think of anything more valuable than time?

By now Henrik, the fireman, had been paid off medically, and it might mean my old friends were also thinking the same idea. We then signed on a Dutch fireman by the name of Jock Decker. He was a big, definitely easy-going chap to get on with, and I confided to him that I was interested in working in Moengo.

DUTCH GUIANA

We were now on our way to Paramaribo, capital of the Dutch territory. It seemed that luck was all my way. We dropped anchor on arrival at the mouth of the river for a four hour wait. Not only was a freighter making its passage downriver, but there was another ahead of us.

On this occasion I reported to the deucer that I wished to visit the quack and pulled a fast one with the doctor. With good acting I was sent to the port hospital for further examination of my backbone. The way I figured it, the *Loke* would be on her way to Trinidad in a week's time, and I could let the visiting medic know that the 'Pain' had gone. All I would have to do was pay a visit to the company agent, pick up my wages and go live with my Dutch acquaintance who spoke about work in Moengo.

It seemed to me that I could leave it to him to guide me through the formalities of legal residence, and he would take care of my employment with Alcoa. What could be simpler? A week went by, and I became restless, more restless than I was by nature. Lying back, waiting for my temperature to be taken by a sympathetic nurse, got me musing in a serious fashion.

Surely the *Loke* must have departed by now. Should I declare myself fit? (as if I had been otherwise.) To be on the sure side, I devised a plan. After 10pm, when only a few small, blue nightlight bulbs filtered enough guidance to see one as far as the toilets, I would bide my moments after the night nurse took final temperatures.

After the fever victims had been seen to, I felt sure that a certain door in this ground-floor ward had been left unlocked for patients, who were allowed out of bed to walk around the garden. It would surely be locked at midnight, the next time the night nurse paid her visits.

Ten minutes past the hour, I hopped out of bed and checked the door; it was unlocked. All being well, I could now sneak out and be back in less than an hour. The walk to Paris Dancing was not more than a quarter of a mile away.

Gently, I fingered carefully beneath the bed for shoes and trousers but never moved rapidly or suspiciously, and then I was through the door and out the main gate in a split second. Soon I was making a wide circle of Paris Dancing, trying not to be noticed by my shipmates, and then stealthily edged myself to an alcove near the outside toilet.

The window faced some drinkers at the bar, and coming out of the shadows, I took a peek. It was easy enough to see through the small chink between filmy curtains without drawing notice to myself.

I recognised the uniform of my gunner friend, Gunnar, on one of the tall, swivel seats. The section of the bar where he sat was not far from the door. Should I pop in and have a quick word with him? It seemed too risky with other crew members at the other end of the bar. The one good thing was that he drank alone.

I took a short stroll into a darker part of the night and lit up a fag to relax my nerves. Time to get back was uppermost in my mind. Looking at customers entering the toilet, I noticed one stranger enter, and when he came out, I was waiting to have a word with him.

One good point about my chances of finding out about the *Loke* was that there was only one person inside wearing a uniform, so when I approached a person with a Dutch accent if he could ask my mate to come out and have a word with me, he was sober enough to assure me that it would be no trouble.

So back to the recess I went and waited, but not with very happy thoughts. I had assumed that the *Loke* had sailed to Trinidad, and having got over that first setback, I now thought on what news would follow. Then out came my friend to relieve my stress. First, I asked him not to pass on to others that he had met up with me.

A nod was enough to put my trust in him. He smiled when he noticed my hospital shirt but spilled out all the information I needed to calm my jumpiness and uncertainty. Instead of lying at anchor, the skipper had brought the ship alongside at the request of the chief engineer for a minor overhaul.

The port surveyor had added it to the repair roster, and as of the moment, she would leave the dock in three days' time. I thanked him for briefing me, and he promised to reveal nothing about me making a trip out of the hospital to talk to him.

Back at the hospital, my timing was good, tiptoeing to my bed at 11pm. With a sheet covering me, I enjoyed the spinning of the overhead fan blades, revolving me into a dreamy, bauxite settlement and residing in a prefabricated hut with all the modern conveniences at hand. Morning came around with a jolt with the realisation that I would still have to act the part of a man with a spinal injury.

I also realised that I had played a very risky game the night before, and had I been caught, it would have meant a very speedy eviction; however, now I had an ace up my sleeve. One more week abed, and my act would have to turn out to be a star turn. My 'complaint' demanded that I remain horizontal except when visiting the toilet.

Most of my chats were with a young soldier in the opposite bed. He was East Indian, and his father had a vegetable stall in the market. From this lad I learned much about the locale.

Then an event occurred that rang a nostalgic bell from my Canadian hospital stay. Converging doors at the end of the ward were opened out wide to receive new patients. Stretcher after stretcher passed up our aisle on trolleys and were placed on waiting beds. There must have been at least a dozen men. They were all basically skeletons, clothed in brown skin, and understandably looking weak and barely alive.

It took little time for stories to pass around the beds. They had survived a vessel sunk by torpedoes near the Panama Canal. What had remained of the survivors was picked off rafts two months later – two months under the glare of the tropical sun, and I thought I was having a rough time in the glory hole?

Thinking back to an R&R of 1942, my elder brother was rising fast in the South Wales Miner's Federation. I don't know if he was a body reader, but during a drink together at my home local, he brought out something that was on his mind. He told me he could use his influence to have me working down in the mines.

I told him I was satisfied with the life I was leading, and there was also a good deal of danger in the mines. "It's not that," he said. "You are suffering from shock since you were torpedoed. I can see it."

On my mind at the time were two things. First, someday the war would come end. Had I accepted what was then offered, from that day on I would be regarded, in one way or another, as a man who had flunked duty to my country, a coward. And I was glad I had gone back to sea and glad of this current reminder in the hospital.

There were also other reasons. Fatal accidents were common in the South Wales coalfields, and they happened often to men fresh in the industry. With my ears and years, it had been regularly commented by seamen that if you were involved in enemy action, and it left you with fear, return to sea for your own good to relive the shock and kill it.

Shock trauma I might have had, and I realised it was a dangerous ailment, but the more dangerous disorder was not fighting back. As far as normal fear was concerned, I counted it as a safeguard. However, what started off this thinking in the hospital was my idea of skipping out of the war. I thought of this until the next morning broke and came out with my conscience letting me know that what I was about to do may have been leaving in a shoddy way, but actually this was the way I was always going to be – breaking rules not in a criminal sense but in a continuing search for adventure.

I was determined to stick with this leisurely existence for a week. After all everyone was attempting to skin out (leave their ship) – the able seamen even more than us. Going up those rivers in the oppressive heat robbed them of appetite, whereas down below, without realising it, that active exercise with the shovel made us eat like horses.

So really I was not getting out of the ship for extra cash or safety of body. Nothing like that was on my mind. As far as cash was concerned, I was already making a heap for an unskilled person, plus seeing the world at the same time. The trouble was very common in wartime – failing to hold onto it.

You could blame the imp in me, and he was indeed a big imp with a capital 'I'. In the hospital there were a few other seamen who would call around to have a chat with me. One able seaman told me he didn't give a tinkers curse about living in warm quarters; it was the mossies he detested when he wanted a nap. Me: "Don't you have mosquito nets on your bunk?" "Yeah, but the eggs always drop through," he replied.

Monday morning found me in a pretty good mood, having stuck the seven day test well. I could now be sure that the *Loke* had sailed over the horizon and out of my life. When the quack questioned me on his morning round, I thanked him for the attention the hospital had given me. I then confirmed that I felt I had a new back and was hoping he would discharge me pronto!

I told him I was yearning to return to the sea, while in my thoughts I was studying what it would be like to be a new resident in the colony. The doc promised to let me go that very morning and kept his word.

Leisurely I enjoyed my final morning tea, a nice green tea. I also shared conversation with the East Indian soldier, and he wished me well when I confided that I might see him at his dad's stall in the market at a future date as I was planning to settle in Dutch Guiana.

Supping away at my warm beverage, my imagination was taking over. I could see me being paid off at the agent's office and strolling along to the house of my Dutch friend without a care in the world. However, that pleasant daydream got sort of wet and melted away when my eyes turned towards the end of the long row of beds.

Who should be walking between the beds and coming right my way but Captain Neilson of the *S/S Loke*. My spine might have been in a strong and healthy state right then, but if the doctor had diagnosed my heart, he would have found it pretty much cracked. The game was up!

Smiling like it was Christmas, the skipper said he admired me for getting well in the nick of time since the ship was due to sail upriver that very afternoon. I found it difficult to return his smile, and after packing my few belongings, followed him out like a sheep going to slaughter.

Why had that damned engineer kept at fighting weaknesses in the effing steam engine? I allowed my anger to ease up; it was pure energy, which I would need very soon. Johan was glad to see me back; however, it was with Jock, the new fireman that I confided my feelings to. From now on the Dutchman was the one man on board who could pass on good advice to me.

My mate, Jock was quite popular with the local people of Port-of-Spain. He seemed to have charisma with them, and for two years he had never sailed too far from the island. During coffee breaks, I was not the only person who listened in when he revealed his ties to the island and promised us all entry to a workmen's club on a Sunday when the rum shops were closed.

He would not stay on a ship for longer than three months and then amused himself ashore for the same amount of time. How did he do it? I was becoming interested in his lifestyle, which I intended to follow. I lay back in my bunk one day when I was off-duty and allowed a little philosophy to enter my head.

I realised that irrespective of the very heated conditions we worked under, a payoff in one of these islands was worth two in the 'civilised' North. In the first place, the cost of living was halved, and if you developed a strong enough mind to choose your company, instead of being magnetised into boozing groups, the world could be yours.

I decided to study big, happy-go-lucky Jock Decker. As both of us were off-duty when sailing into Chaguaramos, we leaned over the ship's rails, planning shore leave. He praised my idea of drawing only sufficient amounts of cash to do more sightseeing than getting lost in the US club.

TRINIDAD

Without my asking him, Jock seemed to read my mind that I was trying to release myself legally from my contract with the ship. Then he opened up and let me know that a few years back, he 'jumped' a Dutch ship here, and now all he wanted to do was linger on this palm-studded island.

For those confused with the phrase 'jumping ship', it has nothing to do with jumping off a ship physically. It is merely a term meaning that a ship crew member has decided to leave his vessel in a foreign port, due to a grievance with an officer or crew member or for some other reasons.

Another popular name used for the same offense was 'skinning out' which was mentioned earlier. After his ship left, the seaman would come out of hiding ashore. If he had deserted over a lover (when the girl might have hidden him to help get him legal residence), he would have to face the Mercantile Authority.

There could be a pattern of excuses for his mishap. The most popular defence was that the vessel had sailed without him, and he could do nothing about the matter. It was a pretty poor alibi because in most cases, if it was an authority other than the consul, the word 'Deserter' would be written opposite his name in the marine register.

You could fight this verdict on your return to your own port. Jock and I, sailing under a Norwegian flag, could actually walk off without a reprimand and leave only a few dollars behind but could spoil it by being refused work on another Norwegian vessel. Additionally, the harbour master for Port-of-Spain was known to cause a great deal of trouble when you rejoined another freighter.

One defence for desertion was to leave your belongings and private documents on board before shore leave to prove that you went astray unintentionally. Had I deserted a British ship here, it would most definitely have incurred a penalty when I returned home because of the gravity of being at war. Although I had yet to desert, in ships' mess rooms it was often discussed, and there were very many different cases, e.g. if a ship was short-handed.

When a seaman joined a ship which was sympathetic to the reason he had deserted, a decent captain might hand in a good report on the man upon arrival at a home port, and anything against him would be quashed. In shipping circles everything was taken into account.

Few people realise that when you sign articles of agreement, you are usually contracted to stay on that vessel for 18 months; the arrangement made in the company shipping office was almost sacred. You had signed an agreement in front of a bone fide witness before leaving home waters, and if you broke that deal, you would pay, and the heaviest payment was in your character report.

Jock was by no means Mr Perfect. He was captured lock, stock and barrel by the rum bottle; however, he possessed the private wisdom of strength of mind. This meant that he would not be turned down by skippers plying a regular route to the island of Trinidad. The talk about Jock in the US mission was that he would never get turned down if there was an opening on any vessel. Skippers never classified him as one of the useless bums that sat on benches at the entrance to the mission, begging for booze money. He was that well-known in the island drinking clubs that he would never be short of a drink.

He explained to me that he had a policy to spruce up when cash in his pocket became scarce and would pace the jetty not far from the club. He would board up to around ten smaller type vessels, some inter-island, and others like Alcoa on regular runs from the States. His policy was to have his documents handy so that when boarding, he was ahead of himself in possessing both deckhand and 'Down below' proofs of ability. However, before even considering seeking work, he would make sure that the vessel would be making return trips to the island.

I was at my ease in such company as his, and now that I had gotten past my failure to bail out in Paramaribo, I could take my time with future planning. Actually, there was nothing to worry about. Now that the engineers had realised that good coal-burning firemen were hard to come by in this hot quarter of the Caribbean basin, we had been allowed to share necessary duties among ourselves.

It was Johan's watch and his time to clean soot, and the only work I needed to look forward to was trimming coal from the recesses. This would give the trimmers a break, and they could clean up in the engine room whilst helping the engineers when needed. Two of them, that is, the other trimmer took his turn to hoist ashes from the donkey boiler and other stokehold jobs. Jock would trim the other side bunker.

Instead of rushing ashore as soon as cash was handed us, our group took things in a less hurried way. What was agreed was that at least one fireman and one trimmer be on board at all times, and we followed the example of the deckhands and cut cards for whoever was to stay on board on whatever day.

No longer did I consider a four day shore leave but just followed the roster. With a weekend off, it just about gave us that amount of time off.

My next time ashore I promised myself to visit a calypso concert. I wanted this fresh kind of singing and music to get into me so that I could sense the feelings of the locals. Their songs changed weekly, noting any interesting events that could be written in satire because that was, or seemed to be, the whole idea of calypso.

The purpose of these musical gatherings seemed to be to cut down any tall poppies that gave themselves overbearing airs. The war had brought good, well-paying jobs and cash, and from what I gathered from the more serious types in the rum shops, there was a new class of educated natives creating a new culture for Trinidad, and in turn calypso was central to this idea.

Whenever possible I went ashore with Jock, and sometimes Johan. I was always eager to go through a learning process under my tutor, Big Jock. This day Johan, Jock and myself, alighted from the bus at the US Mission Club in the early afternoon and entered for cold beers.

I decided to hang out for info before I left to book up in another haunt of mine, the Resid. We sat under the ceiling fan wings of our seafront hang-out, and there I listened to every word of the twenty-six year old Dutchman. Johan asked Jock on how he would fare if he spent all his cash on grog and found that his ship had been diverted to New York in mid-winter.

"That's OK," said the other. "My brother owns a laundry there, so I wouldn't run short of gear; he just passes me a bag of left behinds." With talk like that, he couldn't help but attract company. Jock could have made a living on the stage with such bluff remarks.

His very easy-going presence was something to witness when he came out with his cavalier remarks. I always hoped that tough, stout Gomez, the harbour master, would not get in his way and try to force him out of the colony. It was only when I had met 'Boston Blackie', a Swedish-American, did I learn that my hero had knocked three men on their backs on one occasion when accosted outside the Mission grounds.

Just before our parting, Johan, who had taken glasses back to the bar, overheard the bartend mention that one of the six steamers plying the bauxite run had been sunk by a torpedo on her way from Dutch Guiana. We were obviously still in harm's way.

It was 5pm when I left my mates, but in this eternal summer, the big, white orb in the sky was still shining down its golden rays. Any loose coins in my pocket were handed to one of the half dozen bums sitting on the long bench outside the mission when I passed. Some premonition told me I could find myself in dire straits at a future date. And then into the shade of the fruit and veg market I stepped.

I ogled some skirts in the hopes of company to join me at the evening calypso but received not one return glance. On the way to the other mission, I passed an elderly gent, barking out new calypso verses, which had sold for a penny a piece.

I didn't buy a paper that day. The bad news of the convoy sinking had given me bad dreams of desperate men struggling to swim away from shark-infested waters. At the hostel I learned that the Scotties had taken passage back home, and without them the place seemed pretty empty.

I still did not make it to the music fest but did spend time probing the alleys of the town whilst promising myself further investigation later on. Before boarding ship, I came across Jock in the Waterfront Club. After a couple of beers, he said he felt like a brief walkabout, and I followed eagerly when he told me he would take me along to the nearby docks.

We strolled leisurely along and I counted eight vessels. He also gave me a few pointers to guide me if ever I got beached.

Pointing out the harbour master's office at the end of the jetty, Jock warned me to keep away from Harbour Master Gomez with my sensing in the tone of his voice, there was little doubt that he distrusted the man. Out of the berthed eight vessels, he picked out three that always made regular return trips to the island.

He pointed out where the bauxite trucks had their depot and told me this was where Alcoa ships left on regular runs to Mobile, Alabama with American crews; union rules were very strict, and it was not easy to find a berth on one of them. On our return to the canteen, he threw out a few more pointers, like facing up to a captain of a ship, dressed and looking respectfully clean.

Most important was being sober. Another point mentioned was to never show your documents to the ship watchman but to request passage to the Master's cabin directly. And most important of all, he urged "To walk on board as if you own the ship. This gets you past the watchman faster than official papers. At times a crew member or shore watchman will say that there are no jobs on board, and you lose heart even before you try; however, more times than not, you have caught him in a bad mood and he's telling lies."

He put it this way. "Derelict seamen or pilferers often use the excuse that they are seeking a job when they confront a watchman, so try not to look like a bum, or you may get the bum's rush." He insisted that if I was trying to get myself off the *Loke*, even for a month's break, try hard first to obtain a legal discharge through a medic.

DUTCH GUIANA

Some time passed and our next port of call was Paramaribo. There nothing offered a chance of causing an accident to myself on purpose. A second try might prove embarrassing, so I put aside any ideas of falling down the gangway, which was more popular than swallowing silver paper, in which case you were diagnosed as an emergency ward visitor to have your appendices removed in an operation and would lose something that could not be returned.

We found a pair of tugs was waiting for the *Loke* at the estuary to tow us, stern first, upriver. The fresh trimmer on my watch was a young Norske who lived for the bottle, but that was OK by me as he was capable of supplying me with all the coal I needed. Sticking out these trips with competent firemen, like Jock and Johan, had its pleasant effects.

It really is amazing how a human can condition himself, even to the overuse of the seat pores, so long as one possessed the energy-renewing magic of a young man, and a future focus on playing the girl chaser, or, at least, playing the big mouth in the rum shops. A free and easy life has a lot going for it.

TRINIDAD

On returning to Trinidad, I began to realise that the *Loke* had its good points. It had liberties that more modern type ships lacked. Take days off on an oil-burning steamer or a motor ship, and you could be paid off with bad remarks in your record book. On board an old tub like *Loke*, judgement was more flexible.

Even the deckhand department had arrangements of work practices that would not be tolerated on other vessels. Even so they would not dare take a three day leave, as the firemen did so casually. The skipper was no softy, but circumstances being tough as they were, leniency was even granted to the officers. On a rusty, old tramp ship, there would be no backstabbing for promotion amongst them.

Altogether this easy-going attitude from topside brought a harmony and unity of a sort, and you could classify this ship as a 'Happy' one, and you should think again if you have the idea that this would be the general pattern of crews on merchant ships. On most voyages I have made on tramp ships, there was a balance between hell and harmony.

And Jock helped to make the *Loke* a happy ship. Bench sitters talked of him in popular tones, so admiration came not only from myself. The way he managed to ignore any immigration laws and live ashore on the island at whatever intervals that pleased him baffled many heads. And an obsession with his personality type pulled me in.

One Sunday evening when I joined him in a amble to a local drinking club, so great was his popularity that among the native Trinidadians drinking there, all gushed over him. He was known to have the better of any toughs that crossed his path, yet he was not the brawling type.

But I had my own concerns, as we alternated our trips between Georgetown and Paramaribo, I was already developing a plan as we entered Tiger Bay in British Guiana, preparing to be towed up the Demerara River. From then on my mind was set on a certain gamble I would take on our return to Chaguaramos.

Before arriving back to this port in Trinidad, I had a plan all figured out. I remembered Jock's advice on jumping ship. Most important was secrecy, and second, it was important to leave your possessions on board so you could be classified as 'Missing' the ship instead of deserting it.

It rarely took less than a week for loading time at our discharging berth. When the big chain buckets ceased tipping bauxite onto the white mountain, shore side moorings would be slipped and the *Loke* would continue on to Port-of-Spain for stores and bunkers of coal and water.

Back in town I planned to stay dry in port and play the miser. At six shillings for a bottle of rum, it might seem that one could enjoy inexpensive evenings at the rum shop; however, it never worked out that way, although the bottle size was smaller than average spirit bottles, maybe two thirds the size.

I was really serious about doing a bunk (jump ship), and even wondered if I had lost a shrewd move in letting the second engineer know that I would be staying on board. He would be in the same line as myself in drawing cash from the saloon once we had come alongside and might lift an eyebrow when he noticed me drawing all my wages.

When we did line up for subs, he must have failed to notice anything irregular because we passed smiles as I made my exit. By now he must have realised that the three firemen could be trusted to do necessary tasks before skipping off ashore. He also had reason to smile with one of his hands prepared to stay sober on board in case of emergency.

I spent a somewhat agreeable rest up on board, even if it was a bit lonesome, and had given myself time to catch up with correspondence with folks at home and elsewhere. An influential factor in my planned escapade was that the *Loke* never left the bunkering jetty unless it was under the cover of dark when we would either wait at the anchorage for a few hours or sail straight away to collect more bauxite.

The late, quiet evening when most hands were in their bunks, resting from their shore binge, I distanced myself from the watchman but kept an eye on him. Having made prior arrangements with a native at the rum shop (ignoring Jock's advice about leaving my personal gear on board), the local offered to stash my clothing at his place – there would be no problems.

When the watchy entered the doorway leading to the mess room, I figured he would take a good ten, gulping to down his coffee, and I fleet-footed it down the gangway with my kitbag slung across my shoulder. There was no private gate at this wharf, so I strolled along with an easy mind.

I steered my feet in the direction of my new acquaintance's home. He was wide awake and in no time my things were passed through the door. On my return on board, the watchman was none the wiser, thinking I was a late arrival.

Usually on sailing day, there was a crew headcount on deck after the evening meal, and men were told to be on board at 8pm. It was now an hour later – 9pm – and no headcount. Now that the watchman had seen me, should there be any questions about all the firemen being aboard, the watchman could tell the donkeyman that he had seen the last one board himself.

I knew the shore watchman was waiting for the duty mate to allow him to go pretty soon, so he would be spending most of his time sitting in the crew mess, chatting to the d'man. He would be popping in and out, and so I was in and I was out, stepping swiftly down the gangway for the last time.

I felt free and easy because the ship rarely left the bunkering berth before midnight, but with no alcohol in me, I took things very seriously and left the waterfront area to book into a hotel, ready to go undercover. I checked into a moderately-priced hotel and settled in a comfortable room with a washbowl.

My limbs rebelled against a lie-down at such an exciting time, but that is what I did. I stripped and covered myself with a thin sheet. The room was on the second floor, just high enough to catch the evening sea breeze through the open window which could dilute the humid, tropical night.

I then ventured back to the dock area after midnight, and from a safe distance, spied the bunkering wharf. I looked a long look in that direction to assure myself that the *Loke* had definitely gone. Then I made tracks to the man with whom I had stowed my gear.

I rapped the door of his small, lonely apartment in a sort of tender way, trying not to disturb his neighbours; however, I got no response, so the raps became loud fist bangs that surely would awaken anyone inside. But it didn't. In anger I put my shoulder to the thick, wooden stronghold.

I was happy to find that it moved noticeably. Maybe a good inch, as the nearby street lamp showed. My anger ebbed as I gave the door one more rap, and with no response, I took the impolite step of bunching my right shoulder muscles and crashing in. The door had been sealed more by stiffness than with a lock and key. I was soon putting the tentacles of all ten fingers out, fumbling for an electric switch.

Gaslight from the street lamp streaked through the uncurtained front window, and then I flicked on the electric light which revealed a room meagre of furniture, in which there was only an ancient, large chest of drawers taking up a third of the space of what seemed to be the living room.

On one side there was a doorless entrance to a narrow room with a bed and a child's cot. Most noticeable was what could not be observed by the flat's general atmosphere. Had I been a ship's steward, I might have haphazardly stroked my finger across the window sill and picked up a lot of dust. In other words, I got a strong feeling that this house had not been lived in recently.

I only met with disappointment by rummaging through the spacey drawers of the big dresser and decided that the only property in this cave was invisible space. There was one door at the rear, which entered onto a lane. A very bitter pill had to be swallowed. I had been conned out of my belongings.

Fortunately, I was familiar with the rum shop at the corner of the street. It was open twenty-four hours a day to service late workers at the dockside repair jetty, and with hopes decidedly deflated, I put on a fast trot in that direction. The atmosphere there had always been one of familiarity between dockworkers and seamen.

No doubt many had past sea service themselves, and with any luck I might get into the ear of such a person to aid me in locating my kitbag. It was good to see a few heads nod in my direction. It seemed I was in sympathetic company, and after settling down at a table of rough-hewn timber with a glass of rum and coke, I bided my time.

It took just a little time to mix in friendly talk with two men at the next table. I unfolded my story of the missing kitbag, giving a description of its trustee. With head nods and sighs, the men were surprisingly open to notifying me that such a one as the 'White Carib' (as he was dubbed) was quite skilful at relieving seamen of their belongings.

The way they spelled it out, thieving was his line of business. The way the four other sitters passed me glances of sympathy marked my quarry as definitely a criminal. Then someone dropped a coin in the jukebox, and a calypso tune eased the tension.

I sat it out for a few drinks, and before leaving, felt that the world was not coming to an end after all. It's quite common to hear the quotation

'Sympathy is only words.' But words spoken honestly from any side can make one feel first class. It is the similar kind of honesty that comes from drunks occasionally but also children.

Sitting there in the late hours, I felt that I was not the only one who had such misfortune, and with grudging acceptance, I finished my tippling with a certain peace of mind. I felt that my new stability was owed to these men of Negroid and other racial backgrounds. So I left seven shillings on the counter to pay for some further tippling when these men had their hour or half hour break. And that did my mind good, too.

Returning to my hotel room, the first thing I did before taking to my bed was to ensure that any personal papers and documents were safely stowed in the top drawer of the small bedside cabinet. I might need to buy work trousers and strong boots should I join another coal-burning steamer, but surplus clothing was unnecessary in such an endless summer.

As far as my New York souvenirs and knick-knacks were concerned, they could be purchased when I sailed north again. Most of all I missed the names and addresses of birds I had kept company with in various ports. But on later consideration, I figured they were loose, waterfront chicks of whom I may have been only one of their pickups.

I had been roaming the streets of Port-of Spain long enough to be aware that muggings were practically unknown there, and with so much work and prosperity in the port, the White Carib was not popular with waterfront workers. Strong rays of tropical sunlight struck my face from between the curtains and broke my deep, heavy sleep.

Thankfully, I was not in a hung-over state and met the dawn with a mind to get out of town before the *Loke* returned in ten days' time. It was around 7am and very few cars or carts could be heard in the street.

I lit up a cigarette and lay my head back leisurely on the pillow. My body was tingling with a sense of adventure, and the idea of leaving town became the focus of my thinking. Getting out-of-town and out-of-sight became a priority. Losing my kitbag had its bright side. It gave me more freedom of movement.

Peering at the pockmarked mirror, this man of leisure took a slow shave to play the part, and now smooth-skinned, I walked down after leaving the key in the door. Putting my right foot forward, I set a course to the railway station, stopping only at the market.

The market always opened very early, and I bought myself a strong canvas handbag. The dregs of alcohol had left me with a thirst, so out into the street I went to search for the donkey carter with his wagon of coconuts. He handed me a soft, fresh one for the price of one penny, and I truly enjoyed emptying its milk down my gullet.

I bought a small cluster of bananas off another cart, placed it in my new bag and was off, nicely refreshed with hunger pains yet to gnaw. Then I studied a large island map at the train station. The town of San Fernando looked at a good distance.

That would do me fine. With the thought of a mystery tour in my sights, I booked a ticket to San Fernando at the far end of Trinidad. The engine steamed in, pulling shorter carriages than those back home in the UK. When I stepped aboard, I found no compartments. The seating was more like that of the London Underground or the New York subway, with people facing each other from long benches. Seated just about middle on one side, I faced a cross-section of island commuters. Obviously, most were working people and regular travellers.

As we chugged further into the countryside, I was attracted very much by the panoramic changes of scenery, from tall, elegant groupings of banana plants to squared ditches of paddy fields. Students made up a number of the train travellers. It seemed to me that the Negroid-type preferred to sell his labour rather than take to agricultural husbandry.

For this reason, I learned later that Asian Indians were imported from the East under British administration, and these people preferred making home sweet home beside their cultivated rice paddies, and no doubt gardening vegetables alongside tropical fruits for sale on the side

By observing the East Indian student children on the train, one sensed that the attitude of the new generation was not that interested in rice or mango plantations. Town jobs seemed to be more appealing. Altogether, these healthy West Indian islands seemed to boost the well-being of its people.

Like everywhere, there were a lot of young jobseekers in the train, and the remark I overheard from a young black man, sitting opposite me, caused me to realise that job competition was similar everywhere. After checking the daily newspaper, he remarked to a friend sitting next to him "look at these adverts. They are always asking for young Chinese and Indians." The only conclusion I could draw was that these two races were educating themselves into the employer class, maybe on a small scale, but were providing employment for their own.

After about fifteen stops, we pulled into San Fernando, the second largest city after the capital. I didn't waste time on a long walkabout to try to find a moderately priced hotel. With a good supply of Trinidad currency, I entered the first hotel I set eyes on.

It looked classy, but if the rent was too steep, I would book for a single night and move elsewhere. Stepping through the foyer, I had no need to worry; the room prices were at a reduced rate, very much so, and

I gladly paid for a week's berth. The neutral face of the European, who took my cash over the desk, would be in his forties.

He kept a surprisingly pale face considering there was no lack of sunshine around, and within twenty-four hours I learned from the maitre d' in the dining room that the hotel was run and owned by two Polish brothers, obviously Jewish refugees from Hitler's Europe. The maitre d' was an Indian past his thirtieth year, who looked and acted very capably like his immigrant parents who had trained him.

I found my room equipped with a private shower and spacey. I was excitedly pleased at gaining a first class accommodation at third class prices.

I then decided to purchase a classy shirt to live the part of a new snob in town; however, that would have to wait until after I had showered and eaten. The Indian maitre d' seemed to be running the show, whilst the brothers handled the visitors at the front counter in turns.

The billiard room, jukebox and bar room plus dining hall were two floors up, giving this combo a special seclusion. Enclosed in walls and big windows, it had a surprising décor, considering that the windows were uncurtained. Perhaps the blue-painted skyline had the effect of cooling unruly drinking.

It seemed the thickset yet short Indian tried to make his guests feel at home. He filled me in with info, and learning he was boss over two younger members of his race and a black lady who kept the place tidy, I called him Boss as his name was Ram, the same moniker as one of his help.

Boss told me that most of the hotel's revenue came from the sale of alcoholic drinks, especially to American GI's stationed at the local army depot, some of whom booked in on the weekends. Whether they were charged full-price for a room, I wouldn't know because I saw no printed tariff on the ground floor desk.

Whilst I waited for my first meal, a choice of curry dishes, I stood at a window near my table and peered down on straw hats pacing the main street. Then a big window on the opposite wall pulled me over, where I saw below there were no bathers on a serene-looking beach with only tame waves washing the white sand.

I found the curried something was surely something super-appetising and counted out fourteen small, square tables awaiting the weekenders. Supping black coffee after a banana split, I lit a cigarette. Boss stood at the far door of the kitchen and passed me a smile as the ceiling fan swirled silently, cutting out humidity from the fragrant, salty beach air.

Dinah, the Afro-island girl, would be in her early twenties and was the only female in the small group working at the hotel. Besides her cleaning tasks, she assisted the teenage Indians. She was as good all around as Boss himself and was called on to serve drinks when he was not around.

She was also as talkative and friendly as him, and since there were no others to chat with that first day, I began to learn about the local asphalt lake and the people who worked there. The following day was Friday, and US soldiers on furlough piled in that evening. Dinah was kept very busy, being called constantly to various tables to serve, one after another.

The two young Indians helped her but since they were still in the apprentice stage, the main coping was done by the waitress. Naturally, she picked up the most tips.

The popular song 'Drinking Rum and Coca-Cola' was rising to the top of the charts in the US, yet in Trinidad it seemed to be an even bigger hit. And that evening it captured most of the pennies in the jukebox slot, whilst, incidentally, most of the drinks that were served were just what you might have guessed – rum and coke. Sung by the famous Andrew Sisters, I can never remember tiring of it myself, although it echoed through every cafe and rum shop in Port-of-Spain on a daily basis.

The lighter-skinned and younger of the two lads helped his mate Ram to sweep and mop the shiny floors and passages. There was no family connection between the three Indians, so they must have been picked up at random by the brothers. The youngest was favoured by them. There must have been something in his extremely good looks and intellectual bearing. He was possibly being trained to be an important staff member.

What made me at ease in my new sanctuary was that there was no toxic curiosity into my personal life, even when I was the sole boarder, and friendship could have been used to do so. Life was just good rapport amongst us, and it was good waking up in the morning to feel that one existed in such a protective atmosphere.

The wealth of San Fernando was accrued from the nearby asphalt lake, so I heard from Dinah. Even though there was a war going on, roads and highways had to be macadamised, and there was a ready market in the USA for asphalt. The town could not be considered a port in the normal sense, as there was only one berth, and that was used for tankers to load up their tanks of tar.

And so settled was I in this comfy hotel that when I strolled around the block, I never lingered in cafes or bars. I didn't seem to fit in a town visited mostly by folks of the farming set. What a difference to the capital which was an out-and-out sailor town with a long history going back to buccaneer days.

I might have missed the sight of a dozen or so ships moored at anchorage, waiting for vacancies at the jetties, plus a harbour full of craft – punts and ferries, pontoons, launches, tugs and barges – many transporting welders and boiler makers, crews and sundry. But I was staying well in pocket and that's what counted.

After the first few days, only the silent beach drew me, and I knew it was safe to wade in, as occasionally youngsters came for a dip. Apart from those excursions, I would saunter to the newspaper shop for some reading matter and slink back to my "exclusive" bar, where I was given service with a smile.

Here gathered white-skinned tipplers. They were the skilled men maintaining the flow of asphalt from the lake and happy-go-lucky GI's carousing away the weekend. The only black I chatted with was the sole female in my hotel. Although I pushed myself into the local rum shop to be as chummy as I usually was, I failed to break into its clannishness.

I took a turn at noon day, swimming in the salt brine before an afternoon meal of curry which was always my favourite dish, and which I could not have enough of it. Like everything else in the hotel, times were as flexible as the guest's pleasure wished.

After drenching myself in salt water and sunshine, I would return to find a group of British oil workers from the refinery, and after first introductions, they would request my presence at the table. When I drank with these oilmen, my glass was constantly refilled with whatever I was drinking, and they would not take no for an answer.

If they twigged I had deserted ship, I was certainly unaware of it. When they were in their cups, they let me know they made top cash within the safety of the shoreline. They were real gents and made it known that it was a pleasure to pay drinking money to a man who earned his living stoking furnaces of a steamer in tropical waters. With open reports of shipping losses on the island daily, they were well-aware that enemy submarines were still lurking beneath the calm waters of the Caribbean Sea.

Being pleased with my cash reserve, I rebooked my room for yet another fortnight. Being without a romantic female partner, this was an odd decision; however, it was a sensible move to give my health a full recuperation, now that I had succumbed to cheating a legal shipping contract. If I could nurse my cash through a long leave and successfully rejoin another vessel, there would be plenty of time to act the playboy.

Usually I did little navigation of the streets, spending many daytime hours on the beach at the back of the hotel. Only on one special day did I spend most of the time in the avenues, together with most of the townspeople. Carnival time was making its annual rounds.

Days before the carnival, the hotel staff was excited with the coming event. The two young help related the thrill of past carnivals and insisted I must be a part of the bystanders. Possibly the tranquil atmosphere of the town had reined in their young spirits, and this was a time when they could let loose. The prospect of the colourful street parade had them gripped with anticipation to a point of fever in the way they described past parades.

I returned my loyalty to them by joining the throng of onlookers when the day arrived. Reasoning that I was the only one boarding at the hotel at the time, my absence would ensure that all the staff could make it a holiday.

Yes, I think the staff worked well together and made my stay too much of a pleasure to make me want to leave. Dinah, for instance, always made me feel at ease when serving me drinks. She carried no chip on her shoulder against white folks and gave me an insight into the lives of the oil workers, most of whom had eloped with local girls.

She shared their quarrels in sympathetic tones. There was no doubt that overindulgence of alcohol went with big earnings. Even a balmy, tropical climate could not prevent family upsets, and I felt family quarrels were a universal tag on marriage.

In conversation she spoke to me with more open confidence than the Indians, who preferred being more restrained. Not that they kept me in the dark about local goings-on, but they must have been well-trained not to show the slightest interference in another's business, an excellent trait in itself.

The carnival turned out to be a roaring success. Port-of-Spain, according to talk, held the most splendid local carnival in the whole island. If that was the case, then it must have been a Hollywood super because up to this time, my eyes had not seen anything as spectacular as the San Fernando exhibition.

The actors, prancing and bowing their way along the main street, were clad in more colours of the rainbow than existed. Appropriately spaced between the weaving and dancing talents of both sexes were just as colourful and noisy a bunch of musicians as you could find, yet having a rhythmic beat in harmony with the dancers and prancers.

There was body language behind the masked entertainers that locals seemed able to read. Personally, I was at a loss, especially in the meaning of grotesque, enormous hats that weaved and bowed to some rhythm that carried mystical messages from some past culture. The participants must have counted for one half of the population, whilst the other half looked on.

I took the same childish enjoyment of waving at masked actors from the kerb. On either side of me, voices were erupting with enthusiastic cheering, as were the three Indians from the hotel on the opposite side of the street. With a joyful gleam in their eyes, they must have been hypnotised by the teasing quality of the music, or they understood the language of the dancing, which was new to me.

With just a few days left before departing this cloistered world, I cancelled all beach slumming and kept close to my hotel. I was seriously considering Jock Decker's guidance of finding myself a steamer and shipping out whilst I still had some banknotes.

It was time I made my way back to the main port. Rent was up on Friday morning, the ideal time to depart before getting involved in any weekend drinking bout that might occur. Rising early Friday morning, into the canvas bag went what little clothing I had bought, and I went down for my last breakfast.

Later, after leaving the table, I left a small tip for whoever cleaned my room and was off to the rail station, nursing the taste of bacon and eggs in my mouth. I had not long to linger for the train – just enough time for a coffee, a smoke and the purchase of a newspaper.

The paper was still folded under my arm when I entered the train and sat myself comfortably on the long bench. Then I spread it across my knees. A fresh sense of insecurity caused an intense attack of anxiety at the headlines facing me. The lead article had it all.'108 seamen loose on the island' it read, and in smaller print 'Police would track them down and return them to their ships'. This sudden news did not upset my breakfast really, just jolted the intestines a might. I had made the right move in time. Upon arrival in the capital, I decided I would lose myself in the American Club.

Still on the train, I turned my eyes from a pair of young chicks sitting opposite; there was more serious business to consider. Presently, I got into conversation with an American soldier, sitting next to me. I was happy for this diversion from more serious personal thinking, and we exchanged opinions about the opposite sex.

Arriving at one particular station, most of the commuters disappeared through the train door. There was no one sitting nearby except the two lassies opposite, and I took advantage of the situation to pass on a few, low words to the soldier. With encouraging words and eye language, I drew his attention to the ladies.

He took the cue, walked across and sidled close to one of them; her response was a big smile, and I knew he would find it easy to negotiate a date. I could not help from overhearing the conversation between the GI and his new girlfriend. The girl carried on about her dad earning a living on a fishing smack.

Just in case he mistook the darkness of her skin for that of a Creole, she pointed out that her father was Portuguese. This brought from him, "Yeah! Say! My grandpa's a fisherman, and he's Portuguese too."

Sitting there, I built a firm fix in my mind to follow the lifestyle of my Dutch hero, Jock, for the remainder of my journey. When I stepped down from the carriage at the other end of the trip, my mind was still absorbed in this dream, and although not a little excited at fronting up at the American Club, I took a straight course to the residential one. There was no problem in getting a vacant room for which I paid a week's rent.

All the faces in the club were strangers to my sight, which was just as well, so I could keep personal plans to myself: secrecy aids success. Most of the rest of the day was spent lounging around my new place and reading magazines that cluttered the veranda.

With no alcohol in my system, I appreciated the midday curry taste of well-cooked meat and veg, followed by some ice cream delight; after which siesta time made up for my early activity. It was then a stroll down to the popular club after evening salad and cold cuts of meat.

The boys sitting on the entrance bench were enjoying an evening zephyr of a breeze; I passed the time of day with them and made a donation towards a bottle of rum. One of the five tars requested that I buy him a bottle of beer instead, and I told him to hang on.

No familiar face drew my attention when the bartend handed me two bottles of beer, and I returned to the long bench to enjoy the lowering sun. Handing a bottle to my new mate, I sat beside him; he told me his guts were on the raw side from a lack of appetite for food and was grateful for the ale.

He turned out to be Norwegian, and by his comments, was a good information centre for ships lying at the nearby wharf. I kept my ears flapping as I plied him with a couple more beers. Drawing him out, I learned that a ship by the name of the *Lido* needed a fireman.

That was all I wanted to know. I decided to give this Norwegian craft a visit the following morning. As it was now Friday, it was important that I board early morning before the skipper took his weekend shore leave. I left the bench and walked the streets in the cool of the evening.

I did not want to lose myself drinking in a bar and turned a corner to the melodic sounds of a calypso group. This backstreet quintet consisted of a singer and four musicians. They stood on a small stage in the middle of a green, locked between housing, and I joined the hundred or so in attendance.

The band was made-up of young people of East Indian origin whilst the singer was a typical Trinidadian. Rhyming ditties put to music the latest news about West Indian society. One song I memorised, thanks to repeats, was a satire on the influx of labour to Trinidad from smaller islands to grab the job market.

It went like this – 'You come here in a little fishing boat, and you land on the wharf like a bag of potatoes.' and ended, 'Small island man, go back to where you come from.' Encores were continually requested for this song in particular, which reflected the feelings of the local people.

The musical group deservedly received enthusiastic approval for the two hour concert. It also made me feel one of the crowd. I lingered around under a full moon, meaning to mingle with the young locals, but I had to admit they lost me in cultural small talk.

Most were of the academic set. They were definitely nursing an island pride, and I was at a loss to reply to their intellectual conversation. Some must have been part of Trinidad's elite; however, they made sure I left in a high and pleasant mood.

When passing drinking places on the way home, jukeboxes seemed to give out only one popularised refrain – 'Drinking rum and Coca-Cola'. Nothing could remove it from the top of the pop chart, at least not on the island of Trinidad.

Weary, I slept with a pretty settled mind eager for morning so I could become a new crew member on the *Lido* which was on the familiar bauxite run, and I could maybe meet up with old shipmates. The sooner I joined, the sooner I would lose the shadow of the harbour master which seemed to hang over me. When men spoke of the mysterious Mr Gomez, I really couldn't grasp why they mentioned his name in such low, serious tones, and that was why he appeared so shadowy in my mind's eye. Yet, on the face of things, the only problem I might have was with the immigration department.

The residence's veranda looked out on the harbour since this club was built on a rise, and before digging into my breakfast of bacon and eggs, the sight of so many ships chased away any job problems. Half of those vessels down there could be looking for firemen or sailors. Aroma from the fresh bread rolls at the table started me feeling good.

I left the table without lighting up in case the cigarette took the papaya taste from my mouth. I felt myself moving back into old discipline and being cleaned up, cared not for socialising but made straight down the hill to the port area. I located the *Lido* as the third ship out of twice that number tied up alongside the jetty near the big club.

The blue and white cross of Norway against a red background sagged

171

from the stern ensign staff, as humidity started to claim the morning. No one was on duty watch as I climbed the gangway, and I made straight for the crew quarters aft. This ship had more shine to it than the *Loke* but was no larger.

There was one sole diner at the mess table, a young fellow about my own age named Scouse, (I had met several by that Merseyside nickname in the past.) and when I queried him if there was still a vacancy for a fireman, he nodded his head and introduced himself as a lad from Liverpool. He told me to grab a cup of coffee from the steam geezer on the bulkhead and sit down with him.

I learned that the steamer burned oil fuel, and when I mentioned that I was a stranger to anything but burning coal, he chuffed me up with, "You'll get the hang of things."

It was before 10am when I went up to the bridge and knocked at the skipper's door. I was invited in when he heard that I was after the job down below, and asked me to produce any document of sea service. I took my worn elastic-bound wallet from the rear pocket of my trews, and when he caught sight of the blue pay book from the *Ingerfem*, he told me to visit the cabin of the chief engineer before he went ashore.

I had planned to convince the deucer that the master of the *Loke* had failed to leave my discharge with the agent when I paid off sick. I did not proceed halfway through my statement when he looked me straight in the eye and said in clear tones, "It's not unusual for a man to have too much to drink and miss his ship, but if you promise me that you will not allow drink to interfere with your work, I will ask the captain to sign you on."

He must have read the eagerness in my face to comply because he smiled and told me to turn up at the consulate on Monday. I hurried back to the mess, hoping to find Scouse still there. There he was, still the sole body in the mess room, and I passed on the good word.

He stalled for a minute as if he was developing a short briefing to pass on before I stepped ashore. We took two coffees together, and he told me I was welcome to stay for dinner, provided I didn't mind eating boiled fish. When I nodded, he explained that the best point in oil-burning vessels was that you had an easy time at sea.

"You could sit on the valve box and read magazines once you had gotten used to regulating the oil fuel valve. Apart from that, these jobs are not that easy going in port. Not like coal burners. The engineers work you the full eight duty hours. You are either painting machinery or helping the engineer to repair it."

I didn't buck at this. Every job is uncomfortable to kick off until you get used to the routine, and with experience I could offer myself for work on different types of vessels. Right then all I wanted was a weekend spree to release my tension of insecurity.

We had dined alone, as all hands were lying in their bunks after a Friday night binge in the rum shops. Whilst my new mate went to change his clothes to come ashore with me, I felt rich with $20 in my pocket, and all I needed to buy were work shoes of the lighter type and some work pants. On this job short trews would do. It was also a nice feeling that I would be starting the trip with a good shipmate.

We both strolled to the canteen for a sociable. During ship talk he told me that the *Lido* was replacing the vessel that was sunk seven weeks before on the bauxite run. Then leaving my mate that sticky, hot afternoon, I made it back to the other club. The effect of a couple of beers prompted me to want a nap.

By the time I neared the place, the uphill walk had not felt very strenuous after all. The adventurous side of me wanted to continue the ascent. From my first day of arrival here, I had often wondered what existed on the hill looking down on the port.

Wearing little – only a T-shirt, shorts and good sandals – upwards I climbed on the way to the green summit. I realised that this was the kind of exercise I needed and increased my leisurely climb to a more vigorous one. Eventually, my feet were no longer treading streets but following windy, steep lanes.

Narrow tracks came next, and without looking back, I found my feet tracing dust on pathways, sometimes losing the tracks for a long minute. The sound of streams and rivulets soon entered my ears. Even as I slackened pace towards the brow of the hill, I turned about to view the port's panorama.

However, trees were preventing me from a complete view, so up to the summit I continued, where I would take another look. Wooden habitations merged into shacks, and the shacks began to space out more. There were knock together timber houses, but the people I passed looked healthy and certainly not ill-fed or poor.

I responded to friendly nods and salutations from men with wide-brimmed hats. I saw people throwing scraps of food to fowl, which wandered all over the place. Then I came up on a small stall and this overall friendliness urged me to start a conversation with a shopkeeper standing at an open doorway. I neared him, and looking through the gap he allowed at his entrance, my eyes fixed on loaves of bread sitting on the counter behind him, in company with machetes and the other sundries of a knockabout general store on a small scale.

With a growing smile on his face, he socialised readily with me and allowed me to lean against the outer wall close to the doorpost his own shoulder was leaning against. I took time to ease off and looked back at the slope I had ascended. In its way the tranquillity of pigs and geese rooting around in a background of palm trees gave my sight a glimpse of paradise.

Here I was, with my back resting against a board wall with my knees slightly bent, maybe a mile plus from the island's metropolis, yet I felt I had been transported to another Caribbean island. A customer with a wide straw hat appeared from under the front of a nearby tree, and the proprietor welcomed him into his store.

When his wife left the counter to go through a rear curtain to fetch something requested for the new arrival, the boss joined that person in conversation. The words he used were not English, and noticing my curiosity, I was told that up in these hills, they communicated in a patois going back to slave-holding days.

I wondered if it was a mix of African and Carib which was used as a protection against early Spanish slave masters. I recalled that on the island of Curacao, natives spoke in their own patois, Papiamento, probably grounded in a language from another part of the African continent.

Waving to my new acquaintance when I left his doorway and sauntering around, I found myself on the topmost elevation, so there was only one way to go and that was a pleasant stroll downhill. I came to a clearing and sat myself on thick grass to take in the view of the whole city of Port-of-Spain.

The upward sight of the harbour was more colourful if you can call variations of greenery colourful. Perhaps this colour is so restful to the sight that one appreciates nature to the full. What was revealing was the tremendous amount of shipping anchored in the harbour. I realised that here, at the top of the South American continent, was an important point in the allied war effort; a place where ships were repaired, bunkered, provisioned, and where big convoys of ships formed. An elderly straw hat, sitting on a rattan chair on the veranda of his bungalow, lifted his hat to me and passed an invitation smile.

This smile lured me to join him in talk when he proudly stated that he was a carpenter by trade and had constructed his own dwelling. He said it was nice to meet a white person making a trek into these parts as so few did and showed me around his two large rooms.

One was a combo kitchen-living room, divided from the bedroom by a curtain of thin, clean canvas. The furniture was sparse, but his two teenage offspring, a lad of around 16 years and his sister a bit more mature, looked the picture of health.

Although no words were passed when this pair acknowledged me with faint smiles, it was not just their superb builds and complexion that drew my attention, but it was also their composed, relaxed attitude, played out against the whitish timber in an airy room. A wide open window with a fly screen gave one an impression of a painting.

My host poured me a tot of rum and invited me to sit out on the veranda where he spread his arm in a half-circle. By this motion and a suggestive voice, I understood that he had a sizeable piece of ground to feed his pigs and chickens. Presently I left this family and their home. And overall, I felt I had thoroughly enjoyed the afternoon ramble, and proceeding downhill, I timed it nicely to catch the evening meal at the hostel.

That evening at the US Service Club by the waterfront, I came across a familiar face. It was the Latvian fireman, Lett, who had paid off the *Loke* in Swansea in early August of 1942. He was now sailing aboard an American vessel on the bauxite run between Chaguaramos, Trinidad and Mobile, Alabama. He insisted on buying me drinks the whole night, and I retired groggy from the world. Moneywise, I still held most of my cash. This gave me a good feeling since I could now enjoy a few Sunday drinks before turning up at the Norwegian consul on Monday.

In the meantime, my body decided on a long lie-in the following morning. The cigarette drug was handy, and once in a while I reached over to a nearby chair and blew blue rings to my furniture. My appetite remained nil when I arose in late morning and sauntered to a rum shop near the market for a hair of the dog.

The bar had few customers at the club when I returned, so I took to my mattress again and was horizontal until near 5pm dinner. By this time I was in healthy form and enjoyed a mixed cold salad. At the hostel there was a group of fresh lodgers, and after the meal all hands took seats out on the veranda.

This boded well for me. Instead of returning to the bar, I spent the whole evening spinning yarns with these boys and the next day woke up good and sober. I stepped out, digesting a pleasant breakfast of bacon and eggs and directed my feet to the market. Carrying new work boots and a light quality pair of work trews in a canvas bag, with my other hand I reached around to my rear pocket to feel the bruised wallet enclosing my seagoing documents.

There must have been a morning tide since a pleasing breeze thinned early humidity as I looked at the Coat of Arms of Norway above a typical shop front door. As might be expected, this consulate was a small affair. It was reassuring to find the captain of the *Lido* there behind the counter and all ready to sign me on, and due to my having only recently left my ship, a medical was waived.

The skipper was kind enough to give me a lift in his taxi, and I turned my feet to the crew quarters as soon as I scaled the gangway. The crew were still enjoying an extension of their 10am coffee break in the mess room, and as soon as I was shown my cabin, I joined them and heard the news that we would not shift to the anchorage until the following day, which gave everyone a final chance of shore leave.

A message was passed to me from the Second Engineer that I could spend the rest of the day cleaning my cabin. By early afternoon I was on my way to the club to spend whatever cash I had left over. Lying back on my bunk that night, I congratulated myself on not having to front up to the harbour master Gomez for leaving the *Loke*.

I felt that it had been an agreeable six week break and a wise move to escape to San Fernando. In a normal sense my $200 had not been wisely spent; however, had I stayed in Port-of-Spain, my cash would have slipped away in a third of the time. Vibrant ports encourage one to follow a pattern of orgies and wild spending.

Promptly, I entered the engine room with my three mates at 7am the next morning, and the duty engineer soon let me know he wanted his pound of flesh. On coal burners one fast became used to hard, physical slogging along with an overuse of sweat glands, and while sailors lost their appetite in the tropics – but not stokers and coal-trimmers. We never lacked a big appetite.

During that long 8-hour day of painting and brassoing in the steamy engine room, I gained little appetite to renew these activities. These sorts of light duties under the watchful eye of an officer cause more stress than a hard day's work.

If it hadn't been for the local church sending me a ten shilling note from a collection, I would have stayed on board that night so I would not miss the early morning sailing time, but with the thought of a few cold beers at the club, I was down the rope ladder and into the liberty boat with the rest.

At 6pm we scrambled into the launch and were deposited near the club. I entered to find it jam-packed. Whilst waiting to be served at the bar, I took an attentive view from my high stool and turned this attention to a group in a state of merrymaking. The Latvian ex-shipmate of mine from the *Loke* was among them, and he caught my eye the same time I spotted him and waved me over.

The group were all leaning on ledges of open windows, enjoying the fresh evening sea breeze, but the reason for the party was seated. They were too busy reminiscing for introductions to be much of anything, but the Latvian briefed me. I gathered that the seated person was paying off with a leg injury and was awaiting a boat to give him passage back to New York.

Here I was not allowed to spend my British currency note, which was usually exchangeable behind the bar, and my old shipmate kept feeding me duty-free whisky. The last thing I remember was falling asleep on one of the bunks in one of the cubicle rooms at the club.

I awoke with moonlight slanting through a small window, and this gave me sufficient light to guide me to the electric light switch. My head throbbed, and confused thoughts were trying to make sense out of the situation; anything to let me know where the hell I was. And then things began to register after seeing familiar faces; there were five others in the room, one occupying the other bed, whom I recognised as the New York bound patient with the bandaged leg.

Others were sprawled out on the timber flooring. I needed another drink in order to plan out what course to take in this new misfortune because I realised that my vessel had definitely sailed after midnight. I was unlucky, so I switched off the light and dived into bed before anyone else took it over. My throbbing skull melted into oblivion, as I began the mental battle of surviving the next days, and I soon joined the others in slumber land.

The sun had chased the moon over the horizon when I awoke some hours later. An alarm clock sitting on the window ledge told me it was 7.30 am, yet not a soul in that room moved.

I didn't need any energy to get up; my throbbing head drove me out of bed and on a second search for the hair of the dog, I found a huge snorter from a large whisky bottle and downed it before anyone else awoke with the same urge.

I sat on the bed, and believe it or not, peering around I spotted yet another 'spiritual' find. This time it was a bottle, half-full lurking in a shaded corner. Well, I was sufficiently aware now that this was the day for reckoning with the shipping master, and I stopped the urge for another wee dram. I had no intention of throwing the towel in and joining the bums on the bench at the club entrance.

The ailing person was still asleep, so I sneakily grabbed his soap and towel nearby and went outside to the communal washbowls. I was lucky to meet another there to whom I unfolded my undesirable state, and he advised me to call at the ship agents first before reporting to Mr Gomez, the harbourmaster.

There was time before the ship agents opened at 9am, so I decided to stroll to the early morning market and refresh myself with a coconut drink. Then I realised that the only currency I had was the 10 shilling note. I called into an early hour rum shop to be welcomed by a big, black man, so I decided to sit at his table. He happened to be one of those whom I had met in a cafe after I first jumped ship.

He asked me if he could buy me a drink. I told him I needed to change my British note and would he ask the counter man if he could change it into Trinidad dollars? He rapidly complied, and I told him to get two rum and cokes. At this point my new resolve of keeping to the straight, collapsed after inhaling fumes from other tipplers.

Small talk revealed that the all too infamous white Carib had done the same to him as to myself. He had either gone underground or out of town — good riddance! I had left the club with a splitting headache and that first livener had released all my tension and had put a smile on my face as I related the San Fernando experience to my companion.

I also buoyed him up, expressing my appreciation for the tropical plantations I saw on my rail journey, and the realisation that Trinidad was no small island. This conversation helped to fill in time, but as he had to go to the docks, I removed myself as well and returned to the market to fill up with coconut juice; hoping the agent would smell no accusing giveaway on my breath.

I had a spot of luck at the ship agent's office; the pilot boat had returned my seaman's documents. Scouse had probably thought I had intentionally left the ship and was kind enough to make sure I was in possession of the papers that would ensure me getting another job. The agent told me two days earnings would be paid out to me when the *Lido* returned in a week or two and advised me to visit Mr Gomez.

As I ambled off to the harbour master's office. I felt pleased with my progress so far. Dark clouds had thinned out a lot since my leaving the club, and I was sailing in the stream so to speak. As there was always a shortage of qualified seamen in these out-of-the-way places, who knew, maybe Mr Gomez might offer me a choice of jobs. Perhaps he was not as bad as people made out.

Although the rocks in my head had melted as I entered the big doors, intuition told me good luck was not 100 per cent on my side. It was the first time I had entered there, and it did have a foreboding atmosphere, a sort of gravity in the silent, open-eyed faces sitting around. If only I had my canvas bag with my belongings in it to grip onto, I would feel a cut above the others, who were all schooner-rigged.

I drew my documents from my back pocket, placed them on the low, wide counter and soon drew the attention of Mr Gomez himself. His face did not show any unkindness as he deigned to spread his paunch over the low counter and lend me his ears. I unfolded my story of having missed my vessel through persuasive intoxication, and there was no hope for me being retained as a crew member since my papers had returned with the pilot boat.

He stepped back to consult one of the two clerks scribbling at small desks. I noticed a revolver holstered onto a thick belt drawn around a Wallace Beery belly. He returned to give me attention, providing me no clue as to what had been decided with my fate except to direct me to sit on a long bench against the wall. His tone of voice like his face sent no signals.

The effects of the livener at the rum shop were wearing off, and I felt as flat as a punctured tire. My inner body seemed to evaporate into limbo, and so I started taking interest in my surroundings to keep my mind alert for any job opportunity. Sitting opposite me were three hefty seamen, Norwegians by the look of them. They sat silent with half-bowed heads.

The tallest of the trio, a blonde Viking, was stirred out of his inertia by the voice of Gomez. He barked at him to direct his feet to a certain vessel. The captain was waiting to sign him on. His voice tone was not unfriendly but was meant to be obeyed. The man nodded his head, said goodbye to his comrades and left at the door; however, he was blocked by another stalwart dressed in the gold braid of a captain. As soon as this new face came in, Gomez gave him a friendly wave forward, and the Viking departed. I watched him place a satchel on the counter, and he started to remove documents. I decided that he wasn't interested in my plight, drew a cigarette packet from a shirt pocket and lit up. My attention was then diverted to the doorway by another important looking visitor.

A fresh uniform was wrapped around a short, yet sturdy body, very dark in the face even for a Black. As he walked up to the counter, I tried to figure out who he could be; he didn't have the carriage of a seaman, and he showed an air of importance. I would soon find out because Gomez now found time to turn his attention to myself.

I didn't have long to wait. The uniformed man introduced himself as the chief immigration officer and instructed me to follow him outside. I hadn't gone five yards when a brown uniform stepped in front of me, guided me to the rear of a paddy wagon and requested me to step inside. The steel doors shut out the dazzling white sunlight, and I could hear an iron bar being placed into a bracket from the outside. This was getting serious.

DETENTION

I was the sole passenger with no one to converse with except my own thoughts, and as no intelligible pointer came from my mind, I had nothing to hope for except to sit out this mystery tour in silence. Soon the wheels stopped, the iron bar released and the dark interior lit up as the doors were opened. I found myself stepping out at a police station.

I was respectfully grabbed by the upper arm, guided by my guard into a narrow passage and then entered a bare looking office halfway down. I found myself standing in front of a counter and was requested to produce some identification; some scribbling went on, and I was led off to a larger wing of the building and locked up in a communal cell.

In a way, I did not feel too depressed because at least the mystery was over. In a secluded office, the immigration official later briefed me as to how I stood with the law, and I was relieved to learn that a charge would be brought against me for overstaying my leave in the colony. My case would be held at the local court the following day, which was not too long to wait.

I was far less discouraged than I thought I would be. The five other prisoners in my cell were quite sociable without being nosey and freely passed on information. They explained that if I had cash or cigarettes, some conveniences could be gotten by calling to one of the guards. I inspected the two toilets which I found clean. The taste of the curried rice and yam meals was acceptable, if not too filling, and late that evening our group had increased to ten. No one interfered with me except to pass on useful tips, and everyone generally kept in groups of twos and threes.

Before lying down for the night, I had come to the conclusion that most of the inmates were familiar with the place and being on remand kept themselves the best to prepare their court cases. They looked like your normal citizens, and outside the walls, I would never have taken them for criminal types. Later, I didn't find it too difficult to sleep on the stone slabs, perhaps being in a warm zone helped. I found it more uncomfortable in coolers in the more northerly regions, when I was occasionally picked up for lying around drunk.

As slits of dawn pierced the high, tiny windows, electric lighting was switched on, and the place came alive with low chattering. Locals began sitting up in pairs, probably to discuss their impending court cases. Heavy footsteps became louder and louder as they echoed along the passageway, and conversation became more animated. Into view strode a most robust police officer with the healthy yellow-black face of a mulatto.

Jangling keys were removed from his belt at the gate, and when the gate opened, two trustees wheeled in trays of bread slices next to a tumbled heap of outsized mugs. The luckiest two grabbed the top and side handles of a light metal container and poured out some steamy, brown liquid. Even heavy smoking didn't dent in me the rich smell of cocoa wafting into my nostrils. It was a light-hearted affair for a police station with no lining up, and I was not backward in picking up the well-baked bread and my mug of hot cocoa.

One of the trustees must have noticed the happiness I took from dipping the bread in the cocoa and with a smile, offered another of those thick bread slices which I accepted. Maybe the other detainees could not be bothered eating properly because they were expecting friends' tastier food later. Whatever the reason for abstaining from breakfast, their main interest was definitely in the direction of the guard.

These prisoners stormed the gaoler with questions concerning their particular cases. Their familiar and seductive tones were met only with insulting rebukes. Nevertheless, they didn't cease to band together and pester him. Behind the bellowing malevolence of the officer, I sensed that the aggro attitude was a put on. In his high-handed shouting, there was a humane undertone, which was barely detectable but well-sniffed out by the inmates.

When an opinion was requested by one cellmate, regarding the outcome of his court case, the guard, placing a thumb inside his wide John Brown belt in a pose of authority, bawled out: "You rogue and vagabond; you will be put away for three months!" And later on when I was taken to court, this same prisoner preceded my case and received just that sentence – three months as a rogue and vagabond.

One of the inmates advised me to purchase a packet of twenty cigarettes in reserve should the court not favour my release, in which case I should hide them in my trouser lining just beneath the belt. He had little scissors and directed me where to cut the thread on the tuck of the plaited lining surrounding the top rim of the trews. I accepted his offer to split my hem at the stitching, and altogether manoeuvred seventeen cigarettes through the lining.

I was placed in the box that morning and was puzzled at the charge I was forced to accept. "The accused has overstayed his leave in the colony and will be transported to Kingston, Jamaica for trial." When being escorted to a waiting van outside, I wondered what further mystifying procedure lay ahead. There were no windows in the sturdy, steel bus that I was transported in, and then when I stepped out of the rear door, I looked up above two wooden doors and read HIS MAJESTY'S PRISON.

My escort led me to a narrow side entrance near this fortress-looking front and passed me onto another guard with three other prisoners. He turned the key in the door lock and allowed us to pass through; on no occasion were handcuffs used. The guard was last, ducking his head under the low door, and then took the lead, guiding us through a wide passage in the eerie silence.

The echoing boots of our leader led us further along a narrow passage. This short walkway led us into a large, high-roofed interior with a mass of electric lighting. I joined the tail end of a queue of some forty to fifty men. On both sides of this inner area were cells, and looking up I noticed two more tiers duplicated on the first and second floors. Security men, spaced well apart on either side, leaned against the walls. I felt at ease here, as there were no guards barking orders as I had expected. The only sound was the spirited conversation among the inmates themselves in low tones; all of them coloured males except myself.

It seemed that the officers in charge allowed for a bit conversation to ease tension. Then slowly moving forward, progress became stalled for a long five minutes, and all this time I heard a small voice in a foreign accent calling out "give me cigarette, give me cigarette." The cells to my left were a distance of about ten feet, and my hearing located a small hole in the upper part of a door. When I asked those near if they knew from whom the voice came, the question was passed along, and as heads jerked back, I learned it was from a jailed German captain who had scuttled his vessel across the Suriname River at Paramaribo.

Something subconscious prompted me to fumble beneath my trousers belt, and I drew out a couple of fags. A black face looked over my shoulder and seemed to have an idea of what I was about to do and warned me that one of the screws would get upset. The line was still halted, and talk buzzed more freely and without hesitation. I walked directly over to the talk hole and popped the smokes through.

I returned swiftly into line and asked myself why I had done such a hasty and reckless action for someone who was the enemy and had made himself infamous by preventing vessels from going directly upriver. I feel, however, that the subconscious gives orders for a good reason. After all there might be someone in Germany giving my prisoner brother the pleasure of a cigarette for the same reason.

When there were only seven or eight men in front of me, a guard advanced and requested for me to remove my T-shirt before reaching interrogation. At the desk identification was confirmed and tattoos noted down, and then I was told to turn left and replace my shirt. I was led out of the building alone, and I realised of course that I was still under remand and, therefore, would not be jailed in the main prison building.

I followed my guide back to the entrance but turned left down a side passage and came out onto a cobblestone square, shiny with use. To the right again I faced a big, wooden door, though not as massive as the entrance. Then I was told to step through one of the low, poky doors on the side, and the guard left me in another compartment of the jail, locking the door behind him.

I took in the view of my new surroundings, and the first thing that stood out was that there were no guards and certainly no lack of space. I walked forward some more, and between the very high walls, there were about twenty men – some without footwear, pacing the length of the yard in groups of twos and threes, some more leisurely than others but most in conversation.

To my left the main body of prisoners sat on long benches aside long, bare board tables, taking the shade under a zinc roof high enough to divert heat, and a space was made for me to sit with those others gathered around. Most of the questions directed at me were: "Did Gomez put you here?" "What was the charge?" "Have you got a butt of a cigarette on you?"

"I'm supposed to be sent to Jamaica for trial," I replied. Ripples of laughter were followed by, "That's what he tells all of us, and most of us have been stuck here for over six months, what a joke." Looking around I realised that there were five coloured men at the most, the rest being white, and by their familiar talk and disposition, they seemed to be men having to do with the seafaring business, which I soon found out to be so. "How many men are there in this compound?" I asked and was told that there were sixty-five. One titbit I reserved at the back of my mind was that the guard never entered your cell. It was your private domain; they just stuck their head around the door to see all was OK.

I learned that the evening meal was the same as breakfast, hunks of bread and a cup of cocoa. It was served at 4pm and at 4.30pm we were locked in until 7am the next morning. That evening when the food trolley came around, I was handed a fork and spoon of very light aluminium and a small pudding bowl of the same quality but very battered, and those were my personal possessions. I did not regret being locked in my cell that evening, as early as it was. I had a lot of thinking to do.

After the screw had clamped the thick door of my cell, the first thing I did was to search around the walls for a loose brick or stone to hide my cigarettes. I found nothing moveable; however, there were several niches to choose from plus a Swedish bible. I was pleased with a cell that was not too confined; perhaps those on remand were allowed a few extra feet.

The setting sun faced a lengthwise window which would give me an hour's reading. If it wasn't for the big wall, I would have had light until the sun dipped half an hour on. One good item I had on me which had been allowed was a box of matches, and I soon got to work carefully removing the smokes hidden in my trousers. There was no ledge to place them on so I had to place them beneath my wooden bunk and covered them with a small towel I found on the bunk. Then I lit up, got myself seated comfortably on the palliasse and leaned back against the wall.

Many times I had thought of making an effort to cut the number of cigarettes I smoked; however, it was during times such as these that I found it invaluable to smoke so that thoughts slowed down for a quiet intake of the current situation. These thoughts sometimes came to some agreement on immediate problems. Items of importance surfaced in my mind. I would need a book to escape the reality of my present situation, and the desire to look on the bright side got me thinking that cigarettes were like gold in this place.

There was a small washbasin in the corner of the room, but I had no soap. Then an idea hit me that perhaps I could hide my cigarettes under the recess of the basin and carry out maybe two or three at a time. If no soap was dished out to me the following day, I planned to bargain the use of some soap and a razor in exchange for a cigarette. I dropped off to sleep, wondering if I would be allowed a book from the library; prisons had libraries, didn't they?

The next day, I was awake for maybe twenty minutes. The room was lit up with the rising sun enough to make things clear, when I was prompted to make another effort in rubbing my hands over the walls, and yes, this time I came across a loose fragment of stone which I must have overlooked the first time, and I hid the fags behind it. Just in time too because heavy boots and the sound of dangling chains approached, and one could hear wooden doors thumping against the wall in other cells.

There was no need to make my bunk as I had not needed the blanket folded at the base of my palliasse. Then I joined the pisspot procession down the passage to the toilets at the far end of the square where I washed the pot out and returned. After placing it under the bunk, I went as far away from the door as I could, turned my back on it and furtively positioned three cigarettes into my hiding place in the rim of my pants.

We were all ushered out of our cells with a sharp signal by the guards. I had my hand clamped on my little bowl, fork and spoon. When I approached a new face and asked the breakfast time, I was told it was 7.30am, and he informed me that there was 20 minutes to go. I had splashed my face in the cell and wiped it with the small towel provided.

That would have to do, so I made my way to the toilets and found a group washing and shaving around a circular stone well with several taps.

I pretended to examine another stone basin, quite large and obviously used for washing clothes. But with one eye, I squinted in the direction of the washers, found one raising a German Solingen razor to his chin and bided my time. A couple of men walked off and then another, and seeing my chance, I asked him for a loan of his razor. I thought I had picked a generous face, and I was right. He seemed to catch up onto my state because he handed me a small sliver of soap as well. Before we went out of the door, I held him back and manoeuvred a cigarette from my hiding place and handed him one; he was overjoyed. Then a whistle blew to form a line for breakfast.

The other fellow went ahead of me, whilst I dawdled, and being pleased at the arrangement of the six toilets and other facilities, it seemed the area must have been hosed down by some prisoners in early morning because the concrete floor was still damp. I heard the whistle blow and joined the breakfast line; that dallying had cost me a more forward place in the long snake of men with their bowls held out.

There was not too much talking at the tables as men dipped their hunk of bread into their cocoa. Later seeing the others drift to the corner of the shed where a tap and drain permitted one to wash out the bowl, I followed suit. I had a lot of questions on my mind and sought out the man who had befriended me with soap and razor.

I had spotted him at a table and had asked the person next to me if he knew about him. "That's Sorensen, the Dane," I was informed. "He's been here for four months," I further learned. Wondering where he had gone, I returned to sit on the bench and mingle. At the back of my mind I was thinking where I could find a hiding place to smoke a fag.

Then I passed the time of day with the man next to me, and he seemed eager to enter into conversation by his rushed response. He introduced himself as Spud Murphy, who came from Newport, Wales, yet his accent didn't seem Welsh. I couldn't quite place it. He then went onto say that he had missed a Harrison boat, which I knew always sailed out of Liverpool.

Turning around, I saw Sorensen with three or four others where they were hunched over their table, and I got interested. One of them held small, conical holders of brown paper, whilst the Dane patted the cigarette I had given him. Then he poured the loose tobacco into those paper cups, two of which were sealed by turning over bottoms and tops, whilst a lighted match was stuck in the other corner. I sat down to watch the performance.

Except for the odour of brown paper, they seemed to draw full value out of the cone, sucking it at the bottom, and then passing it around. There was little smoke escaping from the narrow end, and it seemed that one of those cones could last the time it took to enjoy a full cigarette. I watched them cupping hands under the cone for a while, and once the novelty was gone, I returned to speak with Spud.

He filled me in with what went on. The following day, Thursday, you were allowed through the big doors to visit the Salvation Army padre, who had an office there, and he would dole out a bar of soap to each man, and you were then handed a book to read at the same time; if dissatisfied with the title, you could swap it with other prisoners.

I noticed the shade line creeping down the high wall on the opposite side of the yard; then I turned my attention to a pair playing dib-dab-doo inside the overhang of the shed, where the floor was flagstone. They had etched out the square with a sharper piece of one of the stones they were using as counters. The sun line had now reached the bottom of the wall and was slowly advancing along the concrete onto the whitewashed wall. As that white orb rose and slanted over from the shed, I decided that I would enjoy a smoke in the toilets.

I made that fag last for just about as long as I could and enjoyed the fact that there was only one other place in the vicinity to hide away at. When I entered the yard, most of the floor was under sunlight, and men paraded back and fro along the hundred yard length, most of them in shorts. I had only my long trews but, nevertheless, the idea was catching, and I decided to stretch my legs with the rest.

Out of the walkers, I spotted only one black face. It was not long before I fell in step with Sorensen, and soon, like the rest, we passed the time chatting. I learned of the different characters as he picked them out. The only brown man that did the walking exercise was a Panamanian, whom he said everyone liked. The thin, tall fellow strolled between two Danish friends of his the Swede remarked and had been jailed nine months and was taking it bad emotionally, wondering when release would come.

He pointed out the other blacks, consisting of two BG's (British Guianans) – one a young lad of seventeen years and his mate, a small, bony half-Portuguese Black. Both had stowed away on a fishing vessel to seek work with high wages in Trinidad. Of the others there was a Zulu and a West African, both in their twenties and an older, wizened Indian from Calcutta. After an hour's exercise, I decided to sit it out under the zinc roof until the whistle blew for midday eats.

I sat down near Spud to gather more info and mentioned Gomez. I got an earful. "That Gomez is an extremely sly bastard. God knows what he's up to. That poor Panamanian guy has been here for months, and nobody gives a shit about him." Spud himself had been here for three months and told me of his fears. Up to six months ago, he heard that men hardly stayed for longer than a few weeks, but since then no one had been released from detention.

He pointed out the bigger of the two stowaways and referred to him as Jim Jam which brought a smile to my face, as I recalled the golliwog face on a well-known marmalade of that time in the UK. It seemed the Brits must have stuck the name on him. Since the wartime lend-lease agreement between Churchill and Roosevelt, people had been coming from all over the region to work for the American dollar in Trinidad.

My mate passed on unfavourable remarks about the expected meal, saying it was the same monotony every day, always curry and rice. Well, I was ready for it anyway, and when it arrived, I tucked into my little bowl of curried rice and yams with relish. Spud continued to run down the food even as I ate; however, if he had the idea I would pass any on to him, he soon stopped when I showed continuing gusto. The cook certainly knew how to put meat in the gravy at the bottom which I cleaned off with my bread slab. The guard hung around after dinner to make a store of names to see the chaplain.

The only thing I found wrong with the food was there just wasn't enough of it, and Spud never sat beside me for dinner after that. I sat back on the bench to digest and watched the parade of bare legs and torsos as the pacers started up again, most of them wearing the minimum of clothing – short trews and sandals. Had it been the evening, it would have resembled the strollers of any small town in Spain.

I wondered in the following days if Spud seated himself beside a fresh arrival at dinner, hoping the newbie would still be agonising from a bout with the bottle. It seemed to me that many of the prisoners were Scandinavian, the wildest boozers of the lot, followed by the American and British. I would say that in most cases drink was the demon that brought them to this place, and with some negative remarks, Spud might have scored a portion of extra feed.

By moving around and chatting with others, I got the first clue why the harbour master wished us to stay put. It was really an open secret that he was in collusion with the immigration chief in selling seaman's jobs to locals who had cash but little experience, if any. There was always a bunch of really qualified seamen who could not resist the temptation of leaving a ship once they felt they had made enough money on a particular vessel for a few weeks to journey ashore; on British ships one could only draw a small percentage of wages and therefore, less ship jumping. They lived for the bottle and turned up for a job when pockets came up empty. A captain would have definitely preferred them to an untrained seaman.

Later, I had decided to light up a cigarette in my cell, but became drawn to the dib-dab-doh players, as did most of the bench sitters on the front row. Therefore, I got myself a perch at the end of the bench and turning aside, leaned over and lit up, puffing my hands Indian style to make believe I was dragging on old butts. Most of the pleasure came from the fact that I would be one of the very few who was able to have a whiff after the midday meal, when the urge for the weed was strong.

Entering my whitewashed cell after bread and cocoa that evening, the first thing I did was to close the door and rush to the loose brick. With high relief I found the smokes still there, all twelve of them, so now I felt it was true that nobody interfered with one's effects whilst you were away; however, I was still without reading matter so I decided to challenge the Swedish Bible.

I had never been good at cryptic crosswords, but decided to see if I could try and make any sense out of this first page. I read – bygeenel sen var gud og gud var I byggenilsen. I sat on my bunk and thought: I'm not so dumb after all. 'In the beginning was God and God was in the beginning.' Smart me! I tried several more words, but some mental blocks held me up, and I surrendered and was about to throw the bible to the other end of the room, when I decided it might put out the light of one of God's creatures; there were two of them taking a stroll across the room, a big fat cockroach and a smaller one. The prisoner before me must have been in the habit of bringing bread into the room.

My possessions consisted of sandals, long trews, T-shirt and over shirt, plus a single handkerchief, whilst my documents were being held at the main office. I usually left my shirt in the room when I went out in the morning; however, I reminded myself to wear it the following morning to visit the chaplain; fifteen hours without a book is less pleasant than having a read one hour in the early morning and then one hour in the early evening.

After cocoa the next morning, I sat as near the gate as I could, ready for the roll call for a stroll out of the gate to the padre. I watched a few sun lovers pick a place near the far wall where the sun ran down it, and they could sprawl out beneath the early morning rays. Then I heard someone call Jim Jam. I had already realised that that same person was sitting next to me.

He was a big chump of a boy with a real charmer of a face. He had a full clump of curly black hair and resembled the picture on a popular brand of British marmalade (as mentioned earlier). Jim Jam had the big friendly face of a native West Indian. He took no offence when someone shouted his name, and I thought he was an easy-going person to get on with so I chatted with him, and like most British Guiana locals he became very sociable.

Comparing ages, I found he was my own age of 19 years but looked three years younger. Like myself, he was waiting to get hold of soap and informed me that we would be marched out at 10am. He turned out to be intelligent and interesting company. And I felt it unfair to have such a name stuck on him. It would be likely someone from the UK who nicknamed him because that's where the marmalade was sold, but then noticing the West African and the Zulu horsing around and pushing each other in a playful manner, I noticed the mischievous eyes of the Zulu and thought it could be him. Both were young and happy-go-lucky.

The whistle blew. The sun bathers sat up, and there was a general racket; I moved smartly into line thinking there would be a visit for all sixty men. However, it turned out about fifteen of us marched through the big gates into a cobblestone square with offices on both sides. We stood in line opposite a wood and wattle structure. The upstairs section belonged to the Salvation Army.

The guard allowed us up, three at a time. The chaplain, about forty years of age, was a breezy, light-hearted man who passed you a book and a small bar of soap, after which the three descended to allow three others up. And that was it; the gates were opened, and we filed back to our enclosure. The name of my book was called 'Robinson Crusoe,' a tale I had read as a boy but had no wish to exchange it.

Beneath the shade of the dining place overhang, the did-dab-doh game was going on; and another board had been scratched out on the flagstone. The two contestants were bellies to the cold stone and had a good audience. I kept my eyes away, studying whether to join the devout sunbathers, slumming against the far wall. I stripped my shirt and undershirt off, walked over and placed them down for a headrest. Then I changed my mind, left the clothes where they were and joined the strollers' league.

Being leisurely I was overtaken by two others and invited to a walking chat. I felt the benefit of this friendly stroll after the first half hour and promised myself to put in a daily performance. Time went pleasantly by as we passed on interesting info and experiences to each other, plus we got a suntan out of it. The footwork wasn't that active, but neither was it passive. Then the whistle blew for dinner.

I don't know what it is, the way a little sunbathing affects us, but it put me in a optimistic mood when we got locked in that evening. And when I tired myself out reading Robinson Crusoe, I looked forward to a reread of it since his island refuge had a similar climate as Trinidad – at least it seemed so with its background of palm trees. I fell asleep wishing only that I was Rob.

I was now settling in, not being imprisoned long enough to suffer boredom but enjoying the titbits of information around the tables and with spells doing the wall-to-wall walks and talks. Food rations were pretty sparse, but as an afterthought, I am forced to conclude that the sparser the better because in such a hot climate, there would be more than one reason to spark off a riot with any surplus energy.

Not all were sociable here; I was put off talking to the silent Indian after one brief attempt. I think that being married and maybe with a family to keep, he was eating his heart out. He was in the same boat as Spud, except that this man allowed a venomous expression jar his feelings. It was trying for him, as for the other married men, who kept themselves cooped up under the shed, leading an aimless life.

Not that they would have started anything. The spark could be lit between a white American fellow from the South and maybe the West African because that fellow had a troublesome attitude, and it could have drawn in the married men, just as a relief as they fiddled with their thumbs, wondering if the company was still sending a cash allotment to their wives. Then it struck me suddenly; there was only one person who could contact consulates and shipping companies, and that was the Salvation Army chaplain.

A week later, all my cigarettes had been smoked, and I surprised myself that withdrawal pains were not that overwhelming. Perhaps that was because I had a lot of company suffering with me. I found myself being sympathetic to most of the inmates now, including the 2 BG's. They told me they would have preferred to stay in British Guiana; however, it offered little opportunity to get ahead like in Trinidad, and they aimed to get into the big money once they were cleared by immigration. They knew there was a lot against them and were well aware that Trinidadians were trying to deter all other West Indian islanders from entering to keep the labour force more expensive during the American restructuring programme and to ensure their own employment.

Not only were there US agencies hiring civilian personnel, but they also created jobs in the services. Gomez gave himself popularity locally by returning stowaways, and Jim Jam knew this and was very pensive when the matter was brought up.

This tension spilled out in his quite unpleasant attitude to the more fortunate whites. Yes, he did have a chip on his shoulder after all, and our socialising became less frequent. In such a situation, negative vibes were the last thing I desired.

On the other hand, I really never thought Spud Murphy was a bad chap. I don't even think he was that concerned about the food, as he only had a small stature but gnawing thoughts about his faraway wife must have disturbed his mind. She would receive no mail from him, as it was unthinkable that she would even know at what address he was at, and there was the uncertainty as to whether the Society of Friends or the shipping company were keeping her afloat and all this spilled into food friction. The only refuge of thought left to him would be whatever money he had left on the ship when he departed, as this would cover allotment money for a month or two.

One story I heard about a few days after entering the compound was of three men who had spent a week here, and at first I was excited about the news because they were not ordinary men, but men who had been through very desperate circumstances. It was the best yarn going around the week I arrived. These survivors from a raft were picked up in the Harrison Strait, the channel that separated Trinidad from mainland South America, but they were not the victims of enemy action.

They were escapees from the penal settlement of French Guiana, from the notorious Devil's Island. Of course, there was a titbit about the story of the three Frenchies that was passed around quite a lot. On the third day of internment, it was decided by the authorities to give them the ultimate search, and sure enough quite a lot of saleable gold was extracted from three rectums.

I waited for more tales of these three rare species of men who had survived that jungle hell. However, all further talk was speculation on how much gold they had escaped with, and how they came to get hold of the stuff. I had speculations of my own about the precious metal. It was an open secret in the bars of Georgetown, British Guiana that on the upper reaches of the Demerara, there was an area that was fenced in by a South African conglomerate.

It was commonly believed that the reason was that there were oodles of gold in the area; the company, therefore, paid the colony an annual stipend to leave the secluded place unexplored. Not everyone believed this, especially on my ship, where unbelievers outnumbered the others. I'm not sure if I was a mug or not for not turning to the sale of small pieces of gold offered by natives at the corner of shady lanes at very cheap prices, but I did conclude that the three fugitives had first escaped to BG, or British Guiana.

After turning down offers from other readers to swap Robinson Crusoe, my attachment to the book inspired inventiveness in my mind as keen as my hero's. I read it twice over as an escape against a semi-boring existence.

Sadly, not everyone in the camp was friendly, although I found only one who was truly unfriendly, and that was Suwarey, the West African. However, the Zulu youth who played with him was the type I refer to next.

In the talk and actions of the playful, good-looking South African Zulu, I noted something pretty sinister that the smiling face couldn't camouflage, even though he flashed two superb rows of teeth that would have qualified him for a toothpaste advert. Yes, the slim, bronze body had within it a puzzle I failed to work out.

Then there were two other prisoners you felt rude to bring into conversation. They were the type that could almost make themselves non-existent, and it was several days before I even noticed them.

These two Spaniards were as different from one another as you could imagine, and I learned that one of the young men was a doctor, although he looked more like a boyish playboy, being about twenty-four. The other was somewhat nondescript, a little dwarf-like in stature and lacking the refinement of his companion because that is what they were, mere companions brought together by fate in a foreign place, meeting up only to chat in their own language. I soon learned that they had stowed away from Franco's Spain and were on their way to Cuba, when the local authorities caught them and brought them ashore.

Stranger yet was a Welshman, who came from the next valley to my own. He was fit and what you might call a hard case, unafraid to call Suwarey, blackbird, whilst that person remained untroubled and even admired this loner. He was friendly to me in a distant way, and what I learned was that he was a Casanova with the opposite sex.

It seemed the lady who managed the kitchen and rooms in the town's big club was infatuated with him, and this man, who was about twenty-six years old, gave her sexual favours while she had allowed him to live there for free, she being a doughty forty year old. They had split for some reason, and it was rumoured that she had encouraged Gomez to jail him.

And then accidently, I was to break the ice with the loner of loners. This man, who I would say seemed about twenty-eight years of age, was a tall, blonde, well-built man, who never attracted attention or even contact. He walked the wall-to-wall paces; he sat at the table and gave off polite smiles, yet never a word came out of his mouth. Yet, once I saw him speaking with the Spanish doctor and that was about all. Then one time I passed him at a table, far away from the rest as usual, and I made a friendly gesture, and as casually as you like, he invited me to sit down near him, just like that!

In minutes we were chatting away like old friends, and why not, we were both Welshman. What was so strange about it was that it took a month before our associating, even with us living very closely. When I say Welsh, I mean he had Welsh parentage, but his birth place was in Patagonia, a long way down in the Pampas in a southern province of Argentina. I learned that he spoke three languages fluently, but it still was a surprise when he informed me that he had interpreted for the three men who had escaped Devil's Island.

This was my golden chance to hear some inside stories about those intrepid escapees, except I got confused that if he spoke French, then he was a linguist in four not three languages. We drifted into typical small talk. Could he be kidding me? Experience had taught me that with deep-sea mariners, each man was a separate personality, and some had hidden pasts, which general principle told one not to try to unlock.

I learned that he was sailing in the American Merchant Marine. He confided that he was aiming to put in papers to obtain American citizenship when the first chance arose. The first-rate living conditions and big pay packet was preferable to returning to Argentine ships. That night, with plenty of time to think in my cell, a recollection from childhood came back to the Johnny Onion men, who used to come from Brittany to Cardiff in skiffs full of onions which sold well in the valleys. Because Welsh and Brettone were dialects of the same language, they would converse ten to the dozen in ancient Cymric to my mother as she stood on the doorstep. I realised that the three ex-convicts were not typically French at all but from Brittany and that is why my blonde friend could be their interpreter.

Keeping sombre thoughts to myself, I continued to find life not unenjoyable. Here I was in my little, whitewashed cell with fourteen hours of privacy and a few books. The high-barred window welcomed the 6am tropical dawn, and as there were no timepieces in the area as far as I knew, this new world of timelessness had a novel effect on my mind. It was only occasionally that the blanket on the palliasse bunk was necessary. Soap shortage was a minor problem, but with a little extra, one could enjoy two or maybe three showers, a couple of which were always available near the latrines.

Since there was no work required, it meant an A1 rest up for the single men, but maddening boredom for the married seamen. If one's attitude could overcome the monotony and quiet of this life, and enjoy the daily sun bakes, followed by a cooling shower and then strolling along leisurely whilst involved in chat with another, things like the teasing sunlight never bothered one. Like usual events occur out of the blue, just when life is a song, and one afternoon a few days later, I was sunbathing alone in the corner of the yard, and beside my head was a hanky I had just washed and placed there to dry. A small item perhaps, but had this mob of global seamen been fed the energising food received on board ship, this little incident might have sparked off a riot.

I was lying on my stomach when the shadow of an arm appeared before my eyes. Just in time I grabbed the hanky from the black hand of Suwarey, the West African. He snarled and cussed at me. I was up and at him in no time, not because I was unafraid, but because I was afraid – the signals in his eyes told me I had just escaped my face getting kicked in.

Seeing me spring to my feet very rapidly, he took first punch, probably believing I was about to attack, and I returned blow for blow just to retain face. We were about the same build, but he held out longer than me. It was fortunate I weakened first because when the guard's attention was attracted to the scene and blew the whistle, Suwarey was on the attack, and he was taken away immediately for a three day bread and water diet.

The whites were in the vast majority, and although we would point a finger at the hot-blooded, sunnylanders with rich food inside them, white men flared up quicker in hot temperatures, and this was especially so with alcohol. With everyone boasting a slim waistline, the event passed off quietly. Only one comment came my way and that was from Spud. He said I fought disgracefully; I should have downed the bastard. As an afterthought, I wondered if the oily talk of Spud had provoked the quarrel in the first place since Suwarey's company never attracted me.

And a bit of an actor is always welcome in places where entertainment is nil, and Glen, a shrewd Glaswegian, was a natural. You could be sure he would be one of the first three in the line-up for meals, and if you were at close quarters, his antics were worth a study. He read the moods of the screw standing close to the trustees, and because he was skilful in his socialising with the guard and kept him in a good mood, this was favourable for the rest of us. His familiarity with prison jargon would even put the trustees at ease; however, it was only after pivoting my eyes on him several times that I realised how rapid his automated brain would count every slice of bread on the tray.

A fallen spoon, cocoa ladle, tea cloth, or any other item that dropped from the tray table would cause Glen to spring out of line, retrieve the object and pass it back to the trustees with a smile. After receiving his meal, he had ample time to enjoy the bigger part of it, after which the remainder was set aside, and by observing him, I noticed his subtle action of falling in for a second time at the end of the line, knowing full well that the extra slice would come into possession of the last man if an ingratiating smile met the eyes of the important screw.

One Thursday, I went with him to the chaplain's office and noticed he came out with an extra ration of soap, and so I asked him there and then why he was favoured so luckily. I suppose he had weighed me up and decided to take me into confidence as someone who admired him and to whom he could release a little boast once in a while.

"It's quite simple," he said, "just request that you wish to attend his morning service on Sunday," and covertly opened his hand to reveal several cigarettes as well. I did as recommended, and although I never received any smokes, I was pleased with my extra soap.

Sunday came and about ten or twelve of us were escorted through doors to the final door into the prison church, where I made sure to take my pew next to Glen. The Church of England service proceeded as usual. After some praying and hymn singing, the Salvation Army chaplain proceeded into his lecture. It was during the lecture that my mate whispered something in my ear about the chaplain being a secret smoker. Then drawing towards the end of his sermon, the clergyman hesitated, bowed his head a little and allowed his glasses to slip to the end of his nose. He stopped talking and concentrated his sight over the top of his specs to someone in the rear row of pews.

"Is there anything wrong back there?" he asked sympathetically. All heads veered around to enjoy the new centre of interest, and those in the rear area were speaking in hushed tones with an elderly, white-haired American with his hands over his stooped head. Eventually someone scrambled an answer to the waiting ears of the chaplain. "He mentions something about his mother passing away, sir. Says Mothering Sunday has brought it all back to him." The cleric returned a pensive look, and Glen was quick to mimic him, as much as to say 'By God! How did I forget it was Mothering Sunday, even if it was the US version?'

"Tell that distressed person I shall have a word with him when the service is over." "Yes, sir," answered the comforter, seated next to the excited provoker of non-mother lovers.

As the service continued, there was another special Glen whisper tickling my ears: "PB, that yank is a PB!" I kept trying to convey to Glen to pass on another whisper to disclose the secret meaning of PB, but his teeth were fiddling with his lips, and there was no doubt he was very pleased with this mothering business; it had given his mind something to bite on. Then turning his eyes sideways, he read the signals on my face, and cupping his hand over the side of his mouth, he gave me the message, "He's a professional bum, a PB."

Finally, the service finished, and I left for the door minus my mate. He had told me that he had to have a word with the chaplain before leaving the church. It was several days later that I learned about Glen and the American. After they jointly communed with the padre, and he comforted and solaced them with the assurance that their grief would not pass unnoticed by the one above, Glen, spying a large flat cigarette holder under a spare bible on the table, begged religiously for a smoke to alleviate the agonising nostalgia of Mothering Sunday. Then the chaplain nodded consent, and swift as lightning, our man snatched thirteen of the nineteen Players Please cigarettes in the container, parting with half a dozen to his PB friend, in return for one of the two little soap blocks he had received from the chaplain. Later I came to the conclusion that there were two PB's in that morning flock, two professional bums.

With our spartan diet in which everyone was losing weight, it was only the great sunshine and scented sea breeze that prevented depression from eventually setting in. Day followed day, one day the same as the day before. Merchant seamen are experts at relating yarns, and fresh ones continued to spring up like mushrooms. These tales gave a kick to boredom, so life altogether was not too unpleasant. Wouldn't four or five weeks on your average tramp ship be considered boredom without the yarn-spinning on the poop deck?

After six weeks, I was a confirmed, slow stroller for one or maybe two hours of the day, switching partners every now and then to vary discussions. If we had similar thinking, the back and fro leg stretching could go on for a couple of hours, as there was nothing like a pleasant jawbone to make monotony and the hours vanish.

On this morning, I chatted with a Norwegian sailor. Slightly built like myself and unlike a lot of the six foot Vikings I had come across, he had reached a period of disgust after a confinement of four months left him unable to cope with monotony, and that was why his ears were the first to catch on to any fresh rumour. He revealed that a new prison governor was to arrive very soon; a sympathetic guard had passed on this fact to him. The new prominent was called a Barbadian.

That night, I lay on my cot a little fed up with books, not in the mood for Robinson Crusoe, who could expand my imagination so much that when I awoke mornings, I felt sure that the Man Friday was going to bring me some cocoa. I tried to get my tongue around this new word Barbadian, and my mind was still intrigued by who or what it meant when

I fell asleep. The next day it was not a secret; the buzz had got into everyone's ears, and when I got into the walkie-talkie exercise, I found the new prison governor was a white man, born and bred on Barbados, a neighbouring island of Trinidad.

The following day was so breezeless and stinking humid that even the regular pacers sought the shelter of the dining area. All hands sat there oozing sweat, or if they had a surplus of soap, refreshed themselves under the shower. Then through the gate stepped a most ordinary-looking person of a ordinary height reaching about 5'7". He was in immaculately clean and creased light-coloured khakis and white, thin gloves of all things; the new governor was paying us a visit.

His orders were more curt than strict. "Line up, men!" he ordered, with a tone that had army discipline in it. His spoken English was of an colonial elite, an overly-exact pronunciation, but with a definitely sympathetic vein detected in it. Merchant seamen usually take a callous attitude to orders from uniforms, but on this occasion there was eagerness in obeying. Even the warm weather could not dampen the hope that this new, big shot seemed to have brought with him.

The long, silent line of over seventy sailors plus the two BG's, with most only wearing shorts and sandals, stood along the middle section of the yard. There were no bare feet, even by the West African and the Zulu, as the cobblestones may have been walkable, but it looked likely to be a long stand.

The new governor took his time, walking slowly along the line, sometimes studying faces, and then looking elsewhere. He took his time, striding from the centre to one wing of the line, back to the centre and then going in the opposite direction. It was anyone's guess what was going on in his mind. He ended up in the centre area and reversed his footsteps to the rear, hands clasped behind his back, clutching a wooden staff until he got himself centre stage again.

Without raising his voice too loudly, he spoke firmly in a half-bark, "What the dickens are all you seamen doing in here when ships are having to ship out with incompetents picked up on the streets of this port?!" Silence. No one wished to antagonise him, although I'm sure most wanted to cry out, 'Tell that to Gomez!' He bided his minutes, and the next statement that came out of his mouth showed that he respected our silence because his tone was lowered.

"Shortly, the twenty men who have been here longest will be set free under my supervision." The voice was even but firm. The face was a blank, no signals. His family must have been in long residence in Barbados; racial colouring was evident, although faint enough to be unnoticeable at first glance.

A pause was followed by a short cough, and the military bearing came through. "Should any of these men be found still remaining on the island after one week since being set free and without good reason, that person will be detained then in the local internment camp until the termination of the present war."

The internment camp referred to was a set of huts with reasonable comforts, surrounded with barbed wire and would have been fairly vacant. The reason for this was that recently Britain had decided to release all the Finnish seafarers, since they were no longer considered a danger to the Allied cause, and most of the aliens at the camp had been Finns. He did not repeat the threat; he did not need to. The tone of his voice underlined the fact that he was not kidding.

He paused allowing the message to sink in. Then he looked along the long line, eye to eye with each face. Sweat poured from all our necks, including the governor and the two guards flanking him a few paces to his rear; yet the relief was so great with us lot that you could feel it. Had the news been to the contrary, I imagine half the men would have collapsed with heat and utter helplessness; however, as our minds had received such welcome news, it seemed that the body would have been buoyed even if the sun had turned on its most pitiless glare.

Despite the heat, the governor became his cold, unemotional self as he finished matter-of-factly – "Twenty more men will be released a week later," and pointing to the wide gate said, "The final batch will be sent through there when I am satisfied that no ship has left Trinidad without a complement of able sailors and efficient firemen manning it." Making an unconcealed smirk in his almost pitiless features, he about turned and marched through the gate. The two screws followed him into the outer courtyard after locking it behind them.

Five days later the first batch said goodbye and were let loose on Port-of-Spain. And then it was a week later that I happened to be the last name called to go free with the next mob, but it was after the first gang had gone that I lay abed, reminiscing about characters I would probably never set eyes on again. Men who sailed deep-sea tramp ships were a different mob to liner crews, who stayed on the same ship year after year, or coasting men who also saw more of each other. When we finished our voyage, the chance of meeting up with an old shipmate when we joined another ship was next to slim.

When the first batch of names was called out, the first one was that of the tall, slim Panamanian Black with splayed feet. Being the longest resident, he had paced the concrete for ten monotonous months. In the end he had become so weak and frail that one of the guards had passed him a long stick to aid him in his promenades. We liked his affable and friendly manner, and he drew a lot of sympathy.

He had left three blocks of soap on the dining table, and I was not slow in picking one up. I was keeping it ready for my own exit when I would dhobi (wash) my pants and shirt before leaving. A passing thought surfaced concerning the chaplain. He spent most of his time outside the prison walls and only visited the prison on certain days for a few hours at a time.

I had a strong feeling that being aware of his English nationality, it could have been he, more than anyone else, who out of a patriotism, must have contacted Barbados and related the strange story of men being incarcerated while ships were short-handed sailing out of port.

Then there was the blondish, Patagonian Welshman from Rawson in southern Argentina. After our first meeting, I had no desire to dig at him about the Breton escapees who I felt sure he knew a lot about and wanted to tell very little. Was he holding gold for them? They were free men now and would probably rendezvous with him on release and connive for him to stow them away to the USA.

Lately, Jim Jam had got himself into the dumps, yet somehow his mood improved after being named to get released with my group. Being a young chap, the first time away from home, I felt he was trying to hide deep feelings. He had that lost look that drew sympathy, yet when anyone started to converse with him that was not of his colour, he would put on airs and become critical. I drew away from him after a few social meets. If I brought up any of my experience that would be of benefit to him, he was quick to remind me that I had the worst of the fight with Suwarey, a fellow black person.

Most of these characters would drift into thin air a few days after release, but I felt pretty sure that one of them, namely Glen would not disappear from sight. He'd fallen in love with that long bar in the big club and would possibly end up on the scrounge.

The order for our impending release came after cocoa one evening when the warder reminded us to be ready to leave after breakfast the following day. Just to be on the safe side, I had washed my gear two days earlier, so I was surely good and ready. Only half a dozen men possessed Solingen or Sheffield cutthroat razors, and one was always beholden to them to return the favour with soap or the stub end of a cigarette when requested.

On this special morning, however, these items were freely lent out. We were kept in suspense for several hours; everyone wearing long pants if they possessed them plus a clean shirt and a clean chin. It was 11am before the big prison doors were opened, and we were hustled through the cobbled courtyard and bundled most willingly into the waiting paddy wagons, ten men in each.

There were no windows, and as we squeezed together, we found ourselves in semi-darkness, and the only lights glowed from small pilot bulbs on either side, but if I felt jammed up, my thoughts were totally gleeful; we knew it was only a short journey before scrambling to freedom.

The brake was jammed on, and we heard faintly the sound of steam winches. We were home and carefree. When the guards lifted the bar from the rear door and opened up, we were nearly blinded by sudden daylight, as we stepped onto the tarmac. It caught us by surprise to notice Gomez standing beside the main entrance of the harbour master's office, with a peaked cap of authority above his big, brown head and his gun holster at the ready. The harbour master was plainly not a happy man and showed a nasty streak in his look, I had not seen before.

I have heard of much power wielded by certain sergeants in the French Foreign Legion, and I had a feeling this man was in the wrong job, which had been gotten by the wrong means. This gut feeling stuck with a fleeting moment of insight, and I couldn't shake it off. With an island the size of Trinidad with its overcrowded harbour and its tremendous importance to the allied war effort, he knew he held a post of considerable influence. Thinking that the guards had much less power than himself, Gomez barked out an order that the two BG's must be returned to the prison immediately in a tone that implied no questioning. Then the pair of Guiana boys, cowering inside the van, was invited out by one of the guards, and they stepped into the sunlight.

The eyes of Gomez nearly jumped out of his head when one of the guards returned a blank refusal to his order to take the BG's back to gaol. Was it possible that this man had carried on a hand-in-glove relationship with the departing prison governor, similar to his liaison with the immigration department?

If so, that person had informed him of the iron will of his own replacement, and the underlings of this new authority were fired up by Barbadian's example so it seemed. All the seamen were ordered to file into the office where a clerk would attend them. As we filed in, it appeared that for the first time, Gomez was facing cool determination which he had never encountered before.

We were doled out chits for lodgings at either of the two seamen's hostels, and receiving and studying the form I was handed, I learned for the first time the name of the club I was assigned to – The Marine Services Club. When we scattered and made our exit, the confrontation touched off by Gomez had fizzled. If there was any swashbuckling 'I've got a gun' pose', it was acted out most firmly by our two escort guards, who had banded together, called his bluff and outfaced him.

The most senior officer on the waterfront was still against the wall, but in more than one way. There was a dark shadow across his face. He had wavered at the final moment in case he might be stripped of his high position due to the influence of the new prison governor. Ahead of us, alongside the quay, strolled the two stowaways from British Guiana. When they looked back at us, the smiles on their dials were very broad.

The ten of us assigned to the nearby club, walked into the bar and were ushered into the office of the manageress. As I had remembered, there were five rooms and a dormitory at this place, three of the rooms being single, and I was fortunate to be given one.

Once there I sat down on the room's chair to take in the marine atmosphere and to relish for that split second my freedom; then got up and walked around to try and bum a cigarette off someone. I found all the rooms neat and clean, but found only one face I knew, the friendly Panamanian.

He sat on his bed and invited me to sit on his nearby chair. He informed me of the good news that an American vessel sailing to Panama would pick him up in four days' time. With this happy news, he passed me a smoke, and I returned to my room, not to miss out on any messages coming along.

I lay on my bunk, and shortly there came a knock on the door. When I shouted for the messenger to enter, the lad who swept up around the bar area, entered to let me know that those who were recently freed from prison would be expected to take their place at the dining table in ten minutes.

The meal reflected the well-run in-charge of the restaurant; this smallish creature, although a little plump upon entering middle age, was as active on her feet as her job expected her in running such a place. She showed a lot of cool confidence as she invited us to tuck in. One would have thought that after two months of a daily intake of curried food, the diners would have looked forward to a change, but as for myself, the obsession for this spicy ingredient could never be fully satisfied; it has stayed with me that long.

The Sunday type treatment of chicken and veg with mango sauce was followed by a whopper ice cream and some exotic fruit. I felt I had never had such an agreeable meal. Then it suddenly dawned on me that being without alcohol or smokes for the best part of two months had renewed my taste buds no end. Not only that but the slow-moving ceiling fans and the very slight tidal breeze entering the door and open windows, made me appreciate how pleasantly the elements affected one, not through the skin, but by way of the nose; I was eating the perfumed air coming in from the Caribbean.

This gave me serious thoughts of throwing the weed habit, but just then, our hostess threw a packet of Lucky Strike cigarettes on each table (and I postponed my new resolution for later), assisting our after-dinner digestion with a nice puff and chat. It caused us all to linger and talk to beat the band, as we supped from cups of superior American coffee.

Before returning to my room, I learned that out of the first group of twenty released, already fifteen had shipped out, which proved that there was a choice of ships. Sitting back on the bed, I considered that without any strong resolution, I could at least abstain from alcohol in the near future due to lack of cash, but that fertile mind of mine reminded me that there could be a possibility of redeeming some unused rent money from the club on the hill.

Later, studying the layout of the long hall called the bar in my club, I noticed that the dining space was set crosswise against the wall of one end and while sitting against it, one could see who was coming and going through the single door on the middle of one of the long walls. The tables were separate from the rest of the bar by ten feet. I went out of the room with the intention of sitting an hour there, in hopes of recognising a familiar face walking through the door.

I found I had the company of three others and wondered if they had a similar notion. Whilst focusing on the door, I found one eye wandering in the direction of the open space of the kitchen on the opposite side. There were some cute-looking native chicks passing to and fro, and it struck me that my Casanova friend, who had been locked up with me, might have found them irresistible, thus causing the manageress to turn against him.

Just as I was thinking of her, the lady herself came out of her office and asked us if we desired any reading matter, and if so, to follow her. We trailed her to a spacey store-room and selected magazines and fiction books to occupy the afternoon with.

Then I realised that the liberty boat would not be shore side until 6.30pm, and feeling too restless to enjoy an afternoon siesta, there was nothing for it but first to stroll up to the other club and see if there was any back cash waiting for me.

After deduction for lost key money, I returned to my residence five

US dollars richer in Trinidad currency, and although we had been supplied with soap and towel, I found that I would no longer need to borrow a razor or writing pad. I now awakened to the fact that I had neglected writing people at home, as well as a few occasional friends, who might be waiting for news from myself. In some respects, jail had served me in bringing back a bit of inner awareness.

Sitting it out and doing door watching after a feed of good tasting fish, together with a rich salad, really got the blood circulating again. It being a Monday night, most of the crews would be still getting over their weekend hangover, so I sat out the time chatting with my friends and later returned to the magazines and books in my room.

By morning I felt settled in; however, remembering the words of the new prison governor, I felt I should start making headway in trying to get employment, and I decided to have a word with one of my bench bums. Irrespective of their status, they were rich in marine information. First of all, I thought it best to have a chat with men from my prison group and walked around the rooms and dormitory, only to find them vacated. I felt panicky; where had they all disappeared to?

When I strolled into the bar area, none were in sight there too. I realised the rat race for jobs was on already; it was usually this way, men moved swiftly, keeping job tips to themselves. I soon had an idea; I would speculate the small cash I held and buy a couple of beers for the bench loungers, and so out I strode to find only one solitary bloke with a straw hat covering his eyes and sat beside him.

Sensing my presence he lifted the brim and wished me good morning, and I returned it fast to gain his attention. It turned out to be someone whom I had helped before, and recognising me he asked how I was getting on. I replied that I would give anything to get on a ship and would he like a bottle? The Viking gave me a broad smile and told me to hang on a while and he soon would be back. He disappeared into the bar with a – "You wait here."

He returned with two bottles in his hand and passed one to me, then lighting up a smoke, offered me one and told me to begin again, as he was interested in me. I told him I had just been let out of prison, and if I didn't ship out in a week, I may be returned there. He told me that he was on a ship nearby, and watches were set for 4pm, as he was sailing that night, and that was why he was spending his last couple of hours blowing his last few dollars, hoping to meet some friends of his.

Quickly, I asked if there were any vacancies on his ship. "If there was," he said, "I would have let you know right away, but I've heard of a ship that needs a coal fireman if you are interested." "That's just the job I want," I said enthusiastically. "Where is she lying?" He thought for a minute, and then asked, "Have you sailed on Norwegian ships? Well, this is Norwegian, and she's anchored in the harbour but won't sail for several days." "What's her name?" I quizzed. He hesitated and then remembered, "It's called the *Loke*."

That was the one ship I didn't want; however, that thought keyed me up more than ever to go job searching. I remembered what Jock Decker had said about boarding nearby ships, and then it struck me that I was a little late in the race. With all those men let out, they would be swarming aboard them. I decided to report to the harbour master first, get my name on the list and then to scoot around to the shipping agents.

I was about to refuse Olav when he offered to buy another bottle, yet he insisted very strongly so I agreed, and when I sat thinking of my problem, it suddenly occurred to me that there may be some cash left for me from the *Lido*. This memory had been blocked because the Agent Consul had been associated with the name of *Loke*, but now that I knew she was in port, I could avoid offering my services on her.

The thought of obtaining extra cash must have advertised itself on my face because it brightened Olav up to find me in a less despondent mood. I enjoyed those extra few minutes of guzzling and yarning, and as there was about an hour left before dinner, I excused myself to pay a visit to the harbour master. I was expecting little luck and got none, but at least I had my name down on the register, so as to show I was trying to ship out and left feeling at ease.

I left in full sail walking in the direction of the Norwegian consul, and despite the heat and a slight cloudiness in my head, I was in full stride. The two bottles had the same effect that ten would have had after nine weeks of sobriety. When I entered the consulate, I didn't know why the young mulatto at the counter seemed delighted to see me. "Can I help you?" he beamed.

Then he brought up a folder from under the counter referring to back wages, and I was the one that became delighted. I was passed ten Trinidad dollars and loose coins. I couldn't leave the office without asking him on the job situation. He fumbled once more through a clip of forms and replied that there were several jobs on one vessel, which would be sailing to New York in a week's time.

I held my breath, wondering if there were any vacancies in the engine room department, all four of them were. I was as puffed up as an adder now with expectation, and he read it on my face. Then he gave out the details, two firemen and two trimmers needed on a ship that had just arrived from Moengo, Dutch Guiana, with a cargo of bauxite. She had discharged her cargo and was waiting for a berth – and her name? The *D/S Loke*.

He watched me stand there in a pensive mood. The *Loke* did not beckon me, though the fact that she was sailing to New York did. "When will she be coming alongside?" I blurted out. He had the answer on the tip of his tongue. "Neilson has informed me she expects to tie up near the Marine Services Club in three days' time."

My thoughts were speeding up now. What if I turned her down? Wouldn't that mob in the marine club grab the job? He watched the expression on my face, knowing I was trying to develop a response. Not only did I want the job, I wanted to make sure he kept the job open for me especially. He was much relieved when I told him this but frowned a little. Had I worked as a fireman on coal burners before? Had I? When I informed him that I had served on the *Loke* for nine months, he gave me a big smile and promised to keep the job open for me.

Having learned I was an experienced man, he didn't take long to jot my name and info down, and before I left, requested I round up one more experienced firemen and two trimmers if I didn't mind. I certainly didn't. There were more men than enough ready to ship out of the two seamen's clubs.

I returned to enjoy an English dinner of roast beef and veg, feeling as independent as a king. I had cash in my pocket, a job coming up, but most of my closest friends had been sent to the other club, so I decided to pass around the vacant jobs on the *Loke* to those that were with me at my club.

I passed on the good news when we chatted after our meal, and it somewhat deflated me to learn that there were no takers. Only two of the ten declared openly that Gomez had found them vacancies. Two Americans informed me that their consulate would be getting them passage back to the States in about a week or so. The other six excused themselves as belonging to other departments, although I could have sworn that two or three looked like stokers. So I returned to my room and slept off the small hangover from the early couple of beers.

I intended to walk up to the other mission to spread the news of vacancies on the *Loke*; however, when I entered the bar, I lingered, grabbed a chair from the eating table, placed it against the wall and lit up. Taking in the scene, I assumed there were about fifteen drinkers in all, half a dozen sitting on the high stools at the bar and the rest sitting at the small, square tables. Two of those at the bar I recognised as those who had been released from the prison with me.

I had no urge to spend my newly, acquired cash on feeding them beer, as their attitude to me as soon as we settled in had turned very cool, and as far as I was concerned, it could stay that way. There was, however, one new body that caught my eye since the muscles of his long legs stood out below his shorts, even at a distance. He was picking up empty beer bottles from the table and putting them on the counter.

I checked my pocket for keys and cash and went through the door on my way to the mission on the hill. I couldn't understand why, but I never could remember less than three or four no-hopers on the long bench outside. However, for the second day I found only one solitary sitter there. This stocky, little blond waved at me as I passed, and then said, "Hey, cobber, got a smoke on you?" I sidled up to him and got pulled in by his cheeky face.

Before he lit up, he started spinning his tale of woe, which I was sure would end up him asking for a handout, but then he implied that he was fed up looking for a job and was also averse to lying about. I sat beside him and got interested. "Been down below?" I asked. "Yeah, I'm a greaser." "Ever fired coal?" I questioned. "No, but I'm ready to give it a try." I got ready to move off when he mentioned that a friend of his was a coal fireman.

Me: "How can I locate him?" "He's in the bar, helping the barman clean up for a few beers; the cleaner has a day off," he replied. I stood there pondering, then feeling the crisp notes in my pocket, I asked him his name. "Just call me Aussie." "Ok, Aussie. Don't sit there and get yourself blistered with the sun. Come sit inside and introduce him to me," I insisted.

I took him into the bar and called for two beers while he swivelled around, trying to locate his friend. He couldn't find him so we started introductions. He was from Adelaide, Australia and had landed two days earlier after being given passage from Sao Paolo, Brazil with his friend, a Canadian – the one we were seeking out. Presently, he spotted him emerging from the toilet; he was the husky, red-headed bloke I had spotted picking up beer cans.

The tall stranger picked up a broom and started sweeping between the tables when my new friend hollered. "Put that brush down, Red and come over!" The beer was still making me giddy after being absent from the stuff for a few months, so I decided to stand up and gave my seat to Red. I asked him if he had any papers to show he had served with the banjo gang. He let me know that he had discharge papers from the Canadian lake boats in his room at the other mission.

After being let down with my offers to the current residents, I then asked him if there were any coal trimmers where he stayed. He said that he didn't know but questioned me why I shouldn't hire Aussie. "We've been pals for a pretty good while, and I know he has no experience at shovelling, but if, as you say, there are only two to a watch, I'm prepared to have him on mine."

We downed a few more beers, and I thought why not get this business over and done with; so again I brought up the business about the other trimmer's job, and then Red said that during his visit to the US consulate the day before, he had come across an American who would be prepared to take any kind of job. He had experience in working down below but not on coal jobs. Would I be interested? What he meant was would I be prepared to help the American along if he came on my watch. In a beery mood, what could I say except yes and hope for the best. I then probed him about the bloke, and he told me he was a young guy in his twenties like ourselves, and he had jumped a US vessel. Then he told me something I was unaware of. A new law in the States took a very serious attitude to any seaman jumping ship and would face serious charges in a marine court when he returned home.

It was obvious this man was desperate for a job, and Red arranged to contact him; we could all meet the next day here at the canteen. I was feeling groggy by now and wanted to take off with my cash still holding. I thought it worthwhile to keep in with this pair rather than meet up with an offensive type, so I passed them a dollar each which would see both of them OK for another half dozen bottles plus a pack of smokes between them, and I took off for an afternoon snooze.

I was awakened by a rap at the door. It was Aussie, so I asked him in. "Hey, cobber," he burst out, "I've been trying to find your pad for ten minutes. Come out and meet the new Yankee trimmer. He wants to join your ship if he can. What's the name again?" "Hang on, I'll get my keys and be right with you." I answered. Putting my keys in that very useful back pocket, I ripped a page from my new writing tablet, grabbed a pencil, wrote *Loke* on it and passed it on to my new friend. "Now we should all show up at the consulate tomorrow, though if you lie in and prefer to go later, show this at the office."

As we walked out, he commented that he didn't realise the rooms here were so neat and clean; the only difference with the other place is that they supplied mosquito nets. "I know that, but you don't need nets here; the sea breeze is not to their liking." Walking into the bar, it was half full; the liberty boats must have brought the evening crews ashore. And now the atmosphere felt like happier times.

I was introduced to 'Okee', a slim-built guy with a face that showed he was no softie, which relaxed me; coal burners couldn't afford those types, and I was happy I had made the decision to bring him into the group. They had a beer waiting for me at the table, and I sat down. Aussie tried to pass the ship's name to Red, and Okee asked me what the name was on the slip of paper, so I explained it was spelled *Loke* but spoken Lokee, just like his name, Okee. This bit of wit broke the ice, and the reaction of laughs and smiles told me that things augured well; we might sail together after all.

I left the table to visit the toilet, and who should I see cupping a bottle alone at a small table except Glen from the lockup. There was no cunning look in his eyes, and he was as sober as he had been inside. This surprised me, as I figured he'd be bumming a drink off everyone by now. I said I'd have a word with him on the way back, which I did. I felt I was the banker for three dollars right now, unless Okee forked out a few dollars, and I felt like holding back if Glen should ask me for cash.

I couldn't, however, see him nursing a beer all night, so I asked him if he needed a dollar, yet he turned me down saying that he had met a livewire at the other mission, another Scotty, who had paid off sick from a ship and had handed him ten dollars. Being so honest towards me, I felt for him but reminded him about the warnings we received about being put behind a barbed wire fence unless we shipped.

Surprisingly, he took an amicable view of my advice, even thanking me for it. However, he said he was feeling a bit under the weather and mixed up and would visit Gomez as soon as he sorted himself out.

Worthy of special mention! Remarkably, I learned after the war that Gomez had detained able seamen because he was thought to be a Nazi collaborator and wanted to make departing allied ships less seaworthy. That made lots of sense to me considering everything that had come to pass.

Before we parted, Glen shared some advice with me also. After I told him that soon I would sign onto a ship, he reminded me to pay a visit to our old friend, the Salvation Army chaplain, and let him know I was schooner-rigged, and he'd give me some left behind buckshee (free) clothing.

When I returned to the table, I found a full bottle near my chair, together with the half bottle I still had to swallow. I was still holding good but thought it would be a good idea to slow down the others if the next round would be paid by myself, which I knew it would be. Reading the coinage on the table in front of Okee from Oklahoma, I realised he had spent out on the last round and had left change in case the group ran short of cigarettes.

I added a new ingredient into the general discussion by suggesting that we should all go to the Salvation Army the next day. They finished their bottles well before me, and I thought as a wise banker, I should retire without spending up. Loads of other thoughts were also going through my head; I hoped to see Johan and the young Welsh trimmer, Dave, from the *Loke* before going broke, and hopefully, they would step ashore from the launch the following evening.

I was much surprised the next morning, when I was sitting outside on the bench about 9.30am, when who should be entering the mission gate but my three new mates. They really were serious about shipping out. Perhaps the groups that had been released and who stayed at their place may have warned them what could happen to seaman lounging around the island too long.

Anyway, I was glad to see their faces and freely invited them in for a beer before our paying a visit to the consul but told them it would be only one bottle; we didn't want to lose our chances over the smell of beer on our breath. I was glad they felt the same way, and when we did set out together, the talk centred on how much gear we could bum out of the SA chaplain.

We had good news at the office. The same young fellow was there. He made a quick scrutiny of all our documents and was very pleased with me for bringing along the new recruits. He also informed me that the deucer would let bygones be bygones concerning my deserting the vessel, and he was only too glad to rehire a proficient fireman. It was now Wednesday, and before we left, he wanted our promise that we would turn up promptly at 10am on Friday to sign on the *Loke*.

Next I guided the lads to the Salvation Army headquarters which was also a hostel for single men, and as I knew the chaplain personally, led the way inside and was lucky to catch him before he paid a visit to the prison. He really was in a good mood as he would be leaving shortly, so he passed us on to the dormitory manager, giving him a bunch of keys and instructions. The big black man led us down into a cellar and after unlocking a door, led us in and put on the lights.

On some dusty shelves were stacked maybe thirty or forty parcels, which our guide told us hadn't been touched in a long time. They were parcels sent out from well-sympathising friends of sailors.

The manager caught the string of two parcels and passed them to Red and Aussie and another pair to me and Okee. Before leaving the storeroom, we asked him if he had any second-hand boots for wearing in the stokehold. He had no idea what a stokehold was, or if there was any footwear in the building, so we went up and signed for the parcels.

We stood outside in the main street for a minute, wondering where to go next, then someone suggested, "Let's go to the park." The park in Port-of-Spain was quite large and near the port, and as we were all familiar with it, that's where we went. We didn't take long relieving the parcels of string; unfortunately, however, the gear was of the most undesirable kind. All we needed were old boots, a few pairs of socks to go with them and a pair of pants each, plus a singlet to soak in the sweat.

The chaplain had put a pair of trews in each, but they were of the thick, worsted type, which would only increase the output of our sweat glands, and in each parcel there was also a very thick woollen sweater. About the socks, you couldn't get any thicker or more unsuited for wearing in a hot area. I decided we should wrap them back up and return them. However, Red said to hold on a minute. I was thinking that the parcels were meant for Labrador or Iceland, not a tropical destination. However, Red had another idea – Russian convoys to the Arctic.

Spreading the goodies on the park bench, he felt over the material with his fingers. He noted that the wool was particularly good quality and said that anyone in the business would tell you that with wartime shortage of such material, they could command good prices, so why didn't we unravel the sweaters into balls of wool and try to sell them.

To kill time before the midday meal, we all got busy making balls of wool as round as possible. There were always a few, penniless bums hanging around the park, so we left four pairs of trews on the bench for them and took off, letting Red carry our parcel of merchandise. He went off to see the dockers for the sale, and when I met Red that evening, I learned he had gotten a reasonable profit in a local café for the wool.

Red was a good sport. He told me to hang on to my money, and he would pay for the rounds out of the sale. It was midweek, and there were not too many crews coming ashore for booze-ups, so the club was relatively quiet. We discussed the matter of stokehold clothing, and when they asked me when the ship would leave, I told them sometime next week after loading general cargo.

That satisfied their minds that we would be eligible to put our names down on the Friday sub list, on account that we needed to buy gear. All the time we were supping away, I kept my eyes on the door in hopes that Johan or Jock would step through it. At 7pm I gave up looking, and as there was not much to talk about, I left the table and returned to my room.

The day went well on Thursday. I rose late, and finding no one in the canteen, took a stroll to the market for my coconut juice, bought a paper, and returned to my room to remain there most of the day, planning my return to the *Loke* and writing a few letters. Again, that evening I sat alone at the bar, which was already half full even before the evening launches came in with seamen pouring in.

This time as I watched the door I was in luck; I saw Johan advancing alone. He didn't recognise me at first, saying my face had changed and that I was now suntanned, and when I told him where I got the tan, he busted out laughing. I had time to brief him about the new stokehold gang he could expect on board because not long after, introductions were got off easily. Not only that but he had passed me a ten dollar note, so I called the first round.

Johan also reported that as soon as Jock Decker heard the *Loke* was heading for New York, he packed his bags and paid off. And referring to the ship itself, Johan revealed that after six months on the bauxite run, the *Loke's* food lockers, bunks and all the woodwork were infected with roaches. However, more on the tub's structural woes later in NYC.

It was pleasant meeting an old shipmate, but the night was more memorable due to an event that got the whole club excited. Let me not slander PB characters too much since they are part of the human circus. On this certain evening, a drunken argument broke out between a dark-haired Swede called Blackie and my pal, Glen, and they put on a lively performance.

Before they got to blows, a stout American put his body between them. Enclosed within the long perimeter fence of the club grounds was a yard, well-lit at night. The intervener had a kind of persuasive force over the would-be combatants. He must have had experience as an MC at one time because after coaxing the two into the well-spaced area, he called the insiders to come out and form a ring.

With an eloquent voice that might have classified him as a pro, he soon got them swarming around the two opponents. There must have been near a hundred tars that poured out of the door. We picked up our bottles and joined the crowd.

The promoter drew the crowd into a well-formed ring, and without wasting time, brought the two contestants together and built up their egos with constant references to Queensbury rules, though I doubt he knew what they meant being an American. Each of these men were what you might term a Mr Average of around 5'7" in height so it looked like unfairness would not occur; and it didn't, thanks to the polish of our self-appointed referee.

With encouragement from the wide circle, the two pugilists laid into each other. They were your ordinary type of brawlers, but lack of professionalism didn't seem to worry the audience, probably because the pair was fairly representative of themselves. Friendly comments and shouts urging the two fighters on with boosting comments like, "They're a game pair." lengthened the action.

Yet even with all the encouragement, after fifteen minutes the alcohol was wearing off, and clumsy blows became more frequent, so the ref-cum-MC raised the right fist of each contestant, commended them of their performance and ended it calling the match a draw. After that they shook hands and there was a mighty cheer from the silly-looking, grinning fans.

All hands went inside to finish off their carousing, whilst our two heroes mopped the sweat off themselves. It was one of those very hot evenings that only an ice-cold beer could remedy, and if I was not mistaken, the two men were deciding to bring down their temperatures with as much of the stuff as they could bum from those who enjoyed the amusement.

Time passed and it was after midnight the following week when our convoy of ships sailed out of Port-of-Spain, Trinidad, into the Caribbean: destination Guantanamo Bay, Cuba for further orders, which we all knew would be New York. We also knew that there would soon be further reports as the days went by. Johan and his trimmer, Dave, were on first watch taking her out, as they were the most experienced pair; then at 4am Red and his mate, Aussie, did their four hour stint.

It was back to the fish balls breakfast, which went down well for myself, but Okee had no hankering for them. Well, later after work, he should certainly have an appetite for dinner. Red looked all in when we relieved him at ten minutes before eight down in the stokehold and commended Aussie for supplying him with coal. I hoped my trimmer would do his stuff. Red left a good head of steam, and as he dragged himself up the ladder, step by iron step, I checked the water can under the ventilator.

Since Okee was completely new at the job, I didn't expect too much of him the first day, so I handed him the empty billy can and asked him to fill it at the pump outside the galley. By the time he returned, I had made fast work of cleaning two fires and topping them. I showed my mate the two wide-mouthed seawater taps on either side of the stokehold with buckets nearby and told him to splosh water over the red hot ashes.

I then went out into the engine room to fetch a pair of gloves. The Third Engineer opened the top of his desk and handed me two pairs, one of which I passed to Okee, and after drinking from the water can, stood under a vent and tried to cool my body off; however, the breeze was faint, I then told Okee to follow me to the fiddley, where I showed him how to haul up buckets of ashes and dump them over the side.

Okee had a frail body, but he made quick work manually winding up the ash; even an empty bucket could weigh twenty pounds, so I was pleased with the thought that he would keep his word and make sure I had a coal supply. After loafing around on shore a few months and with hardly any wind coming down the vent, that first watch sucked about all the energy out of me.

There were always wash buckets outside the galley pump, and after filling one up for myself, I told Okee to follow suit and follow me to quarters where I showed him the washroom. After dinner I walked up on deck for a look around and noticed that smoke streaking from the funnel made a bare slant; there was so little breeze. We had sailed into a sweltering mid-June day. I returned below and tried to modify the wind chute in the cabin porthole to try and grab what wind a seven knot ship could create.

I felt like I was more back in business during my four hour stint of the evening. As soon as the sunset came, there was an evening breeze, as weak as it was, that breeze gave me the breaks I needed under the vent between stoking hot furnaces. After we had washed at midnight, both of us took a cup of coffee on deck to allow the cool midnight air to waft over us, and we were joined by two ABs who had just finished duties on the bridge.

One sailor brought news that was a tonic to our ears. After leaving our convoy base in Cuba, we could look forward to several weeks in New York, since the _Loke_ was then due for a refit. We had six days more to Guantanamo, and the more north we sailed, the more we could expect cooler conditions. In peacetime the Caribbean was the playground of millionaire yachtsmen, but during these times, a thought always lurked in one's mind that it could be the playground of enemy submarines.

Once I got back into routine, the days moved more rapidly. One thing that I never lacked was an appetite. I got stuck into boiled fish and that other boiled food that Norwegians are partial to, a sort of stringy corned beef that is eaten with mustard. By liner standards you wouldn't call this appetising victuals, but with four hours of continual energy layout twice a day, rough bulk food was maybe the best to replace lost energy.

The best time of day was coming off-duty at midnight. You were already into a brand-new day, and it felt good sitting under the starry sky, holding a cup of dark coffee in your hand, knowing you had conquered another day. Although it was not permitted for any ship to show lights at night, the dark outlines of the armed naval craft, forever circling the convoy, gave a good feeling as ships moved in unison on a quiet sea.

News came through that we could arrive a day early in the Bay; the fifty odd ships of this seven knot convoy had kept a speed of nine knots an hour. One reason was the lack of a headwind, and Red being used to firing lake boats in a much colder climate, welcomed the early arrival, even more so than Johan and myself who had the experience of keeping steam on jungle runs.

After three days at sea, Okee asked why we received no fresh fruit, so I made a point of quizzing the sailors and learned that they knew there was fruit aboard, as they had carried the stores to the steward's cool room. Then I passed this on to the other firemen and trimmers to find out what they thought about it. When I left the table after the midday meal the following day, Red invited me into his cabin.

He told me to kneel down and look under the Aussie's bunk, where I spotted two wash buckets. Red got down with me and drew them up. Both were three quarters full of beautiful oranges. He pushed one back, took the other into the mess room, placed it beside the bench and went to fetch another bucket from the washroom to use for peelings. We gorged ourselves and pushed the two buckets beneath the table.

I rarely slept for more than two hours after dinner and was up at 3.30pm, and when I awoke, Okee and Aussie were taking turns at gorging through the orange supply. I thought I would give myself a second helping before the citrus disappeared and joined in. Normally, I would have taken a walk up to the poop deck and sat down on a bench under a tarpaulin, but the deck was very hot; the big, white orb had so heated the deck plates, it was cool nowhere, and therefore, I returned to my cabin and looked over some old magazines.

Whilst I was thus occupied, I overheard the authoritative tone of the steward's voice booming loudly about stolen oranges. I heard him moving around in the mess room, and then an argument broke out in the next cabin. I heard the voice of Aussie telling the steward he knew nothing about the door of the cool room. From the top bunk, Okee gave me a nod. I took the hint to back up the 4-8 trimmer and stuck my head out of the door.

The steward stood near the door, looking around for evidence, and if he had spotted the bucket of peelings, it would have overwhelmed him, and maybe he had because when I gave the diminutive chief the same brazen answer as my mate had, he stomped up the ladder with his prominent peaked cap pulled down half over his eyes. There was no doubt he didn't believe us.

And there was no doubt that on the whole, the steward was a fair man, yet I remembered an old story that I had heard about him when I joined the *Loke*. That he could act queer at times due to an incident that occurred pre-war, when he was aboard an oil-tanker that had blown up in Rotterdam.

For the rest of that day, there was a sort of silence as we expected trouble if the incident reached the captain's ears, but the only rumour that came through was from one of the sailors that the steward had reported to him that someone had opened up the cool room with a nail. Anyway, for the rest of the trip, there was fresh fruit on the menu daily.

The following morning I was seized with a cramp, but as we were close to our anchorage, I made an extreme effort to wriggle out of my bunk and do my stint. Once I had started stoking the fires, the stiffness disappeared, and I worked at the watch in the usual way. The spasm may have been caused by excess sweat because although we had clean tubes running through the boiler, Yankee slack coal unfortunately had to be continuously sliced and raked for any combustible smoke to flame up through the tubes.

However, a pleasant surprise came after the evening meal. The skipper sent down two bottles of rum, one to the sailors' side, and the other to us. This very kindly gesture was to celebrate the birthday of King Haakon of Norway, and we meant to do him justice.

The tropical sun set just after 6pm, and four of us made our way up onto the gun deck to get the most of the evening breeze. Empty 7lb fruit tins were never dumped overboard, and seizing one from inside a cupboard, Johan went off to see the steward, returning with ice blocks for our glasses. I enjoyed a couple of hours spinning out yarns, but never a mention was made of who might just have forced the cool room door and stolen the oranges. Realising our responsibility not to let down the skipper for his appreciation of us, we left a third of the bottle for the 4-8 watch to polish off.

My brain seemed a bit disordered when I was aroused at 7 bells. The effect of spirits that first hour down below with much perspiring was weakened, and I was really none the worse except for a short headache. I battled blindly against inertia and was soon welcoming Johan and Dave at midnight, as they laughingly related that Aussie had spilled the beans about forcing the cool room lock with a rusty nail while guzzling the rum.

It was my habit to seat myself on an empty five gallon oil drum beneath the vent after pitching coal on the six furnaces to get my breath back and wipe the sweat from my face. However, since leaving Trinidad, the oxygen that blew down only had the force of the nine knot speed of the convoy most times so that I was forced to stand up, head bent back and with an open mouth, gulp in what current of air there was from the air shaft.

It was with pleasure that I was told to reduce steam at 10pm one night, and we steamed into Guantanamo Bay at half speed, slowing down near the anchorage. By the time I had washed up and sat out on deck, I found I had a lot of company. The agent had brought a lot of mail on board, most of it back mail, plus also the news that we would undergo maintenance and refitting in the Brooklyn Navy Yard for at least a month.

There was a whole lot of restlessness and excitement. Some passed on what they planned to do in New York's summer weather, while others confided to each other news from past mail, romancing about girlfriends in faraway places. Twenty-four hours later the anchor was hauled in and with more breezes to help us in the second half of the journey, we reached New York Harbor a week later. Feeling was good all around. Often I passed a sailor coming along the deck singing a shanty. Most faces had wide smiles on them in the hope of a good rest up and plans of socialising in the bars and canteens on the Great White Way of Broadway.

For most of the crew, including some officers, there was the open option of switching to another ship. In other words, because Norway had no home base in big ports like London and New York, men were allowed to pay off if circumstances permitted, and there must have been a lot of thinking about this. On top of this consideration, it was possible to take residence in the city and ship out when one felt like it.

This would not be possible at all in peacetime, because European nations prevented their citizens from leaving a ship in a foreign port, unless paid off sick or after eighteen months when their contract expired. The consul then found them passage home in another vessel. Had I been on a British ship, this would have applied to myself, but sailing under the Norwegian flag, I came under their legalities.

Even I began to dither on whether to pay off or not; the chance was there for the asking. In such a big port, reliefs were easily available, but after I learned from the Second Mate that the ship would definitely make headway back to home waters, I decided to stick it out. But hardship knits good friendship, and it was a little heart-breaking to hear that half the crew had decided on leaving the ship when we arrived.

U.S.A.

Luckily, Johan had not made up his mind and neither had Dave; Okee was determined to stay on rather than face disciplinary action by a marine court. Before long we arrived at the approaches of New York Harbor, and the usual launch came alongside with pilot, doctor and customs officer, and we were soon passing the Statue of Liberty.

It was past 5pm by the time we were securely cradled into one of the seven dry docks at the naval yard, and since the agent brought no cash on board, we settled for a nice rest that night with plenty of news coming through. All hands were instructed to have their personal possessions packed for a bus at 10am next morning. We would be driven to the Norwegian Seamen's Hostel in Pacific Street, Brooklyn.

Most of us were familiar with the nearby diner on the dock, where we had been served the last time we docked, and the arrangement was that there would be no turning-to until 9am, which would give us enough time to eat breakfast. We could leave our work gear in the same change room, even though the living quarters would be overhauled, and the copper coffee percolator would be kept in place at all times.

We were told that all three meals could be ordered daily at the local diner; however, when we arrived at the home, it also had a short-order counter, just in case we didn't want to shift for ourselves on weekends. On the whole, it was a very good set-up with clean, spacey rooms and amenities of the usual type – like a ping-pong table and a reading room with plenty of American magazines.

Our working hours were between 9am and 4pm, but all our gang were early birds on the subway that first morning so we could have a long gab at the diner's table before boarding. It was good we had no cash that morning, or there might have been some beer drinking and that could have spoiled the day as we moved into the sultry June weather which was more enjoyable when sober.

There was quite a gathering at break time. As there was nothing much for us to do in the engine room, which was packed with fitters and electricians doing critical maintenance checks and repairs, and the stokehold had another group of men cleaning back ends and tubes, we just walked around socialising so that by smoke time, Johan and some Norwegian sailors escorted Scandinavian American fitters, etc. to our mess for a cuppa.

A money list had been handed in to the chief officer early on and with 50 dollars in my kit when we knocked off, I intended to linger at the diner for a few hours before going to the hostel. During the midday meal, some of the counter hands recognised our faces from the year before and beamed smiles at us, reminding us to choose any dish we required, while adding, "Don't worry; company pay." And when we entered later, it was not before two Swedish sisters arrived, and Johan played the gent by inviting them to our table and introducing them.

In return we let him take them away from us so he could indulge in his waltzing to the jukebox music. These two hostesses were twins, 29 years of age and entertained us as younger chicks could not. This Tuesday night was an enjoyable return to New York. The girls would not let us overspend, and as an afterthought, they may have enjoyed the sultry evenings under whirling fans more than us, as the jukebox whirled out melodies against a backdrop of spirited conversations in our male group, where the oldest, Red, was only 22.

With first-rate treatment from the counter and evenings with the sisters, we were all present for the following two nights, then on the third day, the breakup started. Okee was called to the saloon to have a word with the captain and was instructed that he would have to pay off the next day. The captain hinted that charges would be brought against him for jumping ship. He returned to let us know the news.

During the coffee break, Red learned that Okee's first call would be at the union rooms and decided to accompany him in a taxi. He intended to try to transfer from the Canadian Union into the National Maritime Union of America which had both the best pay and living conditions of any other merchant marine; however, they were very militant, and discipline was the byword with them.

When they put the cash list in on Friday, there were only four of us left so that Red must have succeeded in shipping out on a US vessel. As usual, the dockworkers entered the mess for a cuppa and interested us in taking a trip to Coney Island. "Just jump on the Brooklyn rattler," said one, "and get yourself a good weekend," added another, and it soaked in. The four of us decided to take the train to that famous beach the next day, and although we stopped in at our watering place, we didn't linger more than a few hours before taking the subway to Pacific Street.

We took a bite at the home before stepping on the train to the sun, sand and amusement centre, only packing a towel and deciding to buy bathing costumes when we arrived there. When we stepped off with the rest of the multitude from the metropolis, we first set a landmark to meet at a certain time, after which we could allow ourselves to get lost in the throng. At first I joined the rest after we purchased bathers and took a dip in the sea. Having cooled off I wiped down and adventured around the tents.

The first tent I reached advertised a scene of wax figures depicting the Rape of Nanking by the Japanese army. While a man lifted the flap to entice a customer, I ducked my head in smartly and found quite a crowd inside soaking in the gruesome, tortured victims, and I walked on to the next tent. The US was deeply involved in a wartime mind, and sympathy went out to those in occupied territories, both in Asia and Europe.

I speculated a dollar on the second tent. It was purely out of admiration for a skimpy-dressed lady advertised outside. She was also advertising some fearsome skin complaint that baffled scientists. There was a sitting room inside, maybe twenty or thirty seats, and when most seats were filled, the flap was dropped, and a Mr Ordinary appeared from behind a curtain – a middle-aged man who made a short speech about a one in a million skin complaint that had marred the life of a poor, yet beautiful Swiss lady.

The curtain was drawn from behind him, and a beautiful teenage doll stepped forth. It was rude to whistle, so sympathy was sucked out of the likes of me, and in a more maternal way, from elderly women. The blemishes on her body seemed to spread across the sexiest parts of her torso, and naturally, she had to bare herself as much as possible, in order to give proof of her disorder, which did not seem to hide or divert from her beauty much; it looked like a plain, light brown rash.

And then back to the emcee, back to the Mr Ordinary, but when he spoke, his voice was not that ordinary; it did things to you. "Ladies and gentlemen, as you all know, everyone has seven layers of skin." He stopped to make a polite cough, and the nodding started. First only a few heads went into action. Not to be left out from the rest of the heads, I took up the up-and-down exercise, very sagely, of course. I managed to break my gaze from this hypnotic chap and switch it to poor sexy, as she made the slightest teasing wiggle of her bum and that brought a nod from myself.

After the nodding ceased, he handed us a line about Miss Poor Distressed, from far away Switzerland, who had to bathe her beautiful body several times a day in a specially prepared liquid, and hoped we shared his sympathy for her. He kept silent for a special second for the message to sink in, but the nods were very subdued this time; perhaps a few felt like they were being made mugs of.

They were. I swear to this day that during the fifteen minute show, he managed to milk a donation from half the audience, and if she had come from a country occupied by the Germans, even I might have contributed. His technique of raising our brain boxes to noble heights by suggesting our high intelligence worked at first, but after being milked of cash, the contributors must have felt like a bunch of apes when they walked out.

Somewhat later I bumped into the gang near a coconut stall, and when we left to take in more scenery, I asked them a poser: "How many layers of skin does a guy wear?" Johan replied. "Two, of course." and I knew by the nods he received, they were genuine ones. We all went back for a swim, and then got ourselves under a beer tent to finish off. We left by the same train, got off near Pacific St and then onto the mission. After a short nap in the train, I had regained my zest and left the mission on my own to adventure in Manhattan to fill out the day.

The music of rattling wheels sent me into another sleepy doze. I was involved with a dream about the lady with the blemished skin, when I was shaken by a guard and found myself seated alone in the train. He told me that all passengers had to get out, as the train was on the way to Harlem where riots were in progress.

Climbing the steps, some memory told me I was in the centre of town. I strolled to the nearest frankfurter stall and asked the man at the counter if he knew of an inexpensive hotel nearby. I had no urge to retrace my journey back to Brooklyn and therefore OK'd his advice and booked in a German hotel in 46th St. It was a reasonable pad for the night, and I made use of the bed right away. As I pulled the sheet over me, I kept trying to think out what the uniform meant when he gave me the order to get out of the subway?

I dozed off to sleep thinking how serious the riots in Harlem were. I must have slumbered real deep because sun streamed in between a split in the window curtains and beckoned me to take a look of midtown New York on that Sunday morning in the beautiful, sunshiny month of July. I took a quick face wash in the bowl provided. I didn't have my razor with me, and chin stubble told me through the mirror that I was not the fairest of them all.

After taking the elevator down to the ground floor, I was soon light footing it through the doors into the quiet of the city. You would think it was part of the British Empire in which cities under the Union Jack stopped in a time warp every Sunday. Come to think of it, at one time little ole New York really was a settlement of the old country until the colonisers decided that their straight, puritan backs would refuse to bend before an overseas despot.

Then I walked myself over to Fifth Avenue and crossed at the light. Without any particular notion of where I was heading, I just bowled along, enjoying the exercise. Then I slowed down to where a queue of people was lined up against something that looked like a big gun turned up at a high angle. There were a lot of people showing interest, and I wondered if it was worth lining up for a peep through this telescope. One man popped his dime in, and as he turned to look away, I pulled him up and requested what famous sight he had in view?

He pointed a finger upwards to where a tall skyscraper zoomed into the blue. "That's what you see," he answered, "the top of the Empire State Building." "Is there anything interesting up there?" "I noticed a telescope up on that roof," he replied, "with people looking down at this street." After that response, I thought I would rather spend a dime on coffee instead and amuse myself watching people walk here on this street and that is what I did.

I strolled on and before long stopped at a Nedick's kiosk, mounted the high sidewalk stool, ordered a coffee and planned my next move. I felt like a beer, but one had to stretch the legs a bit far to get a beer in New York City on a Sunday, so I dropped that idea. I tried to work out the direction of Times Square, and as my mind cleared with the hot beverage, my bearings became clear, and I was soon off toddling on my way to where it was all happening.

There weren't any solitary walkers, just people in bunches; there always was, Sunday included. And here I was staring up at a big corner cinema. Neon lighting was flashing the latest news by the second – ..... M-A-Y-O-R L-A-G-U-A-R-D-I-A V-I-S-I-T-S H-A-R-L-E-M...nineteen people dead in riots...Twenty people now dead.

With a throng of others, I hung around until Harlem fatalities reached twenty-three dead and then left with a fancy for a look-see at the theatres and the other enchanting areas of 42nd St in the cool air caused by the shade of high buildings, and I forgot all about tippling.

I then wandered back up Fifth Avenue, passing the big telescope once more, and after a short halt and by asking questions, discovered that the canals of the moon could be viewed at night, as a result I promised myself a dime's worth one starry evening.

I discovered I was creating an appetite and entered the first subway underground that came my way and took a tube back to Brooklyn. If I caught the boys lingering at the diner, I intended to boast of NEARLY ending up in riot-torn Harlem. Anyway, all yarns were NEARLY ones; else we wouldn't be alive to spin them – Anything to brighten up a Sunday.

I missed my regular stop in Brooklyn, and when I walked out of the station, I came across a bridge. As I stood beneath this raised structure and tried to find a familiar landmark along came a middle-aged gentleman, whom I asked as to the whereabouts of the Navy Yard. He told me that if I followed the bridge exit for half a mile to where it turned off, my destination would only be a block or two further along the highway.

Not only did he give me my bearings, but he also gave me a brief account of Tadeusz Kosciusko, the philanthropist, who donated the structure to Brooklyn. However, years later, I found that his account was definitely wrong. Kosciusko was a Polish-Lithuanian engineer and leader who had become a national hero in Poland, Lithuania, Belarus and who had really helped United States military efforts during the American Revolution (1776-83) against us Brits. The bridge was built in Brooklyn in 1939 over Newtown Creek and named for him to honour and boost the large Polish-American population in the area since Poland was then under German occupation. My new acquaintance was some yarn maker; maybe he had been to sea! I thanked the gent for his directions and took the leg stretch to boost my appetite. But the walk took way longer than he said. Yeah, some yarner that guy was.

At last I reached the boys at our usual rendezvous. I so enjoyed our time together that I was hoping that the four of us would stick with the *Loke* until we reached the UK.

The best thing about this diner was that one could eat at any time between 7am and midnight. The Sunday chicken and veg went down well, and after a few beers, we took ourselves off to the hostel. No one complained of a cash shortage, and it was decided to take a snooze, after which Johan would lead the way to a Scandinavian dance and drink joint in south Brooklyn called the Ragnas to kill off the weekend. After the nap Dave and Aussie changed their minds. They decided on venturing uptown to visit the Pepsi-Cola Canteen in Times Square to try and pick up a date.

I stayed with my old mate, Johan, and we took a taxi to the Ragnas. From hearsay, he had often enthused about this Nordic honky-tonk, and when we arrived, we didn't find it too exciting on the ground floor, so we were advised to go up one floor for the high life. This well-lit area was rather larger with maybe fifty or sixty tables with more than half occupied. Most of the tables we passed had small glasses of a pale liquid set on the mahogany, and Johan enlightened me that the popular drink was called Tom Collins.

When the waiter appeared, we decided to go with the majority and ordered two glasses. At one dollar fifty a shot, it was expensive in 1943, but it certainly was a powerful spirit, bringing a flush to the cheeks. Johan fell in love with the place right away when he found that only waltz music was piped through since that was the only type of dance he practiced. He was in his oils. As for me, I was only too eager to get the second round of drinks, just to feel that happy glow on my face.

My mate downed his second glass right off, caught the eye of some passing bird and went whirling away in his favourite sport. Along came the waiter, and I ordered a couple more to save him time, sat back and studied faces including the actions of the good, the bad and the ugly. Also, I spied some very beautiful blondes to balance the scenery with the staggering slobberers and whirlers. I was aware that with a few more Tom

Collins, I wouldn't be looking at the scene but would be part of it.

After taking a tongue-washer to his glass, my mate was on his feet again, grabbing some willing female and whirling around like a pair of kids. This new brand of short drink made me feel on top of the world. Perhaps the only drawback to all this cutting loose was that whilst the spinning dervishes were creating a lot of heat, the whirling overhead fans had competition in keeping the place cool in the midsummer heat.

Not that it bothered a stokehold boy like me much. I felt kinglike, sitting there plying that magnetic Collins stuff. A slobberer pressed his hands on my royal shoulders just then, and I was about to displace them in a gentle, understanding way but then I turned around to meet a familiar face – none other than Ole, the fireman who had stayed in the same cabin as myself on my second ship, the *D/S Ingerfem*. I guided him to the chair abandoned by Johan and prepared myself for what I expected to be an enjoyable yarn.

Plomp! He was nice and firmly installed on the seat, leaning back and started blurbing away. I drew my chair near him and asked if he was still on the same ship. He started spilling out some story about playing on the gun deck with the ship's dog when a torpedo struck. He then broke off to reminisce sadly about that ship, "Go Habana after I leave my ship in Liverpool...returned back to my old ship later...then the sinking of my friendly, good old ship." Me: "Where?" Ole: "Blurb-blurb." "How many saved?" I questioned. "Only me and dog saved on raft." "But where was this?" I asked. "After Iceland," Ole muttered.

His head began to drop into a weepy state as he got sentimental about himself and the dog playing on their gun deck. I knew there was always a loose raft located on the gun deck and waited for my mate to compose himself so I could drag the full story out of him. Ole's head slumped more forward, and then he allowed it to hit the table. This must have sobered him up a bit because when he raised his head, he looked at me as if he didn't know me, stood up and walked away.

After that "phantom" from my past, it was back to work on Monday morning; we drank extra coffee at the diner and boarded at 9.30am. With most of the work left to shore people, there was little to do, and we were not alone in turning up late. Normally, the shipping company would have paid off all hands on board; perhaps, however, they wished to retain a skeleton crew who knew the working routine of the ship. I think the skipper purposely relaxed the working times – Dave reported to me that he only saw one officer on board when we knocked off for smokes.

By now the quarters were bare of woodwork which had been torn away from the metal plating together with the timber divisions, and if we hadn't become accustomed to finding cockroaches, plop-plopping from holes made in the evaporated milk tins, which were pierced to allow a flow into the cups, the sight would have soured us. The habit was to first pour the milk into a bucket before running it into tea or coffee so that you were sure the floating corpses of the roaches were gotten rid of.

We still had the coffee urn boiling away, and as long as there were none of these creatures on the table or stool, no one worried. It was unbelievable, the sight on deck of such a vast population that had been breeding behind the wooden slats. Where the refuse of wood had been heaped on deck, the inner sides of the slats were of a brown colour – in other words, the closeness of these fertile breeders seemed like brown paintwork.

Over smoking and drinking, the running rumour of the day had it that the *Loke* would return to the Swansea-Canada run after the refit so that settled my future plans. I would do some budgeting from now on and forget about paying off. There were still a few more months to end up with a nice bundle of pound notes when I arrived in the UK and played the bonanza boy. I had three good mates on board which encouraged my plans to stay. Perhaps they would be thinking along the same lines.

Then Aussie disappeared for two days. And while Dave and Johan were pleased to spend their evenings cavorting with the two sisters – I, instead, did some adventuring around Pacific Street, trying to keep off the liquor. I paid visits to soda parlours instead of trying to mix with local youths, most of whom were Hispanic-Americans whose attitudes were cold and unfriendly to an outsider.

Each evening I asked the elderly Norwegian lady at the hostel if she had seen Aussie. He must have gone on a splurge because her replies were always in the negative.

Being alone on the second night drove me to seek comfort in the nearby cinema; it was a forbidding film about some Latin American country. It was called *The Leopard Lady*. I failed to follow the mystery, except it was very sinister, about a senorita with high-heeled shoes, clop-clopping a lonely, cobbled street in the hours of darkness. It was all very tense as she was about to get murdered under a half-moon, yet never did. Considering I lived in an area where Latin gangs roamed the streets at night, I was not too high-spirited when I left the cinema.

I had promised myself to keep away from a thirst-quencher that night, but with the backdrop of such an alarming film, I began to see muggers around every corner, as I made my way to the hostel. The twilight was quickly darkening, and I felt I must have a comforting nightcap and dropped in a bar for a whisky and washed it down with a beer. Later, even though it was a humid evening, I dropped off to sleep easily on top of the bed sheet. A bright light flashed past my eyes, and I automatically clamped hands over them.

"It's only your old Aussie mate," came a voice. I uncovered my face and sat up. "What time is it, Oz?" "Hour and a half after midnight. Do us a favour, Cobber." Aussie said. "What's that?" I inquired. He handed me a sheet of paper with writing on it. It had the address of the Belgian Consulate. He asked me to hand it to the skipper with the request that he send his pay and personal possessions to the address. Being satisfied I would comply, he opened a flagon of beer and passed it to me while he took a pew on the single chair.

I was feeling as dry as hell, so he waited while I took a swig from the brew's neck, and then suddenly he excitedly told me about a forthcoming trip to the Belgian Congo. After handing him back the bottle, he took a swig and continued. He had been in conversation with the captain of a Belgian ship in a late bar and had been offered a job on his steamer which was fuelled by oil. "I took up his offer of a fireman's job and promised him that I would be aboard by 5am," he continued, "and I'm bloody well going to keep it, too."

I was interested and asked him about his new duties. He explained something about atomiser nozzles that were the ends of tubes about 18" in length. They connected into the fuel pipe and squirted oil into furnaces. "You clean a dozen of these each watch and you can sit on your arse for the rest of the time." Me: "How long does it take to clean them?" Aussie: "About twenty minutes." Me: "Is the job all that easy?" Aussie: "Sure, all you do for the rest of your four hour stint is to sit down and read comics and magazines."

"Cop this," he said, handing me the flagon still half full. "Don't forget to pass on my message." With a new kitbag over his shoulder, he made for the door, and before closing it, hollered, "See you in Africa!"

I took one more swig from the bottle and put it under the bed, then lit a fag and blew blue smoke rings into the air. 'Well,' I thought, 'I still have two mates left.' I took a short stroll down the passage to empty myself in the toilet and noticed the air had cooled off, so I slept that night with a sheet over me.

On the subway next morning, I asked Dave and Johan if Aussie had visited their room, but they hadn't gotten back until 2am, so I related Aussie's farewell. It seemed like their hangovers from the Ragnas drinking bout wouldn't lift. Maybe it was the way I told them about Aussie, but soon they were laughing, and that was good for me, too, because when we got to the diner, conversation would be more enjoyable.

Neither of them could eat a bite, just kept swallowing coffees, one after the other. It was now taken for granted that we boarded at 9.30am instead of 9am and knocked off at 3.30pm. I gave up the idea of going on the straight and narrow in the strict sense of the term and gladly fell in for plans for a weekend at Coney. Considering the alien feeling I had about the hostel's part of Brooklyn, I promised myself to be a regular customer at the diner during weeknights

The engine room of the *Loke* was so crowded with shore workers doing repairs and overhauls that there wasn't much room or purpose in employing us firemen, as there was more sitting around and chatting to New Yorkers than cleaning. I'm sure that had this vessel been an oil-running steamer, the company would have paid off all hands as soon as we arrived in port. However, coal firemen it seemed were difficult to pick up here, especially experienced hands. There was also an enormous choice of ships; yet thinking it over soberly, I realised I was in a lucky position. Dave and Johan felt the same way.

Johan spent more time at the Ragnas as time wore on, leaving Dave and myself to flirt with the Swedish sisters. They trained us both into good waltzers, yet there still was that hankering to get away that affects most seamen regardless of the tippling, even though I was eating and living well. In the third week in July, we had already been a month in dry dock, and word came through that we would sail the first week of August for Canada. A few days later, Johan began to crack. He told us that if repairs continued after the first week in August, he was determined to pay off.

He had made a lot of friends at the Ragnas, who had told him he was a mug for staying on a dirty, old tramp ship when the harbour was full of Norske ships he could choose from. For days he kept quieter than usual. One night I paid a visit to his favourite honky-tonk to see if I could again catch sight of my old friend, Ole. I was hoping to meet him in a more sober state of mind so I could get the full story about the *Ingerfem*, while Johan was involved in his dervish exercise.

Then late one night, it occurred again; not one midnight flit but two. Both Dave and Johan entered my room in the early hours, turned the light on and started blabbering excitedly about someone in the Ragnas, who had offered them positions on another vessel. They packed up their bags hastily, picked up their documents and there was no message for me to convey to the captain of the *Loke*, as their new skipper would arrange all other business. They had just popped in to say goodbye. They didn't realise in what a lonely state of mind they left me.

I put the bedside lamp on, switched off the ceiling globe and lit up a cigarette. For a minute I looked forward to an uncertain sailing future with maybe hostile shipmates. Then I began to have second thoughts. Even if I was at loose ends at times, I was proud of my stickability, and a certain confidence grew in my mind that all was not lost. Then my mind altered course to take refuge in vanity, and my imagination took on the boastful, cheap pose of returning to Wales, flaunting American-style clothes in a country where material was scarce.

These vanity parades in my mind were good antidotes for times of loneliness, and pulling my sheet over me, I concluded that blackout nights spent in the friendly embrace of genial company was superior to the bright lights of Broadway where friendship could be weak. And as for those nice, modernised ships, sea time might be easier than on the *Loke*, but in port, when you were out for a good time, most of this time was spent under the eagle eye of the engineer, making sure you did your full eight hour stint. After painting the engine room all day, your energy was too drained to paint the town red. That one day on the *Lido* taught me not to take lightly the advantages of a coal burner.

It was obvious now that ship's repairs could go well into a second month, and although I had to take a couple of days to get over the fact that the donkeyman and myself were the only remaining engine room workers, I began to realise the positive effect of having the whole weekend to myself completely. I would not have to follow suit and spend my time with others just for the warmth of sociability but could take my time on the way home, maybe mingle with new acquaintances and also keep to my own private plans. I found that I had not thought of things this way before.

That evening I took it pretty easy after reaching my hostel in Pacific Street, and for the first time, took a real interest in the library and socialising with one of the other residents, a deckhand somewhat more senior than myself, who bought me a coffee at the counter. He was on the waiting list for a job; however, when I told him the *Loke* was heading for Canada, he said he preferred a ship sailing to the warm and inexpensive places southward. When I told him I was trying to keep away from bars, he suggested to me why not take a visit to the Stage Door Canteen (forgetting it was usually reserved for the military), and I was soon making steps to the subway station around the corner.

I enjoyed the ride to Manhattan, answering any nods and smiles whenever commuters wished to exchange them. Arriving at Times Square, I found the canteen very prominently placed on one corner. I kept up my leisurely pace and entered this famous place to find it over-packed with uniforms of the three services, and although spellbound in the spirit of the atmosphere, I felt a little out of place in my civilian dress and continued on to the Pepsi-Cola Canteen only a block away.

War had brought danger to the United States, but it also brought big pay packets as the men working in the dry dock kept telling us; the labour market had never been so good, and as a result the uptown section of Manhattan was seething with big spenders on weekends As I jostled through the excited crowds of cheerful faces, I felt this was the place to be and with no weekend work, I had two long days to fill in.

I felt more at home at the Pepsi Canteen. It wasn't jammed packed like the other place, and there were plenty of merchant seamen there; the civilian dress might have even outnumbered the uniforms there. Along came the hostesses with trays of orange juice; you went to the counter for coffee and doughnuts, all for free. Then along came plain Jane and asked me to dance, and I felt I glided with her OK after my training at the diner with the Swedish sisters.

Lying back in bed the following day, I didn't consider Friday evening a roaring success but neither was it a real flop. My hostess of about thirty years just didn't charm me all that much. My greatest success was drinking orange juice and eating doughnuts without any desire for alcoholic drinks.

But I decided to call on Jane again. So what was the attraction? She didn't captivate me in the way young chicks did, who got you all feverish; they were sex teasers. It was something else.

If I had listened to a male talk as she did about work promotion and hopes for higher wages, it would have bored me stiff, but waltzing slowly in circles, I felt completely at ease with the tone of her voice over the background music and cheery chatter amongst various groups. I had been stupid not to have made a date when offered. Anyway, I would make up for it and pay her a call that day and ask her to come to Coney Island with me on Sunday.

Monday morning came along, and this time the donkeyman passed a job onto me just to my liking. All I had to do was enter the centre boiler and chip the blisters of rust and sea salt covering the crowns of the three furnaces. He instructed me to take my time and make the job last a week. It was a job I could have completed easily in three days, so I had to find a way of stretching it. The chief engineer was busy at all times with the engine room supervisor, and the deucer was ashore for a week visiting relatives in Pennsylvania and because of all that, I had no interference.

There was only one medium sized fly in the ointment; I had suffered a disappointment on the weekend. When I visited the Pepsi canteen on Saturday, one of the hostesses there informed me that Jane was away until the following Tuesday, and there was nothing for it but to go back on the bottle; therefore, I spent most of my time at the diner, but the company was not the same since the gang broke up, and the two sisters had cottoned on to some other forlorn sailors.

At work there were plenty of long electric leads on the bottom plates of the engine room; I barged into a group of boiler makers, fitters, turners and other repair men who were still discussing the Harlem riots that had rocked New York and were now wondering if it would spread to other cities.

At first I listened in to just get on their friendly side, and when my chance came, I nicely interrupted to let them know I was preparing the centre boiler for testing and could they lend me an electric lead? I suppose they wished to keep in with me as much as I did with them, and they told me to use whatever I saw lying around.

Destination now – the manhole opening at the upper part of the rear of the boiler, so grabbing a lead, I made my way up the ladder and walked the grated platform. It was already switched on so I dipped it inside together with my head, located the hand grip above the hole, turned on my shoulders and hauled myself in. Above me was the dome of the boiler, and level with me were the tubes that carried the smoke through the boiler from the combustion chamber leading to the funnel.

I used the soot tubes as a ladder to descend to the upper surface of the boiler. I sat on top of the furnace crown and felt over it with the palm of my hand, then dangled my globe centrally over this area.

I was about to work on it by lashing a doubled section of the lead around an upper tube. I then took my time and mentally checked on the items I would need without making a second journey down into this awkward place. I would need a chipping hammer, a wire brush and a soft bristle hand brush, together with a couple of sacks to sit on. I wriggled out the same way as I had entered, face upward with hands grabbing the bar to lift my body out.

Beneath the bottom plates, a small gang were cleaning oil, grease and grit from the bilges. There was a mountain of sacks near them, which they used for kneeling on and wiping up, so I grabbed two and stashed them under the engineer's desk where he kept the log book; then I went in the stokehold to pick up my tools. I also grabbed the water can; there would be a lot of dust in my throat when the chipping began. All I needed now was string to tie these items so they didn't keep falling into the boiler.

Then I remembered that there was always twine in the log book desk together with a knife. I put the lot in a bucket and ascended to enter my boiler. Inside the boiler I tried out the sacks for comfort, and they suited me just fine. I had an hour to go before cleaning up for dinner and decided not to start kicking up dust by hammering away until I had eaten, else I would have to have a big clean up. I just sat there in those cool surroundings and wondered if Johan and Dave had regretted leaving the *Loke*. Perhaps those nice, new ships weren't very nice after all, what with the wrong kind of engineer on your back in port. If there were no fans in the engine room, hours of painting, bilge-diving and brassoing were not to my liking.

When I got back to my private room at the hostel, I did a bit of thinking about the job I was on. That afternoon I had made a complete job on one furnace-top, and the donkeyman had told me to make the job last until Friday, so I had a plan I intended carrying out the following day. I would do half a furnace crown in the morning and take a siesta in the cool of the boiler in the afternoon, and that next morning as soon as I had changed into my dirty gear, I went around the base of the dock where a lot of rubbish was strewn.

There were loads of packing cases and other debris around and I picked up just what I wanted – a piece of plywood 3' by 4' and pliable enough to bend through the manhole. After putting it inside the hole, I picked up a fat piece of asbestos packing stripped from a boiler and shoved that through as well. I was arranging a bed for the afternoon. Everything went OK, and when I knocked off for lunch, I used the amenities of the dock to give myself a shower.

I was not accustomed to drinking anything stronger than coffee during my meal hour since I was building up calories for night time activities. I seemed to change as the days crawled by. Perhaps it was nostalgia for losing good shipmates, together with loneliness, plus that glorious New York summer getting sticky warm, but after beers one afternoon, I decided to take a long siesta inside the boiler.

I had not seen the d'man since Monday, and now it was Thursday. Every time I asked other crew members about his whereabouts, the answer was always the same – that he had gone to make a phone call. I concluded he was playing games. Maybe he was spending time ashore. That was why I took the liberty to enjoy a long nap.

However, I did not crawl through the manhole door right away. Someone had taken my electric lead. Being in something of a stupor, my intelligence was not up to the mark. There were no shortages of leads; they were scattered all over the place. I went to the stokehold, found myself a duck lamp and lit the wick.

I wriggled hard into the boiler and after descending to the top of the central furnace, hung the lamp on a cross soot tube and napped off. I was lying back in this half-awake state, when my ears caught the sound of metal rubbing against metal. My worst fears were aroused; they were locking the manhole door.

The thought that I might be boiled alive soon shook off the midday torpor. I was just as alert as could be. Looking upwards, the sight of light being eclipsed from the oval opening really got me panicky; my voice would never get through that thick iron chamber. Scrambling desperately up the cross piping, in my haste I sadly had forgotten to take my chipping hammer.

I very much needed that hammer to send a message through that thick manhole cover. In the eerie darkness, I fumbled my way back down. Fortunately, I had been wise to hang my tools on chords to prevent them dropping into to the nether darkness of the boiler.

Giving a hasty grab at the tool I needed, it swung away from me, and I grabbed it on the second swing back. Removing it from the slipknot, I ascended hastily and was about to strike an almighty clanger. A slit of light shot through. My barrier to life and liberty was being removed. It must have failed to lock properly.

Just to make sure I would be removed from this possible tomb, I went head first and face upwards, with arms ready to grab iron bars above the opening. Outside I pulled my legs partly out of the gap and left two boiler makers to lift my torso out. I noticed that my helpers had two very ashen faces. They took part of the shock from me.

On the bottom deck of the engine room where repair men gathered for a smoke and a chat, I became the centre of attraction that afternoon. I joined in with them as they reminisced about how seamen on the docks, piers and wharfs in the Port of New York lost their lives. I soaked in the chatter, of which I was the central point, and one remark remained sufficiently long enough with me to make me feel shocked at the realities of life behind the veil of everyday existence. During a space of silence, an elderly boiler maker, leaning pensively against a support pillar of the upper platform, made a slow and precise statement.

He declared that up to that point in time of 1943, twenty-two lives had been lost due to workers sleeping inside boilers. New York piers were jam-packed with merchant ships during WW2; even so, this news seemed like an inexcusable loss of life.

That lost number reminds me of when I was hauled off a London dock during the blackout four months later. There I was taken to St Georges East Hospital. I signed my name on the register and when I left a few days later, and as cool as you like, the head nurse said as she was searching for my particulars. "You are the forty-second immersion patient to be taken from the River Thames this year."

After eating in the diner that evening, I failed to shake off foreboding thoughts. I wanted to decide what I wanted to do with all my free time on the coming weekend. By the time I had exited the subway near Pacific Street, my mind was made up to pay another visit to the cinema close to where I lodged.

There were not many seamen staying at the hostel and not many seamen stayed long at the coffee and sandwich counter, although the elderly Norwegian lady who ran the place was always eager to help and advise those needing it. Sitting at the counter with a coffee and enjoying a cigarette, I asked her what was playing at the local flicks.

She didn't know but passed me a newspaper. I did not even turn to the movie ads, as I had the idea that only Manhattan cinemas in 42nd Street and Broadway would be advertised; however, I became very interested in the front page that described a massive armada of landing craft attacking Sicily, forecasting that a new Italian government would soon be set up as Mussolini was losing power.

The counter lady had a flat, circular net for swatting flies and was glad when she trapped a fly against the wall. "I vish it was a Yap," she said. This must have reminded her of something. Having shown her patriotic distaste for the Japanese, she said to me, "Why you don't do around the corner? There is a new film showing."

So off I went. The war film was about Americans fighting their Asian foes in the Pacific with plenty of gunfire and with more than enough gory scenes.

My own boiler escapade was blotted out by the life and death struggle in the movie, although lying in bed a day later I did analyse that particular day when things could have gone wrong. In the first place, once I noticed the electric lead amiss, it would only be sensible to ask the reason why.

Normally, there was a pattern of shipboard discipline that was unique and reliable. The duty engineer was always in close touch with the donkeyman, and the d'man watched over the greasers and firemen. The same applied to the deck. If it was necessary to climb the mast, there was always another deckhand standing by when a sailor went aloft as a witness for possible aid.

At any time during the day, those in charge knew where he could find each man in his department. It became a gradual conditioning that someone was watching someone. I disagree with the modern style of completely relying on radar. There should always be a lookout on deck in case someone slipped overboard.

Friday evening I was cleaning up and rode the subway to Times Square and the Pepsi-Cola Canteen. I surprised myself on how good I was feeling. What was the reason? Jane was no bundle of joy, but she was pretty nice to talk to. I was now on my own, yet did not feel alone. I began to realise that the group binges with mates had their downside. After a time, they could weaken one's own identity.

However, I still needed the company of Jane to make up for my aloneness; she aided my personal aims to surface. Enjoyment by men living in close quarters is certainly a good life in itself but only for so long. Without a break for female company, it becomes artificial.

Why did I feel light-hearted this weekend with no happy group to join with? There's a joy in doing your own thinking. I observed New Yorkers in a very sympathetic manner. They knew they were a mighty nation, and with the national unity they showed towards defeating the enemy, they were devoted to the men in their armed forces.

Whilst they were all working their guts out to make sure the US was short of nothing to deter victory, they were in line with the American vision – the American dream of owning a house and a car by slogging away at overtime. The Great Depression was fading into the past, and irrespective of the tragedy of war, they were determined to turn their back on poverty.

The four or five occasions I had met with Jane, she was not very demonstrative in my company; it was an equal, non-sexual relationship, which could grow warmer if either of us took the initiative. So what pulled us together? Like myself her social status was a nothing.

I was something of a coal miner of the sea, and if I termed her PLAIN Jane, she must have termed me something plainer. The height of her own status was that of being a factory worker, no higher. As we paired up for a waltz or a foxtrot, she was by no means a poky, but there must have been an ever so small voice within her that restrained her from too close contact with my body.

It had something to do, I believe, with the early signs of the gradual revolution that followed the war. The international yearning of western women to secure an independent status from their men folk was opening up to them, and mothering was losing priority.

However, she was my only contact with the female sex, and our Friday night meeting encouraged me to see her the following evening. She was not hostessing that night, and I got that 'little boy lost' feeling, I, therefore, had to make the best of it.

"Take a seat," urged a gawky youth, sitting by himself at one of the tables. Being dressed in civilian clothes, he would be a merchant seaman. I sat down. He was eager for talk. "Who are youse?" "Ted. I'm from the old country." "Jeez, my pal's a Limey, too. Hits the bottle some. Told me to get the hell out and do something for the war effort. And because of that I just joined my first merchant ship." My mind was collecting fast words as he raced along.

The he lapsed into soft talk, recalling with nostalgia leaving his home in Delancey Street in lower Manhattan for the first time. We became our best selves when we wished to buck up the other fellow, and I wished to buck up this Andy.

We scanned around at the dance floor. No one was really dancing; the floor was too packed for that. Although a waltz was in progress, swinging and swirling plainly were out. It seemed the dancers were glued together and were slowly progressing in a circle together with heads lolling on shoulders.

There on the floor, lovesick drunks and homesick youngsters put on their performances. My new mate gazed that way as if he wanted to join them. "I have been here often, Andy." I boasted. "Would you like me to grab you a hostess?" "Can't dance," he replied. "And with all these choice broads floating around. Geez!"

"Only half these guys on the floor can really dance," I answered. "The hostesses know this and guide the other half around." Then I noticed a sparkle in his eye. For the first time I realised he had the guts to give it a try. And the gutsiest people I have known have had some impediment or disability.

Seemed to me Andy had been turned down for recruitment in the services due to not measuring up to the medical standard, and about one of the easiest medicals one could pass was to work in the engine room of a merchant ship. All they tested you for was for a hernia.

Andy had signed on as an engine room utility man. They usually did odd jobs in the engine room and took the place of a trimmer or wiper should that person incur an accident or was paid off for some reason. And so another new acquaintance came and went.

Starting work on Monday, the shore foreman in the engine room of the *Loke* told me I could safely continue working in the boiler and would make personally sure of my whereabouts should there be any boiler testing.

After two months in dry dock, all the deckhands had paid off and out of the down below crowd, only the d'man and myself remained so it was almost a completely new crew who signed on. They boarded, slung their kitbags on the bunks of their cabins and went straight back ashore to catch a couple of drinks before our sailing, which was the following day.

There were no introductions; however, the donkeyman informed me that all the crew had recently taken passage on a Norwegian freighter from Freetown, Sierra Leone, after being saved from a burning tanker that had been torpedoed off the West African coast and had chosen to sail on the *Loke* because, with so many vacancies, it offered the crew a chance to stay together.

Soon we sailed out of the dock, setting course up the Hudson River, and diverted into a canal; all those Manhattan skyscrapers evaporated from sight. As the New York skyline shrank in size, Manhattan looked like a toy town, and the next thing we found was greenery and grazing cattle on either bank of the canal.

One thing was missing from this rural landscape and that was a sea breeze, which would have been very welcome in the month of August, but with clean boilers, even the Yankee slack coal blazed well, and it seemed regulations forbade going faster than half speed. It gave us firemen on duty watch a chance to pop up on deck occasionally to turn the ventilators and take in the scenery whilst the trimmer kept his eye on the steam gauge below.

By the time we entered Boston Harbor later in the sail, the d'man and myself were well acquainted with the new firemen and trimmers. What surprised me most was that all the deck officers had new faces except the skipper, yet the three engineers remained on.

My new trimmer was a lanky lad of twenty-two years, who was doing his first trip on a coal-burning steamer. Together with another trimmer, both had previously held jobs as motormen.

After my first ship had sunk under me eighteen months before, I remembered as I stared in the wardrobe mirror in my room at the Halifax Allied Seamen's Club, my face wore a slight rigidness that was not there before. There is always a certain paleness in the look of men who are below decks, but this same unsmiling stiffness now showed itself in Lars, my trimmer, and it gave me a sleepless night as I tried to figure out what it meant.

It was only later that I fully understood the look in both me and Lars to be the result of shock, and perhaps not such a bad thing, even if unhealthy. From that time in Nova Scotia, my nerves had been on a bowstring, and this nervous strain served as a beautiful alarm system throughout the war. Later, however, it cost me a very upsetting state of mind and a lot of booze to allow my nerves to unwind.

As days progressed on the *Loke* I noticed Lars's mates sometimes looked ill at ease. One of the firemen would have bouts of inflexible staring. That burning tanker they escaped from must have been a rough experience by the writing on their faces.

CANADA

A few days run brought us to a small port in New Brunswick called Carleton-Sur-Mer, where a considerable cargo of timber was waiting. This countrified town was a respite from the big, bustling city that we had left. It was obviously colonised by the French, since most of the people were bilingual.

Like Nova Scotia, New Brunswick was a dry province, but there was a drinking club set aside for visiting seamen. The locals looked and acted like a pioneering type; they were most sociable and friendly, and one evening I was invited into the house of a young couple, who had recently migrated from France.

I found very few shops in the settlement; however, one was piled up with a mix of all conceivable goods, and there was also an excellent barber shop, quite inexpensive. However, there was a hiccup that occurred with the crew and this merchant. The owner of the shop sold sundry items like soft drinks and cigarettes at the rear of his shop with no fencing around it, which vouched for an honest neighbourhood.

One day he stormed up the gangway, demanding to have a word with the captain. The captain was informed that not one stick of ripe Indian corn remained in his garden patch. The night before drunken seamen had boarded the *Loke*, as excited as kids, some carrying beer bottles while others had cobs of corn under their pullovers, which they proceeded to boil in the galley.

In was fortunate that the storekeeper descended the gangway with smiles all over his face. This small port berthed only one ship at a time, and the officers must have gotten wind of the fact that no customs men searched the ship for dutiable goods before they left New York, and maybe stocked up with whisky and cigarettes.

And so the Canadian merchant left the skipper as if he had been well-entertained, swinging a bag out of which stuck a bottle top and the end of a cigarette carton. From that I had an idea that it was no bad thing to have a couple of jokers on board to lighten up those members who were still in shock.

This crew must have decided amongst themselves to keep a code of silence about their traumatic escape from enemy action because after the first couple of days I learned nothing more than was revealed to me on that first day. Perhaps playing the imp was a way of starting life afresh.

The skipper never bothered to bring anyone to book concerning the corn heist, and since New Brunswick was a dry province, the storekeeper had a nice, black market cache of medicine for the coming cold months as we were now into September. After a five day rest up in port, The *Loke* left with timber stacked way up above the main deck level.

We rendezvoused with a convoy 200 miles down the coast at the port of Halifax, Nova Scotia, a place I had known pretty well. Perhaps the skipper wished to gain trust with the fresh crew because I could never remember him allowing a sub list and a liberty boat for those wishing to go ashore in a convoy port before.

During the few days wait for the convoy to build up, I joined the happy group myself for an evening out at the Allied Seamen's Club. It would be the last time I could enjoy bright lights before arriving in the blacked-out UK, although no news had yet come through from the radio operator which port would be our destination.

The capital of Nova Scotia was never as well-lit as New York and met the autumn earlier; therefore, a leather jacket became necessary for a boat ride ashore. One night I returned with the crew in the early 9pm boat, yet all hands were as full as a boot, and when they got up the gangway became very mischievous.

The usual pranksters roamed the deck with that extra energy that forbade sleep, with open bottles in their hands from which they took occasional swigs, and by looks and tones were passing mischievous innuendos. I had an idea that most of this crew came from the same port in Norway and had a gang mentality.

They seemed to be trying to stir up some kind of derring-do to continue the fun of the night. A belly full of Canadian beer, spiced with intermittent whiskies, can build up a lot of bravado, and I felt as drunk and cocky as the rest. I fell for the game. Sticking out my chest, I pronounced that I would dive over the side into those cold waters if they would slip a rope over the side and haul me up.

I was well-backed. With lighting restrictions and the fact that I had dived on the opposite side of the gangway, it got me panicky when I surfaced in the harbour. That 'fre-e-ezing' feeling got me looking up to see where any rope was dangling from. Cold can sober a man as well as heat. That is why drunks are put in coolers.

In the semi-darkness of the split moon, I could just make out blurry figures on deck, but fortunately with a full cargo, the bulwarks were not too far above the water line. Yet the rope that was slung to me was a skinny, heaving line. My clothing pulled me down as I swam sluggishly towards it, and I could barely hold my grip with such cold hands and a thin line. Those hardy Vikings from the frozen land of the north were certainly putting me to the test.

For the next few days I felt the warmth of camaraderie. I had been accepted by the new crew. My initiation was not accepted by the kindly old chief engineer. It was no secret on board that he was concerned for his family back home in occupied Norway.

It was passed on to me via another that he looked at my night dive into the briny as an attempted suicide. What do you do when someone communicates sympathetic compassion? I just had to accept it along with his erratic and moody behaviour; actually, my trimmer could have done with that compassion. Yet, I doubt if he realised that Lars' mental state was unbalanced.

The new *Loke* officers were not the strict yet efficient breed that had gained recognition the hard, industrious way, but rather a bunch of young snobs. Their attitudes were both ignorant and arrogant. I found this new bunch of deck officers difficult to accept and felt glad to be under the engineers.

Wartime personnel shortage enabled them promotion three times as rapid as the norm. I learned of their upper class manners one night when we were a week out of port.

It would be about 9pm and I was on the 8-12 duty watch. Lars had heaved up half the ashes from the two fires I had cleaned out. When a ship rolls, an inexperienced trimmer might lose his grip at the handle when heaving up the iron bucket of ashes. There was no such rolling this particular night, since the convoy was travelling its course in fair weather.

I was unprepared for the heavy thud that hit the stokehold deck when bucket and ashes struck the steelwork, not a foot from where I had been standing, a foot away from a most terrible accident had it occurred. The bucket had crashed down so hard that it buckled the steel plate it landed on.

All my yelling upwards to the man on top of the fiddley got no response, and I was fuming. As I was shovelling the mess of ashes out of my working area, who should enter the stokehold than the chief engineer himself. He called to me, "You must do your best to raise more steam."

His eyes were wide open, and I noticed a look of panic in them. Then he was gone as suddenly as he appeared. The first thing was to attend to raising steam. After raking flat the upper surfaces of the six fires, I cooled under the ventilator after taking a swig from the water can and then lit up a cigarette.

As the red, glowing coals brought up steam in the gauge glass, I wondered what the hell was going on topside with the two incidents invading my peace of mind in rapid succession. But this was no time for easing up. The embers would be crimson, turning to white heat right now so I stubbed my smoke and sprayed a lighter pitch of coal over them.

I took as little time as possible; doors were shut so the slightest heat would not leak out to sabotage my effort. My feet made hurried steps into the engine room to learn the need for extra speed.

The donkeyman was seated on the bench in front of the brass-bound speed telegraph; his eyes were totally fixed on the phone box next to it. No doubt he awaited messages from the navigation bridge. There are so many noises in the engine room of a steamship that a lot of lip reading goes on when people talk to each other. The man in charge waved me over to sit beside him. Once he got his mouth near my ear, I eagerly awaited his comment.

"Not worry," were the first words. "Submarine no want timber. Look inside convoy for oil tanker and ammunition." I was soothed for the moment, but really wondered how this short, stout body always kept his cool on duty watch. Seeing no life jackets around, I suggested I go topside and fetch a few down for emergency, with which he agreed. So up I went, knowing him to be a good Joe, who would not let the steam drop in the boilers whilst I was away.

The timber was not in log form instead it was planking. Even so, with blackout regulations, one had to tread carefully to stop tripping over chains and bottle screws holding down deck cargo.

The timber was lashed to stanchion posts on each side of the cargo deck, and I was as careful as a ballet dancer crossing the afterdeck. There was the exploding thump of depth charges, which destroyers were dropping to strike the underwater menace. A scurrying cloud, passing the face of the moon, gave me enough guidance to reach the poop deck.

So high was the cargo, I stepped down to the quarters instead of climbing the ladder. There I took a breather before entering the living quarters. With the moon now shining like a lantern, my watching the lines of vessels all sailing in formation, made me think that I must have been unobservant this trip.

Not only was the *Loke* carrying deck cargo, there were shadowy outlines of cargo items, showing just above the bulwarks of every vessel. Then I recalled what a deckhand had pointed out to me earlier. "Look over there," he said. "That ship is carrying invasion barges." Yet I had barely given it a glance.

It occurred to me that if every ship leaving US ports now carried invasion barges, it would be the biggest invasion of Europe in human history. Down below in the mess room, all hands sat around the table looking grim and wearing life jackets. I singled out Lars, and without mentioning the bucket of ashes he had allowed to drop down the ventilator shaft, asked him why he never took the trouble to drop down a life jacket as well.

I had spoken harshly to him for the first time, and the petrified expression on his face suggested that further reprimanding would have no sensible outcome. I grabbed a life jacket out of the d'man's cabin and another from my own and ascended on deck to make my way back.

This time I decided to return to the other side of the ship, as descent into the working alleyway was safer. Fumbling my way across the timber, anger flared up in me at the unworthy attitude of my trimmer, but there was to be more disillusionment with the second-rate behaviour to come. Putting one foot in front of the other, I delicately stepped from the planking to the alley entranceway.

The first door I passed was wide open. It was where officers took their coffee breaks during duty hours. It faced directly opposite the doorway where you descended to the engine room, and which I was about to enter. Casting a glance into the place, I found the same serious looks as back aft. All officers sat there in their life jackets except the one on duty at the bridge.

Eyes returned stares, neutral stares. Before I opened the door, one young officer opened his mouth and caught my attention. He wanted to know what I was doing out of the engine room when the convoy was gathering speed. I rebuffed him by responding that some officer had neglected his duty by not supplying the engine room with life jackets.

I was quite surprised how unified the others were behind their spokesman. One of them classified my attitude as impudent for leaving my place of duty at such a critical time. I couldn't win.

Soon I found my d'man in the stokehold finishing off pitching coal on my fires. I was glad to catch him there, as it was quieter than the engine room, and I could let him know the remarks spat at me by those young deck officers. He boiled over when I recounted the verbal abuse I had been subjected to. He realised himself that sympathy was in extremely short supply with that bunch and assured me that he would confront the chief engineer about it first thing in the morning.

Combine an emotional setback with an actual crisis situation and the mixture can drive a person bonkers or 'up the wall' as the saying goes. However, there is another combination to beat it, and that is to keep body and mind busy. The d'man had not been idle in my absence.

He had worked hard with the long poker or slice bar to break up clinker at the back of the fire, and I had the benefit of higher steam with air entering at its most important area. In stokehold terminology, the glass in the steam gauge was touching 'the blood' (or the red mark of top steam) which meant that we were in the correct convoy line and had some steam to spare.

I enjoyed this advantage by smoking my fag down to its veriest beneath the vent. It would be nice if everyone was as cool, calm and collected as my mate in the engine room in trying situations, but I have to spit it out that I am too sensitive and thin-skinned to act out such a noble part. Should I allow my mind to enter a void, I might go off my mental rocker like Lars.

Fantasising was the best defence should the worst come. I would hate to be in the same lifeboat as those up-and-coming Captain Blighs topside, which led me to a dream plan in critical situations. To clear bogeymen entering my mind, I fashioned a state of things that would swallow these invasions.

At first, I imagined being in a lifeboat with those wearing epaulets on their shoulder and could see them cornering the rum bottle. I didn't like that idea. Was there any way out of the situation? I began making imaginary contact with the enemy. In my mind's eye, I heard the captain of a German U-boat announcing as he addressed his crew, 'See here, kameraden, we know what it will be like to be struck by a depth charge under these cold Atlantic waves,' and there would be the general assent of 'ja, ja'. 'Then we must watch out for a ship called the *Loke*,' he continued, 'and must make sure the torpedo misses the engine room and stokehold.'

Then steam started to drop; therefore, I flipped my cigarette butt into an ash pit and sliced the fires. I did this with gusto so I could get back to my dream plan under the vent. However, my imagination kept on course when I looked into one of the furnaces and overheard myself saying half aloud, "Let them all get stuffed. I might end up like that loner on the *S/S Pegasus* and live like a king."

Before arriving at our destination port – Belfast, Northern Ireland, I paid a visit to the skipper and gave him notice to pay me off there. I was the only Brit on board, and actually the sole one permitted to pay off.

NORTHERN IRELAND

We tied up not far from York Street, which was frequented by dockers, and I carried my kitbag there while I entered a pub. While sipping my first pint of porter, I was recommended to a very good address. It seemed that an enemy bomb had been dropped on Donegal Road causing damage to an icon for the accommodation of visiting diplomats and other bigwigs.

This was the Royal Hotel in Donegal Place. The premises had been commandeered by the Board of Trade, who turned it into a seamen's hostel for the duration of the war. I shoved my bag into the boot of a taxi and sped there before drink got the better of me and would not be allowed admittance.

The hotel must have been a showcase of the city's architecture, and I felt very small walking through its entrance. From the main desk, I was directed to a lift after paying a very reasonable rent for a week's room. There were no catering facilities, but even in wartime, Belfast had good eating places, being next door to the non-rationed Eire, with farming being its main industry.

The cleaning lady was passing by as I stepped out on the third floor and directed me to my room. Despite jagged cracks decorating the interior walls, all I could do was gawk at the lavishness and lush material of the huge curtains, draping a massive window in my room, when the lady unlocked my door.

When I was left alone behind the closed door, I felt royal myself as I lit up a fag and flopped back on the vast bed, of which there were two. Blowing a ring of smoke in the direction of the fancy chandelier dangling from the ceiling, I began to understand why it had been leased out.

Belfast was an important naval base in wartime, and together with merchant seamen of all ranks, there would be cash enough to prevent the building falling into decay. Plus there was the fact that it would be paying out a lot for security to stop lootings of the paintings decorating the corridors. And disuse of the carpets might cause deterioration.

Before leaving me, the cleaner let me know that "A nice Canadian lad occupied the other bed." I butted my cigarette and rose. There was a tang at the rear of my throat that asked for a pint of porter. It would feel good to return to a residence where writing paper was embossed with ROYAL HOTEL on top and which was laid out on a shiny, circular mahogany table with two cushioned seats facing each other around it.

I slung my bag on the spare bed to signify occupancy, not even bothering to untie it. From the door I looked back and contemplated my double bed with its double springs. It would certainly make a change from the *D/S Loke* with its straw mattress inside a coffin-deep bunk.

For the next three weeks, I intended playing the sissy, and just like the number of my door was number three, for those three weeks I had three aims—oversleeping, over drinking and looking for a doll, when I sobered up and in that order. The chief engineer had put a lot of extras in my pay packet, which gave me between 60 and 70 pounds sterling.

With dough like this I could live in luxury for two months if I handled my finances with due care, but for my three week plan everything could go hang, and taking a leisurely stroll back to the pub in York Street,

I meant to buy a few drinks for the docker who had befriended me.

He had gone, together with his mate, to do another stint of cargo handling. The dock workers had swapped places with seamen who now crowded the place. All the firemen and half the sailors from the *Loke* were there swallowing down the Irish ale like a lot of crocodiles. I joined my shipmates along the thirsty bar yet turned down too much mingling.

After paying a visit to the toilet, I returned to the bar with the intent to seat myself at a table and be a sightseer of all the excitement that was created in the bar after an Atlantic crossing in wartime. I responded to a wave from another table from a man of about forty years – obviously, a sailor by his dungarees and rubber boots.

He introduced himself as a bosun of a Swedish ship I believe he called the *Gdansk* and asked if he could get me a whisky. I was about to refuse when who should stride over and plant a double whisky on the table but Lars, my trimmer. He wished me luck and returned to his mates, standing at the bar. There was a gleam in the eye of the Swede, "I see you get on well with Scandinavians," he said.

"I'm used to their style of eating and working." I replied. "Why you don't join my ship? Make much more money." the Swede continued. It surprised him when I turned down the offer without even considering and was amazed that my excuse was that I needed a moment to think over such an offer. "Why?" he asked. "Because I am in love with a bed." I answered.

Obviously, he didn't believe me. "Have you sailed on deck before?" he continued. "Only three months." "On my ship we need an ordinary seaman. I'll ask my captain to give the job to you. I am sure it will be Ok if I tell him you have already sailed with Norwegians. Before you come in bar, I already speak with bosun of *Loke*. He said you are good worker."

I knew he expected me to jump at the opportunity of making double wages which were offered on board neutral ships like that of Sweden. He mistook my hesitation since my deck experience was short. "Don't worry," he persisted, "I will help you with any deck problems, and you get paid 45 pounds a month tax-free."

I knew that Swedish consulates in the UK had long waiting lists for men who wished to ship out. Men with the best marine tickets would jump at the lower rating of ordinary seamen, but a bosun might find it awkward to hire someone in a position with better credentials than him.

In subsequent years, I never regretted turning down those 'golden chances', and in retrospect, I find enjoyment in just being well and alive. Neutral ships were safe from enemy action during WW2, with the name of their country painted in huge letters on the hulls of each side of the ship. With a mist in the Irish Sea though, an enemy U-boat would find it difficult to read these markings on a dark night, and it was passed on to me a year later that the *Gdansk* sank in the Irish Sea with all hands.

Leaving my new acquaintance in the memorable action of shaking his head in disbelief, I left the pub and went back to Donegal Place. I bathed my face in the weak October sun, carrying an image in my head of a bosun, who could hardly believe that a seaman would turn down double wages just to luxuriate on a spring bed.

My roommate was in when I opened door number three. He had the tall, well-made body of a lad about 17 years old. He introduced himself as Bertie and had paid off as a ship's galley boy. Through small talk he let me know he was a non-drinker, and after giving it thought, I decided that was not a bad thing for the days ahead when cash ran low. I knew I would last out longer playing the tourist.

After that first night drinking porter and whisky, the hangover stinging my head the following morning almost made me take the pledge. At least I did not shun my new friend, and in a few days entered more cafés than pubs under his leadership and good company; also, I was familiar with Bertie's home town of Halifax, so we got on well.

He led me around fresh streets of Belfast. I followed him to where the offices of the British shipping pool were and watched him draw 3 pounds and 10 shillings, after which we went into a café for a hot drink and a smoke. He advised me to pool myself and draw the same cash weekly. While I had cash to spare, I could make no decision. I wanted to hang out ashore for a spell, and when Bertie concluded that Belfast was one of the slowest ports in the British Isles for shipping out, I was soon back on the bottle with a vengeance as if to make up for lost time.

After three weeks, finances made me eager to follow Bertie to the manning pool and put my name on the register for seamen waiting for employment. I was listening more to the news my young mate was sharing. He had keen hearing for picking up shipping news, even if he didn't seem awfully eager to ship out himself; he had just struck up a friendship with the opposite sex.

We both paid visits to seamen's missions, two of them being close by. I was chomping into a cheese roll there when he came across from a table where he had been chatting and asked me if I was interested in a change of scenery. Then he explained that if he was not so interested in the local lass, he'd accept a passage to Greenock.

IRELAND

He passed on the news that this port, a short distance across the strait dividing the two countries, was where some convoys departed from, and a man could earn a pound a day more than the weekly stipend we got for standing by when a convoy departed, in case a ship was shorthanded just before departure.

In 1943, a pound bought you 30 pints of beer, and it took me only a short time to accept the option. With two other volunteers, I picked up refreshment money and a boat ticket from the pool and sailed that night. Although it was a passenger ferry, it was termed a cattle boat, presumably because cattle were stowed in the hold.

A rep from the manning pool on the other side met us early the next morning when we disembarked. He had brought a van, where we jumped in with our kitbags. Many seamen's missions were reconverted decaying structures, but we were taken to a new, prefabricated wooden bungalow.

It had a kitchen and two small dormitories, housing half a dozen cot beds in each and a manager's office. Our guide told us to leave our gear in the office and follow him. Before leaving the premises, he passed us all a pound each, then led us through the township and entered one of the larger pubs.

He bought us each a beer and instructed us that this was to be our rendezvous every evening without fail. That was what the pound was for. Then he left. We felt at ease and should we go on a binge, a pound note would be handed us each morning. However, after the overnight boat ride with no sleeping accommodations, we returned to our hut for a rest.

We learned that rations here were tighter than across the water, but that fish was plentiful. We found a fish and chip shop with a sitting room, sat out a meal and spent most of the afternoon asleep in our bunks. That evening we cleaned up a bit, took our stand at the bar of a selected pub and washed down a snack of peas and pie in which there was more dough than meat.

I had a good feeling at 8pm which was after blackout time. Surely no hands would be picked up at this time of night. The tallest of the trio and myself took off to the toilet to relieve ourselves, leaving a morose sort of bloke, who seemed to have a chip on his shoulder.

When we returned to the bar, the manager informed us that our mate had been picked up by someone in a uniform. By the look of things, standby men enjoyed only a few brief nights of carousing. Our man from the pool came around after 9am next morning on his bicycle and placed a pound each in our hands. We jokingly asked where his van was and he told us that official orders had told him to cut down on petrol.

We took a walk to our regular fish shop, and later, Lofty, my tall mate, left me to read the daily paper, whilst he took a stroll around town. With no rain in sight it was a good idea. When we met later in the hut, he was not very happy about a vessel lying in the harbour called the *Empress of Russia*.

Like the *George Washington*, they were liners fuelled by coal, which made them unable to compete with modern Atlantic liners. Before WW2 both were laid up, and from what I learned at the waterfront pubs, this pair was the largest coal-burning vessels in the world – one having 120 furnaces to fire up steam and the *Washington* 140 fires.

The *Empress of Russia* had been taken out of mothballs early in the outbreak of war to transport troops, and when the USA became involved, the *George Washington* followed. With the shortage of seamen in 1943, Britain released a number of men from prison to work aboard merchant ships. It was rumoured that most of these ships' stokehold gangs were made up of these men, and we had no desire to fill any vacancy on board. The last thing I wanted was to fire a boiler next to a knife-wielding member of the underworld at the bottom of a ship.

Then, my mate said there was a good film showing in Greenock that night. "It's called 'Gone with the Wind'. Why don't we pop in, see it and give the pub a miss?"

I agreed without hesitation. It was one of the longest films I had ever seen, and when we returned to our sleeping quarters, the manager asked, "Where the hell have you two been. The man from the pool has been chasing around town, looking for the pair of you?" We collected our pound next morning but it cost us a lecture that turned our ears red.

Later on in the Seaman's Mission, we learned from the padre that the shipping master picked up crew members from ordinary lodging houses. The following night I was picked up by the skipper of a large 1,200 ton coasting vessel, the *Benjamin Sherburn*.

CHAPTER 5 – *S/S BENJAMIN SHERBURN*

SHIP NUMBER FOUR

I had a final drink with Lofty and took a launch to my new ship. It was heading for London via the north of Scotland. With seamen sucked out of both missions and the standby hut, I knew my friend would not have to wait long for a berth.

If I thought I had witnessed mad seas in the Atlantic, that wintry November was the most turbulent I had set eyes on – there in the north of Scotland. Even on the lee side when navigating around that northern passage, huge seas scrambled over the deck and battered at the steel door of the fiddley, through which I had to dump ashes in the black of night. Sailing on my first British ship, I found that new regulations gave firemen and trimmers the same pay.

As with the *Loke*, there were only two men on watch. We did the trimming in turns. During the three day trip to London, I overheard more stories concerning the *Empress of Russia*. One tale was similar to another told to me by an ex-crew member of the *George Washington*. In both cases beer stores had been looted by ex-prisoners. Drunkenness and squabbling occurred there.

Our ship tied up at St Katherine's Wharf to discharge a cargo of sacked sugar. We could not be closer to Dock Street in Aldgate, provided we circumnavigated some derelict sailing ship basins.

And the Wapping Underground Station was closer than that of Aldgate East. You could have as lively a night at the nearby Pepper Port and the Captain Kid, a little way up Dock Street. However, that first night I joined the other firemen for a ride in the tube to Lambeth. By going along with them, I realised that they too had prison records because the pals I was introduced to soon showed that they belonged to the underworld fraternity.

Britain was now in the fourth year of the war and was definitely on the winning side. Yet, if you travelled in the tube of the capital city London for the first time during the war, you might question that fact. When you alighted from the train, you walked the narrow spaces between the people camping out from the bombs; men, women and children sprawled out on blankets spread over the stony surface of the platform. Had Adolf Hitler seen the massed British souls huddled together on the whole length of the platforms, he would have jumped for joy.

Midweek, with no cash to go ashore, most hands stayed aboard in the evening. I was watching a game of poker in the fo'c'sle when a clatter of boots came down the ladder. The sailor on duty-watch burst in on the game to let us know that there were fireworks on the skyline. Flashes across the mess room porthole put us on alert and up to the poop deck we all scrambled. On this mid-November night, the sky reflected flames from an area of the city being bombed.

An older sailor assured us that we were berthed at a safe distance since the bombing raid was five miles away by his reckoning. On Friday night I drew cash with the rest and went ashore with Jimmy, a young trimmer from Clydeside, Scotland, doing his first trip and made the arced pathway around the disused wharfs to the Dock Street exit.

The night was black and the wind very blustery as we traced lanterns placed at the corners of each unused dock. Then we both tumbled headlong off a dock. At the time we hadn't realised that a missing lantern was the cause of it, probably blown over with the wind.

A worn overcoat handicapped my efforts to keep afloat and swim around the walls to grip on something. Fortunately, someone above overheard my yells for help, and the rays of a hand torch located me and guided my efforts at swimming to a steel ladder.

I managed to ascend but with difficulty, as the weight of a thick overcoat soaked in brine pulled down on my efforts. Once on top I requested my helpers to look for my mate Jimmy. In the meantime a van pulled up nearby and took me off to a hospital for observation. It was called St George's East. This is where I overheard the report that I was the forty-second survivor from the River Thames that year to be bedded down in St George's. How many others were lifted from the Thames and taken to other hospitals and how many never made it? The facts of ordinary life can scare at times!

Two days later, a sad ending was reported at my bedside that Jimmy had perished. His body had been recovered from a large pipe feeding the dock or feeding out of the dock. If his body had not swelled with the high tide, he would probably have been one more immersion casualty the world would know nothing about.

His death left me with a guilt complex for a long time after, as if I could have altered the circumstances. The irony of the episode was that Jimmy, together with his two brothers, was from a family of expert swimmers – prize winners. As for myself, I had yet to learn the proper way to swim; I made up my own strokes, and my aid on that fateful night was mostly doggy paddling.

In the next bed in the hospital lay a thin boy of eight or nine years. We got acquainted and the young patient confided to me that some of the hospital staff would give him scant attention since he was Jewish.

This aspect in wartime Britain surprised me, after the persecution Jews had suffered under the German dictator, Hitler. I did my best to buck him up. I let him know that most boys his age were not left alone in an adult world to fend for themselves, and if the other boys in the ward were coddled by the nurses, he could stick his chest out and call himself equal to a man.

You can't fool kids, and he must have thought that perhaps other people, besides his own fellow Jews, received negative reactions; I noticed he became more confident in his approach to medics visiting his bed. At that time, how was I to know that forty years later, I was to come across this same person and not recognise him for several months.

For about eighteen months I did a stint working aboard tugboats in a tropical area of Western Australia called the Buccaneer Archipelago, near the port of Derby. We worked out of the iron ore exporting island of Koolan. The skipper of one tug I worked on was a real character called Compass Bob.

He could be very demonstrative if a deckhand disobeyed an order, and one day that is what I did. He flew into a temper and loud-mouthed me. His high-pitched voice echoed back into the mists of time. Then I had an idea, walked up to the skipper and asked, "I know it's a silly question, Bob, but were you ever a patient in a London hospital when you were about eight years of age?" While I spoke, I was alert to any reaction from his face. His response was so immediate that I knew it hit his memory spot on.

I will say this much in favour of that bunch of crims on the *Benjamin Sherburn*. They all paid me a visit and wished me a fast recovery before sailing time. Of course, there was nothing wrong with me, and I was released within four days of entering the ward for observation. After my mate's demise, I was only too glad to pay off this coasting vessel. The crew passed me the address of the company in Leadenhall Street in the city, and when I signed out of the hospital, I headed there to request them to make up my wages.

With my small payoff of 16 quid, I took the Paddington train to South Wales and home. When I registered at the seamen's pool in Cardiff, I decided to turn down any coaster berth and go back to deep-sea work. Perhaps the small pay off was good in a way. After my recent traumatic event, I was glad to enjoy a sober rest up.

CHAPTER 6 – *S/S INGLETON*

SHIP NUMBER FIVE

O n joining a ship, its destination was not known until we weighed anchor and were out in the sea lanes. During the four days that our ship sat at the quayside, it was amazing how the Cardiff crew, in joint discussion with dockers, approximated at which port we would discharge our cargo.

The *S/S Ingleton* was a tramp ship of 7,000 gross tonnage. Instead of carrying the usual cargo of coal on leaving Cardiff, swinging derricks were hoisting general cargo aboard. We were berthed close to the main gate, directly outside of which stood the Mount Stewart Pub.

During midday breaks, most hands would gather there, and there would be a guessing game to pass the time. "Where was the *Ingleton* bound for?" Bright sailors who were familiar with opening and closing hatches had without a doubt studied print on cargo parcels and were unified on one point – that the ship would set course for North Africa.

On the second day of the game, the forecast had narrowed to Algeria, and a fresh game ensued from there. What would be the first port of call? Before sailing time it was generally accepted that Algiers would be it! Even more rapid was the forecast of time, depending on the speed reaching there, it would take between eight and ten days.

We called at Milford Haven Harbour for convoy formation, and we left within 24 hours; it was accepted we would be drinking rosé wine in Algiers in nine days' time.

But there were important things to consider. At the outbreak of war, Germany had two super modern marauders of merchant ships ready to knock the hell out of our fleet. Britain's icon of capital battleships was a victim of one of them. The German *Bismarck* showed its power by sinking the mighty *HMS Hood.*

Bismarck's sister ship, the *Prinz Eugen*, had had very little publicity up to this time. The convoy turned course due south, giving the Bay of Biscay a wide berth. It may have been 4pm when someone passed on to me that the *Prinz Eugen* had left the west coast of France and was heading in our direction. "How far away is she?" I asked. "About fifty miles astern!" Obviously our group of ships changed course, 180 degrees, and steered north, hoping that soon an early winter sunset might give us a degree of protection. We had a bonus. Within the hour, a slight mist grew into fog. By morning Sparky told us we had reversed to due south again. Spotter planes had sighted U-boats waiting for us further north.

It was not nine days but three weeks later that tugs towed us into Bone, Tunisia, which was at the extreme north-eastern end of Algeria. Our deckhand prophets were not totally off; Algiers itself would be the next port of call.

I cannot remember such a zigzagging of the North Atlantic as we did on that voyage, but it was all for the best. With the surrender of Italy, even the Mediterranean was no longer a menace to shipping, and no ships were lost. It was Boxing Day when we tied up in Bone with a not very Merry Xmas spent at sea.

From the time we left Cardiff, there was not the usual camaraderie among the mix of men from different ports of the UK. And after we drew cash, the gaiety about going ashore in a fresh port was missing. It was usually expected that a slight gap existed between married men and the others. Those few lived mostly for letters from the wife, and only went ashore when they earned extra overtime.

Considering the crew as a whole, there was a sinister atmosphere, which I later learned emerged from the criminal element on board. Trouble started on the second day in port, and I became one of its early victims. We all knocked off at midday so we could go ashore to buy sundries.

The exchange rate in Algeria then was 200 francs to the pound. I subbed 1,000 francs and went on a spree. Most of Bone was one huge Arab settlement or kasbah, with French settlers having taken control of the small business settlement, whose shops were pretty bare of anything.

There were other ships in port, and I felt good mingling with crews of more happy-go-lucky natures. I got good and tipsy but not blotto. When I boarded the *Ingleton* at 11pm that night, I ran into trouble right away. One of the firemen on a different duty watch to my own picked a fight with me.

He was a pug from Glasgow, and in normal circumstances, I would have taken a very evasive attitude up to a point, the reason being that I had never learned anything about the boxing game. However, this challenge was thrust on me, so what could I do?

I was into giving it blow for blow with this other guy being about my own size. He pasted me for all he was worth. Whether it was the effects of whisky or wine, I never buckled and kept at it, punch for punch, even though my own were much more haphazard, and I had no idea of defence. The Scotch sailors, most of whom came from Stornaway in the Western Isles, quickly gathered as men do when they see fisticuffs.

And I was glad of their presence since by their looks, they were out to see fair play. Some stood outside the entrance doorway, and a couple more at the back of the small area, which was outside the mess room on the poop deck above the sleeping quarters. There were no other crew members around.

I have never developed a jab powerful enough to knock a man down, but that night, I traded punch for punch without too much puffing and blowing. The blows thrown at me by my opponent were numbed by the effect of wine drinking. I cannot remember how long we fought; however, I was very much surprised when this Ginger Shennan was the first to get exhausted and ceased to trade blows.

It was only in the morning when I awoke from both a throbbing headache caused by drink, plus coupled with the delayed pain caused by the previous night's fracas, that I sadly remembered the mischief. This agony was felt mainly in the head and face. Thankfully, I had managed to get to my top bunk without waking up the other two occupants of the cabin.

When I climbed down and sat on the communal bench, the other two stared hard at me. "What's up?" I questioned. "Look in the mirror," answered Shorty Eddie Riley. I did, and what looked back was not a pleasant-faced person. Unbelievably, there were no scars or blood marks. Just a swollen pumpkin.

My eyelids stretched outwardly, and I was more narrow-eyed than an Asian. After a couple of coffees, I felt well enough to join the others for a day's work in the engine room. My opponent showed much smaller effects on his face from the blows I had struck.

I was pulled up by a big greaser in the engine room while helping the third engineer haul a generator. "Don't you know that you fought an ex-boxing champion?" he remarked sympathetically. And if he felt I was going to feel sorry for myself, he was mistaken. It just gave me an air of vanity.

But it privately also installed in me a need to continue to avoid fights whenever possible. These pugs received cash from their fights. If their scientific blows caused any lasting injury, there would be no cash to pay for my lost working days.

Had I boarded earlier on the night of the brawl, I might have had worst luck than what was handed me because another fireman was taken to hospital with knife wounds. I had no love for him, being a shady character from Liverpool, yet I sympathised with his plight. He was called 'The Bull' and certainly roared like one.

Later we sailed to Algiers to discharge the other half of the cargo. I still had plenty of francs left to spend in that major port; the big cities always drew cash from your pocket at a faster rate, and with the port 'choc-o-block' full of freighters, we would have to wait nine days for a berth. I enjoyed exploring new ports on my own and took promenades ashore alone.

Algiers was under military occupation. Maybe it was under the authority of De Gaulle's Free French forces, but British and American troops made a big showing. What stood out glaringly was that in the shop windows there was not even a rag of clothing to purchase.

If we were going to stay in port more than a couple of weeks, I had no intention of blowing cash, so I accepted to stay on board when the cash list was made up for the weekend and then decided to stay aboard for a week. On Saturday afternoon most of the boys were drinking beer at the Guillaume Tell Sailor's Club.

I was going through all the pockets of my clothes to try and find enough loose cash for a bottle of cheap wine to kill my loneliness. Then I walked on deck that sunny afternoon with barely enough coinage for a litre of cheap red wine when I was addressed by one of the Arab workers hired to unload cargo.

He asked me if I had any items of clothing for sale. I answered only bits and pieces although I might have dirty work gear. He then asked if I would let him to look around the lockers where old clothing from past crews were used for extra filthy jobs below, like cleaning soot from furnaces.

I nodded agreement, and after opening one of the metal doors, I pointed to something in the dark recess. I unhooked the item and showed it to him. It was an ancient waistcoat, which he liked. He asked me how much I wanted for it. It was so covered in coal dust, I was ashamed to take any cash and handed it to him buckshee.

However, he would not let me go until he paid forty francs. These men, with such low wages, were not used to parting with good cash for nothing, and it opened my eyes to the current poverty of even the French ruling class, to whom he might sell it after it was cleaned. But I needed the cash, and he walked away delighted with his bargain.

A bottle of cheap wine cost only nine francs, and I was soon cleaned up and off down the road for a lovelier Saturday. The following week the 'Bull' was released from hospital, and he certainly deserved the tag. The stab wound could not have been that deep because this big bully of a fellow kept picking on me.

All I could do was try and keep away from him as much as possible; fair play was a foreign word on this ship. Then it happened for the second time since we arrived in North Africa. I had returned as before after a night out on the binge.

This time I had really mixed my drinks, and the blows striking my face were not felt in the normal way. I must have lost balance since I awoke lying flat out in an alleyway deck. There was only a fuzzy memory of the night before, and I put the ache in my head down to the usual hangover.

I had an idea that it was morning, but going up on deck, I looked out at a starry sky. The clock in the mess room told me it was 11pm. Perhaps the lack of food and wine had given me an appetite, and as the galley was left open at night so the duty watchman could clean the coal fire, that's where I went to look for some eats.

The able seaman on gangway watch described to me, with a big smile on his face, what had occurred earlier on. He disliked the Bull as much as myself and recalled that a witness had seen me having a fair go at him with my fists until I was struck on the head with a full wine bottle.

In the galley, I found cold stew left in one of the cook's pots, and after swallowing a bowl of it, I decided to retire for a sleep. Feeling a bit crummy about the face, I rubbed it with one hand on the way back to quarters and realised it could be dried blood.

After a flannel wipe in the bathroom mirror, it turned out to be only superficial. But when I awoke the next morning, I was feeling wretched with my hands all ashake. If a ten year old boy had offered me out for a bout, I would have run from him like a yellow dog. So much can booze pull a man down.

At that time I didn't realise that crims study body language closely and know when opponents are at their weakest. Refusing to fight gave me a double dose of jitters and caused me to tread miserably down to the engine room to do my day's stint, but, fortunately, that state of mind didn't last long.

As for our food, galley cooks sailing under the red duster faced greater harassment from the crew than under any other flag. Having sailed under more than half a dozen foreign flags, I can vouch for that fact. On British ships the cook is henpecked, in the male sense of the phrase, on quite a continuous basis.

Yet miraculously, sailing with such a rotten mob as was aboard the *Ingleton*, our cook received only praise, and he enjoyed it, always with a big smile for all hands. Ali was a Chee-Chee, a mix of Chinese and Indian, still a young cook at about twenty-five years.

He was a curry king who could spice your meals in only one way — exotic. There were several Scots in the crew, and they even gave up their morning porridge so we could kick off the day with curry and rice, and after a stint of shovelling coal in the bunker, it gave one a good appetite to enjoy his meals.

When we left Bone in Tunisia, we also left a fireman there, who had been on Ginger's watch and came from the same part of Glasgow. I think the legal system in Bone was run jointly by the British military and De Gaulle's government. One day when the stewards were taking their afternoon siestas, Sanny, the fireman, fled with all the tableware from the officer's saloon.

You could get a good price for just about anything at this time in French North Africa. The captain was swift in reporting the theft to the military authorities, and Sanny was jailed in a French-Arab prison. Our deucer promised double overtime to the other two stokers on his watch if they took the ship to Gibraltar, where a new fireman would be picked up.

Unfortunately, the cook left us in Algiers; he had slept ashore with a prostitute one night, and two days later complained about an irritation in his privates, and when he visited the quack ashore, his complaint was diagnosed as syphilis. Being a cook and handling food, he was paid off then and there.

Algiers was under the occupation of three allied armies — French, American and British — so the chances of romancing with the opposite sex were rare. We had a fireman of my own age from the suburb of Tiger Bay in Cardiff, who had the good technique of dressing well. He was the only one I knew who had a relationship with a respectable-type French mam'selle.

She was the leading lady in a show, and his presents to her were food parcels. At the entrance to the Arab quarters, there were massive notices in English forbidding the occupying armies from visiting the interior. As merchant seamen were exempt from the order, all hands went there to watch the belly dancing.

After my rough-ups in that part of the world, some good news came to my ears before we let go of the ropes on the final day. Bull had been arrested by the military for robbing an American soldier. Good riddance!

More positive news came my way at Gibraltar. On 'The Rock' no qualified firemen could be found. Thanks to that, the British garrison sent us two soldiers who had volunteered, and no doubt were glad to sign off the army and join the merchant service. Our two replacements stressed those very feelings and told us they were sick of the monotonous life on the rock.

Geordie, our soldier recruit became trimmer on the watch with Eddie Riley and myself – three shorties together. There was another Geordie on board. Geordie Summers, who like the new man, came from Newcastle-on-Tyne. He was on watch with Ginger and the other soldier, Big Jack from Kent, to make up a black gang trio.

Our next port of call was Freetown, Sierra Leone, where we would drop anchor in the harbour until a convoy was formed. Destination unknown. I made friends right away with Jack. Or to put it this way, he found me an interesting companion and more happy-go-lucky than the others, as he put it.

There was quite a serious mob in the engine room department on the *Ingleton* as she headed for Sierra Leone. So Jack and I would sit out on the poop deck and pass the time when we had a chance. He came from a farm and told me he was used to hard toil. Because of that, stocking coal in the furnaces didn't worry him, and the further south we went into the tropics, the more we guzzled water to make up for lost sweat. He just took the new job in stride, saying that life on the Rock at times was so boring that a homesick squaddie would finish his army career by throwing himself off a cliff. Obviously an extreme case. Jack was a conscripted soldier and on that account, he did not bring up any nostalgic episodes in his army career.

After only thirty-six hours wait in Freetown Harbour, we joined a convoy going further along the western African seacoast. A cargo was waiting for us at Takoradi, Nigeria. One good thing about this ship was that we had a big, wide canvas awning spread over the poop deck, just suitable for the new weather pattern.

We were not short of wind chutes of a light metal which were fitted for the exact porthole size. As the sea was calm for four days, the convoy must have been steaming at nine knots an hour, which created a fair breeze for the chutes to keep the cabins cool.

As was usual, those not on duty watches gathered each evening under the tarpaulin for a yarn. The *Ingleton* was new for a coal-burning steamer, less than ten years old, and it had flush decks so that the poop was not your normal raised stern deck but was flush with the whole afterdeck, yet called 'the poop' through custom.

I had laid claim to a vegetable crate from the galley and moved from the gathering of sailors and firemen standing around or sitting on bits of bollards. I sat alone and faced amidships. My mind was trapped in a 'Fix'. Call it superstition if you like.

I couldn't understand the mood myself. Then I was prompted to take a stroll further amidships. As the sun set over the stern behind, a shadow was cast in front, and the steel deck was beginning to cool. I stooped before reaching the amidships housing and studied two life rafts, one on each side of the deck. I imagine they would float around in heavy weather.

Then I studied the automatic release catch. Having ensured that I understood it, I moved over to its partner on the portside and checked the release mechanism there as well. It had been rumoured on board that sleeping out on deck in this part of Africa caused one to be moonstruck, leading to craziness or perhaps being dreamily romantic.

Anyway, I there and then decided to bring a pillow, sheet and blanket and sleep on one of those rafts after finishing my four hour duty watch that night. On some reflection I developed a preference to sleeping on the starboard raft rather than the other. Why this could be of importance, I didn't realise at that time.

Whilst my two mates were supping an extra cup of tea in the mess that night after we had washed the coal dust off our bodies, I made a swift move of grabbing my bedding, minus the mattress, and bringing it up on deck. I did not wish anyone to irritate me by asking why I preferred a hard bed on a raft.

I must have some kind of animal sense because I was awakened in the black of night by a flash and a noise I failed to understand. Naturally, I would not have been alone to have my sleep disturbed. Up on the boat deck, extra cabins had been erected there for two stewards.

I bumped into one of them making his way down the ladder, as I sprinted up to the ship's lifeboats, half asleep. I had blocked him and he brought me alive with. "You don't have to go up now. She's pulling away." In the dimness, I turned around to see the bows of the ship reversing from a big gash in the hull of our vessel.

This 'Other' had collided with us. An American vessel, probably departing from a port on the African mainland, had not sighted the convoy due to blackout regulations, and as we were in the outside lane of ships facing the coast, we became the victim of this collision.

It had not occurred at night after all, but because in tropical areas the sun rises and sets in one sudden action, it could be black as night at ten minutes to six in the morning and all sunshiny at ten past the hour, and there in the daylight, surrounding the skipper and chief engineer, were half the crew. Fortunately, the ship had been light and with no cargo was high out of the water. Nevertheless, at the base of where the US freighter had ripped the hull apart, it could be seen by torchlight that the ship was a fraction below the waterline. The skipper gave out orders to pump out the ballast tanks and bilges.

What scared the crew was had the collision occurred two or three seconds later, the living quarters would have been hit. They could share their apprehension; I couldn't. I had moved my bedding back to my cabin without anyone noticing so that no one knew I had slept on the deck.

What is more, only a few pieces of splintered timber remained on deck after the collision. My fear could then be greater than the others. It would have been unthinkable had I chosen the wrong raft, yet I had to muzzle any comment on this. We left the convoy to return to Freetown for repairs. Thankfully, the pumps were coping well with seawater leaking into the bilges.

On the return journey there was no talk of panic, which made me assume that the ballast tanks might have been left full on the starboard side to create a temporary list. With our new and improved crew, I didn't mind the word reaching my ears. After a launch was sent out to examine the gaping cleft in the side of our ship, we could look forward to a long rest up.

The marine supervisor of the port concluded that it would take twenty steel plates to replace the mangled steel, stretching down to the waterline. The American vessel had ripped into twelve feet of the main deck as well. First to arrive at the scene would be a team of skilled locals to set up scaffolding so that welders could burn off the area of the jagged, bent steelwork.

Only six plates were available ashore, and they would be welded to the bottom area first to ensure safety on the ship. The rest would have to be sent from the UK. Only one donkey boiler kept steam, the other two being shut down. We then could look forward to painting the engine room from top to bottom.

Weekend arrangements looked excellent. A liberty launch would take us ashore after evening eats on Friday, and the last launch to return us on board would be Sunday afternoon late. From the second day at anchorage, there was no boredom as far as the stokers were concerned.

We had returned to the harbour on a Sunday and surveyed the water for a sign of sharks. Soon canoes showed up, and locals offered to dive for pennies. Therefore, we knew that swimming was safe. After finishing work Monday, most of us were down the gangway and taking a dip.

By Tuesday there were swimming races around the ship. I may have lagged behind, but the dips were just as enjoyable. At sunset the gangway was hauled up for canoe men to board.

There were other diversions that came under three groups. The married men would gather around one part of the deck and rehash news from home. Then there were the card players who gambled with cigarettes instead of cash. Then there was the majority who one could join at any time. They idled under the stars, swapping yarns as long as your arm. The weekend ashore was a prelude to a pattern that was to follow.

I drew a big five pounds sub from my wages, meaning to play the tourist, as did other younger members of the crew still in the single state. After booking into the Torpedoed Seamen's Rest, we still had a lot of cash to go through. Bed and board cost ten shillings a man.

Then it was off to the Cotton Tree Bar, where we mingled with the crew of a steamer called the *Appledore*. They were all Welsh lads from Barry, a familiar port of mine near Cardiff, and were a fun-loving crowd. This tippling place was a bamboo and timber structure with a veranda that was really spacey and adjacent to a tall, stout cotton tree. It was also positioned next to a rambling shed where the Saturday night stomp took place.

There was only one drawback with the hostel we stayed at. It had a dormitory instead of private rooms. The dorm had about sixty beds, but we learned that no torpedoed crews had entered for the past two months, so in a sort of way, you could give yourself a certain amount of privacy.

The hostel's catering turned out to be excellent, and I was glad I had imbibed normally, drinking only beer on Friday evening. I enjoyed the first two meals of the day there. Saturday morning was spent at the market, trying to flirt with the local belles. There was a large pair of buffalo horns, which I bought to decorate the ship's cabin.

I was back to the Rest after a few beers in the Cotton Tree to catch a midday meal. The matron who ran the staff was the double of the catering lady at the American Club in Trinidad. A very efficient English woman, she had a way with the African chef that brought out the best in him, and I soon took a siesta to rest my full stomach.

The stomp went well, and any sort of dancing was welcome with a lot of do-it-yourself steps. The theme was reflected by the ebon faces of the ladies. 'Just make yourself jolly.' Like most of the others, I enjoyed a long lie-in Sunday morning and learned from other beds that after the Sunday roast, there was a regular trip to Lumley Beach, 17 miles distant.

After an army truck drove up to the mission, one of the assistants then drove us to a beautiful spread of white sand to slum around in for the P.M. That last day made our first weekend ashore an enjoyable experience, and I still had a few pounds left in my pocket.

On Monday the deucer told us to take our time erecting the scaffolding as we would have several months at anchorage to paint the engine room. The most dangerous part was that of the skylights and deck head work; it was the first part to do and could be unsafe if we were slipshod erecting the scaffolding.

There was definitely a lot of harmony in our group that continued the weekend ashore. It was as if our earlier stays in the North African posts had only been a sinister interim. We were going fine into the third week when back mail arrived from Takoradi.

And there was horrible news for Ginger Shennan. His wife had run away with a sailor with the Free French Forces, leaving a small child in care of his mother. Ginger was a real hard case, and the possibility of him causing conflict hung like a dark cloud in the mess. Likewise, a younger greaser also from Glasgow learned his youngest child had passed away.

In the meantime, the pattern of life continued as before except for the swimming sessions. The gangway was close to the galley, and that was where the cook threw scraps of food overboard. The fish learned the times of disposal and waited for it against the hull. A shark was seen beneath the small platform at the bottom of the gangway and our swimming races ceased.

At the evening joke and yarn spinning, Geordie Summers could hold attention the most. He was fifty-six years and the oldest serving fireman. Although he had been married in Swansea, South Wales many years and sailed out of that port, he preferred not to mix with the married group.

We were glad of this since he could certainly let out some good stories. On one occasion he bought a bottle of coconut alcohol off one of the bumboats for two packs of cigarettes, and this loosened his tongue. He had us all spellbound one evening, recalling when a bomb dropped on Bute Road, the main way along the dock area of Cardiff.

He stated that he was witness to the swiping of a large chest containing the carvings of Indian seamen. He mentioned the name of the cafe where it was taken from and describing that night of fires and flying debris, he stated that he was thankful for having a few whiskies in him.

It numbed him to reality. He said a lot of shopkeepers ran out into the street and left doors wide open. Out of a certain cafe, one man pulled a hand truck with another pushing. On the truck was a massive chest. It was wheeled onto the road, empty of traffic and lit only by the moon.

Geordie wondered why they were in such a hurry, running down the street with this metal case. Before walking on, he looked up above the door they had made their exit from and discovered it to be the front of a hostel for Indian seamen. Twenty yards on he stopped when he heard some loud yelling behind him. A large man with a turban came running towards him and asked if he had seen anyone stealing a large suitcase. He pointed in the direction where the hand truck had gone. He said he never saw a man with a turban fly down a road so fast.

I never saw a radio in the crew quarters, but often on an evening, a kind of music would echo from a small reach of land. The beating of tom toms under a starry firmament was far from unpleasant.

One day Ginger had one of his turns. In a half serious tone he told me he would be pleased if I got rid of the bull horns on the wall. When he mentioned it again, in a more serious tone of voice, I told him, "No way." I intended them as a trophy to put on the wall of my sister's house.

The reason was that his friend, the greaser, had received a letter from home that another infant of his had passed away and claimed that the horns might be causing ill luck to his family. To give him peace of mind, I stowed the horns beneath the bottom bunk of Eddie Riley.

One time Big Jack and myself made time to move around the veg and fruit market one Saturday morning, and my mate was full of devilment as he kept urging me to purchase a big baboon, and that he would pay half. After waving him off a couple of times, I decided to speculate my five shillings with his, and for ten shillings the ape was all mine.

I was handed the long, heavy chain, while my partner strolled behind with a big bunch of bananas to keep the creature happy. The welders were busy putting steel plates on the ship's hull, and there was a constant service with launches bringing and taking the equipment they needed. So we stepped into one of the launches, bringing Bimbo, the baboon, with us.

He absolutely raced up the gangway when we came alongside the ship, pulling me with him. I was amazed how strong and powerful the creature was. He stood four feet tall when standing, but it seemed he had the strength of a grown man. I had misgivings about coping with him.

I was aware that the local Africans in the launch kept well away from him. With a big smile, when we reached the deck, Jack passed me the bananas and took the chain, leading Bimbo aft, first instructing me to hand the bananas to the officer's mess boy, and telling him that his friend Jack would like him to feed the monkey while we go ashore.

I found Peter, the sixteen-year-old mess boy, putting a fresh cloth over the table beneath a canvas awning on the boat deck, where the uniforms supped their beers in glasses of ice blocks. Handing him the fruit, he readily complied with Jack's request.

I found Jack near the main mast where he had lashed the baboon to a ringbolt on the deck. He had a good twelve feet of chain to move around. We weren't concerned and off we went to catch the next launch to shore. Jack and I enjoyed our leave, but when we returned Sunday night, we found the bosun fuming.

Peter had done his duty feeding the animal, but being an animal lover, released him when Bimbo attempted to climb the mast. He positioned himself on the crosstrees aloft after grabbing what was left of the bananas.

The bosun was a very fussy type, who washed the deck spotless at weekends. So what did the primate do on Sunday morning but leave droppings all over the place. The bosun blew his top and requested from the captain that the animal be taken back ashore on a launch. There was no question of getting him ashore on a Sunday evening. Sunday was a day of rest with no launches bringing workmen.

No bumboat crew would take this type of animal in their frail canoes. With coaxing and waving bananas, he was somehow brought down. Jack hastily grabbed the chain, and unwillingly Bimbo was led aft. The chain was looped through a loose steel ring in the middle of a hatch combing so people could walk safely on either side of the ship.

One hour later, when his captor came near the primate, it made a desperate lunge at him. According to a witness, my mate shot one fist at him and knocked him clean out. These monkeys have big jaws, and I would have been slow to approach if I saw danger. One bite could end up in incurable hydrophobia, as far as I learnt.

The animal became more servile after that affair, especially towards Jack. Then the worst occurred. The monkey's brain had been clever enough to unpick his knotted chain. With its newfound freedom, it reverted to its natural, fearsome self and chased every human in sight except Jack.

When Jack caught hold of the long chain, he started leading the creature around, and Bimbo was obedient as you like. The master stopped for a while to look up at the admiring officers on the boat. In the meantime Bimbo circled Jack dragging that long chain after him.

Not only were faces topside showing a lot of merriment, but crew members came under the shade of the awning, began to smile and to watch the scene. When Bimbo pulled at the chain, Jack found his legs locked and was unable to shift himself. But never was there such a cool guy! He just pulled a little on the chain and stepped out of the loop.

The amusement did not stop the outcry by all hands to be rid of this dangerous nuisance. Even at that point, Bimbo was showing a lot of disobedience to his lord and master.

The capable second engineer might have been a chief had he not a small impediment — one leg caused him to limp. He also wore thick glasses and had a nondescript face and manner. Yet, out of all the amidships onlookers, he hobbled down the ladder to the main deck and took over the situation. Limping towards the fierce creature, he said to Jack, "You can let go of the chain now."

Most of those hearing the words had patronising smiles on their faces. Believe it or not, our man stooped over towards the animal with his arms open as if beckoning a baby. He coaxed the red-bottomed baboon with some jabber, who then ran into his waiting arms.

The chain dragged behind him, as the deucer carried his burden to the top of the gangway to lash him to a handrail until a launch arrived to carry him back ashore. About ten feet to go and things began to go wrong. Stretching out its big paw, the ape held fast to a stanchion supporting the boat deck.

After struggling to free himself, he was allowed to stand on the bulwarks. There were a lot of men crowding around at this time, seeing that the animal had reverted to childish play. While the deucer started to coax him back into his arms, the monkey's grip on the post was relaxing.

I can't recall who the person was, but he must have had a grudge against Bimbo because the culprit rapidly lifted the long chain over the bulwarks and the monkey lost balance. All eyes followed Bimbo into the briny where he disappeared twenty feet below. The weight of the chain gave him no chance to swim for it. Life went on as usual after this event, except I carried a guilt complex from the demise of my pet monkey.

Then after a month at anchorage, we were given a surprise visit by the commanding officer of the British army stationed in Freetown. We were invited to a concert put up by them.

The captain obliged by ordering a launch for us on a certain Wednesday, when we would be taken to the camp and fed beer and sandwiches after the show. Hot weather can bring out bad tempers, yet I somehow or other had developed a bit of camaraderie with Ginger, and altogether we returned on board an amiable crew.

As for the two new hands we had engaged in Gibraltar, they had a ball mixing with fellow soldiers, but the unexpected always seems to occur when things are going smoothly. Surprisingly, alcohol had nothing to with it. Whilst painting in the engine room, heavy industrial boots were discarded for lighter footwear, but Ginger continued clomping around in his big heavies during working hours.

By this time, scaffolding boards had lowered half-way down the bulkheads. All stokehold workers were occupied with a paint brush. On this particular day two sets of scaffolding were rigged up on one side of the engine room, one above the other, with two men on top and another two below. The pair below adapted to the movements of those above so that if any dangling legs came onto heads underneath, the others shifted in turn.

In the shipping business lots of people are personalised by giving them nicknames. Ken Prewit came from an area in Cardiff, Tiger Bay, yet he was no way tigerish. However, the nickname Tiger got stuck on him, though before joining the *Ingleton*, he had been a total stranger to all hands, and no one on board had seen him in any way be aggressive.

Ken sat below Ginger, and the man on top carelessly kicked him in the head when shifting position with those bug boots of his. Tiger complained, and according to witnesses, Ginger delivered an even nastier kick to the other's head. This wouldn't do, and between them they decided to settle things out on deck. The deucer was consulted by the oldest fireman, and it was agreed that work would be stopped for the rest of the afternoon.

It was now around 2pm. The contestants were permitted time to prepare themselves for a bout in the traditional manner whilst the rest of us made a circle. By the time the fight started, the whole crew were present. It was an excuse to break up the monotony at that anchorage.

Ginger appeared in light shoes, daps worn by sportsmen, and Tiger with his ordinary light work shoes. The barest clothing was worn. Just short trousers, as it was a hot, steamy day. It was a bang wallop into each other without hesitation. There was no refereeing. With all eyes focused on them, it had to be fair.

Both bodies were fairly equal in weight and height, giving Tiger an extra inch in height. What surprised everyone was that the boy from Bute Road was not only giving blow for blow but also better and very active about it, as if he couldn't wait to punish his opponent for the offense, even though the sun blazed down and brought an excess of sweat to the skin.

The several Scots on board, who barracked with Shennan, looked a bit crestfallen. Where were those scientific jabs and digs? That weaving and ducking? Anyone there could see that Tiger was not hitting his mark at times, but his speedy returns forbade the other one to think, even automatically.

Perhaps Tiger realised he was paired up against a professional and what were a few misses anyway. Sometimes desperation brings out the spirit of a past ancestor in the genes, and this spirit is the actual one doing the fighting. There was just nothing dainty or scientific in the way the Welshman beat his fists over Ginger's body.

Both contestants were used to being active with the shovel in the high temperatures of the stokehold; therefore, the afternoon sun didn't really bother either. When the fight started, more than a few expected to see a demonstration of professional manoeuvring from the boxer, but it was the street fighter who took the show. In less than half an hour, Ginger had thrown in the towel.

It turned out that Tiger really was a tiger after all, and I wouldn't mind betting that the nickname stuck for the rest of his seafaring career. I have never set eyes on him since that voyage and that is the way when sailing deep-sea. It's only once in a blue moon that you meet up with old shipmates when sailing on tramp ships.

Fighters were all enigmas! It was Ginger, the professional who ended up as the only one with facial injuries, which showed up the following morning.

Back on shipboard where we had enjoyed our spell in the harbour from the first week in February until April '44, there were comments from the radio that an invasion of Europe was imminent. We waited.

The weather developed a clamminess about it, and sticky weather was ideal for infectious diseases. A message came in from amidships that if anyone suffered from water fleas in the ears or had signs of malaria, he should report to the second mate, who would write him a chit to visit the hospital – a floating hospital. The main hospital in Freetown at this time was the *Edinburgh Castle*, an ex-liner of the Union Castle Line, sailing between Britain and South Africa, yet now in permanent mooring.

Fast forward two months later in June 1944, shortly before we departed Africa, the first reports of actual invasion forces landing in France stirred up a lot of excitement aboard. Yet during April 1944, the welding of steel plates on the hull progressed, and thoughts of all on board turned to home. Once the itch caught on, we couldn't wait to get back.

In the meantime, we still enjoyed weekends at the Cotton Tree Bar, and someone who often accompanied the firemen was a diminutive South American who was tagged 'Joe'. Being an odd one out with the Stornaway sailors, it seemed he could not practice his English-speaking as frequently as he would have liked, since most of the time they were communicating in Gaelic. Although of small stature, he was a terrific swimmer, and on our regular outings to Lumley Beach, this little

Columbian would swim dangerously far. Swimming was his pleasure.

On the prompting of their religious bosun, the deck crowd went ashore every second week, and they were chided by their 'Pope' to save cash to buy land on the island of Lewis. It was wise advice that might have done our mob, the black gang, a great deal of good. At any rate, our withdrawals of cash since the first couple of weeks had been less, and we still had a rollicking time as we became familiar with shore prices. But when sailing time drew nearer, the boys got busy writing to sweethearts. As for myself, I hadn't felt any strong feelings since I had left Gloria, my dream girl, in Paramaribo.

April ended with stormy weather, and it had the good point of blowing away swarms of flies, but sometimes the wind had such force that it often dragged the anchor to different parts of the harbour. One weekend the launch refused to return us on board due to dangerous high winds and waves.

This was when the canoe men made cash. There were offers from several to the anchorage, and as was the custom, we had the choice of haggling for the price of the ride. There was a long, narrow craft that could seat six of us, and we used cheap, duty-free smokes as barter – one packet from each of us.

Halfway there, and the rowers couldn't fail to read the terror in our eyes, as barracudas leapt a foot high into the air on either side of our frail craft. Perhaps this wild weather was their mating time. They were known to disembowel seamen, a fact which classified them as a wild type of the deep.

We and the rowers parleyed that we step up payment to two packets each. All hands readily agreed. Like their 'cousins' on the Demerara and Suriname Rivers in South America, these skilful rowers had developed that unique and impossible task of making progress in the roughest of waters with short and broad-ended oars.

Finally, in mid-June we had orders to sail and after loading a cargo of iron ore at Peebles, eighteen miles upriver, it was homeward bound – Destination Hull! It would be back to the toil in the stokehold but who cared. After five days we would pass the straits of Gibraltar, and then the wide-mouthed ventilators would be pouring down cool Atlantic breezes of the north.

And no more than a day out of Freetown, a sailor passed me a serious message as I was walking on the deck. Joe, the Columbian, had jumped overboard. He added that had he not come aft to read the log, no one else might have set eyes on him. He bucked me up with the comment that Sparky was at his radio contacting the commodore of the convoy.

267

Looking over the ship's side, the tranquil sea boded well for our shipmate's recovery. I was part of the crew leaning over the handrails when the rescue destroyer came alongside. It seemed Joe could not command the energy to scale the slung-over rope ladder.

Sailors got busy — a winch hauled up a derrick and swung it over the side with a bosun's chair on the hook. Joe was made fast into the chair and hauled on board. One look at his face as he landed on deck told us that a different Joe had returned. His eyes looked out, wide-open but without seeing. He was still in trauma.

Questions were asked if he had some kind of mental complaint before joining the ship. He walked aft to quarters without recognising anyone and his eyes looked glazed. I felt for him as a close friend. Hadn't we posed for a photograph together in Freetown? His attitude puzzled a lot of minds.

The most concerned was the religious bosun. Rightly or otherwise, he felt that having him in the sailor's quarters might affect the minds of his gang, and the skipper requested the steward to put fresh linen in the cabin used as a temporary 'Hospital'. The steward was a neutral type of person who had little contact with the crew.

But hadn't the second engineer appeared that way too until he proved himself as a person who understood animals, and for the next couple of days, the chief steward seemed to have a way with his patient. Joe started mixing with everyone, yet words never came from his mouth. He made his silent appearance in our mess room, and the cheerful way in which we treated him must have had some effect because he started moving around the ship like in the following anecdote.

If you ever had visited a stokehold, you would have seen a lot of handy rags and pieces of hessian rope lying on top of the valve box and maybe a spare sweat rag. Although gloves were issued to handle the thick, crowbar-type poker called the slice bar, gloves also often kept heat inside them so men made their own hand cloths.

Under the wide-mouthed sea water faucet, you would also see a bucket of brine. This was not the only water container. Apart from the one dangling on the hook at the rim of the meter-wide ventilator shaft, there could be a few more holding water with a couple of bricks to stop it from falling over with the roll of the ship.

Each stoker would have a sweat rag looped loosely around the neck, knotted slackly across the chest while stripped to the waist. The big, Scotch Marine boilers on the *Ingleton* did not depend on air from the ventilator to help the fires burn. On each side of the fire, you pulled down a handle and that turned on a forced draught.

It was an improvement on a natural draught; however, there was a negative side. When you were bent over the open door of the furnace and slicing beneath the fires to loosen clinker, an occasional flame would blow back in your face, but that was rare. What were frequent were the noxious fumes that blew back into your mouth.

To counter this, each time you spliced and dipped your sweat rag in one of the water cans, you gripped on one of the square ends with your teeth so that it dangled over mouth and chin. If it didn't drip, you would first of all wring it with your hands. With your teeth clamped on the rag, no acrid chemical matter could enter the gullet, and the damp rag was also cooling.

Men had different ways of cooling off. Some would dip their hands in the brine bucket occasionally and leave them a short while the pulse on the wrist would slow down. Another might sit on the valve box bent over with a wet rag on the nape of his neck. It is claimed that this also cools the system.

Imagine a stranger entering this semi-dark area where ash dust and coal dust on electric bulbs caused it to appear like a cave of shadows. Then they're opening two fire doors, allowing bright firelight to streak out. There are two men stripped to the waist covered in sweat and coal dust bent over these open furnaces with rags dangling from their mouths.

It would take an onlooker out of any daydream he might be in, and in this case our visitor turned out to be Joe. When we put our pokers flat on the deck, out of the way, we waved our friend over to join us. For the first time there was a slight smile on his face. That was a small miracle. As the three of us stood under the ventilator, I waited for Eddie to pass me the billy can after he had taken a guzzle of water himself.

And after I had gushed my throat, another miracle occurred. "Me," said Joe holding out his hands, and I passed him the can of water. He returned with a smile on his face to the engine room.

There were some humorous actions performed by our harmless madman. On one occasion he ascended the engine room on the deucer's watch where Joe followed the greaser around and watched him paint grease on moving parts of the main engine. He then made his way to our quarters and asked for a tin of jam. There were two or three open tins of different jams, and he was handed one that was a quarter full and off he went. But not to his cabin.

He took off down to the engine room and pestered the second engineer for a brush, and that understanding person passed him a grease brush and enjoyed a good laugh as Joe went around the pumps greasing them with jam. This was the main topic of yarning under the canvas canopy on the poop that evening.

When the pilot launch came out at the anchorage in Hull, a medic accompanied Joe into the boat, and that was the last we heard of him. He left us still in a dazed state of mind.

We had arrived in June in Hull, England and the weather couldn't haven't been better. It was glorious. Whilst the married men were gloating over their mail, we learned that it would be a week before the cargo could be discharged, and then we would proceed to nearby South Shields on the River Tyne to pay off.

When the company super arrived on board, he was so pleased with all the engine room painted that the deucer was instructed to only keep half the firemen working on board. This meant that every other day, we would be free to do as we wished. With that much time off plus the rest up in Freetown, there was little urge to go on a mad spree.

We took things leisurely and did as much window shopping as carousing in the Paragon Pub. There was a large area of bomb damage in the port of Hull, and if you passed certain areas after a night out, the smell of rotting flesh, warmed up by the summery air, sobered one up to the realities of present life.

Tying up on the Tyne, we were told to turn up at the shipping office in South Shield at a place called Mill Dam at 10am. That evening all hands speculated on what their pay-off would amount to.

Next morning when we arrived there, there was more than one long counter plus also a long shiny table to count out our pound notes. The countermen leaned over and studied the accounts of wages that were handed them on the other side of the counter. If we agreed with the account, we would be expected to sign our names at the bottom, hand it back and receive our pay packets in return. Up to this time there was mostly quiet, then there was an explosive question from the fireman, O'Brian.

Holding his pay sheet in front of the skipper, O'Brian blasted off. "What's this?! What's this?!" The captain took the sheet off him and spoke with the shipping master whilst the rest of us waited for the verdict. After several words passed between the two officials, they returned to the counter with the shipping master clearing the air.

"Do you recall leaving your ship in Australia two years ago?" O'Brian: "Yeah, I remember." The official cleared his throat. "Mr O'Brian, then you must be aware that during those two months, your wife received no allotment of money from you. The Society of Friends rescued her from poverty with weekly payments. Since they were kind enough to support her, 45 pounds have been deducted from your wages to repay them."

"But 45 pounds!" O'Brian fumed. There were a lot of hums and ho's along the counter, and I conferred with my mate Jack. I took him over to the table and said, "What do you say we take up a collection for O'Brian?" He stared me in the face without saying a word. I had no idea what was in his mind. Then he looked around.

There was no one within a distance of six feet. "Come to your senses, Ted; there's something you ought to know. Who do you think visited Bull in hospital and told him you had stolen his clothes?" This piece of spicy news left me stunned!

If O'Brian was the culprit who turned the Bull against me, then he must have been the one who caused the friction between Ginger and myself, and when the squabbling began he would be secluded in his cabin, enjoying it all. Jack's word was his bond. Fortunately, I never had the misfortune to sail with that rat again.

I was paid three weeks' wages leave pay which gave me a healthy payoff of over eighty pounds, and I only spent half of that among friends back home. I signed onto the *S/S Cragpool* three weeks later, together with a second cook who lived in my valley and had worked in a mine quite close to my elder brother, who was an up-and-coming union rep.

CHAPTER 7 – *S/S CRAGPOOL*

SHIP NUMBER SIX

After signing on the *Cragpool*, the second cook and myself walked across Mount Stuart Square in Cardiff to the pub opposite with the same name. Supping our pints of beers on the bar at the Mount Stuart, we quizzed some dockers if they were working on our ship, and we wished to know where she was bound for. Perhaps wartime restrictions had lessened to a degree.

One of the men was a foreman and quite openly let us know that the *Cragpool* would be taking general cargo to Melilla, Spanish Morocco and there it would be loading hides. That was about all he knew. I learned from Victor, the second cook that he had barely five months sea service; for that reason, I thought to put him straight before we went on board. I told him to keep our friendship low-key.

If he blabbed, it might cause jealousy among the other firemen who might think I could be getting hold of special food supplements. Before making our exit, the dock foreman waved us off with a final comment. "She's a rust bucket, and the day the war finishes, she'll be sent to the scrap yard."

We took it as a joke and went on our way. Vic went to the cook's quarters amidships, and I discovered that the crew quarters were up forward of all places. The *Lily* gave me the first experience of what to expect, and once I joined a vessel with quarters on the stern deck, I realised what hell the sailing crew had to put up with.

But I had signed on the dotted line and would complete my voyage, come what may. The actual fo'c'sle meant you sat, slept and walked on a gradient. When I stepped over the storm plates and into the quarters of the *Cragpool*, I lost heart at facing these nineteen century conditions once again. The foreman at the Mount Stuart was close to judgement when he claimed the *Cragpool* was ready for the scrap heap.

Walking up the narrow fireman's alley, I found the first door open. A slim person, who looked to be in his thirties, passed me a smile. He noticed the question mark on my face. "If you are looking for a better cabin than this, you better be lucky! I'm the first of the black gang to board, and you should choose this rat's nest rather than a cabin up forehead, where the bows will be taking big seas if we go through the Bay of Biscay."

He had a pleasant Cockney accent and with a nod from him, I threw my kitbag on the top bunk. As ugly as this compartment was, a friendly partner helped to take one's mind from the surroundings. And were they deplorable! After a quick look around the mess room and toilets, I returned and realised that we had a problem.

Obviously, we would work together on the same watch, and as there was no change room, there was only sufficient space for one man to dress himself. The other man would have to stay in his bunk or stand out in the alley. As there was no water or steam heat pipe from amidships, what took up important space was a coal stove with a skinny pipe leading up through the deck head.

I was glad I had chosen my Cockney mate as a partner because next morning when all hands arrived ready to turn in for duty, experience was already teaching me to look out for the sly ones, and besides my cabin mate, I could be sure of only one straight face. 'More jailbirds,' I thought.

When we cut cards for watches, believe it or not but I was in the lucky three. Just like the *Ingleton*, nine men handled nine fires, and according to the new British wartime system, everyone worked in the stokehold. Every third watch you worked in the bunkers, trimming coal on a rota system.

The rota applied also to the total number of fires you stoked. One watch you took care of five, followed by four the next time on duty. But there is a long custom that the 4-8 watch fill the coal bunker in the galley. As the long stove in the galley burned 24 hours a day except when being cleaned of ashes by sailors on night duty, it burned over a cwt of coal a day.

That meant that we filled the galley bunker with five hundred weights of coal every four days. There was a bonus for this extra duty called 'black-pan'. The 4-8 firemen ate every evening at 8.30pm, after having washed up. They took their meals from the oven, and on top of this, the cook would put away in the locker any special titbits left over from the saloon table where the officers ate.

273

This was called the black-pan and in actual fact, the cook could leave any Madeira cake or other fancy food if the 4-8 firemen found favour with him. This business was left to the second cook and with Vic being my close friend, if any of the main meals disagreed with my stomach, there would be rashers of bacon, a half dozen eggs and tins of paste left for our watch.

Passing Penzance and coming into the open sea, the weather was cold enough to try out the cabin stove. The experiment did not turn out very successful. Trouble was that when you fell asleep, you would wake up totally unable to see through the smoke, which caused eyes to burn and coughing to start up.

When the ship altered course, the wind direction would cause the smoke to blow down the long stovepipe instead of upward. Also, when the bows plunged into the briny, it created such a rattling of the forepart structure that keeping the stove lit was a dangerous measure. As we were making headway into more friendly warm weather, the stove was cleaned out and used as a receptacle for work gear.

In a few days' time, we were abeam the Portuguese coast with blue skies and a fair sea. It was back to evening get-togethers on the open deck yarning and getting away from those pokey cabins. The end of the Number One Hatch faced a steel wall enclosing the quarters, and most of the gathering sat in a row on the tarpaulin cover, swinging legs and passing jokes.

There was a moment of silence, which I filled by lamenting that I had to join such a broken-down rust bucket with disgraceful conditions, when I could be building up a fat bank account with a real cushy job on a neutral Swedish ship. "I think it was called the *Gdansk*," I added.

An interruption came from an able seaman. He asked me to repeat the name. I did. He then had a few words with his partner sitting next to him. "That's the ship," he told the listening group of us. "A Swede we were drinking with in the Ship and Pilot told us she went down with all hands in the Irish Sea. It must have been at night because all neutrals carry big letters on each side." So much for that savings fund I thought.

Melilla, on the north African coast, was where the Spanish dictator, Franco, had his lavish residence. The authorities disallowed any shore leave when they learned that the crew had signed on in Cardiff. The previous Cardiff crowd had written graffiti across the walls of this mansion, giving the dictator some indecent names.

It was a let-down for those who had subbed wages, which were most of the crew. But in a way it was a godsend because soon we were boarded by people selling watches. As usual, the watch experts on board surfaced and passed good quality remarks on the merchandise. The advice given was that they could sell in the UK for five pounds apiece.

All the Arabs wanted for them was just one pound, and a lot of five pound subs were made good use of. I purchased only two watches myself and kept three pounds to squander in Gibraltar, where we would finish loading cargo. The lack of merrymaking in port would mean a good rest up, and the Rock then became something to look forward to.

We docked on Gib on a Friday morning, sub day, and were ready for a weekend spree. The ship was almost empty during the daytime over the weekend as most of us drifted to Irishtown, a street where bands, consisting of females only, were masterful at hip-weaving and playing the clappers.

There was a lot of loose skirt around; perhaps that helped to turn the men's attention to a certain cheap cognac sold on the Rock. By Monday morning all hands were skint, but a certain ceremony that evening brought all hands ashore. We were sobered up by then and were ready to show appreciation for an annual event called 'The Changing of the Keys'.

There was an excellent military band, which every once in a while changed to waltz music. A bystander informed me that the change in tempo was to prevent the horses from kicking up and spoiling the formation. It was the first time that I realised that these spirited animals were as emotionally impressed by music as humans.

Moving on, there was only one man among the crew who owned a radio and during our uneventful evenings in Morocco, he would set it on Number One Hatch so we could all leave those cramped cabins to listen to a station that gave out music; however, after the weekend spree in Gib, very few gathered for an evening, even though the radio was brought out.

Over the weekend I had chummed up with a Bristol deckhand called Bronco. On Tuesday evening with nothing to do, I paid a call to his cabin. It was still warm there in early September, and I wondered why my mate kept his door closed. He invited me in after a rap at the door. Then I saw what he was up to.

He had cut out a stretch of leather and was sewing it into a shopping bag. He stopped pushing the big needle into the hide, laid down his palmer and lifted his bottom bunk mattress. There, doubled up underneath, was a hide. It must have been wrapped around a small bull, as it was thin and pliable.

What kind of hides were these? More important was that it had been cured. I showed interest in obtaining one for myself, and the next day, after finishing work, I found one beneath the blankets of my bunk. I decided to start bag-making later and stowed it under my mattress.

That evening I joined a drinking deckhand of mine from Cardiff on the fo'c'sle head. He had his ear to the tunes coming off the radio and his name was Johnnie Peterson. We both sat on bitts while the radio owner turned the knob of his toy to receive better reception. The air was sweet. At sunset the man took his box below and left us longing for cash withdrawal three days hence.

After the steam winches and cranes had ceased their mechanical noise, with no radio to draw us, we turned outward, looking over the handrails to an inward bay of ships at anchor. It seemed both of us had our eyes trained in the same direction on the same barge. As no one was within earshot, I asked Johnnie, "Do you see what I see?"

He turned his gaze away from the barge, lying alongside a war prize, an Italian cargo ship. There was a nod from him. I happen to be short-sighted but deckhands take a rigorous eye test, so he must have spotted the boxes of wine topped up on the barge. I kept quiet, leaving the next move to him. Stars took over the sky and invited mischief.

The loaded barge would be about forty yards away, crushing wavelets against the cargo vessel, and the small bay was more like a lake – placid, cool and inviting. I helped my mate to think faster. "It's getting darker," I opened. "Do you think we could swim over later and collar a few of those cases?"

"Those cases of sealed bottles will float. The air in the bottles will stop them from sinking. All we have to do is lash a heave line around them and haul away." Johnnie said. "What about the searchlight?" I worried. From the peak of the Rock, a massive searchlight screened the dock area with its powerful, all-seeing beam.

It circled the impregnable fortress in a slow sweep of the base of the Rock after dark, in a repetitive circle until daybreak. Together we arrived at a plan. I was by no means a speedy swimmer, but I wouldn't mind ducking my head if I was caught in the eye of the beam, and my partner was a very confident man in the water.

In Melilla he had taken a dive in the harbour when no one else did, claiming that the pair of sharks swimming on the waterline were only basking sharks and harmless. We decided to descend a rope ladder, only after the circling spotlight had immediately passed (and then later climbed the barge with the same timing), letting ourselves slip under the briny at that moment when the ray passed by.

We needed a third man to haul the cases from the water with similar timing. We decided to cut Bronco in. He was ideal, being the bosun's mate, and knowing where all the deck gear was stowed. He told us to return to our cabins, strip and he would lower the Jacob's ladder over the side at the ready for anything.

There was a force of dock police who paced the area in pairs, and very regular and observant they were. They had to be watched. The bows of our ship leaned over the dock lying at right angles to our berth. We were locked in the corner of the dock, and the only shore space we had to watch was the short length between our bows and the stern of another cargo ship.

The moon was cusped, giving sufficient light to spot the dark-uniformed police. The small shadow of our bows gave encouragement to our piracy. Bronco passed a two fathom rope to each of us with bow lines at both ends. All we had to do was extend the bows, loop it over our bodies and do the same with those beautiful, Italian wine cases.

We stopped in the shadows of the bulwarks as the spotlight passed our light-skinned bodies, and Johnnie went swiftly over the side first. Thankfully, with cargo in the belly of the ship, there was little freeboard. I determined to put all I had into my relays with my partner so as to keep the pace.

I could make that short distance and duck under the shadow of the barge before the spotlight caught my swimming body and that made me confident to time it the other way. My mate could not swim any faster because he had to time himself with the swirling arc light. We had our rests this way and hadn't decided how many cases we would tow – they floated practically weightless.

When Bronco lowered a heaving line, the loop end was ready for hauling up, and both of us must have become greedy with the ease of getting free booze. About the hardest part of the swim was pulling a case down from the stack on the barge, and so low was this vessel in the water that even that proved a breeze.

From above came a loud whisper. "Make this the last box, Ted, when I haul it up, you follow." I did so and up on deck I found a chain gang of half the crew, with the bosun himself in command. The deck quarters were in the portside fo'c'sle alongside the quay and on the opposite side to where the boxes were being hauled up.

The big super torch had caught Johnnie as he was ascending the ladder. Two policemen spotted him and started blowing whistles. The whistles spread like some kind of message to bring a posse together.

The bosun was not a petty officer for nothing; he held his cool, calling all hands to a meeting in the sailors' mess room, as it was larger than the firemen's mess. Standing at the end of the table as cool as you like, he grasped the situation. First of all, he told all hands that they could expect the police at any minute.

He then eased any panic by stating that if we played our cards well, everything would come out Ok. Now he had everyone behind him, ready to take orders. He asked if the deckhand on night watch was present. That person raised his hand, and he was asked how long since he had surveyed the deck?

"Just about a minute ago," the deckhand replied. "Is the duty mate on deck?" the bosun asked. "No, he went into the saloon for a coffee just before the whistles sounded. I only heard them faintly from the galley and came along to find out the reason," the deckhand offered. "Well go back to the saloon and find out if the mate is still inside," the bosun retorted.

While the sailor went swiftly on his errand, he told three men to fetch a case each from the top of the chain locker hatch. After battening down the other spoils, he had purposely left these three cases for display to the police. The men placed the three cases on the mess table.

They were placed at the end near the alleyway leading on deck. "Now spread the playing cards on the table," he instructed, "and some of you pretend to play a game, while the others look on." The duty sailor returned, panting and blowing to report that his senior, the third mate, was still in the saloon watching his fellow officers play a game of cards and entertain themselves with beer and duty-free liquor.

"That will be the best news of the night if the dock police come straight here," said the bosun. "They're already on board," revealed the watchman. "Should be here in a minute."

A posse of five policemen charged into the mess and looked in all directions except the correct one. The wine was standing on the table right in front of them.

They must have expected us to be racing around with stolen cargo and were out to capture us in the act. They cooled down when they seized the three cases. The sergeant moved forward, and laying one hand on a box, asked in an officious way, "Who is the thief?" The bosun stepped forward; he knew his worse fears were over.

Had the police group been joined with a ship's officer, arguments would not have worked, but now he felt on safe ground. "These are the stolen cases," stated the bosun. "You can take them away. If you fine the man who stole it, all of us here will dob in to pay it." The sergeant turned around to consult with his group.

He had the option of reporting the matter to the captain but would lose status. They turned to the table and examined the stolen goods. One of them said that the enemy cargo would not be tallied until it reached the warehouse. The sergeant turned his attention to us.

"You will be let off this time. I will keep silent about this business and you, bosun, will be responsible for not letting this business leak out. Remember that you will not get let off so lightly if anymore cargo is pilfered by your crew. You cannot fool me. I think all of you were involved in stealing. A report will be sent to England next time."

The law picked up the cases and left. The watchman followed and checked if his boss was still in the saloon. It was also fortunate that the catering staff had gone for a night out. Still he was double-questioned by the crew on his return. "In which direction did the law walk?" asked someone. "In the direction of the canteen," he answered, which put all hands at ease.

Then everybody there started talking at the same time until the commanding voice of the bosun broke in and said they could say and do what they like, but on no account must anyone tamper with the hatch cover of the chain locker until after midnight. It was now 8.30pm and during this meeting, Johnnie had remained hidden in the cabin.

He was now told to join us, and the discussion returned to what the police would do with the three cases. "Use them themselves, of course," said the bosun. "That's why they were on the way to the canteen." And to finish off his directive stated, "The only ones who could spill the beans on this affair is one of our own."

"That is why I insist that not a bottle be taken from the chain locker until our gangway watchman has given us the all clear that the officers have left the saloon and turned in their bunks." Even though the air was still on the warm side when the crew took to their cabins to nap off for a few hours, they closed their doors in case conversation was overheard.

At this point, no one bothered getting busy with a palming needle to sew pretty bags for their sweethearts back home. Down in the chain locker, there was surely enough Italian wine to give all the ship's crew a memorable headache.

We really had a ball in the late hour, extending into the early hours of the next day. Everyone was downing the rich, expensive export wine like it was as weak a drink as shandy. Benny, the Maltese fireman, gave us a connoisseur's opinion. His taste let us know we were onto some classy enjoyment.

He vouched the liquid as top-grade and told us this grape juice was meant to be consumed in small, delicate glassfuls, but seeing all the dumb heads sitting around the long table of the sailor's mess, he was persuaded to disobey his own reasoning and walloped it back along with the uninitiated.

At daybreak, the sailor on night watch entered quarters to stir up all hands ready for the day's toil. The only ones he managed to bring back to life were those who had lost their balance and tumbled off the benches, maybe four or five. The crew lay around like cadavers on the hard, wooden deck.

Watchy, the watchman, had to resort to booting the ribs of those logs. Other ways of reviving life had no result. His boot was tired by the time they had gathered the strength to arise and join other butts on the benches. The morning air, breezing through the alley, encouraged the unconscious to rise from the dead.

Having done his stint, the watchman left to wake the cook and the other catering staff. Thankfully, it was the watchman and the bosun who had kept their heads during the boozing orgy, and soon the bosun rallied all the dodos. The few firemen at the table dragged their feet to their own mess room.

There was the easy going British style in port, and as it was yet early, the bosun relaxed, once he found there were no wine bottles in evidence. The night watchman must have disposed of them. There was over one hour to go before the 9am turn-to for work, and there were yet hopes for the bosun to rally his boys.

The table sitters moved to their bunks to rest heads that were still in the process of swelling, and when the watchman had visited the cabins, there was no way he could unglue them from their deep cots, so he left that to the bosun. By 9am those few on their feet could not dislodge their fellow workers.

The only life they showed was to complain to those trying to bring them to their feet that they were medical cases and needed the attention of a doctor. They were left writhing in their agonies. With his sense of command, the bosun visited these ailing men personally, letting them know if they didn't work the shift, the captain might learn of the night partying.

Trays of breakfast food remained untouched as the working day approached. The lads all sat on the mess table benches, bowed over as if in prayer, each man with elbows on the table, holding his head as if he were afraid it might drop off. It was like a bunch of patients waiting for an ambulance, nursing their throbbing brains between hands that should have been used to getting the *Cragpool* shipshape.

Not a seaman's body budged out to deck, and Captain Richards, when he received news from his officers that there was a collective inertia among the crew, took this state of affairs as the beginning of mutiny. He requested the chief engineer and together they walked up forward.

Number One Hatch stretched to within two metres of the crew quarters. The other officers were gathered there waiting for him, and he ordered a low foot ladder. This was placed against the combing and up stepped the master quite nimbly, considering he had one leg made of wood.

The hatch table was going to be his platform to deal out maritime justice. Into the quarters strode the officers and ordered all hands to parade in a line on Number One Hatch

With insistence from the epaulets, a line of bleary-eyed men with drooping shoulders faced the skipper. As this meeting was called on the instant, there was no time to arrange a small dais so that the men in command could look down on the 'mutineers'. The bosun was told to stand aside from the crew.

Richards possessed a face that turned scarlet like a chameleon as his blood pressure rose with his ranting. He spat out the Riot Act in no uncertain terms. He rammed his message into our semi-deaf ears that we had better turn-to for duty.

Then he made a promise that if we didn't, our seaman's record books would be impounded on return to the UK, and we would have to find a new way of making a living once the maritime court charged us with mutiny. We accepted his message and changed into work gear.

If the rest of the crowd felt like myself, it would be hard going. The working day passed as if I was carrying a heavy brick on my shoulders instead of a head. I waded through the tedious day with suicidal thoughts, yet the miracle of it all was that our superiors had no inkling that we had indulged in free grog and had more bottles left over.

That evening we kept our contraband under wraps, and all hands sought the attention of their small mattresses. The bosun advised us the next day that Friday was only twenty-four hours away, and the skipper would expect us to be getting the happy stuff down us after money subs were handed out.

By Monday it was expected that all cargo would be loaded, and then we would be on our way back to Cardiff (only a four day run), so no one wanted to spoil their record books. After work that day, the sewing circle was in full swing. We had no need to draw cash on the weekend except to purchases sundries because most of our drink was on board with the free stuff.

Although Gibraltar used its own special currency, they accepted the ordinary pound notes that the skipper had in his safe. These couple of pounds that each man drew were in most cases kept for arrival in a UK port were in need of ready money for the evening ashore.

For a change, we hit pretty fair weather skirting the Bay of Biscay, but instead of sailing up the Bristol Channel, we were diverted to the English

Channel with our new port of call being Middlesbrough on the northeast coast. It was a peaceful trip with no depth charges dropped by our escorts. Hitler's U-boats seemed to be thinning out by now.

From the galley, the cook could only report good news on all the allied war fronts. However, table talk consisted of boasting about who sewed the prettiest bags. Most stitching I set eyes on looked pretty bloody awful – except my own, of course.

We dropped anchor off Middlesbrough and were surprised that the September air there was just about as balmy as the Mediterranean's. And there the boys made final touching ups to their souvenir bags.

We celebrated that night with one tot each from the last bottle of wine before it was thrown overboard and waited for further news from amidships. The first news was that watches would be kept; we had to be ready to heave in the anchor at short notice. The next news item, brought along by the deckhand on duty, was that no one would be allowed to pay off until all the cargo was discharged.

We were still waiting for further news about docking during our 3pm tea break next day. The bragging and boasting now was not about bags, but how many watches each crew member had acquired in North Africa.

The firemen's cabins were on the starboard side of the bows, and one man spent his leisure time peering through the porthole at the shore to see if any launch was coming in our direction. The porthole was a small circle because the ship was pre-war built and aged. This type of porthole restricted looking in a fore and aft direction.

There was a vessel anchored astern, and the 'sentinel' screwed his eyes at the sound of a motor to find a cutter sort of sneaking up on him from the stern. It was coming from this other boat. He hastily left his port to report the movement to men sitting in both mess rooms, sailors and firemen.

There was the rush of several feet out onto the deck to have a view. As the launch neared, a lot of supposing went on by half a dozen viewers. "Supposing it's the pilot come to take us alongside?" "No, Sparky would have let us know." "Could be the mail." "Yes, that's it for sure," someone agreed.

A glass and metal canopy domed over the forepart of launches for rough weather protection, and whoever was there on board remained hidden, but as she broke foam on reaching our stern and slowed down to half speed, her stern swung over, ready to come alongside.

She cut out the engine, and before drifting to the gangway, the onlookers had seen all they wanted to see. One man let out a cry of panic. "Look at all those uniforms! It's loaded to the gunnels with bloody customs officers." There was a mass stampede of feet into the fo'c'sle.

The threatening warning was spread to others that in minutes a big search would be on for contraband. Men were feverishly uncertain if they had hidden their watches in well-concealed nooks. And then there were the thin leather hides.

The crew began to realise that poaching cargo was a criminal offence, and no problem for the custom's officer to spot. Some men upended their mattresses and grabbed what remained of the unused leather, squeezing the material hard to be small enough to ram through the mini-portholes, with an energy that only panic could supply.

My cabin mate became overwhelmed and threw three wristwatches through the porthole, whilst I sweated it out until the last minute, seated on the small, unheated coal stove. We had a lookout in front of the alley door. The door opened just then, and I tried to read the tread of boots.

The friendly voice talking to the man in the next cabin told me that all was Ok for the moment and both of us relaxed. "It was only our mail," said the lookout. "That boatload of uniforms you spotted were only apprentices of the Customs and Excise, being given a free trip around the harbour."

Early evening the pilot boarded, and we tied up at the Tyne and Tees Wharf after the evening meal. We could see the dock exit from the ship; it was only a short walk, but it was over several sets of steel railway track and a lot of coal dust. It was unfortunate for those who had jettisoned their watches, but like my cabin mate, there were quite a few who had more of the same hidden around the ship. I had retained my two watches, which according to the buzz, would fetch 10 pounds, half a month's wages after tax deductions.

It looked as if it was going to be a dry, crispy September evening when Bronco and myself stepped down the gangway. Rumour had it that the two best pubs were the Captain Cook and the Robin Hood.

There was neither a gate nor a blue uniform to stop us as we walked onto the main street. We certainly did not have to venture far for our night of carousing. The very first two structures on either corner of the street were none other than the same ones where we were advised to 'Have a good time at.'

Piano music reached us from the windows of the Robin Hood, and we opted to become part of that fun, jolly company. The tune seemed an unusual one. Normally, two popular tunes – 'The White Cliffs of Dover' and 'Coming in on a Wing and a Prayer' – could always be heard in pubs throughout the length and breadth of Britain during wartime. Everyone sang these songs, even in the dives of seafaring men, along with renditions of 'Sons of the Sea' and 'Maggie May'.

However, entering the Robin Hood, I couldn't make out the words of a tune that had no connection to war. 'Maisy doats and dowsy doats and little lamsy divey' the words went and 'A kiddley divey too, wouldn't you'. So sang the pickup girls and naughty sailors.

There were no seats, just long wooden benches on each side of plain timber tables with plenty of sawdust to suck up the beer spills. Pints of draught ale were still only nine pence a glass, and in the old currency of 240 pence to the pound, we could last out an hour with the five shillings in loose change that Bronco nursed in his pocket. We both brought two watches ashore with the intent of selling only one each.

The other one we intended to carry on our bodies in case HM customs paid the ship a late visit. We carried our bitter ales to a vacant area near the open window and placed them on the ledge. There was still an hour or two until curtains would be drawn, and windows closed to conform to wartime blackout regulations.

We were quite lucky to catch a slight breeze that blew the smoky atmosphere out of another window. It was a pity to light up cigarettes when we were enjoying the late summer air. And light intoxication, bolstered by finger-gripping a smoke, gave us the boldness to catch the eye of stray females.

Bronco spotted room on one half of a bench where there sat two damsels on their own. There was room to spare and we lost no time to occupy the space. They responded to our company in a very sociable way, and my mate lost no time in going to the counter and bringing back two pints of mild beer.

The girls downed the dregs of their half-pint glasses and thanked him. The black market was busy in wartime, and the bar girls, who were used to the ways of seafarers, knew that if we had little cash, we had something to sell. Bronco sat next to this Doris, who lost no time in looking him up and down.

She must have read something in his eyes because she asked him point-blank if he had anything to flog. He showed her the watch he was wearing on his wrist. Doris removed her butt and paid a visit to a young chap across the room. When both came our way, my mate nudged me to move further along the bench.

Taking Bronco's pew, the young fellow gave nothing away. In a plain, light-grey coat, he was introduced to us, and small talk was passed around as he sipped on his shandy. Then the ivory keys on the piano pumped away again. 'Maisy doats'. The sing-song got all throats exercising in unison, except ours, that is.

Incidentally, this was when the bargaining started. No one could hear our private conversation, even though we chatted loudly over the melodious noise surrounding us. And so the haggling began. "How much you asking?" "Five pounds is top price." Then there were the furtive movements of hands beneath the table.

By the time the pianist ceased banging away, I had parted with two big-faced watches and had crammed one trouser pocket with ten one pound notes, one of which I gave to my new friend, Eunice, whilst Bronco parted with a quid to Doris. I was off to the toilet to fold my currency bills and there placed the bills neatly in the rear pocket of my trews.

Back to the table I went and asked the girls what kind of drinks they liked, then went to the bar and returned with two Bloody Marys. Our kind black-marketer had slunk away to continue his shady business elsewhere, and it was smiles all around with a fun night to look forward to.

That 'Maisy Doats' song must have reached the top of the charts the way customers kept requesting encores from the pianist. It ended with very un-English words like 'A kiddley divy too, wouldn't you?' Bronco turned to his partner and asked "What's this 'kiddley divy' mean, Doris?" Slapping him playfully on the shoulder, he turned to hear her sweet voice say, "It goes like this, silly. A kid'll eat ivy, too. Wouldn't you?"

At 10pm closing time, we took off to the fish and chip shop for hot meals wrapped in newspaper. We promised to meet the girls the following evening at the Robin Hood pub and went our different ways.

We had really gotten the hang of the new song at last, and although we staggered a little, manoeuvred our tiptoes across the railway lines, singing in unison "Mares eats oats and does eats oats, and little lambs eat ivy, and a kid'll eat ivy, too, wouldn't you?"

With beer at only nine pence a pint and 240 pence to the pound, it meant we had enough cash and more to play the big spenders in the Robin Hood for the whole period we were docked in port. And that also meant that our wages would remain untouched. As most are aware, with spare cash easily obtained, cash slips through fingers with no thought of tomorrow. You live it up! Within a week both of us were skint, broke. And the cargo discharge was moving at a snail's pace. It was three more days before we could enter the shipping office to get paid off.

As the first glorious days passed, I had clean forgotten about the hide under my mattress. If the customs were not on board within the first 24 hours of a ship's arrival, it usually meant they had no intention of screening the vessel. I then realised that the leather hide meant a few extra quid in the pocket.

After four years of war, there are very few things a country is not short of, but while I was planning to swap the leather, belatedly, the customs and excise officers paid us a visit. There could have been a good dozen on board, and with all those torches flashing in nooks and corners, the search seemed no less than thorough.

I climbed on deck looking like a chimney sweep after cleaning out soot from the boiler tubes that morning with the intention to make a daring attempt to salvage the goody under my mattress. Luckily, my close friend, Vic, the second cook, was at the doorway of the galley. I let him know that I was in an emergency situation and needed a good potato sack.

I got nervy waiting for the galley boy fetching one from the storeroom. It would soon be the dinner break when the searchers would request crew members to allow them to enter their cabins for inspection, and my mind was set on transferring my booty to shore side before noon.

I could wait no longer and rushed to the fo'c'sle. When I entered our quarters, there was a customs man dawdling along the alleyway between cabins, tapping the above deck head with a rod and carrying a powerful-looking torch. Keeping my distance and putting my feet down one by one, I waited for him to pass my cabin and enter the common washroom.

Slinking after him, I moved as slick and silent as a feline when he entered the room of washbowls and toilets and was soon inside my own room with the door closed. It's amazing how people miss the obvious. After tugging out the leather from its hiding place, I cracked the door open a split.

The bathroom door was open but ajar enough to hide the enemy. I could hear the peaked cap tapping at pipes with his magic rod. I am not very good at walking on my toes, especially down a sloping deck, so I walked delicately on my heels to keep the silence.

Soon, I was stepping over the storm-plate of the open door, losing no time in reaching the galley and having a word with Vic. Here was a good point. With the dockers tugging away at the yardarms and the steam winches screaming plus all kinds of people crowding the deck, one seemed immune to curious eyes.

Unable to find an empty potato sack, Vic passed me a substitute, a flour sack, and a very floury flour sack at that. I stuffed the folded hide inside it and left my mate to sweep up the jumble of soot from my blackened clothes with the flour.

Had not the dockers been busy dispensing cargo and barking at each other, I might have made myself an eyeful for their amusement in my chimney sweep look, lugging a bulky flour sack over my shoulder as I crossed over to the wharfside and descended the gangway.

Desperation to distance myself from a probing gang of customs officers got my feet mobile and my brain active, while darting around stationary coal wagons and tiptoeing over rails and sleepers. Only three wagons blocked my way at first, and I hurried around them.

There was a lengthier line of rail stock meeting my eyes next, so looking right and left and finding no engine attached, I crawled under the buffers separating two trucks, dragging my snowy white bag over coal dust. Hidden behind this long row from the Sherlock Holmes mob, I sat on the sack with a sense of relief, took a breather, and flattened out my contraband at the same time.

However, this was no time to linger. Behind a short row of trucks in front of me, the wide, open entrance beckoned. I carried my light load around the wagons in a relaxed fashion. Twenty yards up the street from the unguarded entrance, I could do a spot of business in a shoe repair shop with the cobbler.

I was not ten yards from the entrance when I skirted around a wagon, dropped my sack to change shoulders and before I could give it a sling, there was a tap on my shoulder. It was Mr Sly himself in a police uniform.

He shot out a straightforward question: "What have you got in that bag, young sailor?" Everything was occurring so fast that I blurted, "Hides." It was immediate surrender. "I had eyes on you when you were crawling. My eyes don't miss much," Sly said

He braced himself up into a commanding manner and rambled on as I awaited my arrest. Blowing himself up to show how smart a cop he was, I gave him the attention he wanted to make him feel even bigger. "Hides, indeed!" he frowned "Who are you trying to kid? On your way and don't waste my time."

And I did, turning my back as quickly as I could to hide my astonishment. Was he afraid to get himself all messed up by looking into a messy flour bag, or did the local sailors 'enjoy' the kidding of the port's local police? I even heard a guffaw from his mouth as I hastily retreated.

I sped my feet to a nightly landmark, Ye Old Fish and Chip Shoppe. The cobbler had his shop next door, and all I wanted to do was get the thoughts of hides off my back, my chest and my mind. After five years of war, there would be hundreds of items of merchandise in short supply, and if I hadn't been unbalanced by the sudden appearance of the law, I might have haggled for double the cash I received. I accepted two pounds, a first offer, on condition he take the flour bag as well.

Bronco was overjoyed at my deal. We could look forward to a few more days tippling, before picking up the payoff and getting on a homeward bound train. If Hull had been savagely bombed, the dock area of Middlesbrough seemed to have taken an even more cruel bashing.

Bombed property housed a bunch of vagrants and itinerants. With limited drinking hours on Sunday, instead of taking a few flagons of beer on board, we would just drop into one of the bombed houses and create a party. Not only pub girls would take part of the entertainment but other skirts on the loose.

The day of paying off a ship is taken very seriously by all hands. It is usually 10am, and booze is gone for cups of tea or coffee in a seamen's mission, which nearly always adjoins the shipping office. The shipping master collects all the crew's smiles, in case the captain decides to mar your record book with a bad stamp of DECLINE TO REPORT.

No one likes this. It means you are a baddy, and you are offered only a coastal ship where you can eventually build up a good record. The only person with authority to revoke that stamp is the Shipping Master, so it pays to be clean, sober and polite.

Not only that. Men were returning to wives, sweethearts and families, and they wished to look responsible. The hour's wait in the mission made one reflective. When would I sail with Johnnie or Bronco again? In a year's time, I would be lucky to come across any of the crew. That's the way it is when you sail deep-sea on tramp ships.

In this meditative mood sitting alone, I began to think about what Winston Churchill had recently spoken about – that victory was not only in our sight but in our grasp – and that was shown in people's reactions and expressions. Even though semi-destroyed buildings pockmarked Middlesbrough, there was a fresh festivity in the air.

They were turning to new light-hearted sing-songs. It was only a matter of time before blackouts would be a non-thing, and prisoners of war would be reunited with loved ones. Newspapers were already reporting that the liner, the *Empress of Russia*, which I had avoided joining in Greenock, was now on a special charter.

She was returning POWs from Germany via ports in Sweden. A man of about 50 years joined me at the end of the table. I couldn't identify him as a seafarer. He wore giveaway clothing, which brought me out of my brown study. The grey sweater was a little too large for him, and the scarf around his neck was an item of clothing that was rare with seamen.

"If you're looking for a spot on a ship, the *S/S Cragpool* signs on tomorrow?" I opened. The washed-out face made a remarkable return statement. "No thanks. I have just been repatriated from Narvik in Norway." I then asked, "Were you included in a recent exchange of prisoners?" "That's right," he answered. "Would you happen to know a sailor called Johnnie Peterson?" I quizzed.

He placed an elbow on the table and cupped his chin pensively. After a few blinks, he replied. "I think I do. He was in a group that escaped from Narvik in 1940." "That's him. Hang on a tic?" I walked to the other side of the room where Johnnie was nursing a cuppa.

He had misgivings following me after I told him an old shipmate would like to have a word with him. After introductions I switched to another table. It was good to watch two smiling faces chattering away and exchanging reminiscences after so many years. I felt Ok sitting alone.

As for me, it was not often that I had left cash in the bank back home where I next visited. And this served me well now that going to sea was a safer business with a reduced U-boat fleet. I drew my three pounds plus from the shipping pool for over six weeks while I awaited a berth on my next ship. Forty pounds was a nice surplus to draw from after a month at home.

In November, 1944, the Manning Pool in Cardiff handed me a slip of paper called a P45 and told me to get around to the shipping office. *Princesa* was written on the slip and that stately building was packed. I soon found that two vessels were signing on crews and mine was the longest line to the counter.

After signing on, I accepted the five pounds advance on wages and changed the advance note with the money changer outside the main entrance. He deducted ten shillings and I was off.

CHAPTER 8 – *S/S PRINCESA*

SHIP NUMBER SEVEN

Entering The Mount Stuart just across from the shipping office, it looked like the two crews had made the bar their assembling point, and as the *Princesa* was the larger of the two ships, most of the drinkers were from her. I soon entered a circle of standing drinkers and learned most of what I wished to know.

I had joined a 10,500 ton freezer boat on a regular run to Buenos Aires, which meant that with two engines, there would be a hell of a big gang in the engine room department. I noticed a person entering the pub who had been standing alongside the note changer. He had a friendly face, came my way and we shook hands.

He introduced himself to me as Bill, the new donkeyman aboard the *Princesa*. Since he had sailed on her before, I decided to stick with him. I listened to a lot of talk about 'Monty' and 'B.A'. Slowly I got a hang of the talk about Montevideo and Buenos Aires. This was the first time I had joined a ship on a regular run, but my new mate was helpful in mapping out the trip for me.

I opened confidences to this person after he had revealed his own family connections. He was the son-in-law of the Portuguese advance note changer. He let me know that the trip was usually three months. "How many boilers on her?" I asked.

"This happens to be a back-to-back job." He saw wrinkles gather on my forehead and cleared the air. "Back-to-back means that boilers face each other and the firemen work back-to-back. Not many firemen do a second trip on her since they get in each other's way, and it's stifling when she gets in the tropics. The run is five weeks – either way from Cardiff."

It was noticeable that as men dropped in for a drink, it was usually for a single pint only. When Bill and I came to the bottom of our glasses, I was about to call for two ales more, but he stopped my hand. Then Bill said, "Pick up your bag; we're off. It's no good facing the deucer first day with the smell of drink on you."

We followed a broken line of men to a lay-by dock, where the Holder Line steamer was waiting for a berth under the coal-loading cranes. Bill's father-in-law would naturally know about shipping movements and times due to his business of changing notes and would pass them on to Bill.

"We won't go under the cranes for four days," he passed on to me. That left me four days to idle around in port. On board he pointed out the quarters for the black gang and took himself off to the petty officers' accommodation. Seeing one fireman throw his kitbag down a staircase, I did the same with my own.

Picking it up at the bottom, I made a careful view of the mess room. It was vast, stretching from one side of the stern to the other. Long benches were on each side of long tables, all of untreated, bare timber. Two geysers of hot water were fixed against the bulkheads.

As men sat on benches, sipping hot drinks and talking about Monty and B.A, I was approached and asked if I was one of the firemen just signed on, and when I nodded, the man took a head count. Then with a raised voice proclaimed that the last fireman had arrived and suggested we cut cards for watches.

The black gang consisted of thirty men, nine men on each of the three watches and three men on day work. Each was divided between five firemen and four trimmers. One of the trimmers was looking for a swap. He had been made a trimmer, as his sea experience was nil.

However, he had done some training in a special school in Cardiff and wished to try his hand at stoking fires. The enclosed stokehold, with two boilers facing three others, would be a scorcher within a week when we had steamed past Gibraltar. What he was throwing away was that on this duty he would be working in the side bunker.

Of the four trimmers on each watch, two worked in each of the side bunkers above the stokehold, where your sweat was created not so much by heat but by shovelling, a natural exercise that gave you a good appetite. You could time yourself and provided you had a good crown of coal over the small opening on top of the stokehold bunker, you could knock off work a half hour early.

Therefore, I was making both of us happy by taking over his job and losing no cash in the deal. In the hatch next to the stokehold enclosure and beneath the foredeck, there was stowed 2,000 tons of Welsh anthracite. It was called the thwartships of the cross bunker since it stretched from one side of the ship to the other.

An iron slide door would be raised at the centre part prior to sailing time so that all twenty furnaces of the five boilers would be used. There was 1,000 tons in each of the long-side bunkers. Basically, we had less coal to trim than the plate trimmers who were supplying coal at the base level.

The decks of both engine room and stokehold are called 'The Plates'. No part of this steel deck is welded together, but flat screws seal these 5' by 5' plates to a forest of stanchions and supports beneath. Normally, two men can handle three boilers in a row. One man would stoke five fires and the other four alternately on each watch.

The inboard fire makes a man walk a few steps, but it's manageable to rely on side bunkers. In the congested heat of two boilers facing three, coping with four fires each is sufficient. One man to a boiler – each side bunker serves only one boiler. The plate trimmers barrow coal between all the boilers so that the firemen working the twin boilers and the centre one need not stretch to pitch coal into the fires.

It was fortunate that I had met up with Bill, who had explained the situation beforehand. With the trimmer's job handed me, there was none of the usual jitters in my stomach, which arises with new kinds of stokeholds. I poured myself a cup of tea from a vast teapot sitting on one of the tables.

I had my ears in readiness for any discussion on work procedure. Listening to talk, I gathered we would go en masse and pay our respects to the deucer. A spokesman was elected – a thickset man in his early thirties. His name was Ted Healy, and he had a rough face and a firm jaw but not a hostile attitude.

He took the lead up the ladder. Next, Ted knew the face coming our way and pulled him up to ask what sort of person the second engineer (deucer) was like. This other person let all of us know that the man in question was basically interested in tasks that were necessary.

Whilst a lot of small talk went on, I socialised with someone who knew more than I did. I remarked that the deucer had a lot of responsibility handling thirty men and a reply came swiftly. "Are you kidding?! What about the six greasers for the two engines and the refrigerator greasers and there're eight engineers with two apprentices."

Our meeting was short with a lot of body language between the deucer and our spokesman, perhaps more understandable than speech. It was obvious that the second engineer wanted to use three of the four idle days for a maintenance check of the engines before the voyage began.

Once in a while he would scan different faces to measure the degree of trust in their eyes. It did not take long to settle him once he realised that the spokesman was a steady, married man and put the ball in our court. After being satisfied that we had arranged watches, he offered us a very decent deal.

All he wanted from us was a promise that by Friday, we would have nine men standing by to shift the ship to the bunker loading berth. It was Tuesday, and that meant that a lot of men might be able to spend the whole weekend at home if the *Princesa* was slow in shifting to the coaling berth.

We returned to our quarters, and I think all hands felt they had chosen the right spokesman. In the mess deck, Ted explained to those unacquainted with such large vessels the necessity of card-cutting to solve on-going problems instantly. Then cards were cut for who was to stand by Friday.

Once that was settled, we all prepared to go our different ways. He boosted our plans with a final statement of assurance. "As for the rest of us, you can be sure that the *Princesa* will not be sailing until the weekend is over." He knew something the others of us didn't know except Bill, the d'man.

Naturally, no one went home right away, although most of the crew were Cardiff boys. We had been on board less than an hour, and we had time for a few ales before the midday meal to get to know each other. With it being wartime, a meal aboard was definitely a thing to look forward to after living on shore rations.

Later, supping beer in the Mount, I overheard that, depending on the speed of convoy, this meat boat burnt between eighty and ninety tons of coal a day. As there were six watches every twenty-four hours, that meant a little less than fifteen tons of coal burnt on a watch or three tons by every stoker, so I would barrow only three tons to the wing fireman every duty watch.

Back on board, volunteers brought several kits of food from the galley, and we stuck into roast beef and Yorkshire pud, followed by plum duff. Up until then I had thought there was only one cooking facility on every ship, but this vessel had two. The crew galley was quite convenient; just below the poop deck.

Up amidships there was a bakery, adjoining the second galley to cater for those who were petty officers or above plus fourteen passengers. The *Princesa* was classified as a passenger-cargo boat. When I carried my kitbag down to the lower deck to find my sleeping quarters, I entered where very visible letters above the door stated 8-12 watch.

I slung my bag on a bed that didn't have one and left the room with a person elder to myself. He told me he disliked sleeping in a cabin with eight others. I totally agreed. He went on to say that he had sailed on the Houlder Line before on the Baronesa. He then passed a casual remark: "Me and you have missed out on the best watch."

I told him I enjoyed working between the hours of eight and twelve. He looked carefully at me before replying. 'The 4-8 supplies coal to both galleys, and after the evening meal, they pick up all those special dishes left over from the passengers table." I then wondered if I could shift on to the 'Black-pan Watch'.

I was not one of the nine men for Friday duty and enjoyed the time I had on my hands. If Healy was correct and obviously the ship would not sail before Tuesday, I had one week in front of me to play with. I took the Bute Street tram into town and hopped on a train up to the valley.

Just as if it was arranged, I had a rail journey in front of me. My brother had just arrived from a prison camp in Germany at Denbigh Infirmary. My elder sister was eager to visit him and asked me to accompany her the following day. I was just a kid when he had sailed away to join the Palestine police seven years previous, and I gladly took the train.

At the private house in Denbigh, where we were advised to put up, were such nice people, and since they were on the religious side, I cut back my alcohol intake which did me more good than harm. I took over the room of their only son serving in the Navy. The farm-style bedroom was inviting, decorative and bright, awaiting the son's return, and I slept like a log in it that night.

War is a series of shocks. Some shocks don't leave the body and tension builds up. Visiting the hospital, I expected to see an emaciated, unrecognisable body lying on the bed. Ken certainly had me guessing for minutes if I hadn't come to the wrong bed, because even though he had been diagnosed as a spinal injury patient, he looked the picture of health.

That's probably going too far. Perhaps I should put it this way. As that ten minutes stretched to half an hour, Ken had both an ease and yet an unease about him. He had been captured in Crete, which had had a terrible bombing. Had I seen him, say five years earlier, I might have met a nervous wreck.

Five years on restricted tobacco and alcohol had benefited him. I was to learn that for several years after the war, some people passed away quietly in their sleep as a result of their shock years before, and others, like myself, came apart from the daily drudge, not knowing what was wrong with them.

Already, I was starting to see the uselessness of life, and the lethargy that could follow, all because I believed that the body and mind has been disturbed by shocks that had never really gone away; they just settled in the bones. Fancy being jealous of a brother who had just ended five years' confinement. However, that tranquil look on his face told me he had been through it all and had overcome the shocks that I and many others would have to get out of their system or decide to sleep the long sleep.

I felt more at ease with him the second day and could understand his unease. With his spinal problem, it would take a few years before he could walk out of hospital and that meant missing out on victory celebrations and drinking it up with friends.

Everyone has a problem – some of them hidden and some self-created, and I can only assume that Ken, who complained not one bit about his medical state, may have yearned for the return of those lost years in an enemy camp like all POWs, who must feel on securing liberty, a feeling of emptiness.

Back aboard ship, we sailed to Milford Haven on Thursday the following week and joined a convoy heading south. With loaded coal bunkers, we trimmers in the side bunkers had a holiday for three or four days, whilst the plate trimmers wheeled their barrows in that sweaty hole below decks.

There would not be much left of the four thousand tons of bunkers by the time we reached Argentina's River Plate, and by the second week I realised that after a month, I would be wheeling my barrows eighty feet from where the coal was stacked. And I would need a row of bulbs from my electric lead lashed to overhead piping.

On this voyage south we left Casablanca at the same time we left the convoy. For sure we were in danger sailing alone without protection, and where orders from the skipper urged the chief engineer to command the black gang to raise even more steam, as much as humanly possible, before enemy subs or other marauders got on our tail.

Seeing firemen collapse on their bunks after a bucket bath following a duty watch, I felt I could walk miles in my side bunker before I suffered the cramps that most of the down below crowd were now going through. The only thing that might upset my work routine would be if the ship started rolling from side to side.

There were a lot of prize cattle caged on the afterwell deck near our quarters, and it was the main amusement of several crew members to adopt one of those bulls and feed him titbits. The 'Race' to the River Plate caused sinews and muscles to seize up among the firemen as the engineers roared for more steam. Soon there was a line of men attending the surgery each morning, awaiting the ship's doctor to issue a swallow of his famous 'Black Jack' for constipation. It was surely with relief when the *Princesa* sailed up the River Plate and berthed for an evening in the southern summer month of December.

We were moored right at the top of the city, near the First and Last Bar. Everyone cleaned up for a wild night ashore. Then the annoying news was passed around that the company agent was already on board but had no cash in his possession. His excuse was that he had left it too late to call at the bank. A really phony excuse!

There would be rare crew members who didn't know that shipping companies had advance knowledge of ship arrivals and prepared for that occasion. Now men walked around the deck in 'Go-ashore' clothes, hoping that the skipper would find a way of handing out cash.

The gist of the problem came from the mouth of a deck officer who had served with the Houlder Line for twenty years. He came aft to check mooring ropes, and chatting with crew members, confided that when the Argentine peso was about to rise in value against the pound sterling, holding back cash always occurred.

On the day of arrival, the peso was valued at sixteen to the pound. The following day, it was fourteen, but the agent was sure to bring money aboard before the local currency dropped. The agent had probably made a deal with the captain to buy all the pound notes he had in the safe.

An hour after tie-up, several were still pacing the deck on this warm, pleasant evening when a small van drew up near the gangway. For amusement's sake men leaned over the rail out of curiosity. A tiny lady of middle age, wearing glasses, stepped out of the driver's seat and looked up.

She waved us down and opened the rear doors of her van. Those few who descended the gangway returned holding trinkets and peso notes. This lured the rest of us down after her explaining the deal. If you were to buy only one peso of her haberdashery, she would loan you ten pesos.

The condition was that she would hold you in trust one day only. The following day you were expected to repay her. For the price of one single peso, I was handed twelve cards of hairpins, each card containing a dozen. Before stepping ashore, I placed them in my kitbag.

A short way from the quay was a wide street. I sidled up one side and there was bar after bar – shiny American-style setups. Without buying a beer, I peeped into the open entrances and each one was putting on a floor show gratis. I crossed the road and made a return walk on a down slope.

It seemed the same pattern, so I entered the second bar down. I enjoyed the stage acts and my cash went a long way, I was not drunk leaving the premises, and I thought I was well-protected returning on board under a starry sky. There were plenty of police, all pacing the street in pairs.

Most people looked at me in a curious way as I passed them. There were more people going in and out of bars than at first, and it was not difficult to notice by the way they walked and dressed to separate seafarers from locals. It seemed to me that the coppers gave special attention to the salts.

I found the bosun leaning against the handrails when I boarded and passed words with him, giving him my recent observations. The bosun had been aboard for several trips and got interested. Then he cautioned me not to get over drunk at night in Buenos Aires.

He continued saying that in a way the police force in B.A. made money out of arresting seamen. They received a percentage of the fines that were collected from drunken mariners. Make any impression with a big show of drunkenness he cautioned, and they would soon bundle you into a wagon that idled around the corner at the bottom of the street.

Policemen were called vigilantes, and after that discussion with the bosun, I kept that name in mind, and my ears were tuned in to any remarks about them during cuppas in the mess. I was surprised to learn that the 'Vigies' were the main topic usually.

There were horse police as well as foot coppers. The tales coming from several crew members who had been on the 'Meat Run' to the River Plate before were eye openers. Some of these lawmen must have been enlisted from the gaucho or cowboy fraternity.

One story was that a disorderly drunk dived into the Seamen's Mission in B.A. The entrance had a fairly high Spanish or Moorish arch, and the horseman ducked his own head, as well as the horse's head, to enter and arrest his target. There was also a gory tale or two, which I will not repeat, in which a man would outdo a pair, or even three vigilantes with sadistic revenge.

I, myself, could not escape the net of these 'Fishers of men', when together with a shipmate, we were jailed in a communal cell with a hundred plus 'Fish'. Among all these nationalities, wandering around in a groggy state and asking each other for a cigarette, one English-speaking person told us to hold tight to our cigarette supply as we would not be released until morning.

On release the next morning, we made a verbal agreement to return and pay a 20 peso fine within the hour. On the way back to the *Princesa*, my shipmate told them they would have to wait a few days until Friday came along when we would sub cash. I agreed with him.

We were both called to the ship's saloon the next day to see the captain. We also were confronted by a vigilante officer alongside him. The skipper made things easy for us by asking us to sign for the fines he would hand to the police, which would be deducted from our wages.

It seemed this was a regular incidence each trip and no hard words passed from the master. We learned to spend our drinking bouts along a stretch of bars facing the waterfront and directly facing the ships. No vigilantes paraded along this strip as it was considered off-limits from the vigorous restrictions of the religious mayor of Buenos Aires.

The area was called 'The Arches', since most of the entrances to these dives consisted of high, wide arches. Each oasis provided a continuous stage show, a space for dancing and rooms for prostitution. Once inside a different law applied.

When you ran out of cash, it was only walking distance to the beach, and as December was the height of the Argentine summer, I joined others going for a swim. South American governments were usually military or semi-military ones, often with bizarre laws, and a police presence was as visible on the beach as in the environs of B.A.

Women, especially, had to be careful about overexposing flesh on the beach or suffer arrest. This big, beautiful city was well-lit at night, making one forget that there was a war on. From the day of our arrival in port, a large notice had been put in the mess room. It urged us to stay clear of a street called Calle De Mayo.

The notice was authorised by the British Embassy, warning us that there was a large German community in this area, some of whom might want to know our sailing time, etc. to pass on to U-boats, lurking on the coast. The sense of adventure drew me to this street, as it did a lot of others on board. I entered no bar, just strolled along, reviewing this wide boulevard.

I was surprised to see three barber shops in a row. All had a barber chair outside. Not the ornate type, just ordinary kitchen table ones. There was some struggling going on in the centre one between three barbers and a customer. Thinking of the warning on board, I had no intention of hanging around and getting involved.

What I did recall was that the trio of barbers were on the burly side. During tea break on board, I mentioned this in small talk. Up spoke a young fireman who had also been up that way. He asked me if I failed to notice two saloon bars on either side of the three chairs.

It stirred my memory. I saw a man come out of one of the bars. He was in a tipsy way but steered clear of the first barber, only to be grabbed by the middle one who forced him to sit in his chair and gave him a haircut, whilst his two friends held him down and extorted the fee, I concluded.

Time passed in B.A. and it took ten days to discharge cargo, and not until the final day did the buyers come for their prize cattle, which I thought was overdue. It was a big affair with a lot of prominent-looking people around and most of the crew looking on.

The cattleman was in the spotlight since he was the one who had tended these creatures during the trip. When the special ramp was put up, he was also the one who coaxed, slapped and ushered the prize stock to awaiting transport. His easiest task was getting his prize rams ashore. As was the norm, Judas sheep preceded the males, who followed in a docile file.

"Around the corner to the Rio Grande," replied a sailor to where our next port-of-call would be 36 hours later, where, unlike the La Plata, we could see both sides of the river. With 100 miles separating Uruguay from Argentina, the River Plate should have been called the 'Big River' or Rio Grande.

We tied up in a cowboy town where ARMOUR AND SWIFT were the names clipped out of a vast stretch of grass on the sloping pampas. The names were prominent as well above the abattoirs. There must have been miles of cattle pens and slaughtering sheds. "Half a million carcases" was mentioned casually.

The police were as noticeable here in what seemed an easy-going town; however, they seemed very polite to seamen. Their glances were different when observing the young, human steers drinking in the bars. Perhaps the lads from the Pampas had some wild blood in them.

As it was, here of all places, I played one of my silliest acts, more like a goat than a steer. It was a hot, sunny afternoon – a Saturday afternoon and only twenty-four hours before I would have drawn a big cash sub from my wages. I sat under a parasol outside a bar not far from where my vessel was berthed.

Fumbling in my pockets I found no more cash to order a drink and looked around for shipmates to borrow from – just enough to last until the evening meal, when I would go on board, eat up and go into my bunk early to sleep off my excess booze.

The week before tying up in Buenos Aires, the trimmers on my watch had an altercation with the fifth engineer, or 'Splasher'. His job was to see that the boilers had the right amount of water. Up till then he had ordered us trimmers in turn to turn a valve on top of the boiler.

You faced stifling heat if only standing one minute on the boiler, and we were advised by an elderly fireman to make a complaint to the chief engineer that we trimmers were being forced to do an engineer's work. After only a few words with our boss, the fifth engineer was reprimanded, and the hot job was returned to him.

And now only one man was drinking from the crew at the same bar as myself and that was the fiver. When he smiled at my table, I thought bygones were bygones and smiled back. I then rose from my chair and walked over to beg him a loan of a few pesos. He was still in the smiling mood but said he was low on cash and then pointed to a well-dressed person sitting alone at a table.

Here was a smart-looking individual in his mid-thirties, wearing a gleaming white shirt with an open collar and classy long pants. In Argentina, you could purchase a dress suit that could be worn on a hot day, but the fabric was as thin as silk. He looked very important.

According to the fiver, he was in truth very important, being the son of someone very high in the Armour and Swift Company. "He has any amount of pesos." These words were purred to me in a very friendly way. "Try him for a few." I built enough nerve to walk over and sit at the stranger's table.

The rich hombre sipped his wine quietly, and I thought the fiver had passed me good advice. When I asked him if he could buy me a drink, he replied in clear English, "Of course" and flicked his fingers at a waiter. The pair of Latins got into confidential chatter, and the waiter went away without asking me what I would like to drink.

Five happy lads visited the table next and started chatting with Mr Fancy Pants. When this bigwig spoke to me the second time, his face was beaming, as were the five burlies. "You go with them. They will give you a drink."

Although the five companions chatted only in Spanish, they urged me along in a most friendly way , and as far as I knew, there was some kind of party going on ahead. It did not take long to arrive at the riverside and into that broad stream I was hurled. It was a very sober man who climbed back through the reeds after his dunking.

For several reasons, I never shared this event with any of my shipmates. One was that I didn't want them to know I had lowered myself to begging, and as there were very few crew on board when I returned, it was only the Argentine gangway watchman who witnessed my boarding.

I also kept the fifth engineer guessing. He never questioned me about what happened when I was led away by the quintet. Had he done so, I would have told him that he missed a grand drinking party. Lies can be very satisfying at times.

A bit of time passed and the massive abattoirs processed cattle into beef with amazing speed. It took only three days to load the gory cargo with modern cranes and more manpower than you could count.

Our next port of call was Montevideo, on the opposite banks of the River Plate estuary, capital and chief port of Uruguay. We anchored in the harbour Xmas Day, awaiting coal bunkers and very few wished to go ashore, but Paddy Fay, who had been locked up with me in B.A. and myself, decided to be among the few.

Those wishing to take the launch ashore were told that the captain had funds enough in his safe to hand out subs. The purser rejected our sub of five pounds but offered us two each, which we took and we were away on the liberty launch at 10am. Other passengers explained to us that the skipper never allowed more than two pounds for shore leave to anyone who had been locked up in B.A. for their own good.

It was really a blessing as prices were sky high. It was almost like open robbery. Half of our money disappeared in ten minutes of leaving the launch. At Boston Dancing, where no one was up dancing but had American-style fittings, they charged the world for a glass of beer.

We lifted our butts from this first place of call and took off for a bar with normal prices. Having missed out on our Christmas dinner on board, we felt peckish and agreed on getting a bite before all our cash evaporated. We dived into a moderate-looking eating house on top of a rise and were served by a middle-aged waiter with a paunch.

Having been well and truly bitten in the previous joint, we ordered the least expensive meal on the menu. It was long and slow in arriving, but when it was brought, it was delivered in sections. We began to panic. Obviously he had mistaken our order. These dishes were large and expensive.

We were the only sitters in his establishment so it was possible to have a rational discussion with him. We both protested and let him know that we were short of cash , and in no way could we reimburse him for such a feast. His face grew into a placid, contented smile as he calmed us down.

"I am Roosian," he informed us. "You are British, are you not?" Smart thinking, I thought, and we assured him on that point. He flapped his arms down several times and then wished us a "Merry Xmas!" while also repeating that he would not take any payment for the costly fare. We sighed with relief.

We tried to express our appreciation when later he came to collect the empty dishes. Again the arm flapped down as if to say 'Forget it'. He then sat down beside us and recollected how he had personally witnessed the Battle of the River Plate from a nearby hill.

It had made headlines at the time, and cameramen in Montevideo had close access to the early WW2 sea battle between German and British naval craft. The British victory at that time was an excellent distraction to cover the losses Britain was suffering in her merchant fleet.

After we digested our dinner on this pleasant summer day, we had a walkabout. Eventually, we did find a cheap bar away from the centre of town. It was sleazy, but we couldn't care less and spent a few hours there before returning to the wharf to await the launch back.

There on the jetty itself, we walked into the Seaman's Mission to join others waiting for a ride to their vessels, one of which was the *Baronesa*, a sister ship to our own. They had a mostly Scotch crew on board. A fireman told us there were frequent outbreaks of hostility in the stokehold.

It wouldn't be difficult to find the reason with boilers facing each other and men getting in each other's way. We had a few outbreaks on the *Princesa*, but they were short and soon ended.

We arrived at the gangway after I noticed a massive floating crane on the other side of the vessel. The grabs dug into the mighty barge containing coal by the thousands of tons. Together with the towering post office in Buenos Aires and the beef plant also in Argentina, my eyes were opening to the modernisation way down in the lands south of the equator.

After two days we had bunkered and were then steaming north to Casablanca, Morocco. After a four day anchorage there, men felt more refreshed to finish the last leg of the journey. Duty-free cigarettes were lowered in buckets over the ship's side and exchanged for hand woven baskets, fresh tropical fruit, trinkets and souvenirs to bring home.

Our destination was London, and as most of the down below crew were from the South Wales area with the deck crowd signed on in Bristol, all talk centred around Paddington Rail Station, where trains left for the West Country. Most had their gear packed in kitbags and suitcases by the time we were half way through the English Channel.

After early morning arrival up the Thames estuary, we moored alongside the Tilbury docks. All hands were up early and sitting around the mess table eager for news of paying off and getting back home. Mugs of tea were being swilled down to ease the excitement.

Every twenty minutes, one of the trimmers would be sent off to amidships to find out the paying off time from the purser, but there was a hitch somewhere, a holdup. It seemed like everyone had to stick out the dreary minutes. Then the report came through that there would be no payoff. The *Princesa* had been ordered to sail off to some part of the continent.

In February 1945 there was more mopping up in the war zones than actual warfare; therefore, it was pretty much understood that we would discharge cargo at some port in France. However, the purser's office was open for cash withdrawals at 10am. By the time we had drawn money from our wages, we learnt that everyone must be aboard by midnight.

We would be told our destination after midnight and were kept guessing about the final report before going ashore and that a North Sea pilot would board at that time. It seemed it might not be France after all.

With only a day to kill, I decided to visit a brother in the area. At sixteen years my elder brother went to work in Woolwich and lived in nearby Abbey Wood. He was now in the RAF and spent leaves at his old digs. I took a train up to London in the hopes of catching him there and took with me a very cheap present, the twelve dozen hairpins I had bought in B.A. I was almost ashamed to take them as a present to his landlady, but I had nothing else.

When I knocked at the door, I did not receive the usual welcome from Mrs Luxford. Her face was ashen and she seemed in a state of shock. She then informed me that a doodle bug had exploded in the vicinity only five minutes before. Then I noticed jagged streaks of glass in one window.

The flying bomb or doodle bug was the final hurl of defiance at London before Germany collapsed. I dug out the pile of hairpin cards from my pretty cheap Argentine leather coat pockets. I thought it a measly present but better than nothing and placed them on the table before Mrs Lux.

The kettle was on the boil, and she brewed a pot of tea, told me to get seated and left me to it. She then took some pins from her hair and compared them with the ones I had brought. I was rewarded with a smile from Lux as she was fondly called by my brother.

"These pins are much better than our'n, Ted," she muttered. "Must have cost you a shilling a piece?" "It cost me a shilling for the whole blinking lot," I replied. She eyed me in a funny way. "Go on, I don't believe you, these pins I'm wearing are four pence apiece, and they're not a shade as good as the ones on the card."

It was with difficulty that I forced the whole lot on her without her opening her purse on the mantelpiece and handing me a few quid. Amazing how that cheap present had succeeded in taking her thoughts off that dreadful rocket explosion. Her husband, Len, must have left work early on hearing of the bomb, and when he hurriedly entered, he found his wife more at ease than he had imagined.

I learned some gratifying war news upon the arrival of my brother in bomber command, and after a very short visit, I boarded a train back to Tilbury and my ship. Then an incredible thought arose in my mind. What had come to mind, in that compartment where I was the sole passenger, was the scene on the quay near the gangway in Buenos Aires and that little old lady with her van of haberdashery.

Not on that first occasion when we bought a trinket or two for the loan of ten pesos, but on the following day when men descended to pay back that loan, they were I knew by their faces men who had sailed on this ship for several years. And the van was chock a block with hairpins and other sundries.

Among the dozen or so waiting their turn and carrying bags were officers, petty officers and men in the catering department; men who would never leave the ship. Even though I had a hangover, I couldn't help seeing them pile their bags up with these goodies.

However, my drink habit had prevented me from coming to a conclusion. Those men were not buying trinkets for family and friends. If those hairpins were selling for a shilling each in the UK, just one pound's worth of them would give someone a return of one hundred pounds!

And customs officers couldn't care less about sundries; they were not assessable goods, and for a crew member to give them a dozen packets costing little over a shilling, would indeed be more than a modest gesture. Here was one of the countless ways of making easy cash in wartime in the international transport business.

Later I hopped off the train at Tilbury too early in the evening to board and walked to the jetty where ferries took one across the river to the good time pubs of Gravesend but then had second thoughts at the last minute. After getting too much drink on the other side, I might miss the ferry and chose to regale myself in the pub right there on the dock, The End of the World.

I was due to go on watch at midnight and after leaving my glass on the counter at the 10pm pub closing time caught a nap for one hour before duty called. We sailed before 1am, still without knowing our destination. And when we did get underway, the engines were turning at slow speed for an hour.

By then I had my bunker already topped up and went down into the stokehold for a chat with the firemen and trimmers. They were enjoying nice breaks for the first time in that long voyage. After sitting a while on the long valve box yarning, the firemen asked me to go topside and find out where the ship was heading.

So up on deck I went and in the blackout waited at the bottom of the ladder leading up to the navigator's bridge. I thought I might catch a sailor coming down after being relieved at the wheel. I didn't feel like fumbling my way aft on such a dark night. Down came a deckhand we called Champagne Charlie, a shorty Irishman with a wide brogue.

"Get hold of your life jackets – all of you!" he urged, as I asked him about our destination, then as he was hurrying to tell others the same thing, answered, "Tell all the boys we're going up a dan'rus channel!" A fireman had followed me up to turn the ventilators OFF the wind. This is rare because the stokehold is always a hot plate, but that wintry February air blowing hard down the vent must have been a bit much for a ship going at slow speed. I passed him the news.

"According to Charlie, we're going up a Danish channel and you have to have your life jacket handy. Go down! I'll collect them and throw them down the vent." "Hang on," he responded. "I'll give you a hand." We found another trimmer drinking tea aft, and he helped us to haul the life jackets amidships. We dropped down seven and the other trimmer and myself kept two.

Around 9am in the morning, it seemed all hands had turned up for breakfast; the news was too exciting to keep us in our cots. A big part of the crew gathered to the open stern deck and looked around at the fresh scenery. Everyone wore leather jackets purchased in South America.

There was a nip in the air as a morning fog lifted through the hazy portside; an industrial complex then came into view. Willy Savage, a Cardiff fireman with long service, shaded his eyes and cupped his hands. All us younger men kept quiet and waited for any sensible comment from Willy.

"That's Flushing over there; we're going to Holland, not bloody Denmark," he declared. I sat on that remark a bit and mentally tried to decipher Champagne Charlie's message again, and it was a little later confirmed: "We're going up a dangerous channel!" Along came the young apprentice deck officer to hoist the red ensign on the stern, and we gathered around for info from amidships. The young fellow seemed to enjoy giving out news, and before we left, everyone clearly understood that we would tie-up in the Belgian port of Antwerp.

Further up the River Scheldt news trickled back that we would tie up at the New Albert Dock. Willy was accosted for information about the girlie bars. Before retiring below decks for a nap, he returned the magic reply – Skipper's St. Weather broke crisp and clear, and into view came an officer to let us know that the purser would be dishing out subs at 10am.

I had spent less than a pound of the ten pounds I had drawn in Tilbury, so it didn't worry me, but before the young officer left, I asked him why the ship was stopping and starting on her progress up river. He mentioned something about a mine that was attached to a ship's propeller that had to be avoided by making short stoppages.

Skinny masts were sticking up along the river bed; witness to ships that had been mined. Every mile or so, one caught sight of a group of tugs of that sturdy Dutch type with white foam boiling around their props, making efforts to remove sunken wrecks or at least to remove the more obstructive hulks from the main channel.

Then we sighted our first doodlebug breaking through a cloud. It was aiming for the river in the direction of our ship but changed direction at a ceiling of about a thousand feet and exploded on the far bank. Before we arrived at the Albert Dock, four more flying bombs were sighted.

We passed close by a dry dock before berthing, and I read part of the name of a ship being repaired. On the stern the reading was something Hill and below, Newcastle, her port of registry. A bomb had struck her on the journey up from what we had heard.

During those ten days and ten sleepless nights, another bomb struck a day before she was due to leave after the refit. During the course of each day, we came to expect a V2 bomb every half hour. The deucer kept his word and only expected the black gang to do essential work in port.

One morning he detailed me to clean soot from the backs of four furnaces. I completed the lot by 10am, but as usual, it took a long hour scrubbing grime off my body. How soot sticks! After dressing in my go ashore clothes and wrapped in my brownish-yellow Argentine leather jacket, I took off to the purser to swap a few pound notes for Belgian francs.

On the way a trimmer said he wanted a word with me. Very furtively, he led me under the cover of a sloping ladder in the well deck and plopped a wad of francs in my palm. At a rapid count, I found it to be valued at twenty pounds at the current exchange rate. He cautioned me to keep mum about the cash.

Bandy Luke, a trimmer, had flogged a ton of coal to a barge man by way of the hydraulic hoist used for disposing ashes. The takings from the black gold were distributed equally among the black gang. That meant I had no need to spend my own cash. I played the big spender up and down Skipper Street, only allowing liquors of the best to oil my gullet.

Whilst reeling towards the dock gates that cold and frosty night, a flying bomb struck in the vicinity. I was fortunate not to be injured by flying debris. Then, from the direction of the blast, a huge black man, obviously an American seaman by his talk, whose utterances of "Lordy!" "Lordy!" stopped when he heard me trying to get my breath back. I handed him an uncorked bottle of cognac and advised him to take a big swig. Sometimes it's good to slip into a degree of oblivion, especially in emergencies. It seems to weaken future repeats of trauma.

In the nightly forays ashore, I spent evenings drinking in one of the main boulevards instead of adventuring into the dives on Skipper St. My venue was the Cafe Roma. Whereas there was live music in all the haunts in the street of salts, accordion along with violin players, the Roma was a modernised drinking place with a jukebox.

It also had an escape staircase into the cellar when the sound of V2s became too loud for comfort. The bar was central with nowhere to lean, just a clear walkway where waitresses served seated patrons at tables at each wing of the bar. The central walkway had a trapdoor in the centre, which was lifted by the burly Madame herself on occasions.

The hostess would yell, "Fly bomb! Fly bomb! Everyone go down cellar." Her voice would boom above the noise of the jukebox as she lifted the square, wooden door and went down last, proceeded by six waitresses.

These were only five minute affairs, and we were asked to sit on beds, in what seemed a large, spare room. Then the boss would use her strident voice, ordering all hands to climb the stairs. One long, nervous evening we were up and down three times, and the more curious soon found other rooms down there.

The keyhole boys discovered that some were lit up with people moving around in them. It wasn't difficult to assume that coupling was taking place in the forbidden rooms. On the last alert, Madame herself had to coax the more tipsy upstairs; she too had lingered to spy around.

Two years later, when I returned to Antwerp, I entered the Roma and hardly recognised the place. With a new interior décor and a thick, new carpet spread, it was a different Cafe Roma. My arrival there was in the afternoon when patrons had to hurry back to their offices.

As the establishment cleared, I recognised the sweeper and asked her over. She put aside her broom and sat at my table. She may have recognised me, too because a smile grew on her face. After her helper brought drinks over, I asked her how long she had worked in the cafe. "Long time," she answered. "Why?"

"Isn't there a trap door under this carpet," and I pointed to the centre area. I expected her to reply in shortcut bar talk, 'How you know?' She didn't; she wasn't vocal at all. I tried to read her face, and she responded by staring keenly at me and slowly nodding her head, as much as to say,

'You knew what went on down there?' She couldn't hold back and broke into laughter, so I bought two extra drinks to share the memory.

Apart from the flying bombs, most of the ship's crew had a ball in Antwerp but getting back to Wales' Barry Docks eased our nerves a lot. Only seven miles from Cardiff, where we were home and dry.

The war in Europe was soon coming to a close. People sensed it and breathed more freely. On a sunny day in the first week of April, I took myself to the Manning Pool in Cardiff. I accepted a fireman's job on a 600 ton coasting vessel called the *Gem*. The cook on board briefed me about the run.

There were regular trips between Cardiff and St Malo on the Brittany coast. After learning that the quarters were up forward, that's where I went and plopped my kitbag on an empty bunk. I shared a cabin with two others, who had not yet boarded. I spoke with the man I was relieving. He was all packed, ready to return to his home twenty miles away. This person sat on a spare bunk finishing off a bottle of beer before leaving while I sat on my own and lapsed into thoughts of pleasant times.

CHAPTER 9 – *S/S GEM*

SHIP NUMBER EIGHT

My thoughts were interrupted as the other fellow was about to leave. He mentioned that German commandoes from the Island of Jersey had landed in St Malo the previous trip. When the enemy group disembarked from their launch, they strode along the quay and up the gangway of the S/S *Gem*. He quickly learnt that the commandoes aimed to take the *Gem* back to Jersey with whatever cargo was left unloaded.

Their effort backfired. It was during the ebb tide, and like the Channel Islands, it meant a rapid drop of thirty feet into the mud. However, they did make the attempt. Coasters of this size have two smaller type marine boilers, and the engineer usually tends the donkey boiler in port.

My source said that he was lucky not to be chosen by one of the soldiers to go below to get up steam. The chosen fireman was unable to raise enough steam to beat the tide. Having gone through such an experience, the three of them paid off in Cardiff. The fireman showed me souvenirs left by the enemy – indentations in the steelwork above my bunk! The soldier had fired his revolver as a persuader to urge the other fireman off his bunk. It assisted in coaxing and convincing the man to go below and raise steam.

When this last fireman had left the cabin, I lay back in this very same bunk that the steam raiser had occupied and asked myself how I might have fared in the same situation. Even if the tide had not been on the rise, it would not have been difficult to outwit the soldier standing by with his pistol cocked. Steam is not created solely by furnace heat. There is a soot pit at the rear of the fire called the combustion chamber, where smoke breaks out in flames that shoot through boiler tubes.

The best steam coal is surely Welsh anthracite. If it is piled in one black heap with just enough space between the top and the inner crown of the boiler for a stream of grey smoke swirling back; then you sit down on your butt for a half hour. The steam can only go one way, and that's up from the soot chamber in one ball of flame.

All you would have to do to reduce steam was to push clinker to the rear and show the soldier a bright red flat furnace to please him, and then leave the furnace door slightly ajar so cold air could penetrate the tubes instead of the flame. I didn't meditate on this too long or I might have been tempted to follow the other seaman to the shipping office and get paid off.

An Irishman and a small, slightly built Japanese plus myself were the new replacements. I never passed onto the other two what I had heard. After a few days on board there was some abuse aimed at Sam the Jap. I liked the way he stuck up for himself.

One day I was walking behind him on deck when he received a nasty scowl from an enormous passing deckhand. Sam, small as he was, faced up squarely to this mastiff. "You think me Japanese. I am not Japanese; I am British! I've been British from 1918." After that incident everyone on board socialised with Sam, now known as Shorty.

Paddy from Wicklow and myself got on famously. After our first trip, we got our heads together. We decided to speculate our wages on as much chicory coffee as we could buy. Chicory coffee was one item of food that was available through the war. I don't know why, but we bought a kitbag full of these tins.

There was no need of ration cards to buy the stuff, which made it easy to come by, and what a handsome profit we made. Our next speculation was briar pipes. This was indeed a merry life.

Like a pair of fools, we were guzzling away the profits, only to have burned-out guts from that potent Brittany spirit called Calvados. During this stint, President Roosevelt passed away. But so much news was clamouring for the headlines, people tended to forget this figurehead who had pioneered the Keynes Plan to pull America out of depression, and when it was adopted at San Francisco in 1946, helped save a ruined world.

If the commandoes had taken the *Gem* to Jersey, they could have taken a large gang of Germans with them, as they worked the cargo under the supervision of the US army. St Malo was under American occupation.

Then I wondered why should I stay on the *Gem* when the extra cash I was making went through my fingers like grains of salt? After five weeks, I paid off the ship.

My leave home became notable. In the local pub, the wireless was kept in the background and titbits of news were fed sometimes to the tipplers. One night was especially memorable as I sat in the back room lounge of that local pub.

You had to bring your pint in through the pub's door. Thinking back to this month of May, the weather could not have been better. If you have balmy, summery weather in the valley, there is a complete change of scenery from a dump to a landscape that brings poetry to the heart. And here I was sitting down and feeling at ease with myself.

There was only low, quiet chatter from those around me when in strode the landlord. Small tables lined the walls at which drinkers sat. He walked to a large, oblong table in the centre of the spacey room. He grabbed a chair and set it on the table. Then he climbed on the table by means of another chair.

He was obviously in an agitated state because the barman followed with a glass of beer with maybe something stronger inside. He took a sup from it and placed it on the higher chair. Then he made his short but important speech. In a hoarse voice he declared, "The war in Europe is over!"

"It's official! It has just come through on the wireless!" He then stepped down to prepare for a surge of bodies stepping towards the outer bar. There was pandemonium as customers called for short drinks and all at the same time. People just splurged with their cash and didn't give a tinker's curse.

On this very special evening, no one was going to worry about a policeman knocking at the door to caution people about blackout infringements. The weather was perfect for dancing in the street. People went utterly mad, bonkers!

With plenty of the happy stuff going down gullets, people wandered around or coupled up for a dance. I meandered half a mile to the larger township of Treorchy and found the main square chock-a-block full of dancing, shouting people. By midnight it was more of the same instead of less.

Someone told me that a party was going on in a vast barn near my very own street, and the mile walk there kept me from getting the worse for the drink. It was already 4am before I left the decorated barn, surrounded by tiers of hay, where a lot of people had collapsed.

It was a good place to end up just in case you had not the energy to find your way home. In this place full of so much joy, I familiarised with long forgotten friends.

As I pulled the blanket over my head that night, my thoughts must have joined millions of others. 'Thank God, this bloody war is over!'

But it was not over yet. Japan still held out. Although the pool paid you three pounds plus a week, there was little choice of ships or jobs. What I wanted was another deep-sea ship. On coasters it was hard to hold onto cash, you were too often in port. But I was ordered to sign on another one called the *S/S Joffre Rose.*

CHAPTER 10 – S/S JOFFRE ROSE

SHIP NUMBER NINE

Before I signed on this boat, I was lucky to catch my brother Jack, who was a rear air gunner on Lancaster bombers. Already he had demobilisation in his sights. He had left the merchant ships as an ordinary seaman in 1941 to enrol in the RAF and couldn't wait to get back to sea.

As for me, the *Joffre Rose*, a spud boat obviously carrying potatoes, was another 600 tonner but this one didn't carry a cook. I now had the opportunity or was it the agony of learning to cook for myself on the unsteady cooking range of a floating kitchen. When I boarded the ship, I learned that we were bound for Belfast and were given a day off to buy groceries with a seaman's ration book, something I had never set eyes on before.

The ship had only recently come down from Liverpool, and as she had been carrying potatoes from Belfast to that port, there were several bags of that staple still on board. The other two firemen and myself decided to live on boiled spuds until we arrived at Belfast and spent our day off in a bar.

The *Rose* had come to Cardiff for a minor engine repair and we sailed a light ship. Give me the steady roll of a deep-sea vessel to a coaster empty of cargo.

In wartime Belfast there had been no such thing as rationing. At least not for us. You never met kinder people in the shops. The fact that across The Free State border, there were farmers only too ready to sell their produce helped a lot. However, there was an ugly side with reports that the IRA were blowing up food stores.

As I had been in this port several times during the war, I was well aware that shooting went on all the time, even though it was never mentioned in print. I always remembered to keep away from Falls Road from earlier experience. When a fight started, the women got their fists flying as good as the men.

I was also familiar with Liverpool, where we unloaded our cargo, though I had always made tracks to Lime Street and its dives. I was not familiar with Scotland Rd, which was the neighbourhood where we unloaded spuds. After the first trip on the *Joffre Rose*, I had a decided preference for this supposedly rough street. All I found there was friendliness and help.

We did our grocery shopping at a small, corner shop run by a lady called Mrs Grundy. She was definitely a character, standing behind the counter wearing a man's cap and reminiscing about the time she spent in the WAAC's during the First World War.

The customers enjoyed her brand of humour, as well as I did, and one day I noticed she was short of potatoes. Soon I spied a local docker walking through an opening in a fence, close to where the *Rose* was tied up. So one Saturday morning when there was less bustle in the area, and possibly less plainclothes spies, I carried a bag of potatoes through this opening and deposited it inside Mrs Grundy's shop whilst there were no customers being served. I restricted my price to the minimum and repeated this each time I crossed the Irish Sea. Mrs Grundy would carry on, thanking me no end.

On my previous coaster, the skipper had paid me off without question. I didn't realise that if he wished, he could have kept me aboard for six months under the wartime agreement.

I learned this when the skipper of the *Joffre Rose* refused to pay me off. Wartime regulations were still in force. Six months after I joined her, we were back in Cardiff and I did the only option I felt I had. I left the ship with my gear one quiet evening after drawing my fortnightly pay and went home for a week.

The port where I was registered at that time was Barry, seven miles from Cardiff, and I had to report there to claim pool money, which I then picked up in Cardiff. Somehow I claimed it, but not until a very red face gave me a roasting with some silly threat that if I missed another vessel, I would be sent packing to fight in Japan.

He may have pulled that baloney on criminals that have been released from prison during the last year of the war, and while I have always respected shipping masters, there were even among their ranks an occasional clod. In major ports those men took a more realistic attitude.

In the first place, they would have studied my personal record and would have considered this affair trifling, now that ex-naval personnel were queuing up to get into the Merchant service. Whilst I was waiting for my next job, I paid a visit to the Cardiff Infirmary, where my brother Ken had been transferred from the hospital in North Wales.

It was an enjoyable visit, even though he never mentioned anything about his experience in the German prison camp, which would have interested me. Before leaving, his friends in other beds pressed me for a sea yarn. For the sake of Ken, I couldn't back out.

I related the antics of the baboon I had bought in Freetown. Once I got them smiling, I began enjoying my own humour, and as there were no female nurses around, I expanded on the fact that the greatest enjoyment for Bimbo was eating bananas and dropping them out at the other end from the crosstrees of the main mast. Half the ward was laughing, letting out a lot of tension – so much that I left in case the surgeon would blame me for opening their wounds.

Being home I cut back my beer intake to keep up a respectable front. Plus the July weather was just too delicious to enjoy indoor entertainment anyway.

As sometimes happens, if you want to hang around, they find you a job, and if you are eager to ship out, waiting time drags on. I soon signed on a ship of around 8,000 tons deadweight, and now that the war was far away, they even told you where it was heading for. It was your usual tramp ship but no older than five years.

This new assignment meant modern conditions with a plumped-up mattress and a changing room, as well as updated toilet facilities and bigger portholes in larger cabins. Every ship has a snag, and what I heard in the Ship and Pilot pub in West Bute Street did not bode well. A former fireman on her told me he had made a crossing to Canada with her.

He told me that you couldn't get top steam in the boilers even in a slow convoy. When I asked him for the reason, he told me she was an enigma – a real puzzle. The donkeyman had been on her several trips and told him and his mates not to bust their guts. Even with Welsh anthracite, she never reached a speed higher than eight knots even though she was a ten knot ship.

The problem had baffled the company super, who had paid several visits to the stokehold. In his last report, it was stated that it could be due to the stokehold being a couple of feet narrower than regulations in order to claim more cargo space.

If it wasn't for the reprimanding I had received over the spud boat, I would have walked off the *Empire Darwin* there and then, as she was heading for hot South Carolina with a cargo of coal, and where I could look forward to a roasting of a different type.

CHAPTER 11 – S/S EMPIRE DARWIN

SHIP NUMBER TEN

I have heard that a ship with excessive vibration could in time loosen its rivets. Then the company super arrived on board, made an examination and advised that a certain section of the propeller blades be given a degree of shaving.

This procedure was given out and no vibration. Although nothing man-made can equate with the mysteries of the human body, the science of shipbuilding is not shallow. I was amazed to find that the structural defects of a stokehold could affect steam pressure in a boiler. It almost bordered on Feng Shui

On a more personal note, there are only two things worth aiming for on the male side. Marriage and adventure. I was reared in a normal environment in which you matured to a courting stage with some lass and settled for a married state. My parents died when I was an early age and I was taken into care by elder siblings.

I may have lost a degree of parental love and guidance, but the individual inside me certainly had time to blossom. My eldest brother belonged to the fledgling Communist party. He was ten years my senior and turned out as much a dictator as my religious father.

But religion still flourished in the house, championed by the elder sister, a little younger than him. That was good fun, living with two opposing dictators. I ended up doing my own dictating. This seeding time I have never regretted. I always had an antidote for whatever situation I was in.

When I signed on my new ship on one bright Thursday morning in July, I knew what I was in for. Old timers in the stokehold had often told about peacetime competition between shipping companies, and that the engineers were never satisfied with enough steam. They always wanted more. I was going to put in a load of sweat and I really needed to be compensated.

The *Darwin* was still undergoing engine room maintenance, and it would be Monday before she could go under the cranes to load coal for South Carolina. I was told to be aboard, ready for duty that Monday.

I had to work out some kind of solution before I sailed in a cabin with two or three others where you couldn't plan clearly. With over three pounds I had drawn from the pool, I decided not to return to the valley. A brand new club for merchant seamen had opened in Cardiff, diagonally opposite the general rail station.

For the cost of thirty shillings I could book a private room of semi-luxury for four nights. And that is what I did and still had two pounds left over. Most of my actions throughout that long weekend were mental and at night. During the day, I spent intervals in the bar below but drinking at slow speed.

On Saturday, with the weather still glorious, I spent time in Roath Park. I should have brought another mate with me since there were birds there just asking to be partnered. I couldn't work up enough nerve myself to pick up any of these cherry blossoms and ended up rowing my own canoe across the lake.

Each night I lay in bed, knowing only too well that the war in Japan would soon be over, and being twenty-two in a week's time, should I pick up a steady girlfriend in the valley? I realised this was the turning point in the pattern my life would take; I fell back on experience for advice.

The Trinidad affair of acting the playboy had been semi-successful, and it invited me to do more of the same and scrap ideas of marriage. Many times, sitting around the poop deck, men had given out ideas of what they might do when war was over. They were all adventurous aims.

Jumping ship in Australia and starting a new life was often brought up. However, in a way, even that idea seemed like settling down. I gave that away. I wouldn't go steady with a local girl or break out altogether. I would have a good look around the world – get into the playboy act, be the wild rover and be a scenery bum. You only have one life.

If I jumped ship in Charleston, I could cop a nasty report on return. But returning, in say maybe three months, might put a different complexion on things. The war would be over, and punishment would be reduced to a three month suspension from shipping out.

The immigration department shouldn't be a hurdle. Once my ship had gone, I would naturally report to the shipping agents to see if any documents had been handed in by my skipper and put my name down with the Norwegian consul to ship out, taking any job that was offered. They were never queasy about paying men off in foreign ports, as long as it was Ok shoreside.

We sailed out of port Tuesday, and on this ship there was an open gap between the two mess rooms. The Bristol sailors socialised with the Cardiff firemen, nine hands on our side and ten on theirs.

We were a bunch of feelers, a good sociable mix with the oldest being a Cornish fireman of about twenty-six years. Even the bosun was younger. Just my luck though to have the watch with the odd man out, a young bully who knew it all. Perhaps it was best I took the flak.

I say this because the others noticed I could brush off his taunts and at the same time, give out a few songs on the afterdeck at the request from the sailors. I was not a bad pub singer at the time except for the difficulty of maintaining tempo with the pianist due to strong drink.

Yes, it was all as I had guessed with the engineer on watch chasing us up for more steam. However, with the combination of an excellent cook and a shipping company that stocked the steward up with the best provisions, the best course to take was to loll around under the canvas awnings during duty breaks and try to find out how long the voyage would be.

Naturally, I kept mum about my personal plan; we learned that we would discharge our cargo in 24 hours and then load a similar coal cargo for Genoa in Italy, this time American coal. When I learned that the skipper would allow us a large cash sub for such a short stay, what could I do but whistle away those arguments with the bully in the stokehold on each watch.

Naturally, putting in for a big sub might raise eyebrows, so I reduced my ten pound sub to eight. Like a fool I had hesitated at taking a five pound advance note when signing on, as my plan had not been seeded yet.

Perhaps it was best I didn't or I might have gone on a spree. When I heard that the return was on American coal or 'Yankee slack' as we called it, I was glad I had decided to leave. We were making poor speed with the best coal in the world, Welsh anthracite.

We tied up in Charleston with the local temp at 110 Fahrenheit. Thankfully, bullyboy was trimming in the bunker on the 8-12 watch that morning with us coming up the river against an ebb tide. Try as we could to liven up the furnace by continual levering beneath the coals with our long slice bars, our speed was never more than two knots against the six knot current.

I was now more serious than ever to be rid of this slaver. I was one of the first ashore, and I was certainly alone, with no intention of joining a get-together of knocking back ice cold beers. I was up to serious business.

We were moored beneath vast new machinery, which actually sucked the cargo out according to reports. I didn't hang around to watch but patted the back pocket of my best trews. Nestling there in the wallet was $30, which I intended using wisely. It was not far to town, and I missed the cafe-bars on my way to the Greyhound Bus Station.

It took me a while asking around about the nearest town before buying a ticket there – a short distance of nine miles. Just as the usual horseshoe bars were missing in Charleston, hotels were non-existent in this neighbouring small township, but I passed several veranda-style rooming places being advertised. Three nights lodging would be my biggest investment.

It cost me all of $12 to book a room and I made use of it right away. The room was spacey with decor, though a little on the expensive side. I could probably have gotten a decent place in the town centre for less than half the price; however, I wanted to remain unseen for the next 48 hours when the ship was due to leave.

I lit up a Camel, and the warm air caused it to give off a flavour I have never tasted in other smokes. I needed a drug that would keep me in a sober state. I placed the fag on the bedside cabinet ashtray and lay back to test the bed, which proved to be bouncy.

The mosquito net dangled on a light, square frame above me. Before falling into a siesta, I felt good about one thing. Although I had my best shirt, pants and footwear with me, this time I had been sensible enough to leave all other gear in my cabin. This was thinking ahead.

There was little doubt that when I returned to the UK and picked up my Seaman's Record Book, now safely on board in the skipper's safe, those famous words would be printed in it: WHEN THE SEAMAN FAILED TO REJOIN HIS VESSEL, a discharge that was termed a 'Baddy' or 'Burn down' in more colourful language. By leaving gear on board, it could have a favourable effect on the maritime panel judging my conduct. I might still be able to cling onto the shipping industry after jumping ship.

I satisfied myself with a cup of coffee and a couple of doughnuts around the corner that evening after a snooze. It was not the first time I was playing the hermit, and it was pleasant enough as long as I had a packet of smokes on the table besides me. Being well and truly left alone in this quiet town, I slept with only my undies on. Any extra dress would have caused undue sweat.

With some reading matter, I could stick out this isolation a couple of days and even enjoy it. Next morning I bought a paper and sought out an eating place. After ordering breakfast, I checked the date on the paper – August 9, 1945. Then I overheard talk from the next table.

It was certainly a morning of happenings. First these elderly gents were talking about an atom bomb being dropped on Hiroshima, Japan. I had no radio in my room, so I listened to their southern drawl chatter with interest. Chances were that Japan would now sue for peace.

The cafe had seats at the counter as well as table service, and later, when I went to pay my bill, the boss told me to take a seat and have a coffee on him. He must have guessed I was a seaman from my dress because he asked me if I was off a ship. Then he confided that he had jumped ship at Charleston years ago. I stayed put, interested.

I realised that he was a trustworthy type, but still caution told my feet to get mobile. When I was leaving, he advised me that he could be of assistance should I need any. By those words I realised that he read something in my face that alerted him I was his kind. There's a lot of jabbering in small townships, and in the US, police mixed in with cafe talk.

Instinct told me to remain unsociable for the time being rather than betray my intention. Then the most unexpected happened when I stepped into the hot, silent street with air so scorching it siphoned one's breath away, who should I meet but a shipmate, Don, a fellow fireman off the *Darwin*. It's incredible that the two of us held the same idea of clearing out in port and ended up meeting in such a small town.

I walked him down the street to a bar. We called for a few drinks and chose a tune on the jukebox haphazardly. Out came a voice, 'Back to those Oklahoma hills where I was born'. Another fellow at the bar, in the uniform of the US Navy, raised a drowsy head off the bar counter and told everyone "That's where I come from."

We shifted our glasses of iced beer over to a table to discuss mutual plans. His room cost the same as mine except he had booked it for only two nights. Then he told me I would be safe to return to the port tomorrow. "How come?" I asked. He came back, "The *Darwin* was only berthing for twenty-four hours; it only takes four hours to suck the coal from the holds."

"I thought she was in port for forty-eight hours, so I booked in for three nights," I muttered. Don suggested, "Let's go back to your place and ask the landlady if she'll give back some rent and stay at my place. That big bed of mine could sleep three people." "Same as mine," I answered, "but your idea is best."

I got a rebate of $6 rent and moved in with Don for the night. It was a cinch that our ship had gone, and all we had to do was bus it back to the port the next morning. Feeling so free and easy that morning, we decided to hitchhike instead, just for the fun of it.

When we hailed an old truck with a wide front, two young black men squeezed us in between them. We opened the conversation but with no response. They remained tight-lipped and told us to make a quick getaway as soon as we were in the big town. What we did get out of them was that it was not at all customary in this area for black and white to mix.

Once in the big city, we decided to have a cold beer before visiting the shipping agents. The white people in the bar we entered could not have been friendlier or more sociable, but we took it as policy not to mention the free ride we had with the black driver.

Both of us were in top spirits, coasting along in the direction given us where the shipping firms were located and telling each other that we could be sent on a free ride to the British Consul in New York, where we would have a choice of ships to join. We entered the first building with the wording of a shipping company.

After mentioning the ship's name, we were advised to try another building further up. We entered that office, and a young lady there told us to follow her upstairs to yet another office. When she ushered us through the door, we felt all our troubles were over. This feeling was increased by the warm, comforting drawl of the man we were introduced to. There was no doubt of a free trip to New York. And we were not mistaken; after showing consolation for our desperate condition, these were his very words, "I may have to fly you to New York."

It was early afternoon and he asked us to return in a couple of hours so that he could get in touch with the British representatives. We were so full of satisfaction, we made fast tracks to the nearest bar. We became loose with the cash we had hoarded for an emergency and knocked back a few whiskies in celebration at having escaped that workhouse of a ship.

We were wise enough to gobble a few hot dogs on the return walk to the agent, and when we entered his office, he received us with his face all smiles. He was glad to report that the *Empire Darwin* was being towed upriver by a pair of tugs. Our faces dropped.

We wondered what went wrong. By the time we were driven to a jetty to board a launch, we sighted the *Empire Darwin* at anchorage. We may have entered the craft's cabin sheepishly, but as our boat moored alongside, there was wild cheering from the crew on board. This eased our attitude of being returned prisoners having to face up to a very burly master.

I appreciated the briefness of our interview. Our names had been entered into the official logbook, and we would be dealt with as deserters back in the UK. Nothing could be done to erase the data.

Then sitting under the canopy of the poop deck, we learned of interesting events when the ship went sailing downriver firing on Yankee slack coal. Two able seamen had volunteered to take our places in the stokehold. The *Darwin* had sped rapidly downstream, yet in the open sea, the fastest speed the propellers could make was only five knots, or half her projected limit. The chief engineer advised the skipper to return to port and ask for advice in burning this slack coal.

And there I was back in the stokehold. Experience had taught me well how to burn the stuff, but it took a lot of continuous effort even with the best of boilers. Half a dozen shovels at the most needed to be pitched on each fire and then followed up with slice, bare and rake at five minute intervals. Not even time for a smoke.

With flat fires and the continuous opening of doors, there was an additional adverse effect. On the way out, we had been doing eight and nine knots at times and the engineers had been clamouring for more. Since it was up to the tugs had to tow us upstream, the other firemen had conceived a plan.

With the inferior fuel we now used, we could make sure the engine would not go faster than seven knots. We would pitch coal in the fires every twenty minutes, and not before, so that the firemen off-watch would monitor the slower progress by observing smoke rising out of the funnel every twenty minutes. No one broke the rule.

Slow going! Instead of reaching Genoa, Italy in three weeks, we would arrive there a month later. I was on the 8-12 watch when we finally left, and some days later, about 9pm, just after we finished pitching, in walked the engineer, not to ask for more steam but to let us know that the war with Japan was officially over.

We celebrated with a guzzle of water, lit up a cigarette and sat on a valve box. From then on, the bully boy was no longer bossing around. As a matter of fact, when this hefty engineer came into the stokehold during one watch to ask for more steam, he received verbal abuse of a kind that only the criminal classes can inject with so much venom. The request never came again. An odd crim on board is good medicine, but they are so skilful at psychological warfare that three or four together can ruin harmony on board.

Eventually, we arrived in northern Italy with a lot of joy in the streets and bars of Genoa. A onetime enemy, once allied troops set foot in Sicily, the anti-fascist movement of the north gave them a lot of support.

It was the north of Italy that had resisted at times the dictatorship of Mussolini, and the people of Genoa had seized power from the fascists themselves before American troops arrived; they, therefore, enjoyed the final victory celebrations as much as we did.

Weather-wise we could not have arrived in a better seaport. Early September in Savoy, with gentle breezes and a sun not too hot to burn, makes you want to enjoy things. The way people greeted you in the streets with 'Buon Giorno' or 'Good Day', it seemed more in the nature of a small town than a city.

We tied up at the Ponte Ethiopia near the lighthouse at the far end of the dock. No customs officers boarded to search our vessel, and I truly hoped I had successfully stashed away well more than the three cartons I had hidden. You could use them for barter or get a good exchange rate in liras.

Quite a few men boarded to buy, sell and change this and that. I opted for the barber first, who charged me one packet of cigarettes. I then had a good price for a carton of duty-free cigarettes. With the rest of the boys, all young, single fellows without a care in the world, I drew a sub, but with luck it might be changed back to British currency by the way prices stood.

Beer, spirits (except Scotch whisky), and wine were one-third the price one paid in the UK, and service was first class in the glittering bars. Jukeboxes played the most up-to-date American hits and smiling young ladies gave you their attention. You would be a sad sack if you didn't feel at home.

And this port, due to ship congestion, was slow loading. We could be sure of remaining tied up for over a week. I don't know if the skipper was afraid of losing firemen in this port after what had occurred in the US, but he must have instructed the chief engineer to let the firemen take all the time off they wished. Labour was very cheap, and a shore gang did the back-ends and tubes soot cleaning.

Every night was a spree. We strode ashore in the mellow evenings and drank Cinzano wine inside plush bars, returning on board during the early hours. One good thing about the heat of a stokehold – aching heads and painful tummies were soon cured with stiff exercise.

Then we put to sea, bound for Freetown, Sierra Leone, to load a cargo of iron ore at Peebles, near Freetown. It was uneventful. There was a good understanding with the engineers. Once we were loaded, there was a three day wait at anchorage in Freetown for some adjustments in the engine room.

One of the natives boarded with a small monkey. He kept plaguing me to buy it for two packs of smokes. Eventually I gave in. To make my monkey comfortable, I secured a 44 gallon oil drum from the engine room, gave it a good scrubbing out and found a good place to suspend it.

The alleyway outside my cabin led to the steering flat where there was an empty space with only a coil of rope dangling from a ring bolt overhead. I threw the rope around and suspended the drum from the bolt after making four holes in the side.

The drum now swung lengthways with the open-end facing the alley and the small breeze that blew along it. A long, thin rope was looped around a small post and was made fast to the primate's ankle to give him room for some exercise. When the ship rolled when we were homeward bound, the drum would roll with it.

That way the monkey would not get seasick. I had a good supply of bananas for him, which were hung upside down in another part of the ship's quarters from a thick pole and were covered with a blanket so they wouldn't ripen too quickly.

Later the *Darwin's* next port of call was Glasgow, Scotland where the October weather was mild when we tied up there one afternoon. The following morning after breakfast, everyone was donning their best clothes to call on the shipping office to pay off. Someone came to tell Don and myself that the captain would like us to visit his cabin.

He handed an envelope to Don with the address of the shipping agent we were to visit in Broomielaw. The skipper insisted that we make it snappy as the offices were expecting us. Broomielaw was quite close and we stretched our legs to get this mysterious errand over.

A door was opened for us and we were invited in. We walked up to the reception counter and Don handed over the envelope. After reading the contents, the lady receptionist took the envelope into a room behind her, and then returned followed by two gents in police uniforms.

We were passed into their custody to be escorted out and led to an awaiting van down the street. We never dreamed that the black van was for our exclusive use. The driver stopped at the entrance to a prison, and we were then incarcerated in the same cell, without preliminaries like answering a series of questions or signing our names.

When midday came around, we were brought out to the remand section, where we inquired of the stout warder, escorting the trustee food handlers, the details of our case. He was very obliging and let us know that in a couple of days we would face charges of desertion in the sheriff's court.

He was of a sympathetic nature. My mate noticing this pleaded that our case be brought forward, as arrangements had been made for his marriage. This authority must have had a grown family of his own and responded favourably saying, "I'll try and get you in the sheriff's court tomorrow. You will probably pay only a fairly small fine," and added a crucial final remark: "Plead guilty."

The following morning I found myself in luck since both of us took our place in court. Cases were dealt with rapidly, so we did not have to wait too long. We didn't even have to stand up. All I heard was an exaggerated wording of a statement that implied that we had defied wartime regulations by fleeing from our vessel in a foreign port.

Before we knew it, the same policeman who had ushered us to our pews, tapped us on the shoulder to follow him to where we would pay our fines of two pounds each. A farce really, yet had it been six months earlier, it could have meant us spending six months behind bars.

We returned to the ship and the only one we met on board was the cook. He smiled all over his face when he learned of our good luck. Our kitbags had been left in his cabin, and after we picked them up, he told us to visit the chief mate to collect our pay off.

When the cook let me know that a customs officer had borrowed my monkey to show to his girlfriend, I told him he could be the new owner if he wished or sell it to the small zoo next door to the seaman's mission in Broomielaw.

And then soon after a train trip we arrived back in dear old Cardiff. I left Don at the station and proceeded up the valley. Drinking in the local with my brother, now demobbed from the RAF and a few other long-lost faces, made my leave break enjoyable.

But how Cardiff shipping had changed in the short period that had brought world peace! There was very little shipping in port. I heard it was because of the high cost of docking, which government funding had covered during the war years. When I called in a Maltese cafe near the pier's end, I told the dockers sitting there with their cuppas that down the whole long mile of Bute Road, out of maybe thirty cafes, I passed only two open for business.

At the pool I found that most men were being sent to Barry to join ships. Although only seven miles away, the berthing rates for loading coal there were very much cheaper. As one fellow remarked, "It's only a mud bank."

Instead I was sent to a job in the Cardiff docks. But it was not the same Cardiff docks I was familiar with where ships were in a tight line, bow to stern and no space between.

My new assignment, the *Empire Condicote*, looked small and alone among the row of idle, giant cranes that hoisted coal up in the air by the truckload. However, she was big enough to start me on more adventures with the world no longer at war, and I would then continue to sail on a host of various vessels.

But for now, 'Anchors aweigh, *Empire Condicote*! We've got some serious travelling to do to meet some new people, new places and new adventures!'

<u>GLOSSARY</u> (Mainly nautical terms)

Abeam: Alongside or abreast – opposite the centre of the side of the ship.

Aft: The part of the vessel behind the middle area of the vessel.

Afterdeck: The weather deck of a vessel behind the bridge house or amidships section.

Amidships (Midships): The middle section of a ship referring to its longitudinal plane, as distinguished from fore or aft.

Athwart: At right angles to the fore and aft or centreline of a ship.

Ballast: Heavy material that is set in the hold of a vessel to provide stability.

Batten down the hatches: To prepare for nasty weather by securing the closed hatch covers with wooden battens so as to prevent water from entering from any angle.

Berth or moorings: A location in a port or harbour used specifically for mooring vessels while not at sea.

Bilge: The bilge *is* the lowest compartment on a vessel, below the waterline, where the two sides meet at the keel.

Boatswain or bosun: The non-commissioned officer who issues "piped" commands to seamen (in order to hear over the sound of the ocean) and is responsible for the sails, ropes, rigging and boats on a ship.

Black gang: The engineering crew of the vessel – crew members who work in the vessel's engine room, fire room, and boiler room – thus named because they would be covered in coal dust during the days of coal-fired steamships.

Bollard: A substantial vertical pillar to which lines may be made fast. Found generally on the quayside rather than the ship.

Brassoing: Polishing the brass.

Bulkhead: An upright wall within the hull of a ship. Bulkhead is particularly a watertight, load-bearing wall.

Bulwark: An extension of a ship's sides above the level of the deck.

Bunker: A container for storing coal or fuel oil for a ship's engine.

Capstan: A capstan is a vertical-axle rotating machine first developed for use on sailing ships to apply force to ropes, cables, and hawsers.

Clinkers: Waste residue often formed as loose, black deposits that can consist of coke, coal, slag, charcoal, grit, and other waste materials.

Coal trimmer: The person responsible for ensuring that a coal-fired vessel remains in 'trim' (evenly balanced) as coal is consumed.

CWT: A hundredweight is a unit of measurement for weight used in certain commodities trading contracts. In the UK, a hundredweight is 112 pounds and is also known as a long hundredweight.

Deckhead: The under-side of the deck above.

Deucer: Second engineer

Dockyard: Place where vessels are built and repaired.

Donkeyboiler: A small auxiliary engine used either to start a larger engine or independently, *e.g.* for pumping water on steamships.

Donkeyman (D'man): One of the vessel's engineering crew who is working on any machinery other than the main engines. On some ships, this Petty Officer is in charge of engine room ratings.

Doodlebug (Buzz bomb): V-1 flying bomb.

Engine Room: One of the machinery areas of a vessel, usually the largest one, containing the ship's main mover (usually a diesel or steam engine or a gas or steam turbine). Larger vessels may have more than one engine room.

Fire room (also boiler room or stokehold): The compartment in which the ship's boilers or furnaces are stoked and fired.

Fiddley: The uppermost part of the stokehole of a steamship or an alleyway across this on a level with the between decks and roofed usually with a grating for ventilation

Fire Bars: Replaceable cast-iron bars that form the base of the furnace and support the fire. These wear out frequently, so designed for easy replacement.

Fo'c'sle or forecastle: Partial deck which is above the upper deck and at the head of the vessel; traditionally the sailors' living quarters.

Following sea: Wave direction matches the heading of ship.

Forepeak: The extreme forward lower compartment or tank usually used for trimming or storage in a ship.

Freeboard: The height of a ship's hull (excluding the superstructure) above the waterline.

Glory Hole: See Fire room.

Greaser: (also known as an "oiler") A worker whose main job is to oil machinery.

Hawsehole (hawse pipe): The hole through which a ship's anchor rope is passed.

Job and Finish: British slang for work without scheduled hours.

Keel: On vessels the keel can refer to either of two parts: a structural element that sometimes resembles a fin and protrudes below a boat along the central line, or a hydrodynamic element.

Lee: Area sheltered from the wind.

List: A vessel's angle of lean or tilt to one side.

Lugger: A small sailing vessel widely used as traditional fishing boats, particularly off the coasts of France, England and Scotland.

Merchant Marine: A collective term for all merchant ships registered in a given country and the civilians (especially those of that nationality) who man them; the ships and personnel in combination are said to constitute that country's merchant marine. It's called the Merchant Navy in the United Kingdom and some other countries.

Offsider: Assistant

Palliasse: A thin mattress filled with straw or sawdust.

Petty Officer: A petty officer (PO) is a non-commissioned officer in many navies.

Poop Deck: A high deck on the aft superstructure of a ship.

Prow: Alternative term for bow

Rating: A naval rating is an enlisted member of a country's navy.

S.S. or **S/S:** Prefix for "Steam Ship", used before a ship's name. *D/S:* Designation for Norwegian ships.

Slagging: The vitreous (glasslike) mass left as a remainder by the smelting of ore.

Slice, bare and rake: Slice – A long handled steel shovel for removing clinkers which have been levered from the fire bars with a *Dart or Rake* The rake is used for raking the fire to one side during cleaning. *Bare* was for clearing the area.

Spurling: A pipe or tube through which an anchor chain passes to the chain locker below the deck of a *ship*.

Steering flat: A compartment holding steering goods among other things.

Stepping the Mast: Raising the mast.

Stern: The extension of the keel at the forward end of a ship.

Stokehold: See Fire Room

Sublist: Allocation of pay

Tramp Ship: A boat or ship engaged in the tramp trade is one which does not have published ports of call. This is opposed to freight liners.

Trim: Relationship of ship's hull to waterline.

Trimmer: Person responsible for making sure that a vessel remains in 'trim' (that the cargo and fuel are evenly balanced).

Well Deck: A space on the weather deck of a ship lying at a lower level between a raised forecastle or poop and the bridge superstructure.

White Horses: White caps on top of the waves

Rank order in Fire Room

On a coal burning ship the following crew are in rank order (lowest to highest): Trimmer, Fireman, Greaser, Donkeyman, and Storekeeper. The head Donkeyman or storekeeper also makes sure deck winches keep working.

ACKNOWLEDGEMENTS

Bangkok:

I would like to first thank Ashley Priest for his unending championing and devotion to getting my wartime memoir into print. Without him this finished book would never have happened. And there's Anita Fromm with her tireless editing, proofing, researching and fact checking which turned my words into a more polished legacy. I consider Ladda Priest my strong aide-de-camp; she has been very, very helpful in so many areas. Recognition for Arme Navee Chumpalee who did a fine front cover drawing. Thanks to Giles Clark, a published author, for his advice and expertise in initiating publication. Kudos is in order for Chris Rodgers for his keen photographic eye. And there's Dave Jarrell for inspiration plus my gang in Soi 4 who always share their enthusiastic support.

Elsewhere:

Credit goes to U.S.-based Deborah Wheaton for her overall skilled cover design. Plus both Howard Hogan in Australia and Steve Robbshaw in Wales deserve thanks for corralling early versions of my manuscript in those distant places and passing them on to Bangkok.

ABOUT THE AUTHOR

Edward "Ted" Jones Whitehead, now 94, was born in the Rhondda Valley of South Wales in 1923. Orphaned at nine he spent time with older brothers and sisters until he left school at sixteen. While attending secondary school, his English master would give him the day off for superior essay writing – a talent he has maintained throughout his life.

At eighteen after leaving a literally rubbish job in England, Ted found himself at the Swansea seaport in South Wales. There is where his ocean going began during World War II in the dangerous engine rooms down below and his globetrotting journeys lasted for the next forty years. Ships took him to every continent except Antarctica and as a senior his wanderlust has not stopped. Through the years some of his adventures have included the French Foreign Legion and service on the Queen Mary.

For the last thirty years, Ted has lived first in Australia and now has made his home in the tropics of Bangkok, Thailand. He has been profiled in Perth (The West Australian) and Fremantle (Herald) Australian newspapers while also writing several of his wartime experiences for them. As early as 1942, his local Welsh newspaper, Pegler's, in the Rhondda Valley, reported several ship mishaps that had already plagued the young seaman.